STUDIES IN
SELF AND IDENTITY
SERIES

THE
SELF IN
SOCIAL
JUDGMENT

EDITED BY

MARK D. ALICKE
DAVID A. DUNNING
JOACHIM I. KRUEGER

PSYCHOLOGY PRESS
NEW YORK • HOVE

Published in 2005 by
Psychology Press
Taylor & Francis Group
270 Madison Avenue
New York, NY 10016

Published in Great Britain by
Psychology Press
Taylor & Francis Group
27 Church Road
Hove, East Sussex BN3 2FA

© 2005 by Taylor & Francis Group, LLC
Psychology Press is an imprint of Taylor & Francis Group

Printed in the United States of America on acid-free paper
10 9 8 7 6 5 4 3 2 1

International Standard Book Number-10: 1-84169-418-5 (Hardcover)
International Standard Book Number-13: 978-1-84169-418-4 (Hardcover)
Library of Congress Card Number 2005004443

Library of Congress Cataloging-in-Publication Data

The self in social judgment / edited by Mark D. Alicke, David A. Dunning, Joachim I. Krueger.
     p. cm. -- (Studies in self and identity series)
  Includes bibliographical references.
  ISBN 1-84169-418-5 (hardback : alk. paper)
  1. Social perception. 2. Self-perception. I. Alicke, Mark D. II. Dunning, David (David A.) III. Krueger, Joachim I. IV. Series.

BF323.S63S43 2005
155.2--dc22
                                          2005004443

Taylor & Francis Group
is the Academic Division of T&F Informa plc.

Visit the Taylor & Francis Web site at
http://www.taylorandfrancis.com

and the Psychology Press Web site at
http://www.psypress.com

Contents

v

Contributors

Melissa Acevedo
Valencia Community College, USA

Mark D. Alicke
Ohio University, USA

Emily Balcetis
Cornell University, USA

David Dunning
Cornell University, USA

Nicholas Epley
University of Chicago, USA

Kai Epstude
University of Würzburg, Germany

Lowell Gaertner
University of Tennessee, USA

Thomas Gilovich
Cornell University, USA

Olesya Govorun
Ohio State University, USA

Karlene Hanko
Cornell University, USA

Sara D. Hodges
University of Oregon, USA

Joachim I. Krueger
Brown University, USA

George Loewenstein
Carnegie Mellon University, USA

Bertram F. Malle
University of Oregon, USA

Thomas Mussweiler
University of Cologne, Germany

Sabine Otten
University of Groningen,
The Netherlands

Katja Rüter
University of Würzburg, Germany

Constantine Sedikides
University of Southampton, UK

Leaf van Boven
University of Colorado, USA

INTRODUCTION

1

Self as Source and Constraint of Social Knowledge

JOACHIM I. KRUEGER
Brown University
MARK D. ALICKE
Ohio University
DAVID A. DUNNING
Cornell University

> *Every man is pent up within the limits of his own consciousness, and cannot directly get beyond those limits any more than he can beyond his own skin.*
> —Schopenhauer, 1901, *The Wisdom of Life*, p. 5

A s Arthur Schopenhauer realized, and as common sense confirms, human thinking and feeling happens on the inside. Departures from the strictures of self seem to be reserved to altered states of consciousness or to artful imagination as in the movie *Being John Malkovich*. Otherwise, as pop icon Paul Revere observed, "no matter what you do, you'll never run away from you." Judgments about things out there are tied to events in here—there simply is no place else to go. It is the *self* that makes evaluations, reaches inferences, and has emotions.

To say that the self is involved in judging others is in one sense a truism. Because experiences of other people involve the perceiver's own thoughts and feelings, social judgment necessarily depends on the self. The interpretations and inferences are subjective inasmuch as they arise from the perceiver's own thoughts and feelings. Rather than simply asserting this truism, the task of psychological research is to illuminate the specific ways in which the self influences social judgment and the consequences of that influence for perceivers and their interaction partners.

Social judgments contain an element of subjectivity, and the exact nature of this subjectivity depends on biases arising from the egocentric limitations of the self. This is not to say that people always expect others to share their beliefs or to use the same values as a basis for moral judgment; nor does it guarantee that people always evaluate the characteristics of others less favorably than their own, or that they expect others to be at greater risk for misfortune and disease. Research has established, however, that the self tends to influence social judgment in all these ways and more. People's own histories, preferences, desires, goals, beliefs, and self-views, as well as the emotional, physical and environmental states they find themselves in, exert a powerful influence on the way they see others. To be sure, social judgments are also sensitive to the particular behaviors of others and the attitudes they hold (Jussim, 2005), but the role of these "objective" social stimuli is only a part of the story. The goal of this volume is to explore the various egocentric sources of social judgments and the various similarities and differences between self- and social-perception that they produce.

A HISTORICAL PERSPECTIVE

Many of the founding figures of modern psychological thought recognized that perceptions of others are systematically tethered to perceptions of the self. William James (1915), for example, noted that people view their "own lusts in the mirror of the lusts of others" (p. 314). Students of abnormal psychology also recognized the intimate connection between understanding others and understanding the self. Sigmund Freud (1924/1956) believed that people project onto others those impulses that are too threatening to be admitted into consciousness. Moving away from a psycho-pathological perspective, Karen Horney (1939) believed that projection is "not essentially different from the tendency to assume naïvely that others feel or react in the same manner as we ourselves do" (p. 26). In Carl Rogers's (1951) humanistic framework, basic similarities between self- and social-perception were also critical because Rogers assumed that people's social experiences are organized into a "self-structure." Those experiences, however, that are too discrepant to be assimilated into that structure are distorted to be made to fit or are ignored altogether.

Pioneers such as McDougal (1908), Mead (1934), and Sullivan (1947), who worked within a more sociological framework, also recognized the linkages between the self-concept and social perception. Krech and Crutchfield (1948) emphasized that the *relation* between self and others was the critical component of the psychological field, and Combs and Snygg (1959) asserted that the characteristics and actions of others are perceived and judged using the self as a frame of reference. As they put it, others "are not really fat unless they are fatter than we" (p. 145).

These theoretical efforts were reflected in work on methodology and measurement. Thurstone and Chave (1929) sought to create equal-interval attitude scales by having judges assign scale values to various attitude statements. An important assumption of this procedure was that judges can assign values without interjecting their own attitudes. Thus, when assigning a numerical rating to the statement: "Women should not be allowed to hold political office," people who agree and disagree should arrive at the same value. Hovland and Sherif (1952) questioned this assumption by showing that judges with extreme attitudes tend to contrast discrepant positions away from their own. Personal attitudes thus emerged as anchors or standards against which attitude statements were compared. In this sense, social judgments are no different from psychophysical judgments of stimulus height or weight. In either case, readily available knowledge of one stimulus shapes judgments of other stimuli as the person encounters them. In a compelling demonstration of this anchoring effect, Dawes, Singer, and Lemons (1972) showed that during the Vietnam War era those considered to be Hawks judged Dovish statements to be more extreme than did Doves themselves, and Doves judged Hawkish statements to be more extreme than did Hawks (see also Robinson, Keltner, Ward, & Ross, 1995).

SIMILARITY AND DIFFERENCE

This brief historical excursion shows that two themes predominated in the early work on social perception (as they still do today). These are the themes of similarity and difference, or, put differently, assimilation and contrast. Overall, work on perceived similarities has received the most attention. This line of research has focused on how people use their attitudes, preferences, and likely actions to make predictions about others. Since Floyd Allport (1924) introduced the concept of *social projection*, hundreds of studies have demonstrated that people begin by assuming that others are similar to them. Allport himself found striking evidence for social projection when surveying students' attitudes at Syracuse University. The more students admitted to cheating on exams, the more they felt that cheating was common among their classmates (Katz & Allport, 1931). This was an important finding because Allport originally believed that projection was limited to public behavior, and especially to behavior in crowds. With its premium on privacy, cheating is the antithesis of a group mentality.

Subsequent work has continually found that people's own behaviors predict how common they think these behaviors are in the group (e.g., Wallen, 1943). In a study that has become a modern classic, Ross, Greene, and House (1977) recast the concept of social projection within the framework of Kelley's (1967) theory of causal attribution. Kelley proposed that social consensus is a cue for understanding the causes of behavior. When consensus is high (i.e., most people act the same), it is likely that aspects of the social situation call forth this behavior. If, however, there is a minority of dissenters, it is appropriate to attribute their dissenting behavior to internal properties, such as idiosyncratic personality characteristics or attitudes. Ross et al. suggested that social projection leads people to perceive high consensus for their own behaviors, and thus to assume that the behaviors of others who act differently stem from idiosyncratic factors within those people. Although Ross et al. (1977) called this consensus bias "false," researchers by the late 1980s proposed that it is reasonable for people with scant information about others to assume that their own behaviors are common (Dawes, 1989; Hoch, 1987).

However, researchers sometimes found that the story involved perceptions of difference rather than of similarity. Most of this research concerned with perceived differences, or contrast, converged on the conclusion that people do not simply exaggerate the differences between themselves and others, but that they also perceive themselves to be better than others. This finding too was anticipated by some of the great intuitive theorists of the nineteenth century. James (1890) rejected the idea that people are exclusively motivated by selfish instincts, saying that "I might conceivably be as much fascinated, and as primitively so, by the care of my neighbor's body as by the care of my own" (p. 325). He recognized, however, that the former passion, which he termed the "sympathetic instinct," is less powerful than the latter, which he termed the "egoistic instinct." James's conclusion that "the pure Ego, *per se*, can be an object of regard" (p. 325) was stimulated by German philosopher Adolf Horowicz (1878), whom James quoted at length on the issue. Horowicz summarized his own views in the rhetorical question of "how much more intelligent, soulful, better, is everything about us than about anyone else?" (p. 267). This insight was as prescient as it was accurate.

THE SELF EXALTED

Modern empirical research on the theme of perceived self-other differences is particularly indebted to studies by Alan Edwards (e.g., Edwards, 1959), Neil Weinstein (e.g., Weinstein, 1980), and Ola Svenson (e.g., Svenson, 1981; see also Greenwald, 1980, or Taylor & Brown, 1988, for influential reviews) who demonstrated what has become known as the better-than-average effect, or self-enhancement more generally, in which people express exalted beliefs about themselves that are arguably too positive to be objectively possible. As in the case of social projection, research on self-enhancement evolved to address fundamental questions concerning the rationality and the adaptiveness of human judgment (Kwan, John, Kenny, Bond, & Robins, 2004), and questions concerning the role played by the cognitive and motivational processes that underlie these phenomena (Pronin, Gilovich, & Ross, 2004).

Research on self-enhancement phenomena has been guided by the assumption that self-knowledge is richer and more diverse than knowledge of others. This view can again be traced to Horowicz and James, who believed that "our own things are fuller for us than those of others because of the memories they awaken and the practical hopes and expectations they arouse" (James, 1890, p. 327). During the recent era of research on social cognition, this idea found expression in studies on self-schemas, which suggested that the self-concept is a particularly well-encoded knowledge structure (e.g., Bargh, 1982; Kihlstrom, Cantor, Albright, Chew, Klein, & Niedenthal, 1988; Markus, 1977; Rogers, Kuiper & Kirker, 1977). A study by Markus, Smith, and Moreland (1985), which showed that well-articulated self-views indeed shape perceptions of others, is an excellent example of work during this period.

ALTERNATIVE VIEWS

Although the idea that self-perception shapes social perception has become widely accepted within the field of social cognition, the claims of alternative theories must be noted. Following Cooley (1902) and Mead (1934), symbolic interactionism stressed the supremacy of the "generalized other." According to this view, people represent social knowledge in highly compact images of what others are like and what they expect. The self-concept is seen as contingent on social perception, as adaptable, as perpetually renegotiated, and as reconstructed as needed (Stryker & Statham, 1985). Emerging from social identity theory (Tajfel & Turner, 1979), self-categorization theorists (e.g., Turner, Hogg, Oakes, Reicher, & Wetherell, 1987) proposed the related idea that individual self-concepts are grafted onto social identities or "collective selves." Most recently, Karniol (2003) articulated the idea that collective social representations can wield primacy over individual self-concepts in a sophisticated theory of "protocentrism" (as opposed to egocentrism). While there is arguably some truth to both the egocentric (or individualist) and the protocentric (or collectivist) approach, the objective of research is to test and model the various interdependencies of human judgment and to take a close look at what is meant by the claim that some kind of knowledge is more primary than another.

THE CHAPTERS

Each chapter in this volume provides a snapshot of recent research on the relation between self-beliefs and social judgment. By bringing these snapshots together in this volume, we hope to sketch a mosaic of contemporary theory and evidence that begins to piece together how self- and social-judgment coexist and influence each other.

Social Projection

The objective of the first two chapters following this overview is to examine how the self-concept influences judgments and predictions of others. In chapter two, Krueger and Acevedo extend a Bayesian framework developed by Dawes (1989), and discuss the conditions under which projecting self-behavior onto population estimates increases the accuracy of social perception. Going beyond previous research, they explore the question of how social projection may affect choices among alternative courses of action. The model they present suggests that projection can lead people to act in socially desirable ways on the assumption that others will reciprocate. When applied to social dilemmas, such as the famous prisoner's dilemma, this analysis suggests that social projection can reduce the perceived conflict between self-interest and the collective good. In other words, social projection may improve both social judgment and social behavior.

In chapter three, Van Boven and Loewenstein then ask how people make predictions about others who are in a different situation than themselves. According to their dual-judgment model, people first imagine how they would act in the situation the others are in. In other words, people simulate their own hypothetical behavior by anchoring it on their present behavior or mental state. In a second step of inference, they anchor their predictions of others on their own predicted behavior in the situation. Van Boven and Loewenstein find that both inferences fail to account for differences between situations and differences between people. As a result, cross-situational social predictions leave sizeable *empathy gaps*. These gaps are theoretically noteworthy because they help explain other well-known judgmental pitfalls, such as the hindsight bias or the curse of knowledge, which can detract from effective interpersonal behavior (as, for example, in the context of sales negations).

Self-Enhancement

Whereas perceptions of self-other similarities lie at the core of research on social projection, research on self-enhancement explores how and when people perceive themselves to be different. A pervasive finding is that self-evaluations are more generous and optimistic than evaluations of others. What processes produce this difference between perceptions of self and others?

Chapter four is dedicated to an exploration of the cognitive processes involved in the perception of self-enhancing comparisons. Building on current theory and research on two-process models of judgment and decision making (e.g., Kahneman & Frederick, 2002), Gilovich, Epley, and Hanko attribute self-enhancement to a simple—and largely automatic—form of reasoning about the self. These authors propose that most self-concepts are automatically associated with perceptions of desirability. When predicting their own behavior in a different situation, for example, people's own good intentions and high hopes for success come to mind easily. With this anchor of optimism in place, predictions are corrected only reluctantly and with effort. Even when engaging the more deliberative and slower second reasoning system, people tend to test their optimistic self-views by favoring evidence that supports them. Inasmuch as this set of biases, that is, the combination of automatically positive expectations and selective testing of these expectations, is unique to the self-perspective, it follows that perceptions of others are often more accurate.

In chapter five, Alicke and Govorun continue to examine the nature of self-other comparisons by honing in on the well-known "better-than-average effect." These authors review several recent models that seek to account for this type of self-enhancement by a variety of "cold" cognitive mechanisms. One of these mechanisms is egocentrism, which states that people view themselves more favorably than others because positive self-attributes are readily accessible and are accorded greater weight in social comparisons than others' attributes. According to the related notion of focalism, greatest weight is given to the attributes of whichever person is the focus of attention, which is usually the self. Alicke and Govorun note, however, that none of these mechanisms can explain the full range of self-enhancement phenomena. For example, the finding that self-enhancement is greatest for attributes that people feel they can control suggests the operation of motivated reasoning (Alicke, 1985).

Self and Others Compared

Social projection and self-enhancement are two sides of the same coin. Whereas social projection creates perceptions of self-other similarities, self-enhancement creates perceptions of differences. The two are not mutually exclusive; indeed they may be observed in the same studies (Krueger, 2000; Van Boven & Loewenstein, chapter three).

In chapter six, Mussweiler, Epstude, and Rüter present a comprehensive model of comparative judgments, of which self-other comparisons are specific instances. Their model can predict when people assimilate judgments of others to their own self-concepts, and when they contrast those judgments away from the self. Likewise, the model assumes that self-judgments are mutable in that they can be assimilated to or contrasted away from salient social standards. The model describes social judgments as occurring in two stages. In the first stage, people form holistic impressions regarding the overall similarity between themselves and others. Then, in the second stage, whatever information is more consistent with the initial assessment becomes more accessible. Testing hypotheses of similarity and dissimilarity by reviewing biased samples of accessible information results in final judgments that are assimilative or contrastive depending on whether similarity or dissimilarity is first assumed.

Mussweiler and colleagues note that perceptions of similarity and dissimilarity depend in part on the relative number of matching and mismatching features between targets of comparison (Tversky, 1977). In chapter seven, Hodges builds on Tversky's classic model to show that judgments about the self and others involve two kinds of asymmetries. The first asymmetry occurs in judgments of similarity. Here, the self-concept serves as a habitual reference point. Overall, judgments of similarity are higher when people assess how similar others are to them than when they assess how similar they are to others. The second asymmetry occurs in comparative judgments. Here, people come to evaluate others only in terms of their unique features. When evaluating themselves, they make use of both their own unique features and those they share with others. Both of these asymmetries are consistent with the view that the self-concept enjoys a place of psychological prominence, from which, in Hodges's words, it is not easily dislodged.

Delving deeper into the different ways in which people think about themselves and others, Malle describes a "folk-conceptual theory of behavior explanation" in chapter eight. According to this theory, it is far from sufficient to look for differences between self-related cognition and other-related (i.e., "social") cognition along single dimensions. Instead, his model postulates that selves (i.e., actors) and others (i.e., observers) hold radically different perspectives. Again, it is assumed that the self-perspective is unique in that it rests on a richer and more accessible foundation of relevant knowledge and in that it is more closely linked to motivational concerns, such as impression management. Malle reviews empirical support for these basic assumptions, and then proceeds to review the evidence for a whole family of asymmetries that affect the ways in which people account for their own behavior and the behavior of others. Following Heider (1958), Malle argues that more can be gained from the distinctions between intentional and unintentional behaviors and between observable and unobservable behaviors than from the classic dichotomy of personal versus situational causes.

Integrative Approaches

The next three chapters cut across the traditional phenomenon-based research areas. In chapter nine, Balcetis and Dunning present a parallel-constraint satisfaction framework that aims to account for both perceptions of self-other similarities and differences. In this connectionist approach, personal characteristics, behaviors, and preferences are nodes in a cognitive-emotional network. These nodes may excite or inhibit one another automatically and in parallel. Working from the assumption that the personal self-concept holds a place of prominence among people in individualist societies, Balcetis and Dunning develop the idea that the self-concept sets the constraints within which social perception can operate. Backed by a wealth of earlier research evidence, their model assumes that (a) people construe other's characteristics in ways that enhance self-esteem, and that (b) relevant aspects of the self-concept are automatically activated whenever people set about making judgments about others. With these theoretical and empirical assumptions in place, the model can represent the ways in which people come to perceive similarities and differences between themselves and others, and how they fill in missing information.

However, there can be more than one way to construe the self. The *individualist* self is a vehicle that allows people to see themselves as unique. In contrast, a *collective* self construes a person as a member of an important social group (e.g., family, friends, college peers). In chapter ten, Gaertner and Sedikides compare the power of individualist and collectivist selves to influence social thought and action and confront head-on the question of which self is primary. Gaertner and Sedikides review evidence that leads them to conclude that the individual self-concept enjoys psychological primacy. The most direct evidence is that people are more distressed by threats to their personal self than by threats to groups they belong to and care about.

Two additional findings challenge the presumed power of the collective self even more directly. One is that members of collectivist societies self-enhance just as much as members of individualist societies. What matters is the characteristic at issue. People with a collectivist self-construal claim to be superior to others in domains that are valued in a collectivist culture (e.g., "I am more modest than the average person!"). The other finding suggests that discriminatory behavior in *ad hoc* laboratory groups can be explained without reference to the somewhat circular idea that people discriminate because they need to differentiate the ingroup from the outgroup. Instead, it is sufficient to suppose that people expect ingroup members, but not outgroup members, to reciprocate their own generosity.

Pursuing this egocentric perspective on ingroup bias in chapter eleven, Otten carefully reviews the claims of several theories built around the notion of collective self-construals (i.e., social identity theory, self-categorization theory, and their most recent variants). After noting that collectivist explanations of ingroup bias face empirical difficulties, such as the lack of evidence for the idea that the expression of ingroup bias raises a person's self-esteem, Otten explains ingroup bias more parsimoniously with the idea that self-knowledge is quickly accessed and easily projected to appropriate social targets (e.g., members of one's own group). According to this view, ingroup bias necessarily occurs among people whose self-images are positive (i.e., self-enhancement) and who expect members of their own groups to be similar to them (i.e., social projection).

In the concluding chapter twelve, we review the emergent themes in this volume and address some controversial issues. Of central interest is the question of the extent to which the individual self-concept is involved in judgments of others. The chapters in this volume suggest that the self has considerable causal power, but a prominent alternative to this view asserts that generalized beliefs about people (or "protocenters") guide both judgments of individual others and the self (Karniol, 2003). A second important question is how perceptions of personal superiority can lead to self-defeating judgments and behavioral outcomes. Here we refer an emerging line of research on *moral hypocrisy* (Alicke, 1993; Batson, Thompson, & Chen, 2002). We conclude by considering directions for future research on the interplay of self- and social perception.

In doing so, we try to fulfill one goal that inspired this volume. Work on the relationship between self and social judgment appears often in the historical terrain of psychological research, but usually in a fragmentary and isolated manner. It is our hope that by bringing current research on the topic under one roof, we can begin to identify integrative principles that explain the relation of self to social judgment, point to new research questions, and most importantly, identify this topic as an important and coherent one that represents an integrated body of work.

REFERENCES

Alicke, M. D. (1985). Global self-evaluation as determined by the desirability and controllability of trait adjectives. *Journal of Personality and Social Psychology, 49*, 1621–1630.

Alicke, M. D. (1993). Egocentric standards of conduct evaluation. *Basic and Applied Social Psychology, 14*, 171–192.

Allport, F. H. (1924). *Social psychology*. Boston: Houghton Mifflin.

Bargh, J. A. (1982). Attention and automaticity in the processing of self-relevant information. *Journal of Personality and Social Psychology, 43*, 425–436.

Batson, D. D., Thompson, E. R., & Chen H. (2002). Moral hypocrisy: Addressing some alternatives. *Journal of Personality and Social Psychology, 83*, 330–339.

Combs, A. W., & Snygg, D. (1959*). Individual behavior: A perceptual approach to behavior.* New York: Harper & Brothers.

Cooley, C. H. (1902). *Human nature and the social order.* New York: Scribner's.

Dawes, R. M. (1989). Statistical criteria for establishing a truly false consensus effect. *Journal of Experimental Social Psychology, 25*, 1–17.

Dawes, R. M., Singer, D., & Lemons, F. (1972). An experimental analysis of the contrast effect and its implications for intergroup communication and the indirect assessment of attitude. *Journal of Personality and Social Psychology, 21*, 281–295.

Freud, S. (1924/1956). Further remarks on the defense neuropsychoses. In *Collected papers of Sigmund Freud* (vol. 1, pp. 155–182). London: Hogarth Press.

Edwards, A. L. (1959). Social desirability and the description of others. *Journal of Abnormal and Social Psychology, 59*, 434–436.

Greenwald, A. G. (1980). The totalitarian ego: Fabrication and revision of personal history. *American Psychologist, 35*, 603–618.

Heider, F. (1958). *The psychology of interpersonal relations.* Hillsdale, NJ: Erlbaum.

Hoch, S. J. (1987). Perceived consensus and predictive accuracy: The pros and cons of projection. *Journal of Personality and Social Psychology, 53*, 221–234.

Horney, K. (1939). *New ways in psychoanalysis.* New York: Norton.

Horowicz, A. (1878). *Psychologische Analysen auf physiologischer Grundlage* [Psychological analyses on a physiological basis]. Magdeburg, Germany: Faber.

Hovland, C. I., & Sherif, M. (1952). Judgmental phenomena and scales of attitude measurement: Item displacement in Thurstone scales. *Journal of Abnormal and Social Psychology, 47*, 822–832.

James, W. (1890). *The principles of psychology* (Vol. 1). New York: Dover.

James, W. (1915). *Psychology: Briefer course.* New York: Holt.

Jussim, L. (2005). Accuracy in social perception: Criticisms, controversies, criteria, components and cognitive processes. In M. P. Zanna (Ed.), *Advances in experimental social psychology.* San Diego, CA: Academic Press.

Kahneman, D., & Frederick, S. (2002). Representativeness revisited: Attribute substitution in intuitive judgment. In T. Gilovich, D. Griffin, & D. Kahneman (Eds.), *Heuristics and biases: The psychology of intuitive judgment* (pp. 49–81). New York: Cambridge University Press.

Karniol, R. (2003). Egocentrism versus protocentrism: The status of self in social prediction. *Psychological Review, 110*, 564–580.

Katz, D., & Allport, F. (1931). *Student attitudes.* Syracuse, NY: Craftsman Press.

Kelley, H. H. (1967). Attribution theory in social psychology. In D. Levine (Ed.), *Nebraska symposium on motivation* (Vol. 15, pp. 192–240). Lincoln: University of Nebraska Press.

Kihlstrom, J. F., Cantor, N., Albright, J. S., Chew, B. R., Klein, S. B., & Niedenthal, P. M. (1988). Information processing and the study of the self. In L. Berkowitz (Ed.), *Advances in experimental social psychology* (Vol. 21, pp.145–178). San Diego, CA: Academic Press.

Krech, D., & Crutchfield, R. S. (1948). *Theory and problems of social psychology.* New York: McGraw-Hill.

Krueger, J. (2000). The projective perception of the social world: A building block of social comparison processes. In J. Suls & L. Wheeler (Eds.), *Handbook of social comparison: Theory and research* (pp. 323–351). New York: Plenum/Kluwer.

Kwan, V. S. Y., John, O. P., Kenny, D. A., Bond, M. H., & Robins, R. W. (2004). Reconceptualizing individual differences in self-enhancement bias: An interpersonal approach. *Psychological Review, 111*, 94–110.

Markus, H. (1977). Self-schemata and processing information about the self. *Journal of Personality and Social Psychology, 35*, 63–78.

Markus, H., Smith, J., & Moreland, R. L. (1985). Role of self-concept in the perception of others. *Journal of Personality and Social Psychology, 49*, 1494–1512.

McDougall, W. (1921). *An introduction to social psychology.* Boston: Luce.

Mead, G. H. (1934). *Mind, self and society.* Chicago: University of Chicago Press.

Pronin, E., Gilovich, & Ross, L. (2004). Objectivity in the Eye of the Beholder: Divergent Perceptions of Bias in Self Versus Others. *Psychological Review, 111,* 781–799.

Robinson, R. J., Keltner, D., Ward, A., & Ross, L. (1995). Actual versus assumed differences in construal: "Naive realism" in intergroup perception and conflict. *Journal of Personality and Social Psychology, 68,* 404–417.

Rogers, C. P. (1951). *Client-centered therapy.* Boston: Houghton-Mifflin.

Rogers, T. B., Kuiper, N. A., & Kirker, W. S. (1977). Self-reference and the encoding of personal information. *Journal of Personality and Social Psychology, 35,* 677–688.

Ross, L., Greene, D., & House, P. (1977). The "false consensus effect": An egocentric bias in social perception and attribution processes. *Journal of Experimental Social Psychology, 13,* 279–301.

Schopenhauer, A. (1901). *The wisdom of life.* Washington, DC: Dunne.

Stryker, S., & Statham, A. (1985). Symbolic interaction and role theory. In G. Lindzey & E. Aronson (Eds.), *Handbook of social psychology* (3rd ed., Vol. 1, pp. 311–378). New York: Random House.

Sullivan, H. S. (1947). *Conceptions of modern psychiatry.* Washington, DC: William Alanson White Psychiatry Foundation.

Svenson, O. (1981). Are we all less risky and more skillful than our fellow drivers? *Acta Psychologica, 47,* 143–148.

Tajfel, H., & Turner, J. C. (1979). An integrative theory of intergroup conflict. In W. G. Austin & S. Worchel (Eds.), *Psychology of intergroup relations.* Chicago: Nelson-Hall.

Taylor, S. E., & Brown, J. D. (1988). Illusion and well-being: A social-psychological perspective on mental health. *Psychological Bulletin, 103,* 193–210.

Thurstone, L. L., & Chave, E. J. (1929). *The measurement of attitude.* Oxford, England: University of Chicago Press.

Turner, J. C., Hogg, M. A., Oakes, P. J., Reicher, S. D., & Wetherell, M. (1987). *Rediscovering the social group: A self-categorization theory.* Oxford: Blackwell.

Tversky, A. (1977). Features of similarity. *Psychological Review, 84,* 327-352.

Wallen, R. (1943). Individuals' estimates of group opinion. *Journal of Social Psychology, 17,* 269–274.

Weinstein, N. D. (1980). Unrealistic optimism about future life events. *Journal of Personality and Social Psychology, 39,* 806–820.

SOCIAL PROJECTION

2

Social Projection and the Psychology of Choice

JOACHIM I. KRUEGER
Brown University
MELISSA ACEVEDO
Valencia Community College

> *We certainly use our knowledge of ourselves in order to frame*
> *hypotheses about some other people, or about all people.*
> —Karl R. Popper, 1957, *The Poverty of Historicism*, p. 138

We humans enjoy some awareness of our temporary states and enduring properties. We feel that we are in a particular mood, we know that we have certain preferences and traits, and we intend to behave in certain ways. Outside observers often validate such introspective knowledge, but sometimes there are discrepancies. These discrepancies can be particularly distressing if they involve the results of professional psychological assessment. After in-depth interviews, for example, clinical psychologists may conclude that a client is depressed, although the client denies being in this state (Shedler, Mayman, & Manis, 1993). Likewise, social psychologists may claim on the basis of an implicit attitude test that a self-described liberal research participant is prejudiced against a certain group (Greenwald, McGhee, & Schwartz, 1998).

When professional assessment and subjective experience diverge, many psychologists assume that self-reports are in error (Wilson & Dunn, 2004). One prevalent perspective is that preconscious neural activity is a sufficient cause of behavior (Bargh & Ferguson, 2000), and that self-perception arises only as a set of fallible inferences and constructions (Wohlschläger, Haggard, Gesierich, & Prinz, 2003). With such doubts about the value of introspection, one important goal of psychological assessment is to do without it. For three reasons, however, self-reports have withstood attempts to eliminate them. One reason is that objective measures (e.g., human observers or sophisticated apparatus) often lack the desired reliability. Another reason is the classic argument of privileged access, according to which there are many mental events for which there are no adequate objective measures.

Last but not least, self-reports remain attractive because of their economy. When mental events lie close to the surface of consciousness, interested researchers need only ask what they are. Self-reports can then be compared to represent individual differences. Attitudes regarding a certain proposition, for example, may range from strong support to stiff resistance. To the average person, such variation may not be evident. Indeed, the idea of privileged access implies that social knowledge is more fragile than knowledge about the self. Nonetheless, knowledge of others is vital for accurate self-perception (see Alicke & Govorun or Mussweiler, this volume) and effective social interaction. Lack of dependable social knowledge hampers efforts to understand one's place in the social world.

How do people get around the relative inaccessibility of social knowledge? This chapter suggests that social projection is a judgmental heuristic that leads people to expect that others will behave as they themselves do. The first part of this chapter is a review of how this heuristic operates when the self is seen as a fixed structure. Noting that social projection is a type of inductive reasoning, we show that expecting others to be similar to the self improves the accuracy of social predictions (see Van Boven & Loewenstein, this volume, for some of the risks involved in projective reasoning). We then extend this analysis to show that when the self changes, social predictions change too. The second part of this chapter offers an analysis of strategic behavior in social games. On the assumption that social projection enhances the accuracy of predictions, we suggest that projection serves a person's self-interest by facilitating adaptive behavior that also promotes the common good.

A BAYESIAN FRAMEWORK FOR SOCIAL PREDICTION

Self as Entity

Floyd Allport (1924) introduced the idea of social projection; other prominent social psychologists (e.g., Asch, 1952; Heider, 1958) as well as psychometricians (Cronbach, 1955) transformed and elaborated upon it. Allport theorized that by using information about the self to generate social predictions, people come to assume that others are much like them. As the introductory quote from Popper shows, even a philosophy of science concerned with the problem of inductive inference acknowledges the pivotal role of self-knowledge as a source of social hypotheses. If people have only one bit of readily accessible information, why should they not use it to make predictions about others? Sometimes, even a sample consisting of one observation can make a difference. A microbe discovered on Mars refutes the idea that only Earth bears life. At other times, such samples change current views very little. A photo showing nothing but rocks makes it *more likely* that Mars is barren, but does *not prove* it. One can make a sport of thinking up novel activities,

2: SOCIAL PROJECTION AND THE PSYCHOLOGY OF CHOICE **19**

such as making an omelet without cracking an egg or completing the first nude ascent of Mt. Everest. Once executed, these activities refute the idea that they are impossible, and the question becomes how easily and how often they will be replicated. However strange an activity might seem, social projection will make it quite doubtful that one would be the first or the last to do it.

To Popper, the goal of empirical observation was to weed out poor hypotheses. People would learn the most if they found evidence that others are different instead of similar to them. According to the Bayesian approach to induction, however, outright falsification is rare. Instead, most observations gradually alter the credibility of certain hypotheses or beliefs (Howson & Urbach, 1989). When evidence becomes available, all hypotheses consistent with it become more probable, and all inconsistent hypotheses become less probable. Suppose there are two hypotheses regarding the prevalence of a certain attitude in a particular social group. According to one hypothesis, 70% of group members believe that, say, brown eyes are more attractive than blue eyes, but according to the other hypothesis only 30% hold that view. If there are no grounds to favor either of these hypotheses *a priori*, a state of indifference prevails, in which each hypothesis is equally likely to be true (i.e., $p(H1) = p(H2) = .5$).[1]

When a person is selected at random from a group, the probability that this person has the attitude in question is either $p(A|H_1) = .7$ or $p(A|H_2) = .3$. Because the two hypotheses are deemed equally likely to be true, the overall probability that the person has the attitude, $p(H_1)$, is .5. Now suppose that this random person actually has the attitude. Bayes's Theorem gives the revised probability of each hypothesis as the product of the probability of the attitude under that hypothesis and the ratio of prior probability of the hypothesis over the overall probability of the attitude, namely

$$p(H_i | A) = p(A | H_i) \cdot \frac{p(H_i)}{p_1(A)}.$$

Because in the present case the ratio is 1, $p(H_1|A) = .7$ and $p(H_2|A) = .3$. The probability that the next randomly selected person will hold the attitude, $p_2(A)$, can be computed by multiplying the revised probability of each hypothesis with the conditional probability of the attitude under that hypothesis and by summing the products. Thus,

$$p_2(A) = p(H_1 | A) \cdot p(A | H_1) + p(H_2 | A) \cdot p(A | H_2) = .58$$

and the difference between p_2 and p_1 captures the effect of past evidence on future expectations.[2] Here, observing one instance of the attitude increases its estimated prevalence by 8 percentage points.

The degree to which observations change beliefs depends on the hypotheses being considered and their respective prior probabilities. Consider a scenario in which the attitude is thought to be either extremely rare (i.e., $p(A|H_1) = .1$) or extremely common (i.e., $p(A|H_2) = .9$). In another scenario, the attitude is assumed to be either moderately rare (i.e., $p(A|H_1) = .3$) or moderately common (i.e., $p(A|H_2) = .7$). In both scenarios, the initial probability of the attitude is $p_1(A) = .5$. Now suppose that the prior probability of the hypothesis that the attitude is rare, $p(H_1)$, ranges from .1 to .9 (with $p(H_2) = 1- p(H_1)$). Figure 2.1 shows belief revision, $p_2(A) - p_1(A)$, across levels of $p(H_1)$. The steep line represents the scenario of $p(A|H_1) = .1$, and the shallow line represents the scenario of $p(A| H_1) = .3$. The difference in elevation between the two lines shows that the degree of belief change corresponds to the extremity of the available hypotheses. The prior probabilities of the hypotheses also matter. Beliefs change the most when the hypothesis which suggests that the attitude is rare has a high prior probability.[3]

Now let's return to the question of social projection. A person may wonder: "What does my having this attitude tell me about how others feel?" If there is no information about how others feel, the probability of finding the attitude in a random other person, $p(A|H_j)$, may be anywhere between 0 and 1. The person is in a state of indifference if there is no reason to assign different prior probabilities to these hypotheses. In this idealized state of affairs, the revised probability of the attitude can be shown to be $(k + 1)/(n + 2)$, where k is the number of positive instances (e.g., people with attitude A) and n is the total size of the sample (see Howson & Urbach, 1989, pp. 42–45). Following this logic, a person with the

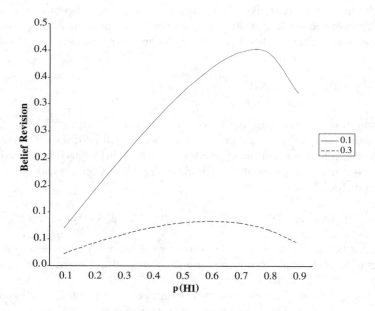

FIGURE 2.1

attitude will estimate its probability to be .67, whereas a person without it will estimate its probability to be .33.

When two people make different predictions, they need not be mistaken in their thinking. Both could have made the best estimate given the information they had (Dawes, 1989). Even scientists often draw different conclusions from different observations in the laboratory. When information is shared, however, predictions should converge. Only when people continue to depend primarily on what they know about themselves, can it be said that their social predictions are egocentric (Krueger, 2000). By the same token, scientific disagreements should diminish when data are integrated as they are, for example, in meta-analyses. But here too, a risk of egocentric prediction remains. Some researchers question whether disparate findings can be aggregated, claim special status of their own findings, or simply ignore the results of others (Tetlock, 2002).

The idea that people base social predictions on their own responses assumes that this sample information is random. But is it possible for people to regard their own responses as random samples of behavior? Compare the ordinary person's perspective with that of a research scientist. Researchers seek to sample randomly from a domain so that, on average, their observations are unbiased. Their statistical inferences depend on this assumption. Ordinary people cannot develop a comparable sense of how random their own responses are with regard to the group. Nothing in their phenomenal experience represents the idea of randomness. It does not seem to make sense to say that a single behavior or attitude is random. Indeed, statistical assessments of randomness require knowledge of the process by which a sample is drawn. If the process is free of bias (as in a drawing of the winning lottery ticket), a single observation may be considered random. But it is this insight into the sampling process that individuals do not have when they reflect on their own attitudes or behaviors.

To summarize, the statistics of belief revision can serve as a model for the psychological heuristic of social projection. According to this model, people hold prior beliefs about the social world, they consult their own attributes or behaviors, and they revise their social beliefs accordingly. The statistical properties of this model say nothing, however, about the underlying mental processes people use to access, weigh, and integrate their prior beliefs with new observations. The detection of such processes has been the task of experiments (Krueger, 1998). One interesting finding concerns the type of cause people identify to explain their own behavior. When people conclude that some aspect of the social situation controls their own behavior, they tend to believe that the effect on others will be similar. When, however, they see their behavior as a reflection of their personality, they project less (Gilovich, Jennings, & Jennings, 1983).

This difference resembles the pattern in Figure 2.1. The top line represents the prior belief that behavior will be relatively uniform. In a scripted social situation, people will do one thing or another, although one may not know which beforehand. Once a behavior is observed, it strongly affects further expectations.

The bottom line represents the belief that people are variable (as, by definition, in their personality differences), and thus new information has little effect. This example illustrates how the statistical modeling of social projection can be reconciled with experiments searching for its psychological sources. At minimum, experimental findings yield estimates of the prior assumptions from which people generated their predictions.

WHEN THE SELF OR THE GROUP CHANGES

Many researchers working in social cognition regard the individual self-concept as a rather stable structure (Gaertner, Sedikides, & Graetz, 1999; Markus, 1977; but see Onorato & Turner, 2004, for a contrary view). In particular, evidence suggesting that judgments about the self are more stable than judgments about groups is critical for the social projection hypothesis (Krueger, Acevedo, & Robbins, 2005). If group judgments were stable and self-judgments were malleable, any perceived similarities between self and group would indicate that people self-stereotype.

Nonetheless, self-judgments are hardly carved in stone. Consider a person whose political orientation shifts toward more conservative views over time. Perhaps this change simply reflects the jadedness of middle age or improved financial circumstances. More importantly, we suspect that a change of social projection will go along with a change of attitude. If both liberals and conservatives see themselves as a majority, a person changing sides may believe that the new attitude is indeed the more common one.

Longitudinal changes are difficult to track and research does not attempt it very often. It is far easier to introduce new attributes to the self-concept and to change them. When personal feedback comes from a credible source (e.g., when it is ostensibly based on the person's scores on a psychometric test), most people gladly accept it (Forer, 1949). When the feedback changes, they come to believe that they now have a particular attribute that they lacked before, or vice versa. Consistent with the social projection hypothesis, social predictions change in correspondence with the changing feedback (Clement & Krueger, 2002). Similarly, when transient drive states, such as hunger or thirst, are induced, people project these states to others, even to those whom they know to be in a different situational context (Van Boven & Loewenstein, 2003).

CONSTRAINTS ON THE SPREAD OF PROJECTION

Until now, we have assumed that the self is a sample from a particular group. Like other statistical models, the Bayesian induction model assumes that inferences about the properties of a population should rest on samples that were drawn from this same population. This raises the question of whether people use their own attributes as sample information to make inferences about groups to which they do *not* belong.

Generalization across category boundaries is a general problem. Research psychologists face it every time they ask whether their results obtained with undergraduate students at a particular university generalize to students at other institutions or even to people of different ages or cultures (Sears, 1986). Searching for answers in the discussion sections of research articles usually reveals little about this matter. The issue of generalizability is typically ignored except by authors of handbook chapters, who urge investigators not to overestimate the external validity of their findings.

One popular remedy is to perform replication studies using different participant populations. The current interest in cross-cultural research is an important attempt to find a broader basis for generalization. Here, the effects observed in participating groups are viewed as samples from the most inclusive social category, the world's population. When the variability of these effects is not greater than what one would expect from chance, investigators can claim they have discovered a human universal. Otherwise, cultural differences are the story to be told (Nisbett & Norenzayan, 2002).

The scientific criteria for the random sampling of individuals or groups are idealizations that scientists strive to meet but often cannot. Still, some opportunities to generalize remain even when the data are not fully random. Findings from social-psychological studies, for example, are commonly generalized beyond the population of college students from which the research participants are sampled. Even before the classic studies were replicated elsewhere, it was reasonable to think that cognitive dissonance (Festinger & Carlsmith, 1959) and destructive obedience (Milgram, 1963) are phenomena that occur outside of California and Connecticut, respectively.

Like scientists, ordinary perceivers need to figure out just how far beyond their own groups they may project their own attributes or behaviors. Suppose you were a participant in the classic projection study by Ross, Greene, and House (1977). The experimenters asks you to estimate in a study on mass communication. If you agree, you need to walk around the Stanford campus with a sandwich board reading "Eat at Joe's," or, more ominously, "Repent!" Once you have made a decision, the experimenters ask you to estimate the percentage of Stanford students who agree to participate. As a good Bayesian, you think that about two thirds of the students decide as you did, whatever that may have been (which is what Ross et al. found).

Now suppose you are asked to estimate the percentage of compliance among students at Berkeley or among students at the University of Tobago. What to do? One option is to look for the smallest category that subsumes both groups. Berkeley students can be grouped with Stanford students as students in California, and Tobago students can be subsumed in the category of, well, students. Inasmuch as larger groups tend to be more heterogeneous, inferences from a sample should lead to smaller changes in belief (see Figure 2.1 or Krueger & Clement, 1996; Rehder & Hastie, 1997, for empirical findings). Stanford students might be less inclined to project to students in general than to students in California, and thus, they may project less to Tobago than to Berkeley students.

Alternatively, one might suspend projection altogether to any group that does not include the self. This does not seem practical, however, because many outgroup members also belong to ingroups according to other schemes of social categorization (Mullen, Hewstone, & Migdal, 2001). Research shows, for example, that women project their own attitudes to other women, but not to men; men project their own attitudes to other men, but not to women (Krueger & Zeiger, 1993). But suppose the same effect occurs when people are categorized by sexual orientation. Now straights only project to other straights, and gays project only to other gays. Next, suppose the effect occurs for categorizations of age, then of race, and so on. The weak projections to outgroups (meta-analytic r between .1 and .15; Robbins & Krueger, 2005) suggest that people overlook alternative ingroup categorizations. This raises the interesting possibility that people may perceive the same individual other as being similar or different from themselves depending on which social category they apply to that person.

The selective application of projection to a salient ingroup matters when the perceiver's own group membership changes. In one study, participants learned that they belonged to a hitherto unfamiliar social group made up of people of a particular psychological type. These participants assumed that others of the same type (but not others of a different type) shared most of their attitudes. When some of these participants were later informed that they belonged, after all, to what they thought to be the outgroup, their pattern of projection reversed itself. Now, they projected to the new ingroup, but not to the new outgroup (Clement & Krueger, 2002). A social-science equivalent of this result is that of a researcher generalizing findings only to freshmen students when thinking that the participants were recruited from this pool, and of generalizing only to juniors when informed by a research assistant that the study participants were, in fact, juniors.

FROM PROJECTION TO CHOICE

The heuristic of social projection is easy to use and it makes social judgments more accurate. If, however, "thinking is for doing," in William James's famous words, one must also wonder how social projection affects behavior. And if projection influences behavior, what are the consequences for the person's well-being and social adaptation?

Everyday predictions are often made under circumstances that are more complex than the sanitized ecology of the research laboratory. Often, a person's own behavior depends on what others do, or on what one thinks they will do. As long as the behaviors of others remain unknown, these behaviors need to be simulated in the perceiver's mind. The question is no longer "What will others do given that I have done X?" but "What will others do *if* I do X, and what will they do *if* I do Y?" Questions like these lie at the heart of game theories of social behavior. "Players" in social games evaluate an array of outcomes that can result from their own choices in conjunction with the choices of others (Colman, 2003).

The Prisoner's Dilemma

The most famous game is the prisoner's dilemma (PD), which has baffled scientists since it was first proposed (Flood, 1952). The canonical story involves two suspected criminals whom the prosecutor can get convicted for a minor offense. To get them convicted on the major crime, however, she needs a confession. The suspects are held separately and they cannot communicate with each other. The prosecutor visits both and makes the following proposal: "If you confess and your accomplice does not, you will go free and he will go to prison for 12 years. If you confess and your accomplice does too, you will both go to prison for 8 years. If neither of you confesses, you will both be convicted on the lesser charge and sentenced to 4 years."

The sharp suspect, who is motivated to serve as little time as possible, knows that the prosecutor hopes to elicit two confessions allowing her to put both criminals away for a total of 16 years. To avoid jail, he needs to confess while hoping that the other will keep quiet. But because the other receives the same offer, he too hopes to go free by confessing. There is a chance that both suspects confess hoping that the other will not, and thereby end up giving the prosecutor what she wants, namely two sentences of 8 years. Would it not be better for both to refuse to talk? The outcome would be more desirable to the suspects and rather frustrating to the prosecutor. But then again, if the other's silence were somehow ensured, or even merely assumed, each suspect would be tempted to confess in order to go free (Shafir & Tversky, 1992).

Social scientists have not been able to reach a consensus on how a choice ought to be made. Their recommendations come from two schools of thought. One is concerned with the way in which inductive inferences inform choice. This view is related to the ideas discussed earlier in this chapter, and we will elaborate on it shortly. First, we consider the alternative approach, which suggests that a player in the PD (or any other experimental game of this sort) will select the *dominating* option. A dominating option is one that yields the best result regardless of what the other player does. In the PD, a confession yields the best outcome if the other confesses (i.e., 8 years instead of 12), and it also yields the best outcome if the other does not confess (i.e., freedom instead of 4 years). If by confessing the player is better off regardless of what the other player decides to do, confession is a "sure thing" (Savage, 1954), and choosing the sure thing is the rational way to go for a person interested in his own welfare (Dawes & Messick, 2000).

This approach to rational choice brings out the dilemma. If both players choose rationally, both will be worse off than if both refuse to confess. The PD not only pits individual rationality against the collective good, it also leaves the individual player with the sinking feeling that he would have been better off if he and the other had refused to choose rationally. Yet, both know that they cannot act unilaterally. Realizing that individual rationality tells both to make a confession, the individual player cannot change his mind and decide not to confess. If he did (while the other presumably would not), he would multiply his own years in prison, while letting the other go free. In other words, he would reap the "sucker's outcome." Thus, this theory of rational choice predicts that everyone will confess. Bilateral confession is an equilibrium state because no player can improve his outcome by a unilateral switch.

This is a grim picture, and one wants to applaud the prosecutor for coming up with such a shrewd proposal (or rather Professor Albert Tucker for imagining such a prosecutor; see Poundstone, 1992). From the perspective of dominance reasoning, the PD is a dilemma because players can always wonder how they could have done better if neither one of them had confessed. But then again, they should not wonder too much, because both did exactly what had to be done. More problematic for dominance reasoning is the empirical finding that many experimental players do not seem to care about it. Nearly 50% of players cooperate (i.e., select the dominated option; Komorita & Parks, 1995; Sally, 1995). Because players choose independently, 25% of games result in mutual cooperation, 25% in mutual defection, and half in a split outcome.

Consider the consequences of cooperation for the players (and the experimenter's budget). Figure 2.2 shows three payoff matrices. All payoffs may be thought of as dollar amounts. Each player chooses between "cooperation," which is analogous to keeping quiet in the original game, and "defection," which is analogous to confessing. The four possible payoffs can be termed as follows: T is the "Temptation" payoff, representing what happens when the defector successfully exploits a cooperator. R stands for "Reward," which is the payoff for mutual cooperation. P stands of "Punishment," which is the payoff for mutual defection. Finally, S stands for the "Sucker" payoff, which is left to the unilateral cooperator. The defining characteristic of the PD is the inequality $T > R > P > S$.

In the three matrices displayed in Figure 2.2, the values for T and S are the same (12 and 0, respectively), whereas the difference between R and P becomes smaller from the top to the bottom matrix. In the top matrix, unilateral defection yields only a small improvement over mutual cooperation, whereas in the bottom matrix, the difference is considerable. This suggests that defection is more compelling in the bottom than in the top matrix. One way to quantify this difference is to divide the difference between R and P by the difference between T and S. According to dominance reasoning, differences in this K statistic do not matter as long as the definitional inequality among the four payoffs holds (Rapoport, 1967). All players should defect, and the individual payoffs would be $1, $3, or $5 for the top, middle, and bottom matrix, respectively.

The grand mean of 50% cooperation is somewhat misleading because of the considerable variations from study to study. Figure 2.3 shows the sums of the obtained payoffs for probabilities of cooperation ranging from .1 to .9. If there is

Matrix 1: $K = .833$, $1/(1+K) = .545$

		Player A: Cooperate	Player A: Defect
Player B	Cooperate	11 11	12 0
	Defect	0 12	1 1

Matrix 2: $K = .50$, $1/(1+K) = .667$

		Player A: Cooperate	Player A: Defect
Player B	Cooperate	9 9	12 0
	Defect	0 12	3 3

Matrix 3: $K = .167$, $1/(1+K) = .857$

		Player A: Cooperate	Player A: Defect
Player B	Cooperate	7 7	12 0
	Defect	0 12	5 5

FIGURE 2.2

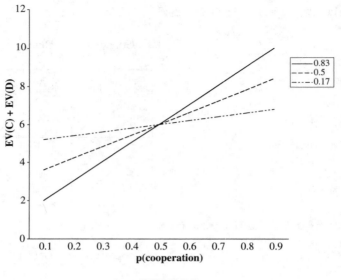

FIGURE 2.3

any cooperation at all, the total success of the players, as defined by their summed payoffs, is always greater than it is when all defect. This is so even if there is only a single cooperator among a million defectors. For the cooperator, the difference between P and S is smaller than the difference between P and T for the defector. The cooperator loses less than the defector gains. As the percentage of cooperators increases, so does the sum of all payoffs, and these gains increase more sharply as K becomes larger.

With the moderate to high levels of cooperation routinely observed, dominance reasoning fails as a descriptive model of human choice. This failure is troublesome in two ways. Not only does it leave a gap between normative choice and actual behavior, it also fails to explain why people reap greater benefits when they act irrationally. Dominance reasoning is thus at odds with the many aspects of culture and social policy that are geared toward encouraging cooperative behavior.

When a normative theory of human behavior fails as a descriptive model, there are three options. First, one can insist that people are simply irrational and proceed with research to uncover the psychological sources of this irrationality. Second, one can "repair" the model by introducing auxiliary assumptions. Third, one can look for an alternative model to bring normative rationality into alignment with observed behavior (Gigerenzer & McElreath, 2003). An example of the first type of response is work on the "disjunction effect" (Shafir, 1994). This work suggests that people miss a sure thing because they fail to think through all possible combinations of choices and outcomes. As such, the disjunction effect results from limited attention, effort, or intelligence. An example of the second type of response focuses on individual differences in how people transform monetary payoffs into personal values. Inasmuch as some people place a greater value on mutual cooperation than others do, they are more inclined to cooperate themselves (De Cremer & Van Lange, 2001). This approach is limited to the extent that it needs to postulate preexisting tendencies toward cooperation or defection, which are then realized once a person enters a game. In other words, cooperation is explained by a cooperative disposition (see Rachlin, 2002, who explains altruism with prosocial habits, or Parfit, 1984, who explains cooperation with values attached to benefits reaped by others). To elaborate on an example of the third type of response, we now return to the question of how inductive reasoning might help.

Cooperation after Projection

Now recall the lessons of the Bayesian analysis of social projection: A person may infer that others are similar to him or her even if (or rather, especially if) the sample used to make this inference is a single, self-generated event. We have also seen that social predictions change when the nature of the person's own information changes. In a one-shot PD, one player does not know what the other will do. Both are anonymous, they cannot communicate, and the information they have (i.e., the payoff matrix) is as sparse as the experimenter can make it. Each player only knows that the other is in exactly the same situation, that he faces the same skeletal information, and that he is as ignorant about this player's strategy as this player is about the opponent's strategy. The knowledge of their interchangeability is their common psychological ground (Lewis, 1969; Nozick, 2001).

Up to this point in the analysis, the PD resembles an ordinary prediction situation in which nothing is known about the behavior of others. The difference is that the player has not chosen yet between cooperation and defection. The logic of induction only says that whatever the player will ultimately choose, is—by definition—more likely to be the choice of the majority than the choice of the minority. In other words, it is more likely that the other player will match rather than mismatch his choice.

Now the question is whether a player's choice may be affected by the knowledge that the choice is more likely to be matched than mismatched. Inductive reasoning suggests that a player might as well choose to cooperate when the expected value of cooperation is greater than the expected value of defection. The argument against this idea is that such a choice amounts to the magical belief that one's own cooperation can induce the other to cooperate too. When, however, the absence of any such causal effect is guaranteed, as it is in the standard PD set-up, a return to defection seems obligatory, just as dominance reasoning demands.

To have merit, the inductive approach must respond to this critique. The answer we present has two parts. First, we show that people are sensitive to the probability that others will respond as they themselves do. That is, they generate projective expectations of reciprocity that remain fluid until a final decision, which maximizes the expected value of the outcome, is made. Second, we suggest that projection-induced choices are valid because they can unfold without implying beliefs in magical causation.

Expectations of Reciprocity

Thinking inductively, a player expects that it is more likely that his opponent will match rather than mismatch his own choice. If the player chooses cooperation, he will expect the other to cooperate; if he chooses defection, he will expect the other to defect. These expectations are purely statistical. The perceived probability of a matching choice, p(M), depends on the hypotheses the player brings to the task. As in the context of a stable self discussed earlier, a player might (but is not obliged to) take a stance of indifference by regarding all hypotheses to be equally probable *a priori*. Then, as we have seen, p(M) = .67.

Whether this expectation leads to cooperation depends on the K value of the payoff matrix. For the matrix at the top of Figure 2.2, K = .83. The expected value of cooperation, EV[c], is $7.33 (i.e., and the expected value of defection, $11.67 + .$) (1 −.67)), EV[d], is $4.67 (i.e., $12 (1 − .67) + .$1.67). The difference, EV[c] − EV[d], is $2.67. It pays to cooperate. As K diminishes, EV[c] becomes smaller and EV[d] becomes larger. For the center matrix, the two expected values are the same, and the player is therefore indifferent. It can be shown that this point is reached when p(M) = 1/(1+K) (Acevedo & Krueger, 2005). Finally, a player will choose defection for the bottom matrix because the difference between the two expected values is $2.67.

The induction model does not prescribe choice. It only asks players to integrate their own expectations of reciprocity with the given payoff values. The result may be cooperation or defection depending on the player's level of projection and the incentives set by the experimenter. In contrast, the dominance model uses only the relative differences in payoffs. Although the use of less information may seem desirable because it is parsimonious, the fact remains that the data from experimental games are far more consistent with the induction model. Rates of cooperation tend to be intermediate as one would expect from intermediate levels of projection, and rates of cooperation increase with K (e.g., Komorita, Sweeney, & Kravitz, 1980).[4]

According to the induction model, people who project more also cooperate more. This hypothesis was supported when the probability of reciprocity was manipulated in an experiment. Participants played several rounds of a PD against a computer (Acevedo & Krueger, 2005). Before each round, they were told the probability with which the computer would match whichever choice they had made. When there was no expectation of reciprocity, cooperative choices were rare (23%). In contrast, cooperation was common when reciprocity was ensured (93% for p(M) = 1). Here, the Temptation payoff and the Sucker payoff were no longer available. The players faced a choice between the payoff for mutual cooperation and the payoff for mutual defection. The most interesting result emerged for the intermediate level of expected reciprocity. When p(M) = .75, most choices were cooperative, and the rate of cooperation rose with the K value of the matrix (54%, 65%, and 80% respectively for K = .17, .50, and .83).[5]

In this study, social projection was independently manipulated in terms of the predetermined probability with which a player's choice would be reciprocated. Players found themselves in a position in which they could make choices *as if* they were projecting at a particular rate (see also Baker & Rachlin, 2001). A separate study measured individual differences in social projection independently of the PD situation and to test whether greater projection was associated with a greater willingness to cooperate. Participants rated themselves on a series of personality-descriptive trait adjectives and they estimated the percentages of others who would endorse each trait. The correlation between self-ratings and percentage estimates represented each person's strength of projection. When presented with the PD, those who projected more were also those who more likely to cooperate (r = .18, Krueger & Acevedo, unpublished).

In large-scale social dilemmas, social projection can also be beneficial. Quattrone and Tversky (1984) found that participants in a simulated election expected their own political party to fare better in a national election if they themselves voted (i.e., cooperated) rather than abstained (i.e., defected). Moreover, the strength of this expectation was associated with participants' willingness to vote. They seemed to reason that "If I vote, more supporters of my party will vote than if I abstain. Therefore, I should vote." Note that this reasoning can make a voter hopeful of victory only if intentions are projected selectively to supporters of one's own party, but not to supporters of the opposition. As we saw earlier, projection to ingroups is stronger than projection to outgroups, which makes this possible.

Reasoning Inductively Without Causing Anything

If people were to cooperate in hopes that they could make others cooperate, their thinking would indeed be more magical than normative. Morris, Sim, and Girotto (1998) detected such thinking among players who were more willing to cooperate in a PD when they made their move before the opponent did. Consistent with the induction model, however, expectations of reciprocity predict cooperative choices even when the behavior of others has already occurred (Acevedo & Krueger, 2004). It is sufficient that players assume that their own behavior is *diagnostic* of the behavior of others (see Dawes, 1991, for further distinctions between diagnostic and causal reasoning).

How can inductive reasoning enable cooperation without simultaneously fostering false hopes of exerting a causal influence? To find an answer, we explore two ideas. The first idea is that players can generate different probabilities regarding opponent cooperation depending on whether they themselves are currently contemplating cooperation or defection. The second idea is that players may then choose that behavior which offers the best value.

Changing Predictions

Inductive thinking suggests that one's own choice will be matched with a prob-ability greater than .5 (with p = .67 under the principle of indifference). When players make such estimates after they have committed themselves to their own choice, they are not faulted for projecting. A cooperator's expectation that the other player cooperated is considered as optimal as the defector's expectation that the other player defected (Dawes, McTavish, & Shaklee, 1977; Messé & Sivacek, 1979). But the cooperator and the defector need not be different people. A single individual can anticipate the predictions he would generate if he were a cooperator or a defector. Before settling on a final decision, the player can ask "What is the probability of receiving cooperation if I cooperate?" and "What is the probability of receiving defection if I defect?" In either case the answer is the same (e.g., .67). The expectations generated by one player at two times are as optimal as the expec-tations generated by two players at the same time. There are no separate statistical rules for the predecisional and the postdecisional phase.[6]

To refute this idea, one would have to deny the equivalence of predecisional and postdecisional induction. One would have to show that there is a separate logic of induction for contemplated behaviors and for enacted behaviors. Alter-natively, one would have to deny the validity of induction altogether. This can be a lot of fun as Hume showed, but it makes it difficult to get up in the morning to greet the sun.

Choosing by Expected Value

If the expected value of cooperation is greater than the expected value of defection, a player who is motivated by self-interest will cooperate. The logic of induction is the same regardless of *how* a player generates an expectancy. All that matters is whether one's own cooperation is introduced as evidence. Bayes's Theorem works the same way for a player who cooperates because it makes him optimistic, a player who cooperates to placate a guilty conscience, and a player who cooperates because he does not grasp the dilemma.

In contrast, these distinctions among a player's possible mental states are critical to a defense of dominance reasoning. Hurley (1991), for example, argued that if one "finds oneself [cooperating], that is good news, because of the statistical correlation of such symptomatic acts with the desired symptomatic outcome, but it would be irrational to [cooperate] for the "news value" of that fact that one has [cooperated]" (p. 174). This argument condemns a player for choosing coopera-tion because of its statistical implications. The player is supposed to have chosen differently. In contrast, a player who *finds himself* cooperating is considered lucky because even devotees of dominance expect him to be a winner.

When a distinction is drawn between the mindful and the unwitting coopera-tor, a problem arises that is much like the one that is often discussed with regard to the induction model. Recall that a criticism of the induction model is that by cooperating, players cannot generate a statistical similarity between their own be-havior and that of others. They can only experience it. With regard to dominance reasoning, the equivalent charge is that by defecting, players cannot eliminate that same statistical similarity between themselves and others.

Choice in a Deterministic World

Perhaps the focus on a player's mental states does more to obscure than to clarify. The logic of induction unfolds the same way from an observer's perspective. An observer knows that the two players in the PD are interchangeable. With respect to the game, they are both randomly selected specimens. If their choices are revealed one at a time, the first is diagnostic of the second. If the first choice is coopera-tion, the probability that the second one is also cooperation is .67 (assuming the principle of indifference). In the language of decision theory, the prediction of cooperation is a hit, H, if the second player's choice is indeed cooperation. If the second player defects, the prediction of cooperation is a false positive, FP. Likewise, if the first player defects, the second player is expected to defect with a probability of .67. If the second player defects, the outcome is a correct rejection, CR; if he cooperates, the outcome is a miss, M.

The power of one player's choice to predict the choice of the other can be expressed as an odds ratio, namely the product of the probabilities of correct predictions divided by the product of the probabilities of false ones, or (H · CR)/ (FP · M). When the probability of reciprocal choice is .67, as presently assumed, projective predictions are four times as likely to be correct than incorrect. Just like an observer can predict the second player's choice from the first player's choice, each player can predict his opponent's choice from his own. What is more, each player can assume that the opponent's choice predicts his own. The affair is sym-metrical, which is easily understood by an observer, but a player is constrained by having to witness his own decision first.

We noted before that the induction model is not concerned with how players arrive at a decision. We now need to qualify this point because, clearly, players (and inmates in Professor Tucker's penitentiary narrative) experience having—and making—a choice between cooperation and defection. They feel the pull of greed (i.e., of being able to reap the Temptation payoff for unilateral defection) and the push of hope (i.e., of achieving mutual cooperation). They may even (falsely) be-lieve that they can make an opponent cooperate by cooperating themselves. These and other mental activities are critical for induction to work because they ensure that players do not make choices at random. If they said, "Since I cannot find a good reason for either option and since I cannot control what the other will do, I might as well flip a coin," the probability of a matching choice would be .5. Only by thinking about the game can players achieve a majority response of some kind. When their choices are strategically nonrandom, a majority will end up favoring one alternative, and an individual player's choice will be diagnostic of it.

An observer who knows this may conclude that the optimistic prediction made by a cooperative player is invalid because of all the cogitation and agitation this player has experienced. Again, this argument invokes dominance reasoning, which warns that "Thou shalt not make predictions based on thy own behavior if thou chooseth this behavior in order to make that prediction." Yet, this argument overlooks the brute fact that regardless of their individual hopes and fears, most people end up choosing like most others. A champion of dominance reasoning would have to find a way to help a player beat the logic of induction.

How might this be done? Suppose a contemplative player thinks through the changing predictions while considering cooperation and defection. When considering cooperation, opponent cooperation seems likely; when considering defection, opponent defection seems likely (Kay & Ross, 2003, show how imagination can be primed to make it so). The dominance champion now advises the player to make a final switch from considering cooperation to actually defecting. This maneuver must be swift and unilateral. That is, the strategic player must believe that he is faster than the opponent, thereby replacing the belief in interpersonal similarity with the belief in own superiority (Alicke & Govorun, this volume).

Acting more decisively, the dominance champion could offer her mentee, but not the opponent, an opportunity to reconsider his choice after the game is ostensibly done. However enticing it may be to the individual player, this arrangement also destroys the game by violating the premise of common ground. Perhaps the most damaging argument against any such attempt to outflank other players is the impossibility to extend these kinds of special offers to many players without making the unattractive payoff for mutual defection the disappointing norm. Try as one might, induction cannot be outrun. Whatever a player's choice inclination is at a given time, that is what ought to be seen as the most common one.[7]

Projection has the appealing property of acting as a brake on undesirable behavior in social dilemmas. More generally, strong projectors should find it difficult to cheat in a variety of social situations. For would-be cheaters with a conscience, intentions to cheat trigger an unpleasant state of arousal, which then, by virtue of projection, they fear to be obvious to others (Gilovich, Savitsky, & Medvec, 1998). Hence, these intentions are less likely to become actions. For cheaters who act on their designs, projection spoils the fun because now suspicions of others cheating run high (Katz & Allport, 1931; Sagarin, Rhoads, & Cialdini, 1998).

Although a brake on cheating is arguably a good thing, the same logic applies to some desirable behaviors. Creative thinkers and artists, for example, can venture to go where no one has gone before only if they manage to keep projection at bay. If they can't, no idea will seem novel enough to be worth working for. If a creative project is completed nonetheless, projection can spoil it by invoking the "curse of knowledge," which makes the hard-won fruits of imagination and labor obvious in hindsight (Camerer, Loewenstein, & Weber, 1989).

Newcomb's Problem Reconsidered

The clash of inductive reasoning and dominance reasoning highlights the paradox of human choice in a deterministic world. Most of the relevant philosophical arguments have been made with regard to a mind-bending scenario known as Newcomb's Problem (Campbell & Sowden, 1985). This problem features a person, or player as it were, who is presented with two boxes labeled A and B. Box A is known to contain $1,000. A demon with awesome predictive powers placed $1,000,000 in box B if she predicted that the player would take only that box. If the demon predicted that the player would take both boxes, she left box B empty. What is the player, who is assumed to prefer getting more rather than less money, to do?

The payoffs in Newcomb's Problem show the inequalities familiar from the prisoner's dilemma (Lewis, 1979; Nozick, 1969; 1993). The top panel of Figure 2.4 shows the payoffs for the canonical scenario. Dominance reasoning mandates taking both boxes because the player will be better off by $1,000 regardless of the demon's prediction. In contrast, inductive reasoning suggests taking only one box

Matrix 1: $K = .998$, $1/(1+K) = .5005$

Demon's Prediction

	1 box	2 boxes
1 box	$1,000,000	$0
2 boxes	$1,001,000	$1,000

Player's Choice

Matrix 2: $K = .5$, $1/(1+K) = .6667$

Demon's Prediction

	1 box	2 boxes
1 box	$750,750	$0
2 boxes	$1,001,000	$250,250

Player's Choice

FIGURE 2.4

because of the demon's impressive record of making accurate predictions. Because the K ratio is a whopping .998, any p(M) over .5005 can induce a player to forego the second box. The bottom panel shows payoffs for $K = .5$. Here, a greater level of accuracy would be demanded of the demon to justify taking only one box (i.e., p(M) > .6667). Just as inductive reasoning does not demand cooperation in the prisoner's dilemma, it does not require a player to settle for one box in Newcomb's problem. The choice between taking only one box or both boxes continues to depend on the expected values of the two alternatives.[8]

Taking only one box in Newcomb's Problem signals the belief that the omniscient demon stocked it, but it does not imply an illusion of influence. From the perspective of induction, the presumed timing of the demon's prediction (i.e., before, after, or concurrent with the player's choice) is irrelevant. The paradox is that a player who cannot claim control over the demon's decision cannot simultaneously believe both that the demon most likely made a correct prediction and that there is still freedom of choice. A player who accepts the statistical association between his own choice and the demon's prediction, and who knows that he cannot influence the demon, must also admit that he cannot influence his own choice. Having to refer to a common cause underlying both the demon's prediction and one's own choice may be a jarring realization for a player who has a strong sense of being in charge of his own decision (Eells, 1985).[9]

A truly free choice is unconstrained by the past; it remains undetermined in the sense that it can still favor either one of the available options. If, when the choice is made, it turns out that the demon was again correct, as she was so many times in the past, the player's experience of free choice can only be an illusion (Wegner, 2002). In dilemmas such as these, people need to act *as if* they had choice, and to do so, they need to think hard before deciding. By accepting the responsibility of choice in the face of determinism, people can discover what they were meant to do.[10] By taking this Taoist path, they can let go of the dilemma, come to understand that they are not unique, and reap the rewards. Cooperating *en masse*, most individuals do well for themselves, while doing good as a collective. Indeed, they do better than they would if they "rationally" sought a behavior that dominates.

CONCLUSION

We began this chapter by noting that there exists an inductive rationale for social projection. Most people are, by definition, members of social majorities. When they know nothing about other group members, their own responses are valid cues to what the majority does. The use of these cues is a "fast and frugal heuristic" (Gigerenzer & Selten, 2001) that leads to more accurate social predictions than a strategy of random guessing. We extended this analysis by noting that the same projective inferences can be made when the properties or preferences of the self change, and to some extent, when the social group does not include the self. Our main objective was to show that social projection may affect one's choices when no preexisting preferences exist. The one-shot Prisoner's Dilemma served as the paradigm for this discussion. In it, players are said to face a conflict between self-interest and collective interest, and researchers are faced with choosing between irreconcilable theories of rationality.

Our analysis addressed both conflicts. From the player's point of view, social projection offers an opportunity to cooperate out of self-interest. This is so because cooperation has the highest expected value when projection is strong. The fact that the opponent also benefits is of no consequence. Of course, this view does not imply that altruistic motives, commitments to do one's duty, or the limitations of mindful thinking never play any role in social interaction. It simply asserts that many choices in the PD can be predicted without recourse to any of these psychological variables. From the researcher's point of view, it should be reassuring that the logic of induction in general, and the psychological phenomenon of social projection in particular, apply to both selves as entities and selves in flux.

Perhaps most importantly, the framework of induction offers an explicit way to think about how people make choices in a deterministic world. But a difficulty remains: How can people accept determinism as a scientific doctrine, and continue to act as if they had freedom of choice? The pragmatist William James declared that his first act of free will was his decision to believe in it. Edward Lorenz, the founder of modern chaos theory, offered a less paradoxical strategy. "We must then wholeheartedly believe in free will. If free will is a reality, we shall have made the correct choice. If it is not, we shall still not have made an incorrect choice, because we shall not have made any choice at all, not having a free will to do so" (Lorenz, 1993, p. 160). This is good advice to inductive thinkers. It allows them to cooperate in social dilemmas and to bet on a single box in Newcomb's problem without having to worry about being accused of magical thinking.

ACKNOWLEDGMENTS

We are indebted to Theresa DiDonato and Alexandra Freund for their insightful comments on a draft version of this chapter.

NOTES

1. Laplace (1814) suggested that all hypotheses be regarded as equally probable before evidence is gathered. This (controversial) idea is variously known as the principle of insufficient reason or the principle of indifference (Keynes, 1921; see Howson & Urbach, 1989, for review and discussion).
2. Alternatively, the degree of belief revision can be expressed by a ratio of p_1 over p_2, but this choice in metric has little effect on the present analysis because

$$\frac{p_1}{p_2} = 1 + \frac{p_1 - p_2}{p_2}.$$

3. It can be shown that belief revision is at its maximum when the prior probability of the hypothesis, $p(H_1)$ is equal to

$$\frac{p(A \mid H_2) - \sqrt{p(A \mid H_1) \cdot p(A \mid H_2)}}{p(A \mid H_1) - p(A \mid H_2)}.$$

4. Extreme sets of payoffs readily illustrate this effect. If T, R, P, and S were, respectively, 100, 99, 1, and 0, cooperation would come more easily than if the payoffs were 100, 51, 49, and 0. According to the dominance model, the differences between these two sets should not matter because both satisfy the inequalities that define the PD.

5. The induction model assumes that people compute expected values for cooperation and defection, as well as the difference between the two. When the difference is positive, they cooperate. If these computations were error free and $p(M) = .75$, everyone would cooperate if $K > .33$. Because estimates cannot be completely reliable, cooperation drifts toward 50% as p approaches $1/(1+K)$.

6. When social projection is recognized as a mental process that affects choices in the PD, postgame predictions of the opponent's choice appear in a different light. For cooperators, the inductive model suggests that projection led them to cooperate, whereas defectors may be attempting to justify their choice after the fact by claiming that others would do the same (see Arndt, Greenberg, Solomon, Pyszcynski, & Schimel, 1999, for research on defensive projection).

7. Many motorists try to outrun induction (and traffic) by deftly and frequently switching lanes. If they projected more, they would be less surprised when ending up in the most clogged lane more than 1/k of the time (where k is the number of lanes). Unnecessary frustrations in the grocery check-out line stem from the same source (Surowiecki, 2004).

8. Also analogous to the prisoner's dilemma is the fact that the odds of making a choice that matches the prediction are the same as the odds of making a prediction that matches the choice. In Newcomb's Problem, p(demon 1-box|player 1-box) differs from p(player 1-box|demon 1-box) if p(demon 1-box) ≠ .5 (Levi, 1975). In the PD, the principle of indifference ensures that these two conditional probabilities are the same.

9. Although the PD and Newcomb's Problem pose a similar prediction paradox, there is a difference. Newcomb's Problem does not make the assumption of common ground. The demon and the player are different creatures, with the demon being the one who knows more. Therefore, the unilateral advice for switching (here, to take both boxes) will not work as well. The very definition of Newcomb's Problem entails that the demon foresees all factors influencing the player's decision, thereby including the advice of those who believe that the demon can be tricked.

   In an informal survey, we found that participants ($N = 84$) were more comfortable taking only one box in Newcomb's Problem (68%) than they were cooperating in the prisoner's dilemma (37%). This difference may be explained by the huge K ratio (i.e., .998) of Newcomb's payoffs, and the fact that the demon's powers were touted as great. The same difference may also explain the lack of a correlation between choices in the two contexts (= −.05).

10. As Schopenhauer (1985) advised, "From what we do we know what we are" (p. 98).

REFERENCES

Acevedo, M., & Krueger, J. I. (2004). Two egocentric sources of the decision to vote: The voter's illusion and the belief in personal relevance. *Political Psychology, 25,* 115–134.

Acevedo, M., & Krueger, J. I. (2005). Evidential reasoning in the prisoner's dilemma game. *American Journal of Psychology, 118,* 431–457.

Allport, F. H. (1924). *Social psychology.* New York: Houghton Mifflin.

Arndt, J., Greenberg, J., Solomon, S., Pyszcynski, T., & Schimel, J. (1999). Creativity and terror management: Evidence that creative activity increases guilt and social projection following mortality salience. *Journal of Personality and Social Psychology, 77,* 19–32.

Asch, S. E. (1952). *Social psychology*. Oxford: Prentice-Hall.

Baker, F., & Rachlin, H. (2001). Probability of reciprocation in repeated prisoner's dilemma games. *Journal of Behavioral Decision Making, 14,* 51–67.

Bargh, J. A., & Ferguson, M. J. (2000). Beyond behaviorism: On the automaticity of higher mental processes. *Psychological Bulletin, 126,* 925–945.

Camerer, C., Loewenstein, G., & Weber, M. (1989). The curse of knowledge in economic settings: An experimental analysis. *Journal of Political Economy, 97,* 1232–1254.

Campbell, R., & Sowden, L. (1985). *Paradoxes of rationality and cooperation: Prisoner's dilemma and Newcomb's problem*. Vancouver: University of British Columbia Press.

Clement, R. W., & Krueger, J. (2002). Social categorization moderates social projection. *Journal of Experimental Social Psychology, 38,* 219–231.

Colman, A. M. (2003). Cooperation, psychological game theory, and limitations of rationality in social interaction. *Behavioral and Brain Sciences, 26,* 139–198.

Cronbach. L. (1955). Processes affecting scores on "understanding of others" and "assumed similarity." *Psychological Bulletin, 52,* 177–193.

Dawes, R. M. (1989). Statistical criteria for establishing a truly false consensus effect. *Journal of Experimental Social Psychology, 25,* 1–17.

Dawes, R. M. (1991). Probabilistic versus causal reasoning. In D. Cicchetti & W. M. Grove (Eds.), *Thinking clearly about psychology, Volume 1: Matters of public interest* (pp. 235–264). Minneapolis: University of Minnesota Press.

Dawes, R. M., McTavish, J., & Shaklee, H. (1977). Behavior, communication, and assumptions about other people's behavior in a commons dilemma situation. *Journal of Personality and Social Psychology, 35,* 1–11.

Dawes, R. M., & Messick, D. M. (2000). Social dilemmas. *International Journal of Psychology, 35,* 111–116.

De Cremer, D., & Van Lange, P. A. M. (2001). Why prosocials exhibit greater cooperation than proselfs: The role of social responsibility and reciprocity. *European Journal of Personality, 15,* S5–S18.

Eells, E. (1985). Causality, decision, and Newcomb's Problem. In R. Campbell & L. Sowden (Eds.). *Paradoxes of rationality and cooperation: Prisoner's dilemma and Newcomb's problem* (pp. 183–213). Vancouver: University of British Columbia Press.

Festinger, L., & Carlsmith, J. M. (1959). Cognitive consequences of forced compliance. *Journal of Abnormal and Social Psychology, 58,* 203–210.

Flood, M. M. (1952). *Some experimental games. Research Memorandum RM-789*. Santa Monica, CA: RAND Corporation.

Forer, B. R. (1949). The fallacy of personal validation: a classroom demonstration of gullibility. *Journal of Abnormal and Social Psychology, 44,* 118–123.

Gaertner, L., Sedikides, C., & Graetz, K. (1999). In search of self-definition: Motivational primacy of the individual self, motivational primacy of the collective self, or contextual primacy? *Journal of Personality and Social Psychology, 76,* 5–18.

Gigerenzer, G., & McElreath, R. (2003). Social intelligence in games. *Journal of Institutional and Theoretical Economics, 159,* 188–194.

Gigerenzer, G., & Selten, R. (2001). *Bounded rationality: The adaptive toolbox*. Cambridge, MA: The MIT Press.

Gilovich, T., Jennings, D. L., & Jennings, S. (1983). Causal focus and estimates of consensus: An examination of the false-consensus effect. *Journal of Personality and Social Psychology, 45,* 550–559.

Gilovich, T., Savitsky, K., & Medvec, V. H. (1998). The illusion of transparency: Biased assessments of others' ability to read one's emotional states. *Journal of Personality and Social Psychology, 75,* 332–346.

Greenwald, A. G., McGhee, D. E., & Schwartz, J. L. K. (1998). Measuring individual differences in implicit cognition: The implicit association test. *Journal of Personality and Social Psychology, 74,* 1464–1480.

Heider, F. (1958). *The psychology of interpersonal relations*. Hillsdale, NJ: Erlbaum.

Howson, C., & Urbach, P. (1989). *Scientific reasoning: The Bayesian approach*. Chicago: Open Court Publishing.

Hurley, S. L. (1991). Newcomb's Problem, Prisoners' dilemma, and collective action. *Synthese, 86,* 173–196.

Katz, D., & Allport, F. L. (1931). *Students' attitudes.* Syracuse, NY: Craftsman Press.

Kay, A. C., & Ross, L. (2003). The perceptual push: The interplay between implicit cues and explicit situational construals on behavioral intentions in the Prisoner's Dilemma. *Journal of Experimental Social Psychology, 39,* 634–643.

Keynes, J. M. (1921). *A treatise on probability.* London: Macmillan.

Komorita, S. S., & Parks, C. D. (1995). Interpersonal relations: Mixed motive interaction. *Annual Review of Psychology, 46,* 183–207.

Komorita, S. S., Sweeney, J., & Kravitz, D. A. (1980). Cooperative choice in the n-person dilemma situation. *Journal of Personality and Social Psychology, 38,* 504–516.

Krueger, J. (1998). On the perception of social consensus. In M. P. Zanna (Ed.), *Advances in experimental social psychology* (Vol. 30, pp. 163–240). San Diego, CA: Academic Press.

Krueger, J. (2000). The projective perception of the social world: A building block of social comparison processes. In J. Suls & L. Wheeler (Eds.), *Handbook of social comparison: Theory and research* (pp. 323–351). New York: Plenum/Kluwer.

Krueger, J. I., & Acevedo, M. (unpublished). *Person perception in the Prisoner's Dilemma.* Brown University.

Krueger, J. I., Acevedo, M., & Robbins, J. M. (2005). Self as sample. In K. Fiedler & P. Juslin (Eds.), *Information sampling and adaptive cognition* (pp. 353–377). New York: Cambridge University Press.

Krueger, J., & Clement, R. W. (1996). Inferring category characteristics from sample characteristics: Inductive reasoning and social projection. *Journal of Experimental Psychology: General, 125,* 52–68.

Krueger, J., & Zeiger, J. S. (1993). Social categorization and the truly false consensus effect. *Journal of Personality and Social Psychology, 65,* 670–680.

Laplace, P. S. (1814). *Essai philosophique sure les probabilities.* Paris: Courcier.

Levi, I. (1975). Newcomb's many problems. *Theory and Decision, 6,* 161–175.

Lewis, D. K. (1969). *Convention: A philosophical study.* Cambridge, MA: Harvard University Press.

Lewis, D. K. (1979). Prisoner's dilemma is a Newcomb problem. *Philosophy and Public Affairs, 8,* 235–240.

Lorenz, E. N. (1993). *The essence of chaos.* Seattle: University of Washington Press.

Markus, H. R. (1977). Self-schemata and processing information about the self. *Journal of Personality and Social Psychology, 35,* 63–78.

Messé, L. A., & Sivacek, J. M. (1979). Predictions of others' responses in a mixed-motive game: Self-justification or false consensus? *Journal of Personality and Social Psychology, 37,* 602–607.

Milgram, S. (1963). Behavioral study of obedience. *Journal of Abnormal and Social Psychology, 67,* 371–378.

Morris, M. W., Sim, D. L., & Girotto, V. (1998). Distinguishing sources of cooperation in the one-round prisoner's dilemma: evidence for cooperative decisions based on the illusion of control. *Journal of Experimental Social Psychology, 34,* 494–512.

Mullen, B., Migdal, M. J., & Hewstone, M. (2001). Crossed categorization versus simple categorization and intergroup evaluations: A meta-analysis. *European Journal of Social Psychology, 31,* 721–736.

Nisbett, R. E., & Norenzayan, A. (2002). Culture and cognition. In H. Pashler & D. L. Medin (Eds.), *Stevens' Handbook of Experimental Psychology: Cognition* (3rd ed., vol. 2, pp. 561–597). New York: Wiley.

Nozick, R. (1969). Newcomb's problem and two principles of choice. In N. Rescher (Ed.), *Essays in honour of Carl G. Hempel* (pp. 114–146). Dordrecht, Holland: Reidel.

Nozick, R. (1993). *The nature of rationality.* Princeton, NJ: Princeton University Press.

Nozick, R. (2001). *Invariances: The structure of the objective world.* Cambridge, MA: Harvard University Press.

Onorato, R. S., & Turner, J. C. (2004). Fluidity of the self-concept: The shift from personal to social identity. *European Journal of Social Psychology, 34,* 257–278.

Parfit, D. (1984). *Reasons and persons.* Oxford: Clarendon Press.

Popper, K. R. (1957). *The poverty of historicism.* New York: Harper & Row.

Poundstone, W. (1992). *Prisoner's dilemma*. New York: Doubleday.

Quattrone, G. A., & Tversky, A. (1984). Causal versus diagnostic contingencies: on self-deception and on the voter's illusion. *Journal of Personality and Social Psychology, 46,* 237–248.

Rachlin, H. (2002). Altruism and selfishness. *Behavioral and Brain Sciences, 25,* 239–296.

Rapoport, A. (1967). A note on the index of cooperation for prisoner's dilemma. *Journal of Conflict Resolution, 11,* 101–103.

Rehder, B., & Hastie, R. (1996). The moderating influence of variability on belief revision. *Psychonomic Bulletin and Review, 3,* 499–503.

Robbins, J. M., & Krueger, J. I. (2005). Social projection to ingroups and outgroups: A review and meta-analysis. *Personality and Social Psychology Review, 9,* 32-47.

Ross, L., Greene, D., & House, P. (1977). The false consensus effect: An egocentric bias in social perception and attribution processes. *Journal of Experimental Social Psychology, 13,* 279–301.

Sagarin, B. J., Rhoads, K. L., & Cialdini, R. B. (1998). Deceiver's distrust: Denigration as a consequence of undiscovered deception. *Personality and Social Psychology Bulletin, 24,* 1167–1176.

Sally, D. (1995). Conversation and cooperation in social dilemmas: A meta-analysis of experiments from 1958–1992. *Rationality and Society, 7,* 58–92.

Savage, L. J. (1954). *The foundations of statistics*. New York: Wiley.

Schopenhauer, A. (1999). *On the freedom of the will*. New York: Blackwell.

Sears, D. O. (1986). College sophomores in the laboratory: Influences of a narrow data set on social psychology's view of human nature. *Journal of Personality and Social Psychology, 51,* 515–530.

Shafir, E. (1994). Uncertainty and the difficulty of thinking through disjunctions. *Cognition, 50,* 403–430.

Shafir, E., & Tversky, A. (1992). Thinking through uncertainty: Nonconsequential reasoning and choice. *Cognitive Psychology, 24,* 449–474.

Shedler, J., Mayman, M., & Manis, M. (1993). The illusion of mental health. *American Psychologist, 48,* 1117–1131.

Surowiecki, J. (2004). *The wisdom of crowds*. New York: Doublday.

Tetlock, P. E. (2002). Theory-driven reasoning about plausible pasts and probable futures in world politics. In T. Gilovich, D. Griffin & D. Kahneman (Eds.), *Heuristics and biases: The psychology of intuitive judgment* (pp. 749–762). New York: Cambridge University Press.

Van Boven, L., & Loewenstein, G. (2003). Social projection of transient drive states. *Personality and Social Psychology Bulletin, 29,* 1159–1168.

Wegner, D. M. (2002). *The illusion of conscious will*. Cambridge, MA: MIT Press.

Wilson, T. D., & Dunn, E. W. (2004). Self-knowledge: Its limits, value and potential for improvement. *Annual Review of Psychology, 55,* 493–518.

Wohlschläger, A., Haggard, P., Gesierich, B., & Prinz, W. (2003). The perceived onset time of self- and other-generated actions. *Psychological Science, 14,* 586–591.

3

Cross-Situational Projection

LEAF VAN BOVEN
University of Colorado, Boulder
GEORGE LOEWENSTEIN
Carnegie Mellon University

> *I go eyeball to eyeball with some other creature—and I yearn to know the essential quality of its markedly different vitality... Give me one minute—just one minute—inside the skin of this creature... and then I will know what natural historians have sought through the ages... Instead, we can only peer in from the outside, look our subject straight in the face, and wonder, ever wonder.*
> —Stephen Jay Gould, 1998, p. 377

Although Gould lamented naturalists' inability to gain an insiders perspective of sloths and shrews, this fundamental barrier is not unique to interspecies perspective taking. Humans face a similar barrier when they try to understand what it feels like to be another human. We cannot step inside the skin of another human. Just as naturalists facing sloths and shrews, we can only peer in at other humans from the outside, look each other in the face, and wonder.

This problem of Other Minds is something of a hassle in everyday life. Most of our behavior is social, so many of our actions require at least a guess at other people's hearts and minds. It is not surprising, then, that many areas of social psychology are deeply concerned with perspective taking activity and ability. Impression formation, causal attribution, group dynamics, romantic relations, stereotypes and prejudice, negotiation and conflict resolution all relate in one way or another to people's attempts to predict and understand the psychological states of other people.

How and how well do people take others' perspective? Psychologists have long recognized that the self is the gravitational center of social judgment, and that people's judgments about other people tend to be egocentrically biased. Katz and Allport (1931), for instance, found that the more students admitted to cheating on exams, the more they expected others to cheat. Mintz (1956) found that children's age was correlated with their estimate of Peter Pan's age. Psychologists typically assume that this social projection reflects an overestimation of the true correlation between the self and judgments of others (Krueger, 1998).

The now classic, if not the first, demonstration of social projection was a study by Lee Ross and colleagues in which university students were asked whether they would "walk around campus for 30 minutes wearing a sandwich board sign which simply says: 'Repent'" (Ross, Greene, & House, 1977). The 50% of students who said that they would wear the sign estimated that 61% of other students at their university would also agree to wear the sign, whereas the students who would not wear the sign estimated that 43% of their peers would wear the sign. Students' own decision regarding sandwich board attire was thus correlated with their estimate of the percentage of their peers that would agree to wear the sign. This pattern, known as the "false consensus effect," is robust, widely replicated, and multiply determined (see Krueger & Clement, 1997; Marks & Miller, 1987).

Research on the false consensus effect has focused primarily on people's judgments of how other people would react to a similar situation faced by the self—faced with a similar choice about sandwich board attire, asked similar questions about the embarrassment elicited by various situations, asked about music preferences, and so on. Indeed, many researchers define social projection as an overestimation of the similarity between self and others. The horizontal dashed arrow in Figure 3.1 represents research in this tradition.

Notice, however, that in many, if not most, of the circumstances that require perspective taking, the perspective taker is in a different situation than the target of perspective taking. How severely does an employer think an employee will respond to criticism? How quickly does a teacher think students will learn a lesson? How nervous does a search committee think a candidate is during a job talk? In situations such as these, the task is to predict how another person reacts to a different situation than the situation the self is currently in.

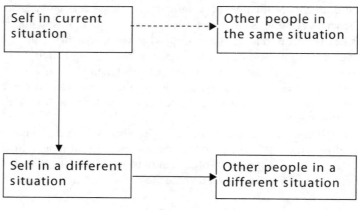

FIGURE 3.1

In this chapter, we outline a simple, dual judgment model of such cross-situational perspective taking. We suggest, essentially, that predictions of others' responses to different situations are based on predictions of one's own responses to different situations (represented by the two solid arrows in Figure 3.1). We report recent research, primarily from our own lab, that demonstrates the egocentric nature of cross-situational perspective taking, and show that biases and errors in self-predictions are closely associated with, and, we argue, cause biases and errors in social-predictions.

DUAL JUDGMENTS IN
CROSS-SITUATIONAL PERSPECTIVE TAKING

Mature adults typically realize that other people who are in a different situation may have beliefs, perceptions, preferences, and behavioral inclinations that differ form their own. We know, for example, that culinary aficionados perceive distinctions between fine cheeses that are lost on our own, untrained palates. We expect that someone who has not eaten in several hours is hungrier than we are, having just gorged on Ritz and Velveeta. And, even though we may have just learned that our manuscript was rejected, we expect someone whose grant was just funded to feel elated. In each case, perspective taking requires the realization and anticipation that because other people are in a different situation than the self—whether that difference concerns expertise, bodily drives, or emotional reactions—they will think and feel differently than the self.

We contend that cross-situational perspective taking entails two judgments, summarized by the two solid arrows in Figure 3.1. First, people predict what their own reactions would be to someone else's situation (the solid vertical arrow in Figure 3.1). Second, people moderate these self-predictions to accommodate perceived differences (or similarities) between the self and others (the solid horizontal arrow in Figure 3.1).

Several initial studies support the proposition that perspectives taken across different situations entail predictions of how the self would react to being in another's situation. In one, we showed participants a picture of three hikers (the two authors and Douglas Harsch) trudging through an Alaskan mountain meadow (Van Boven & Loewenstein, 2003). Accompanying the picture was a scenario describing how, because of a harrowing encounter with a bear, the three hikers were forced to travel through the wilderness for four days without food. After spending a few minutes estimating what the hikers were thinking and feeling during their ordeal, participants described in their own words "the processes and strategies you used to imagine what the hikers were thinking and feeling." Coders who were unaware of the hypothesis indicated that most participants (79%) explicitly described mentally trading places with the hikers, predicting how they would think and feel in the hikers' situation, even though hardly any participants reported having been in a similar situation.

A follow up study suggests that using the self as a basis for social predictions has intuitive appeal even when the self might seem highly dissimilar from others (Van Boven, Loewenstein, & Dunning, 2004). We asked males and females to read about the emotional experience of one of two protagonists. Some participants read about Tom, who experienced a bout with testicular cancer that required aggressive chemotherapy treatment. Other participants read about Sheila, whose son nearly died during a difficult and prolonged childbirth. After reading about Tom or Sheila, participants were asked to spend a few minutes estimating the protagonists' thoughts and feelings.

One might expect participants' gender to moderate their use of self as a basis for judging the protagonists' thoughts and feelings. Because female participants cannot have testicular cancer, they might judge their self-predictions to be less informative about Tom's experience than male participants; and because male participants cannot give birth, they might judge their self-predictions to be less informative about Shelia's experience than female participants. Indeed, when asked whether they mentally traded places with the protagonist, males reported trading places with Tom (87%) more than females did (75%), and females reported trading places with Shelia (87%) more than males did (74%). Notice, however, that most participants reported trading places even when the protagonist was of a different gender: Most males mentally traded places with Shelia, and most females mentally traded places with Tom.

These studies of perspective taking with hikers, cancer survivors, and birth givers suggest that self-prediction is an intuitively appealing starting point for cross-situational perspective taking. Just as people naturally use themselves as a standard of comparison when evaluating others' performance (Dunning & Hayes, 1996), they naturally use their self-predictions as a starting point when making social-predictions. The intuitive appeal of self-predictions, we suspect, stems largely from the self's high accessibility and people's well-developed (if incorrect) mental models of the self. It may simply be easy to form a rich mental picture of how the self would respond to being in different situations. It may even be difficult *not* to imagine how the self would react to being in a different situation (Hodges & Wegner, 1997).

Imperial though it may be, the self is not the only basis for cross-situational perspective taking (Karniol, 2003). In some cases, people may have well-developed mental models of how specific individuals respond to different situations ("Gary has quite an appetite, so losing his food would probably make him very hungry"). Or people may have stereotypes—i.e., mental models about groups of individuals—about how groups of people would respond to particular situations ("Women have a thing for chocolate, so I bet Ginger would prefer Godiva to grapes"). To the degree that people view others as dissimilar to the self, they make them more likely to use stereotypes as a basis for making predictions about others (Ames, in 2004a, 2004b).

CROSS-SITUATIONAL PROJECTION

People's use of self-predictions as a basis for making predictions about other people who are in different psychological situations implies that the accuracy of social-predictions depends critically on the accuracy of self-predictions. The accuracy of cross-situational perspective taking, in other words, depends largely on people's predictions of their own reactions to being in different situations. Previous research indicates that such self-predictions are biased. People tend to project their current perceptions, preferences, and behaviors onto their predictions of what their reactions would be in a different situation (Fischhoff, 1975; Gilbert, Gill, & Wilson, 2002; Hawkins & Hastie, 1991; Loewenstein, 1996; Loewenstein & Schkade, 1999). Based on this research, our model implies that these biases in self-predictions, which we refer to as "empathy gaps," should produce corresponding biases in social-predictions. We have tested this prediction in cross-situational perspective taking involving different nonemotional situations, and different emotional situations.

Hindsight Bias and Nonemotional Projection

Good teaching is difficult. As a teacher, a central challenge is judging how much (or how little) the students know about the subject at hand. Students poorly versed in twentieth century European history can hardly be expected to understand comparisons of the stability of governmental structures in the United States and Europe. Students who have little understanding of probability can hardly be expected to appreciate concepts such as statistical reliability. Students with little understanding of Game Theory can hardly be expected to comprehend references to games of Beauty Contests, Chicken, and Dictators.

Other social interactions require similar predictions. Giving directions, writing papers, having conversations—these interactions, and many more, require a judgment about the knowledge of other people who have less information of the self. Teachers, directors, writers, and speakers obviously recognize that their audience has less knowledge than themselves. But how much less? Answering this question requires perspective taking across different informational situations.

Perspective taking across different levels of information is complicated by the fact that what is clear in hindsight was often less clear in foresight. Hindsight is 20/20, the saying goes, but foresight is not. A large body of evidence indicates that even though people know that hindsight does not equal foresight, the clarity of hindsight nevertheless makes them think that foresight was clearer than it was (Fischhoff, 1975; Hawkins & Hastie, 1991).

According our dual-judgment model of cross-situational perspective taking, the hindsight bias in self-predictions should produce a corresponding bias in social-predictions. That is, people with unique knowledge should expect that knowledge to be more obvious to other, uninformed people than it actually is.

Several studies have demonstrated such a "curse of knowledge" (Camerer, Loewenstein, & Weber, 1989; Keysar, Ginzel, & Bazerman, 1995; Nickerson, 1999; Nickerson, Baddeley, & Freeman, 1987). In one, participants who observed a negotiation and were told that the motives of one of the negotiators (e.g., to be assertive or to be accommodating) overestimated how clear those motives were to the other negotiator (Vorauer & Claude, 1998). In another study, participants who were told the "true" meaning of archaic English idioms (e.g., "the goose hangs high") overestimated how clear the meaning would be to uninformed participants (Keysar & Bly, 1995). These results indicate that just as people project their private knowledge onto predictions of what their perceptions would have been without the knowledge, they also project their private knowledge onto other people who are not "in the know."

We suggest that the curse of knowledge stems partly from the hindsight bias. That is, informed people's biased predictions of the knowledge of uninformed individuals stems from informed people's biased "postdictions" of what their knowledge was before being informed. We conducted a taste test to examine this thesis (Van Boven, 2005). Participants tasted unmarked drinks of Coca-Cola and Pepsi. Participants in the uninformed condition were asked to indicate which drink they thought was Coke and which was Pepsi. These participants could not "taste the difference," correctly guessing the drinks' identities 50% of the time—indistinguishable from chance. Participants in the informed condition were told the drinks' identities before tasting them and then made two predictions. They were asked to imagine that they had not been told the drinks' identities and to predict which they would have guessed was Coke and which was Pepsi. Consistent with previous research on the hindsight bias, most participants (85%) predicted that they would have correctly identified the two drinks—substantially more than the 50% that were actually able to taste the difference. Informed participants were also asked to predict the answer of a randomly selected person from the uninformed condition. Consistent with previous research on the curse of knowledge, most informed participants (89%) thought that their uninformed peers would be able to taste the difference.

Our thesis that informed participants' hindsight bias produced a corresponding curse of knowledge is supported by the close correspondence between self- and social-predictions. Most participants (82%) predicted that others' identification of Coke or Pepsi would match their own judgments of the drinks' identity. The correspondence suggests that the hindsight bias in self-predictions contributes to the curse of knowledge in social predictions.

Of course, there may be other explanations for the results of the taste test study. It may be the case, for instance, that the hindsight bias did not cause the curse of knowledge. Instead, some other variable (e.g., perceived obviousness) may have caused both the hindsight bias and the curse of knowledge. An important task for future research is to compellingly demonstrate that the hindsight bias in self-predictions contributes to the curse of knowledge in social predictions.

Empathy Gaps and Emotional Projection

We have tested our dual-judgment model most extensively in perspective taking across different emotional situations. A growing body of evidence indicates that people in one emotional situation project their current preferences and behaviors onto their predictions of how they would respond in a different emotional situation. Specifically, when people are not emotionally aroused, they underestimate the impact of emotional arousal on their own preferences and behaviors. However, when people are emotionally aroused, they overestimate how much their preferences and behaviors in an unemotional situation state would resemble their current reactions.

These *empathy gaps* (Loewenstein, 1996) have been documented for several emotional states. For example, people who do not own an object underestimate how attached they would be to the object and how much they would require to part with the object if they owned it (Loewenstein & Adler, 1995; Van Boven, Dunning, & Loewenstein, 2000). People who do own an object overestimate how attached they would be to it and how much they would be willing to pay to acquire the object if they did not own it (Van Boven et al., 2000). People who are temporally removed from an embarrassing public performance think they would be more willing to perform in the "moment of truth" than they actually are (Van Boven, Loewenstein, Dunning, & Welch, 2005). People who are just about to exercise and are in a relatively neutral state predict they would be less bothered by thirst if they were lost without food or water than people who have just exercised and are thirsty and warm (Van Boven & Loewenstein, 2003). Men who are not sexually aroused predict they would be less likely to engage in sexually aggressive behavior than men who are sexually aroused (Loewenstein, Nagin, & Paternoster, 1997). People who are sated because they have just eaten are less likely to choose a high-calorie snack to consume at a well-defined time in the future than hungry people who have not eaten (Read & van Leeuwen, 1998). And people who are hungry because they have not eaten expect to be more interested in eating a plate of spaghetti for breakfast than people who are sated (Gilbert et al., 2002).

According to our model, empathy gaps in self-predictions should produce corresponding empathy gaps in social-predictions. In other words, people in one emotional situation should project their current preferences and behaviors onto other people who are in different emotional situations. We have tested this prediction in a variety of emotional states, including bodily drives and fear of embarrassment.

Bodily Drives

In one study, we asked participants entering a campus exercise facility who were going to engage in vigorous cardiovascular activity for at least 20 minutes to answer a few questions in exchange for a bottle of water (Van Boven & Loewenstein,

2003). Participants were randomly assigned to answer questions either immediately before or immediately after exercising, which we assumed would influence their state of thirst and warmth. Participants read a description of three hikers lost in the dry Colorado mountains without food or water. Participants were asked to predict whether hunger or thirst would be more unpleasant to the hikers (and to themselves), and whether the hikers (and themselves) would regret more not bringing water or not bringing food.

As expected, participants projected their momentarily aroused bodily drives onto their judgments of the hikers' feelings. Participants who had just exercised, and were presumably in a state similar to the hapless hikers, expected the hikers to be more bothered by thirst and to regret not bringing water with them more than participants who had not exercised (see the right side of Figure 3.2). This empathy gap in social-predictions mirrored participants' predictions of how they would feel in the hikers' situation (see the left side of Figure 3.2).

Subsequent analysis provides further support for our thesis that participants' self-predictions were the basis for their predictions about the lost hikers. According to our model, exercising arouses participants' thirst, which, along with their hunger, influences their self-predictions. Those self-predictions, in turn, influence their predictions of the lost hikers' feelings. To test this pattern of associations, we conducted a structural equation model (SEM), which assessed the relationship between variables in the model, controlling for all other (indirect) relationships between variables (see Figure 3.3). The model included five variables: the average of participants' two self-predictions (self-predictions), the average of their two

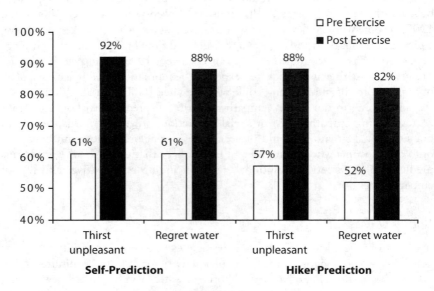

FIGURE 3.2

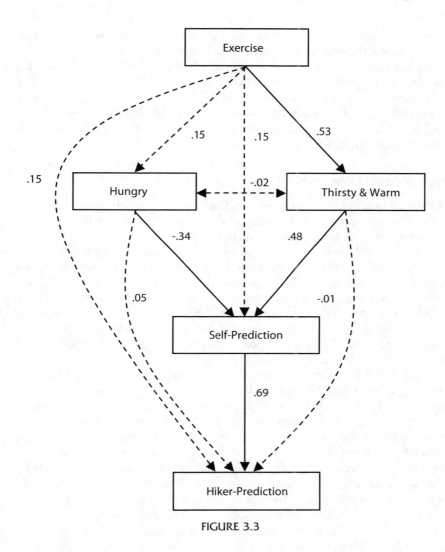

FIGURE 3.3

predictions of the lost hikers (hiker-predictions), participants' average ratings of their current thirst and warmth (thirsty & warm), participants' ratings of their current hunger (hungry), and a binomial variable indicating whether participants completed the survey before or after exercising.

The pattern of associations within the model is consistent with our thesis. The exercise manipulation was positively associated with participants' feeling thirsty and warm, confirming the success of our experimental manipulation. Participants' thirst and warmth was positively associated with, and their feelings of hunger negatively associated with, their self-predictions. Their self-predictions, in turn, were positively associated with their social-predictions. In fact, participants' self-prediction was the only measure reliably associated with participants' predictions of the lost hikers' feelings. These results indicate that the influence of exercising on participants' predictions of the hikers' feelings was fully explained by the impact of exercising and the resulting feelings of thirst and warmth on participants' predictions of their own feelings. These results strongly suggest that people's biased predictions of their own feelings play an important role in producing biased predictions of others' feelings.

Fear of Embarrassment

We have also tested our model in situations involving social anxiety, or fear of embarrassment, a potent self-based, social emotion. Fear of embarrassment is a powerful barrier to social behavior. Although it can prevent people from taking actions they might later regret (e.g., karaoke to Marvin Gaye's "Sexual Healing" at an office party), fear of embarrassment can also be problematic, preventing people from taking beneficial but embarrassing social actions. Indeed, many important failures to act have been partly attributed to fear of embarrassment, including nonintervention in emergency situations (Latané & Darley, 1970), nonopposition to unpopular policies or social norms (Miller & McFarland, 1987; Prentice & Miller, 1993; Van Boven, 2000), obedience to authority, and conformity to social norms (Sabini, Siepmann, & Stein, 2001).

Given the frequency with which people confront embarrassing situations, they might be expected to accurately predict their own responses to such situations. We found in previous studies, however, that people experience empathy gaps when they predict how they would respond to embarrassing situations. When embarrassing public performances are purely hypothetical or in the psychologically distant future, people overestimate how willing they would be to perform compared with when the performances are real and immediate (Van Boven, Loewenstein, Dunning et al., 2005). For instance, asked hypothetically whether they would be willing to perform a mime in front of a classroom filled with people, participants in one study predicted that they would be more willing to mime for $5 compared with people who were actually given the choice of miming for money. Because facing a hypothetical performance is less emotionally arousing than facing a real performance (Frijda, 1988, 1992), participants overestimate how willing, at the moment of truth, they would be to perform in front of a classroom audience. Buttressing this argument, we found that experimentally arousing people's emotions reduced their willingness to engage in performances that were hypothetical or in the distant future. Better in touch with the power of emotional arousal, people more accurately predicted the impact of fear of embarrassment on their willingness to engage in embarrassing performances.

According to our dual-judgment model, this *illusion of courage* in self-predictions should produce a corresponding illusion of courage in social predictions. We tested this prediction in one experiment by asking some of the students in a large lecture class to state the least amount of money they would have to be paid to dance by themselves on a stage in front of an auditorium full of people for five minutes to Rick James' 1981 song "Super Freak" (Van Boven, Loewenstein, & Dunning, 2005). We asked the other students in the class to imagine that they had been given the option of dancing for money, and to predict the least amount of money they would have to be paid to dance. These students facing a purely hypothetical performance exhibited an empathy gap in fear of embarrassment: They predicted that they would have to be paid less to dance ($21) than did students who actually faced the prospect of dancing ($53).

In addition, both groups of students predicted the minimum performance price stated by a randomly selected student (other than themselves) who faced the actual choice of dancing for money. As expected, students exhibited an empathy gap in social-predictions that mirrored their empathy gap in self-predictions. Students facing a purely hypothetical performance predicted that other students would be willing to dance for less money ($13) than students who themselves faced a potentially real performance ($19). Students who faced a real performance themselves thus rendered more realistic predictions of other students' willingness to perform.

Notice that both groups of students expected that other students would be willing to dance for less money than they would themselves, independent of whether students themselves faced a real or hypothetical performance. This self-other difference is consistent with previous research indicating that people believe others are less influenced than themselves by fear of embarrassment in particular, and by self-conscious emotions generally (McFarland & Miller, 1990; Sabini, Cosmas, Siepmann, & Stein, 1999; Van Boven, 2000). In terms of our model, students' expectation that others would be more willing to dance than themselves is important because it distinguishes the two judgments we suggest are involved in cross-situational perspective taking. Students' expectation that others' lowest performance price would be lower than their own illustrates their assessment of similarity—or dissimilarity, in this case—between self and others (the horizontal solid arrow in Figure 3.1). The fact that students who faced a purely hypothetical performance expected that other students would perform for less money than students who faced a real performance illustrates how self-predictions influence social predictions (the vertical solid arrow in Figure 3.1).

Students' predictions of their own and others' willingness to perform also affords a further examination of the judgments involved in perspective taking across emotional states. In our previous research, we found that, compared with students who faced a purely hypothetical performance, students who faced a real performance reported focusing their thoughts more on how they would be evaluated by their peers (the emotional costs of performing) than on the money they could earn (the monetary benefits of performing, Van Boven, Loewenstein, Dunning et al., 2005). To examine whether students would project this emotional focusing onto others, we asked them to report how much the student whose performance price they predicted thought about being evaluated by other people, and how much that student thought about the money. Students also reported how much, while stating their own lowest performance price, they thought about being evaluated and how much they thought about the money.

As an index of how much students focused their thoughts on being evaluated, we calculated the difference between reports of how much they thought about being evaluated and how much they thought about the money. Consistent with our previous results, students who faced a real performance focused more on being evaluated ($M_{\text{difference}}$ = 1.86) than students who faced a hypothetical performance ($M_{\text{difference}}$ = .91). As expected, students projected this emotional focusing onto the other student whose performance price they predicted. Students who faced a real performance themselves thought that the other student facing a real performance would focus on being evaluated more ($M_{\text{difference}}$ = 1.41) compared with students who faced a purely hypothetical performance ($M_{\text{difference}}$ = .73). These results indicate that, in addition to projecting their performance price, students projected their thoughts about the costs and benefits of performing for money.

These data allow further examination of the degree that people use their self-predictions as a basis for making predictions about other people. According to our model, students' predictions of their own performance prices should be the best predictor of their expectations of others' performance prices. We examined this possibility by conducting a SEM, displayed in Figure 3.4. The model includes: a variable indicating whether students faced a real or hypothetical performance (coded 1 or 0, respectively), the difference score reflecting students' focus on being evaluated by their peers (Own focus on evaluation), the difference score reflecting students' prediction of others' focus on being evaluated by their peers (Others' focus on evaluation), students own lowest performance price (Own performance price), and their prediction of the other students' performance price (Others' performance price).

Consider students' own performance prices first. The variable most closely associated with students' performance prices is students' focus on being evaluated by their peers. This is consistent with our other research on the illusion of courage in self-predictions: The emotional arousal caused by facing a real and immediate embarrassing performance causes students to focus on being evaluated by their peers; this shift in focus makes the performance less desirable, so students state higher performance prices than they predicted they would when the performance is purely hypothetical (Van Boven, Loewenstein, Dunning et al., 2005).

Next, consider students' predictions of other students' performance prices. The only variable independently associated with these prices is students' own performance prices. Notice that students' prediction of others' focus on being evaluated is not independently associated with students' prediction of others' performance prices. This is remarkable given that students' own focus on evaluation was the best predictor of their own performance price. Thus, students' prediction of other students' preference is more closely associated with their self-prediction than with their prediction of what other students' think about. This pattern of associations provides strong evidence that self-predictions are the basis for cross-situational perspective taking.

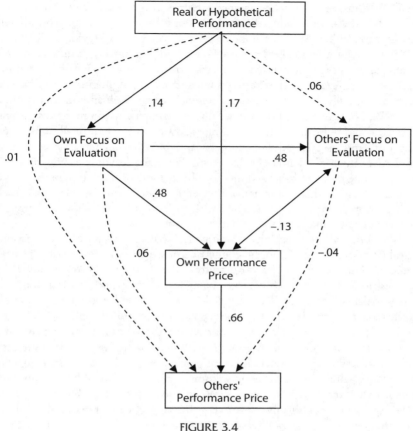

FIGURE 3.4

DISCUSSION

Our studies of cross-situational perspective taking suggest that predictions of how the self would respond to different situations are the basis for predictions of how other people would respond to different situations. The importance of self-predictions for social-predictions, and the resulting cross-situational social projection, has implications for at least three domains of social judgment and behavior.

Projection and Uniqueness

One intriguing aspect of cross-situational projection is the apparent contradiction with other, well-documented perceptions of uniqueness such as pluralistic ignorance and false uniqueness. Pluralistic ignorance occurs when most people erroneously believe that an unpopular norm or attitude or belief enjoys more public support than it actually does (Miller & McFarland, 1987; Prentice & Miller,

1996). False uniqueness occurs when people erroneously perceive themselves to be unique (Goethals, Messick, & Allison, 1991), possibly out of a desire to be different (Snyder & Fromkin, 1977) or to be better than one's peers (Taylor & Rachman, 1994). This contradiction between projection and perceptions of uniqueness may be more apparent than real, however. For one thing, projection is often operationalized as a positive correlation between self and social judgments. Uniqueness, in contrast, is usually defined as a mean difference between self and others (Sabini et al., 1999). These two measures are not directly comparable. In many cases, "false consensus" and "false uniqueness" may reflect conflicting operationalizations more than conflicting psychological phenomena, and the two tendencies may even occur simultaneously (McFarland & Miller, 1990). For example, while people think that they would be more embarrassed in a socially awkward situation than their peers (false uniqueness), their estimates of how embarrassed other people would be in that situation are positively correlated with their prediction of how embarrassed they would be (false consensus, Sabini et al., 1999).

Projection and perceptions of uniqueness may also reflect different psychological processes. Projection occurs largely because people believe their current or predicted responses are unbiased reactions to the situations they encounter, be it a request to wear a sandwich board or being lost in the woods without food or a request to dance for money. Because people's perceptual and emotional apparatus is, for the most part, similar to others' perceptual and emotional apparatus, it follows that other people will experience similar reactions to the same situations (Griffin & Ross, 1991; Pronin, Gilovich, & Ross, 2004; Ross & Ward, 1995). However, most people realize that their preferences and perceptions of the world are somewhat constructive—that their own desires, knowledge, and personal history uniquely influence their reactions to situations (Wegener & Petty, 1995; Wilson & Brekke, 1994). Being metacognitively aware of constructive processes opens the possibility that other people engage in different constructive processes than the self, and may therefore experience different reactions than the self to a given situation (Pronin et al., 2004; Pronin, Lin, & Ross, 2002). Thus, to the extent that one's responses are experienced as natural, unbiased reactions to the inherent properties of the stimulus, other people should be expected to respond similarly. But to the extent that one's responses are recognized as constructed reactions to the situation, other people may not be expected to respond similarly (cf, Krueger, 2000, 2002).

Consider the case of fear of embarrassment. Although most people have a wealth of evidence consistent with their own fear of embarrassment, evidence about others' fear of embarrassment is less accessible. The differential accessibility of one's own and other people's fear of embarrassment may make it seem that others are generally less concerned about embarrassment than the self (Miller & McFarland, 1987; Schwarz & Vaughn, 2002; Tversky & Kahneman, 1973). People's prediction of how willing other people are to engage in an embarrassing performance is thus a function of (a) the fact that public performances are inherently embarrassing and undesirable, and (b) the belief that others react to embarrassing situations somewhat differently than the self. Exploring the factors that moderate simultaneous perceptions of consensus and uniqueness, we believe, is an important task for future research.

Behavioral Consequences

One consequence of cross-situational projection is that it can lead people to behave toward others in ways they would not if they had an accurate understanding of others' psychological state. A homeowner might fail to appreciate how attached she is to her house simply because she happens to own it (Kahneman, Knetsch, & Thaler, 1990, 1993; Knetsch, 1989) and consequently demand too much money to sell it, incurring costs of time and opportunity. Or a buyer might fail to appreciate how much a homeowner values her house simply because she owns it and consequently offer too little money to purchase the home.

In previous research on empathy gaps between owners and nonowners, we have shown that nonowners' underestimation of owners' selling prices can lead them to behave in ways that cost them money (Van Boven et al., 2000, Study 3). We created a situation in which nonowners, assigned to the role of "buyer's agent," would benefit monetarily from accurately predicting how much owners valued their possessions (a plastic coffee mug), and then making an offer to purchase owners' possession. However, because buyer's agents were not themselves owners, they experienced empathy gaps, underestimated how much owners valued their possession, and made offers that were too low, resulting in a loss of money compared with what they could have earned if they had made higher offers that were more likely to be accepted.

Our analysis of social projection in producing costly social behavior implies that reducing social projection would produce more optimal social behavior. Corroborating this analysis, salespeople who can accurately discern the thoughts and feelings of customers tend to make more sales (Comer & Drollinger, 1999). Negotiators who try to see things from the other person's point of view are more likely to succeed, resolving more issues and reaching more optimal agreements (Neale & Bazerman, 1983). In our research, buyer's agents who were themselves given mugs to keep (but not sell) more accurately predicted what their own selling prices would be if they were an owner, more accurately predicted owners' selling prices, and consequently made higher offers that were more likely to be accepted (Van Boven et al., 2000). This last finding is important because it indicates that behavior toward other people can be improved by increasing the accuracy of self-predictions.

We suspect that these examples of misbehavior stemming from social projection are just the tip of the iceberg. The potential for projection-based misbehavior arises whenever the behavior of socially interacting individuals is based on their judgments about other people. Notice, too, that the potential for misbehavior is strongest when the difference between individuals' situations is robust and large. The disparity between drug addicts' and (nonaddicted) policy makers' psychological states, for instance, is strong and wide, so the potential for misguided policies looms large. Or consider a recent analysis of the Bush administration's erroneous conclusion that Saddam Hussein's antagonism toward United Nations weapons inspectors in the late 1990's and early 2000's implied the presence of weapons of mass destruction (Dowd, 2004). This erroneous conclusion, the analysis goes, was based on the administration's assumption that if they were in Saddam's situation, their own failure to cooperate could only imply they had something to hide. In other words, the George W. Bush Administration assumed that Saddam's behavior was guided by the same calculations that guide the Bush administration's own noncooperative behaviors. The resulting misconclusion that Saddam held weapons of mass destruction was a major justification of the 2003 Iraq war—a behavior increasingly considered to be misguided and wrong.

Person Perception Consequences

Just as projection may cause people to misbehave toward others, it may also cause people to misexplain others' behavior. As Ross and colleagues observed, "The intuitive psychologist judges those responses that differ from his [or her] own to be more revealing of the actor's stable dispositions than those responses which are similar to his own" (Ross et al., 1977, p. 280). In one of their studies, for instance, students who themselves chose to wear a sandwich board sign extolling viewers to "Repent" made stronger inferences about the dispositions of other people who chose not to wear the sign ("they must be shy") compared with students who themselves chose not to wear the sign (Ross et al., 1977, Study 4). Because people tend to view their own reactions behavior as unbiased, reasonable responses to situations, they naturally infer that different reactions reflect something distinctive about the others' underlying disposition.

A similar logic underlies cross-situational perspective taking. Our studies of empathy gaps across different psychological states suggest that people's explanations of others' behavior are influenced not only by the choices they actually make, but also by the choices they *think* they would make if they were in a different situation. For example, a student facing a hypothetical decision who overestimates her willingness to dance is likely to make overly strong inferences about the shyness of a nondancing student faced with an actual performance. That is, the student might use her (biased) self-prediction of how she would behave in a different situation as a basis for evaluating the behavior of people actually in that situation (Reeder, Fletcher, & Furman, 1989). Consistent with this possibility, we found in our studies of owners and buyer's agents, that individuals who did not reach an agreement—i.e., pairs in which the owners' selling price was higher than the agents' offer—attributed the other person's behavior more to dispositional greed than to a basic psychological difference between owners and nonowners (Van Boven et al., 2000, Study 4). We suspect that such projection-based misexplanations of others' behavior are common and contribute to projection-based misbehavior toward others.

In one sense, the logic underlying people's attributions is perfectly reasonable, given their projection. If people perceive a behavior to be relatively unique, then they *should* make stronger inferences about the dispositions of others who engage in that behavior compared with individuals who engage in more common behavior (Kelley, 1967; McArthur, 1972). A Democrat who perceives Democratic voters as relatively common should make stronger inferences about the dispositions of Republican voters, who are perceived as relatively unique. And owners should make inferences about the dispositions of buyers when buyers' behavior does not match the owners' reasonable expectations.

In another sense, this attributional logic is misguided. Because they socially project, Democrats' misestimate that Republicans are more unique than they are, and owners' mispredict that buyers will find their commodity to be more valuable than they do. In addition to many other attributional biases (Gilbert, 1998; Gilbert & Malone, 1995), social projection means people have unrealistic expectations of others' social behavior. When the behavior people observe violates their (biased) expectations, they make (biased) inferences about the dispositions of the behavior rather than something about their unrealistic expectations (Reeder et al., 1989).

Learning About Social Projection

One consequence of misinterpreting behavior because of social projection is that individuals may have difficulty learning about their own social projection. To learn about and correct social projection requires prompt, unambiguous, accurate feedback about one's biased judgments (Einhorn, 1982). Such feedback may be rare. And, as discussed in the previous section, even when people do receive feedback about their biased or erroneous judgments, they are likely to misinterpret the mismatch between their judgments and the behavior of others as evidence of others' underlying dispositions, rather than something misguided about their prediction.

Several studies indicate that people do not learn about social projection, even when given ample evidence suggesting that their projection is inappropriate or erroneous. In one such study, participants projected their own decision to wear a sandwich board or not, even after learning that a large number of other students had agreed to wear the board (Krueger & Clement, 1994). Thus, people continue to project their own reactions even when they have unambiguous information that their own behavior is uninformative.

In studies of projection between owners and buyer's agents, we have found that costly, projection-based behavior persists even in the face of feedback that projective predictions are incorrect and produce costly behavior (Van Boven, Loewenstein, & Dunning, 2003). As in earlier studies, agents made an offer to purchase an owners' possession (coffee mugs or other trinkets), and owners stated their lowest selling prices. Owners and agents repeated this exercise four times, each with a randomly selected person in the other role. Agents' offers increased

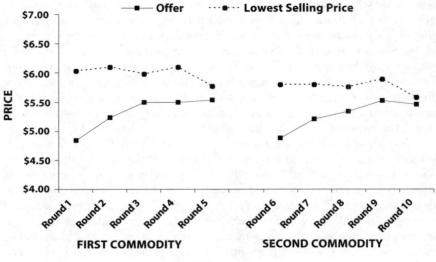

FIGURE 3.5

over time while owners' selling prices were stable (see the left half of Figure 3.5). Agents thus appeared to learned to correct their projection-based misbehavior.

This learning was rather specific, however. After five rounds, owners and agents were told that the market for that particular commodity was closed. Owners were then given a second, different possession (a trinket of similar value as the first commodity), and agents and owners were told they would repeat the buying and selling procedure, exactly as before. Notice what happened in the first round with the new commodity. If agents had learned that owners tend to value their possession simply because they own them, then their first offers for the new commodity should resemble their final offers for the first commodity. To the contrary, agents' first offers for the second commodity were once again substantially lower than owners' selling prices (see the right half of Figure 3.5). Agents thus started at square one, transferring little or none of their learning about owners' value of one commodity to owners' value of a (superficially different) second commodity. This finding is consistent with other research indicating that even when people learn to change their behavior to produce desired outcomes, they have difficulty understanding the psychological processes that produce the desired outcome so that superficial situational changes eliminate their learning (Bassok, Wu, & Olseth, 1995). The fact that social projection occurs in the face of contradictory evidence points to the subjectively compelling nature of social projection.

The results of these studies indicate that learning about social projection is difficult during the relatively short time span of a psychology experiment. But what about over the course of a lifetime? As people age and learn that others' reactions and mental states sometimes differ form their own, it seems reasonable that they may learn to reign in their projective tendencies (Royzman, Cassidy, &

Baron, 2003). Several studies hint at a decline in social projection over time. In one, children's age (range 7 to 9) was negatively correlated with a false consensus effect (Wetzel & Walton, 1985). In another, older university students (M age = 76) exhibited a smaller false consensus effect than middle-aged adults who, in turn, exhibited a smaller false consensus effect than adolescents (Yinon, Mayraz, & Fox, 1994). Other studies suggest that the curse of knowledge also declines with age. In a study with 3-, 4-, and 5-year-olds, younger children exhibited a larger curse of knowledge than did older children (Birch & Bloom, 2003). Another study conceptually replicated this developmental decline in curse of knowledge, and found that the curse of knowledge was smaller among university students than among young children (Bernstein, Atance, Loftus, & Meltzoff, 2004, Experiment 1).

These developmental findings are intriguing and raise many questions. Does social projection across different emotional situations decline with age? Does social projection decline linearly with age? Or are early declines more substantial than declines later in life? Does declining projection reflect a qualitative shift in psychological processes? Or does it reflect greater facility in correcting one's initial, egocentric judgments? These open questions, and the increasing interest in psychological processes among the elderly, suggest that developmental patterns in social projection will be an important and active topic of future research.

CONCLUSION

Cross-situational projection is a mixed blessing. Like many judgmental tendencies, projection frequently yields accurate assessments, and is often an efficient way of making social judgments (Dawes, 1989, 1990; Hoch, 1987; Krueger, 1998). When little or nothing is known about others, the self is a reasonable basis for judging others.

The problem is that self-knowledge is often limited, biased, and sometimes just plain wrong (for recent reviews see Wegner, 2002; Wilson, 2002). We suspect that most of these biased and erroneous self-judgments have corresponding biased and erroneous social judgments. If the key to knowing others is knowing the self, it is unfortunate that self-knowledge is so limited.

REFERENCES

Ames, D. (2004a). Inside the mind-reader's toolkit: Projection and stereotyping in mental state inference. *Journal of Personality and Social Psychology, 87*, 340–353.

Ames, D. (2004b). Strategies for social inference: Projecting to the similar and stereotyping to the different attribute prevalence judgments. *Journal of Personality and Social Psychology, 87*, 573–585.

Bassok, M., Wu, L. L., & Olseth, K. L. (1995). Judging a book by its cover: Interpretive effects of content on problem-solving transfer. *Memory and Cognition, 23*, 354–367.

Bernstein, D. M., Atance, C., Loftus, G. R., & Meltzoff, A. N. (2004). We saw it all along: Visual hindsight bias in children and adults. *Psychological Science, 15*, 264–267)

Birch, S. A. J., & Bloom, P. (2003). Children are cursed: An asymmetric bias in mental-state attribution. *Psychological Science, 14*, 283–286.

Camerer, C., Loewenstein, G., & Weber, M. (1989). The curse of knowledge in economic settings: An experimental analysis. *Journal of Political Economy, 97*, 1232–1254.

Comer, L. B., & Drollinger, T. (1999). Active empathetic listening and selling success: A conceptual framework. *Journal of Personal Selling and Sales Management, 19*, 15–29.

Dawes, R. M. (1989). Statistical criteria for establishing a truly false consensus effect. *Journal of Experimental Social Psychology, 25*, 1–17.

Dawes, R. M. (1990). The potential nonfalsity of the false consensus effect. In R. M. Hogarth (Ed.), *Insights in decision making: A tribute to Hillel J. Einhorn* (pp. 179–199). Chicago, IL: University of Chicago Press.

Dowd, M. February 1 (2004). The mirror has two faces. *The New York Times*, p. 11.

Dunning, D., & Hayes, A. F. (1996). Evidence for egocentric comparison in social judgment. *Journal of Personality & Social Psychology*, 213–229.

Einhorn, H. J. (1982). Learning from experience and suboptimal rules in decision making. In D. Kahneman, P. Slovic & A. Tversky (Eds.), *Judgment under uncertainty: Heuristics and biases* (pp. 268–286). Cambridge, MA: University of Cambridge Press.

Fischhoff, B. (1975). Hindsight is not equal to foresight: the effect of outcome knowledge on judgment under uncertainty. *Journal of Experimental Psychology: Human Perception and Performance, 1*, 288–299.

Frijda, N. H. (1988). The laws of emotion. *American Psychologist, 43*, 349–358.

Frijda, N. H. (1992). The empirical status of the laws of emotion. *Cognition and Emotion, 6*, 467–477.

Gilbert, D. T. (1998). Ordinary personology. In D. Gilbert, S. T. Fiske, & G. Lindzey (Eds.), *Handbook of social psychology* (Vol. 2, 4th ed., pp. 89–50). New York: McGraw-Hill.

Gilbert, D. T., Gill, M. J., & Wilson, T. D. (2002). The future is now: Temporal correction in affective forecasting. *Organizational Behavior and Human Decision Processes, 88*, 430–444.

Gilbert, D. T., & Malone, P. S. (1995). The correspondence bias. *Psychological Bulletin, 117*, 21–38.

Goethals, G. R., Messick, D. M., & Allison, S. T. (1991). The uniqueness bias: Studies of constructive social comparison. In J. Suls & T. A. Will (Eds.), *Social comparison: Contemporary theory and research* (pp. 149–176). Hillsdale, NJ: Erlbaum.

Gould, S. J. (1998). Can we truly know sloth and rapacity? In *Leonardo's Mountain of Clams and the Diet of Worms* (pp. 375-391). New York, NY: Three Rivers Press.

Griffin, D. W., & Ross, L. (1991). Subjective construal, social inference, and human misunderstanding. In L. Berkowitz (Ed.), *Advances in experimental social psychology* (Vol. 24, pp. 319–359). San Diego, CA: Academic Press.

Hawkins, S. A., & Hastie, R. (1991). Hindsight: Biased judgments of past events after the outcomes are known. *Psychological Bulletin, 107*, 311–327.

Hoch, S. J. (1987). Perceived consensus and predictive accuracy: The pros and cons of projection. *Journal of Personality and Social Psychology, 53*, 221–234.

Hodges, S., & Wegner, D. (1997). Automatic and controlled empathy. In W. J. Ickes (Ed.), *Empathic accuracy* (pp. 311–339). New York: Guilford Press.

Kahneman, D., Knetsch, J., & Thaler, R. (1990). Experimental tests of the endowment effect and the coase theorem. *Journal of Political Economy, 98*, 1325–1348.

Kahneman, D., Knetsch, J., & Thaler, R. (1993). The endowment effect, loss aversion, and status quo bias. *Journal of Economic Perspectives, 5*, 193–206.

Karniol, R. (2003). Egocentrism versus protocentrism: The status of the self in social prediction. *Psychological Review, 110*, 564–580.

Katz, C., & Allport, F. (1931). *Students' attitudes*. Syracuse, NY: Craftsman Press.

Kelley, H. H. (1967). Attribution theory in social psychology. In D. Levine (Ed.), *Nebraska Symposium on Motivation* (Vol. 15, pp. 192–238). Lincoln: University of Nebraska Press.

Keysar, B., & Bly, B. (1995). Intuitions of the transparency of idioms: Can one keep a secret by spilling the beans? *Journal of Memory and Language, 34*, 89–109.

Keysar, B., Ginzel, L. E., & Bazerman, M. H. (1995). States of affairs and states of mind: The effects of knowledge on beliefs. *Organizational Behavior and Human Decision Processes, 64*, 283–293.

Knetsch, J. (1989). The endowment effect and evidence of nonreversible indifference curves. *The American Economic Review, 79*, 1277–1284.

Krueger, J. (1998). On the perception of social consensus. In M. Zanna (Ed.), *Advances in experimental social psychology* (Vol. 30, pp. 163–240). San Diego, CA: Academic Press.

Krueger, J. (2000). The projective perception of the social world: A building block of social comparison processes. In J. Suls & L. Wheeler (Eds.), *Handbook of social comparison: Theory and research* (pp. 323–351). New York: Plenum/Kluwer.

Krueger, J. (2002). On the reduction of self-other asymmetrie: Benefits, pitfalls, and other correlates of social projection. *Psychologica Belgica, 42*, 23–41.

Krueger, J., & Clement, R. W. (1994). The truly false consensus effect: An ineradicable and egocentric bias in social perception. *Journal of Personality and Social Psychology, 67*, 596–610.

Krueger, J., & Clement, R. W. (1997). Estimates of social consensus by majorities and minorities: The case for social projection. *Personality and Social Psychology Review, 1*, 299–313.

Latané, B., & Darley, J. M. (1970). *The unresponsive bystander: Why doesn't he help?* Englewood Cliffs, NJ: Prentice Hall.

Loewenstein, G. (1996). Out of control: Visceral influences on behavior. *Organizational Behavior and Human Decision Processes, 65*, 272–292.

Loewenstein, G., & Adler, D. (1995). A bias in the prediction of tastes. *The Economic Journal, 105*, 929–937.

Loewenstein, G., Nagin, D., & Paternoster, R. (1997). The effect of sexual arousal on predictions of sexual forcefulness. *Journal of Crime and Delinquency, 32*, 443–474.

Loewenstein, G., & Schkade, D. (1999). Wouldn't it be nice? Predicting future feelings. In D. Kahneman, E. Diener, and N. Schwarz (Eds.), *Well being: The foundation of hedonic psychology* (pp. 85–108). New York: Russell Sage.

Marks, G., & Miller, N. (1987). Ten years of research on the false consensus effect: An empirical and theoretical review. *Psychological Bulletin, 102*, 72–90.

McArthur, L. A. (1972). The how and what of why: Some determinants and consequences of causal attribution. *Journal of Personality and Social Psychology, 22*, 171–193.

McFarland, C., & Miller, D. T. (1990). Judgments of self-other similarity: Just like other people, only more so. *Personality and Social Psychology Bulletin, 16*, 475–484.

Miller, D. T., & McFarland, C. (1987). Pluralistic ignorance: When similarity is interpreted as dissimilarity. *Journal of Personality and Social Psychology, 53*, 298–305.

Mintz, E. (1956). An example of assimilative projection. *Journal of Abnormal and Social Psychology, 52*, 270–280.

Neale, M. A., & Bazerman, M. H. (1983). The effects of perspective taking ability under alternate forms of arbitration on the negotiation process. *Industrial and Labor Relations Review, 36*, 378–388.

Nickerson, R. S. (1999). How we know—and sometimes misjudge—what others know: Imputing one's own knowledge to others. *Psychological Bulletin, 125*, 737–759.

Nickerson, R. S., Baddeley, A., & Freeman, B. (1987). Are people's estimates of what other people know influenced by what they themselves know? *Acta Psychologica, 64*, 245–259.

Prentice, D. A., & Miller, D. T. (1993). Pluralistic ignorance and alcohol use on campus: Some consequences of misperceiving the social norm. *Journal of Personality and Social Psychology, 64*, 243–256.

Prentice, D. A., & Miller, D. T. (1996). Pluralistic ignorance and the perpetuation of social norms by unwitting actors. In M. Zanna (Ed.), *Advances in experimental social psychology* (Vol. 28, pp. 161–209). San Diego, CA: Academic Press.

Pronin, E., Gilovich, T., & Ross, L. (2004). Objectivity in the eye of the beholder: Divergent perceptions of bias in self versus others. *Psychological Review, 111*, 781–799.

Pronin, E., Lin, D. Y., & Ross, L. (2002). The bias blind spot: Perceptions of bias in self versus others. *Personality & Social Psychology Bulletin, 28*, 369–381.

Read, D., & van Leeuwen, B. (1998). Time and desire: The effects of anticipated and experienced hunger and delay to consumption on the choice between healthy and unhealthy snack food. *Organizational Behavior and Human Decision Processes, 76*, 189–205.

Reeder, G. D., Fletcher, G. J., & Furman, K. (1989). The role of observers' expectations in attitude attribution. *Journal of Experimental Social Psychology, 25*, 168–188.

Ross, L., Greene, D., & House, P. (1977). The "false-consensus effect:" An egocentric bias in social perception and attribution processes. *Journal of Experimental Social Psychology, 13*, 279–301.

Ross, L., & Ward, A. (1995). Psychological barriers to dispute resolution. In M. P. Zanna (Ed.), *Advances in experimental social psychology, Vol. 27* (pp. 255–304). San Diego, CA: Academic Press.

Royzman, E. B., Cassidy, K. W., & Baron, J. (2003). "I know, you know": Epistemic egocentrism in children and adults. *Review of General Psychology, 7*, 38–65.

Sabini, J., Cosmas, K., Siepmann, M., & Stein, J. (1999). Underestimates and truly false consensus effects in estimates of embarrassment and other emotions. *Basic and Applied Social Psychology, 21*, 233–241.

Sabini, J., Siepmann, M., & Stein, J. (2001). The really fundamental attribution error in social psychological research. *Psychological Inquiry, 12*, 1–15.

Schwarz, N., & Vaughn, L. A. (2002). The availability heuristic revisited: Ease of recall and content of recall as distinct sources of information. In T. Gilovich, D. Griffin & D. Kahneman (Eds.), *Heuristics and biases: The psychology of intuitive judgment.* (pp. 103–119). New York: Cambridge University Press.

Snyder, C. R., & Fromkin, H. L. (1977). Abnormality as a positive characteristic: The development and validation of a scale measuring need for uniqueness. *Journal of Abnormal Psychology, 86*, 518–527.

Taylor, S., & Rachman, S. J. (1994). Stimulus estimation and the overprediction of fear. *British Journal of Clinical Psychology, 33*, 173–181.

Tversky, A., & Kahneman, D. (1973). Availability: A heuristic for judging frequency and probability. *Cognitive Psychology, 5*, 207–232.

Van Boven, L. (2000). Pluralistic ignorance and political correctness: The case of affirmative action. *Political Psychology, 21*, 267–276.

Van Boven, L. (2004). *The hindsight bias in self-predictions and the curse of knowledge in social-predictions.* Unpublished data, University of Colorado, Boulder.

Van Boven, L., Dunning, D., & Loewenstein, G. (2000). Egocentric empathy gaps between owners and buyers: Misperceptions of the endowment effect. *Journal of Personality and Social Psychology, 79*, 66–76.

Van Boven, L., & Loewenstein, G. (2003). Social projection of transient drive states. *Personality and Social Psychology Bulletin, 29*, 1159–1168.

Van Boven, L., Loewenstein, G., & Dunning, D. (2003). Mispredicting the endowment effect: underestimation of owners' selling prices buy buyer's agents. *Journal of Economic Behavior and Organization, 51*, 351–365.

Van Boven, L., Loewenstein, G., & Dunning, D. (2004). *Changing places: A theory of empathy gaps in emotional perspective taking.* Unpublished manuscript, University of Colorado, Boulder.

Van Boven, L., Loewenstein, G., & Dunning, D. (2005). The illusion of courage in social-predictions: Underestimating the impact of fear of embarrassment on other people. *Organizational Behavior and Human Decision Processes, 96*, 130-141.

Van Boven, L., Loewenstein, G., Dunning, D., & Welch, N. (2005). *The illusion of courage: Underestimating the impact of fear of embarrassment on the self.* Unpublished manuscript, University of Colorado, Boulder.

Vorauer, J. D., & Claude, S. (1998). Perceived versus actual transparency goals in negotiation. *Personality and Social Psychology Bulletin, 24*, 371–385.

Wegener, D. T., & Petty, R. E. (1995). Flexible correction processes in social judgment: The role of naïve theories in corrections for perceived bias. *Journal of Personality and Social Psychology, 68*, 36–51.

Wegner, D. M. (2002). *The illusion of conscious will.* Cambridge, MA: MIT Press.

Wetzel, C. G., & Walton, M. D. (1985). Developing biased social judgments: The false consensus effect. *Journal of Personality and Social Psychology, 49*, 1352–1359.

Wilson, T. D. (2002). *Strangers to ourselves: Discovering the adaptive unconscious.* Cambridge, MA: Belknap Press of Harvard University Press.

Wilson, T. D., & Brekke, N. (1994). Mental contamination and mental correction: Unwanted influences on judgments and evaluations. *Psychological Bulletin, 116*, 117–142.

Yinon, Y., Mayraz, A., & Fox, S. (1994). Age and the false consensus effect. *Journal of Social Psychology, 134*, 717–725.

PART *II*

SELF-ENHANCEMENT

4

Shallow Thoughts About the Self
The Automatic Components of Self-Assessment

THOMAS GILOVICH
Cornell University
NICHOLAS EPLEY
University of Chicago
KARLENE HANKO
Cornell University

*I*t is not our intent to coin a new term, but any review of the pertinent social psychological literature leads to the conclusion that people are prone to an illusion of personal strength. That is, people's assessments of their own abilities to meet various challenges exceed the best dispassionate analyses of those abilities. People read about Milgram's obedience experiments and come away convinced that they, unlike the majority of actual participants in those studies, would be strong enough to stand their ground and disobey the experimenter (Bierbrauer, 1979). People read about the various bystander (non)intervention studies and likewise remain convinced that they would have sufficient strength to overcome the fear of embarrassment and come to the rescue. And people's assessments of their own traits and abilities have been shown, time and time again, to be overly optimistic (see Alicke & Govorun, this volume).

Our aim in this chapter is to shed light on why people are prone to such an illusion of personal strength. This aim is likely to make some readers wonder whether we are prone to the illusion of personal strength ourselves. After all, there are already perfectly satisfactory explanations of the various manifestations of this illusion. Do we really have anything useful to add? Is another perspective likely to advance our discipline's understanding of these phenomena? Does the discipline really need yet another explanation of the above average effect?

We believe there is still much to be learned about the processes that give rise to the various manifestations of the illusion of personal strength. In particular, we believe that recent theoretical developments concerning the automaticity of everyday behavior (Ferguson & Bargh, 2004) and the "two systems" that people bring to bear in making judgments (Chaiken & Trope, 1999; Epstein, 1994; Kahneman & Frederick, 2002; Sloman, 1996) can shed new light on overly-optimistic self-assessments. One system of judgment, sometimes called "System 1," is associationist and produces rapid, effortless assessments in parallel fashion. The other, "System 2," is rule-based and deductive, and produces more effortful, deliberative assessments in serial fashion. Our aim in this chapter is to explore how recent work on automaticity and dual-process approaches to judgment might provide a more complete understanding of various forms of personal overconfidence such as the above average effect.

The guiding insight is that such optimistic self-assessments typically result from, or at least begin with, a minimum of reflection and the shallowest of thinking. Unless there are unusually powerful incentives for deeper analysis (Tetlock, 1992), individuals will typically offer "snap" self-assessments that arise automatically from a set of rudimentary mental processes involved in understanding the particular self-assessment context at hand. The question, therefore, is why such System-1-based snap assessments tend to be optimistic. What is it about this sort of shallow thinking that leads so often to an illusion of personal strength? We devote the bulk of this chapter to precisely that question.

We begin by reviewing evidence consistent with our proposition that people's assessments of their traits and abilities—and how their traits and abilities stack up to others or the demands that must be faced—are of a rapid-fire and rather cursory sort. We then examine the kinds of thoughts that are likely to spring to mind when people ask themselves such questions as "Would I have obeyed the experimenter if I were a participant in Milgram's studies?", "Would I become as loony as Elvis Presley, Michael Jackson, or Kim Jong II if I were surrounded by obsequious aides and my every whim were indulged?", or "Where do I stand among my peers in terms of my ability to get along with others?" We show how the very nature of these thoughts are likely to lead to the kind of favorable verdicts consistent with an illusion of personal strength.

We also contend that the optimistic biases that result from such thoughts are likely to remain even when the deliberative processes of "System 2" are called upon to inspect and perhaps modify the output of System 1. System 1 gets there first, and so its products are likely to channel subsequent System 2 processing, with the result that any corrections to one's initial assessments are likely to be insufficient. Finally, we conclude by discussing sources of variability in self-assessments and by examining the circumstances under which people's self-assessments are likely to be less positive.

EVIDENCE OF THE SHALLOWNESS OF SELF-ASSESSMENT

Most traits and abilities are inherently comparative. To say that one is a terrible carpenter but a competent writer, for instance, requires a comparison of one's own efforts at a table saw and computer terminal to the efforts of others. So too with personal traits: a person is tall because others are short, witty because others are dull, or attractive because others are less so. Yet research indicates that most people pay scant attention to others' traits or abilities when assessing their own, making the modal subject in the modal self-assessment experiment look anything but deep and reflective.

Most people, for example, believe that they are happier than their peers because they simply ignore how happy their peers might be and answer the comparative question by consulting only their own absolute happiness (Klar & Giladi, 1999). The answer to the simpler question, "How happy am I?" is substituted for the more challenging, "How happy am I compared to others?" Similarly, people's assessments of whether they are above or below average in the ability to meet various challenges or accomplish certain tasks are based primarily on a simple read-out of their own relevant capacities or life histories (Kruger, 1999). Because most people can ride a bicycle without difficulty, most people consider themselves to be above average bicyclists. But because most people would have trouble keeping a unicycle upright, most people think they are below average unicyclists. Owning a home strikes most people (most college respondents at any rate) as likely, and so most think they are more likely than most people to own a home; owning an island strikes most people as something of a pipe dream, and so most think they are less likely than others to own one (Kruger & Burrus, 2004).

To be sure, the comparative nature of these sorts of assessments is not always emphasized, making some degree of shallow thinking understandable. However, similar effects have been found in contexts in which the comparison between oneself and others is explicit—and obvious. For example, people in performance competitions act as if shared impediments and facilitators will have a bigger impact on them than on their rivals. Thus, people think that they have a better chance of winning a trivia contest if the questions are easy—even though they know that their opponents will be fed the same easy questions. And people bet more on a round of poker if there are more wild cards in play because the wild cards make better hands easier to obtain—never mind that they make such hands easier for one's opponent to obtain as well (Windschitl, Kruger, & Simms, 2003; see also Moore & Kim, 2003).

Not all self-assessments require an interpersonal comparison of oneself and others; some require a comparison of the costs and benefits of a decision, or the strengths and weaknesses of one's case. The outcome of a romantic relationship, for example, depends not only on its joys and other positive features of the relationship, but also on its sorrows, annoyances, and other negative features. And yet people appear to base their predictions of the health and longevity of their own relationships almost exclusively on its positive elements, all but ignoring the negative (MacDonald & Ross, 1999). It is small wonder, then, that people's forecasts of what's in store for their relationships are so often optimistically biased.

On the basis of results like these, it is hard to argue that most people's assessments of their personal traits, abilities, or futures are the product of deep thought and an exhaustive consideration of the pertinent evidence. Quick, cursory thought about such matters appears to be the norm. The question, then, is why such cursory thinking tends to produce overly optimistic assessments.

WHY ARE SHALLOW THOUGHTS ABOUT THE SELF SO OFTEN OPTIMISTIC?

The key to understanding why people's quick assessments of their traits and abilities are typically so positively skewed is to recognize that most people regard themselves positively and have good intentions. These two facts steer people's initial thoughts down paths that predispose them toward an illusion of personal strength in the overwhelming majority of domains they might consider.

Implicit Self-Esteem and Optimistic Self-Assessments

Ideas advanced in numerous areas of psychology—from balance theory (Heider, 1958), to connectionism (Rumelhart & McClelland, 1986; Smith, 1996), to work on the Implicit Association Test (Greenwald et al., 2002)—converge on the prediction that when two items in a mental network are each strongly linked to a third, the two will tend to become linked themselves. Thus, people who regard themselves favorably and have a positive stance toward, say, recycling are likely to connect themselves and recycling behavior more strongly than those who either lack self-esteem or don't value such behavior. This initial link—however weak or tentative—then serves to "lean" such individuals toward a positive assessment of their recycling efforts.

When the question is fully engaged—"How do I compare to my peers in terms of my recycling habits?"—most people go beyond this initial association, but the association can nonetheless steer these additional efforts in a particular direction. Because people tend to test hypotheses by trying to confirm them (Klayman & Ha, 1987; Slowiaczek, Klayman, Sherman, & Skov, 1992), they are likely to answer questions about their capacities by searching for evidence that they have them, at the expense of evidence that they do not. Note that this search for confirmatory information need not be effortful or deliberate. People do not need to deliberate and *choose* to search for confirmatory information; they just do. When one considers the question, "Am I good hearted?", the search for evidence consistent with that proposition is reflexive; it is the search for evidence *inconsistent* with the proposition that is effortful and uncertain (Crocker, 1982; Skov & Sherman, 1986; Ward & Jenkins, 1965; Wason & Johnson-Laird, 1972).

In extensive programs of research on both anchoring and social comparison, Thomas Mussweiler has shown just how rapid and effortless such confirmatory searches can be (Mussweiler, 2003; Strack & Mussweiler, 1997). This research has demonstrated, for example, that anchoring effects are obtained in the standard anchoring paradigm through a confirmation-based heightened accessibility of anchor-consistent information. When individuals are first asked a comparative question (e.g., "Did Mahatma Gandhi live to be more or less than 140 years old?"), they begin by asking themselves whether the target value is the correct value ("Could Gandhi have lived to 140?"). Because they tackle such questions by engaging in a confirmatory search for pertinent information, information consistent with the target value (in this case, a very aged Gandhi) is disproportionately accessible when the critical question is addressed ("How old was Gandhi when he died?") As a result, people estimate that Gandhi lived longer after first considering whether he died before or after the age of 140 than after first considering whether he died before or after the age of 9. It is the enhanced accessibility of anchor-consistent information that gives rise to the anchoring effect.

It would be hard to maintain that people spend much time or effort searching for evidence that Gandhi lived to be 140. Rather, facts consistent with an elderly Gandhi simply spring to mind. They are elicited automatically from the details of the question and the confirmatory-search routines we habitually use to examine propositions. Indeed, the magnitude of these anchoring effects are not influenced by manipulations that increase or decrease the ability to engage in effortful thought (Epley & Gilovich, in press; Mussweiler & Strack, 1999; Wilson, Houston, Etling, & Brekke, 1996), attesting to the rather shallow and automatic nature of these effects. The same confirmatory search process is likely to occur when we examine the possibility that we are good drivers, are kind to our coworkers, or are likely to help someone in distress. If our view of ourselves and of these behaviors are both positive, such that we engage the question by asking whether we have the capacity in question, we are likely to search for evidence that we do indeed have such capacities.

A variety of factors collude to ensure that when people search for such evidence, they are likely to find it. Because people are typically able to choose their battles, most people experience more success in life than failure. People who lack a talent for stringing words together are unlikely to write much after completing school. People with two left feet are unlikely to take many ungraceful turns on the dance floor. To be sure, people seek out challenges and engage in risky enterprises, and none of us is a stranger to failure (Lewin, Dembo, Festinger, & Sears, 1944; Csikszentmihalyi, 1990). Still, life is short, and most people choose to spend their time engaging in tasks for which they have some talent, and avoiding those at which they are inept. This has the obvious and happy result of filling our lives with more triumphs than tribulations—even if the tribulations occupy more of our attention and exert disproportionate influence on our emotional lives (Rozin & Royzman, 2001).

This also gives most people a history of success from which they can draw when searching, in confirmatory fashion, for evidence that they possess some desirable trait or ability. Many traits and abilities can be interpreted in numerous ways and research by David Dunning and his colleagues has shown that people tend to interpret them—often automatically—in self-serving ways (Dunning, Meyerowitz, & Holzberg, 1989). Someone who buys recycled paper for his home printer but tosses glass bottles and aluminum cans in the trash may be justified in thinking that he scores high on his recycling efforts. But so would someone with the opposite tendencies. Even someone who engages in neither action but donates money to an environmental organization that advocates recycling may be similarly pleased with his efforts on behalf of recycling. More generally, if each person excels on one component of a given trait or ability and weighs that component heavily in the pertinent self-assessment, everyone can walk away feeling above average.

In other words, our most rapid mental processes are associative, and among the quickest associations to spring to mind are episodes from one's past history with the domain in question. Because we try our best to structure our lives to produce positive experiences, the associations that are most accessible are likely to be positive. And because we have some leeway in how we construe various traits and abilities, these initial positive associations will often be taken as decisive and we end up with a favorable assessment of our abilities.

But what happens when associations to past episodes of directly-relevant experience do not arise? What happens when one has little or no direct experience that speaks to the ability or trait in question? In these situations people are likely to fall back on more general beliefs about themselves and how they fare on related qualities and abilities. Ehrlinger and Dunning (2003), for example, have shown that people judge their performance on many tasks by consulting chronic self-views that strike them as relevant to the task at hand. These chronic self-views, furthermore, are likely to spring to mind as unbidden products of the associative system. So when asked to judge how we might do in a novel domain, such as running a company, we automatically reframe the question as whether or not we possess the broader traits that we believe promote success at such an enterprise, such as communication skill, a strong will, or an ability to delegate effectively.

To the extent that such chronic self-views are both accurate and germane, consulting them can lead to accurate assessments. But these broader self-views may be inappropriately applied for a number of reasons. Most important for present purposes, the general self-view that is brought to bear on the particular assessment at hand may be shaped by asking confirmatory questions, engaging in a biased search for evidence, and defining which traits are relevant in a self-serving manner—just like more specific beliefs about one's abilities.

Intention as a Proxy for Action

Perhaps the quickest assessment we make, and we make it all the time, is whether a given stimulus is positive or negative (Fazio, 2001; Zajonc, 1980). Connected to this assessment is a proto-intention, a stance toward the object as something to approach or something to exert immediate energy to avoid. This is as true of conceptual representations of, say, personal traits as it is of perceptions of physical objects like Koala bears and Gila monsters. "Stalwart," "charitable," and "lively" are traits instantly seen as positive, and yield something of an approach tendency and an impulse to link them with the self. "Weak," "stingy," and "dull," in contrast, are instantly seen as negative, and yield something of an avoidance tendency and a desire to distance them from the self. Thus, the consideration of any trait or ability carries with it something of an intention—sometimes primitive and cursory, sometimes elaborated and strongly-held—to exhibit the trait or possess the ability when it comes to positive attributes or to disavow the trait or ability when it comes to negative attributes.

Because our intentions are arrived at so quickly and are often so unambiguous in character, they sometimes substitute as input to the real question at hand—whether one will actually exhibit the behavior in question (Kahneman & Frederick, 2002; Koehler & Poon, 2005). Because people know they would *intend* to disobey Milgram's experimenter, they believe it is likely that they *would* disobey. And because people often intend to be brave, thrifty, kind, clean, and reverent, they often believe that they possess these traits in greater-than-average abundance. It is only when the barriers to fulfilling their intentions are particularly formidable—and obvious—that this simple substitution is over-ridden and more deliberate analysis is engaged.

Consistent with this account, people's estimates of their likelihood of completing a number of tasks are tightly coupled to their intentions to complete them, and relatively insensitive to various situational variables that actually influence whether or not they get done (Koehler & Poon, 2005). In one experiment, for example, participants estimated the probability they would participate in a future Web-based experiment to help out a student research project. Some participants were told their participation was crucial to the student's ability to complete the project whereas others were told it would merely be helpful—a manipulation that substantially affected their intentions to participate and their estimates of how likely they were to do so. In addition, half of each group of participants were told they would receive a reminder to participate just before the experiment began, and half were not. This reminder manipulation, in marked contrast to the importance manipulation, had a minimal effect on participants' estimates of the likelihood they would participate, but a substantial effect on their actual behavior.

Kruger and Gilovich (2004) provide even more direct support for the idea that people's willingness to seize on their own good intentions—while remaining unaware or insensitive to the intentions of others—contributes to overly optimistic self assessments. They demonstrate, for example, that people exhibit more of an above average effect on traits for which one's intentions are seen as particularly relevant. Intentions strike most people as a more integral component of being "appreciative" or "kind-hearted" than "popular" or "brilliant," and people tend to assign themselves higher ratings relative to their peers on the former. This result, furthermore, holds true when other variables known to affect self-enhancement—such as trait ambiguity, desirability, and observability—are held constant. If intentions are seen as a significant determinant of whether or not one possesses a given trait, people factor in their own good intentions and conclude that they will possess the trait in greater measure than most of their peers—ignoring that others are likely to have the same intentions and thus are likely to strive just as hard to possess the trait in question.

TABLE 4.1 Participants' and Observers' Ratings of Participants' Cold-Pressor Submersion Time, Altruism, and Altruistic Intent

| | Percentile estimate of | | |
| | Submersion | | Altruistic |
Rater	time	Altruism	intent
Self	41%	62%*	63%*
Observer	54%	54%	59%*

Note. Values significantly greater than average (the 50th percentile) are indicated with asterisks; from Kruger and Gilovich, 2004, p. 9.

In an experimental test of this idea, Kruger and Gilovich provided participants an opportunity to earn money for their favorite charities by the quality of their performance on a cold-pressor test. The longer they kept their hand submerged in painfully cold water, the more money they earned for their chosen charity. Afterward, participants rated their performance relative to how they thought the average participant would perform, and also rated how "altruistic" they had been in the study and how strongly they had intended to behave in an altruistic fashion—again, both relative to the average participant. As the data in Table 4.1 indicate, participants' ratings of how altruistic they had been closely matched their ratings of altruistic intent but diverged from their assessments of their actual performance. When rating the self, intentions count a great deal.

But note that this is not true when assessing others. Another group of participants watched a videotape of an individual undergoing the cold-pressor test and then made the same three ratings of that person. In this case, ratings of how altruistic the person had been were tightly coupled to the ratings of the individual's actual behavior, not the ratings of altruistic intent. When rating others, intentions count for less. Examined differently, when ratings of the target person's altruism are predicted from ratings of cold-pressor behavior and altruistic intent, regression analyses reveal a marked divergence in the views of targets and observers (see Table 4.2). The cold-pressor participants' own ratings of how altruistic they had been

TABLE 4.2 Relative Weights Placed on Submersion Time and Altruistic Intent in Judgments of Target's Altruism by Targets and Observers

| | Rating | |
| | Submersion | Altruistic |
Rater	Time	Intent
Target	−.13	.85*
Observer	.59†	.09

Note. †p < .10. *p < .05; from Kruger and Gilovich, 2004, p. 10.

were heavily influenced by their altruistic intent and unconnected to their actual behavior. The relative weights of observers' ratings were just the opposite.

This pattern of weights can explain why we sometimes predict the behavior of others more accurately than our own. When intentions happen to be poor predictors of behavior, access to our own intentions can only serve to pollute our estimates of likely behavior. Being free of such knowledge about others allows us to base our predictions on more determinative information. In a clear demonstration of this phenomenon, Epley and Dunning (2000) asked Cornell University students how many daffodils either they or the average Cornell student would purchase during a campus fund-raising drive for the American Cancer Society. The students substantially overestimated how many they personally would buy, but their estimates of the average student were right on the money. The students certainly intended to contribute to the cause and that intention apparently got in the way of making an accurate assessment of their true likelihood of participation. These intentions, furthermore, were likely to have arisen quickly and effortlessly. A daffodil, after all, is an unambiguously positive stimulus for nearly everyone—so positive it could doubtless serve effectively alongside such stimuli as kittens and ice cream cones in affective priming experiments. And what scourge does one more quickly and effortlessly develop an intention to stamp out than cancer?

Notice that a tendency to focus on intentions when considering oneself but behavior when considering others is likely to leave people feeling even more positive about themselves when confronted with the actual selfish behavior of others. Hearing, for example, about the behavior of participants in the Milgram obedience study does not convince people that their intentions to disobey are off the mark, but rather serves as evidence that others are less compassionate and resolute than one thought. Or hearing about yet another instance of bystander nonintervention does not clue people into the difficulties of intervening in an emergency, but further strengthens preexisting beliefs about others' callousness.

This idea receives support from a follow-up experiment by Epley and Dunning (2000), one in which participants were asked to make hypothetical predictions about how much money they and the average person would donate to a charity after receiving $5 to complete an experiment. Not surprisingly, participants thought they would donate considerably more money than the average person. The participants were then shown, one at a time, the amounts donated by participants in a previous experiment who actually had been asked to donate to charity. These actual donations were considerably less generous than the hypothetical predictions, which resulted in participants making progressively lower predictions about the amount others would donate as they learned more and more about others' actual donations. Participants did not, however, alter their predictions about their own likely donations in any way, such that the difference between self and others grew as more information about actual donation levels was obtained. The reason for this was made clear from the results of a final questionnaire: participants reported that they had predicted their own behavior by taking stock of their personality traits and "character," but not the actual behavior of previous participants.

WHAT HAPPENS UPON FURTHER REVIEW?

We have discussed how a number of automatic assessments produced by System 1 lead most people down the path toward an illusion of personal strength. But fortunately for the health of our species, System 1 does not work alone. These initial assessments can be altered or overridden by the more deliberate, reflective processes of System 2. How are the shallow assessments discussed above likely to be altered by the deeper output of System 2?

Because these quick, shallow thoughts slant people's self-assessments in an overly positive direction, more reflective assessments might reign in this optimism and moderate people's judgments. It is a simple matter, certainly, to demonstrate that there is "room" for such moderation. Toward this end, Williams and Gilovich (2005a) asked one group of participants to make the standard ratings that typically elicit the above average effect—to rate themselves relative to their peers on such traits as creativity, thoughtfulness, sophistication, and so on. A second group was asked to provide, not a single percentile score, but a pair of percentile scores representing the upper and lower bounds of where they could *possibly* fall among their peers. Across these domains, the first group's mean "point estimate" fell at the 65th percentile, nearly identical to the second group's mean upper bound at the 67th percentile but considerably higher than the mean lower bound (49th percentile). The typical self-assessment is clearly one that gives the person making it the benefit of a rather substantial doubt. Where people conclude they fall on a given trait distribution is at the very highest level they believe they could possibly fall.

That the typical self-assessment is right at the subjective maximum implies that closer scrutiny might motivate people to moderate their assessments. The key questions, then, are how often do people engage in such scrutiny and how substantially does it moderate their assessments? As we shall see, there are reasons to believe that this sort of closer scrutiny is rarely engaged and, even when it is, it may only rarely lead to substantially less optimistic self-assessments.

Further Review: The Exception, Not the Rule

Fortunately for fans of the National Football League, the tedious "further review" devoted to controversial plays is only rarely enacted. And fortunately for the self-esteem of the average person, there is reason to believe that further review of one's initial, shallow assessments of personal strength may also be rare. The effortful processes of System 2 are most likely to be devoted to such assessments when there is some problem to devote them to. But when it comes to everyday self-assessments, there is typically no problem to signal the need for System 2's assistance. The reflexive confirmatory search for evidence of personal strength does not have the feel of a biased search, and the quick elicitation of one's intention likewise feels like an aide to accurate assessment, not a contributor to biased assessment. There is therefore little in these initial mental operations, or in the product of these mental operations, to trigger corrective efforts. More generally, automatic cognition is experienced as unbiased because there is no trace of the sort of effortful mental work that people associate with biased reasoning.

The fact that many of the sources of biased self-assessment are automatic and thus inaccessible to introspection gives rise to an illusion of personal strength that folds in on itself—the illusion that we have the strength to stand up to the temptation to be biased. Given that people think they are above average on so many desired traits, it is no surprise that they tend to believe they are above average in resisting bias. Pronin, Gilovich, and Ross (2004) present data indicating that people believe they are less prone to bias than their peers in part because they tend to "look inward" to try to detect traces of bias in themselves, but consult abstract theories of bias when assessing the judgments of others. Because many biases—like those discussed here—result from processes that operate outside of awareness, the inward search for bias turns up empty. Indeed, the inward search for bias is as likely to turn up evidence that one acted or decided as one did in spite of potentially biasing considerations, not because of them (Ehrlinger, Gilovich, & Ross, 2005). People are thus frequently blind to biases in themselves that they readily detect in others.

Further Review is More Often Triggered by Negative Initial Assessments, Not Positive Ones

An intriguing program of research on motivated reasoning by Peter Ditto and his colleagues makes it clear that people are unlikely to engage in further review of their initial automatic assessments if those assessments are positive (Ditto & Boardman, 1995; Ditto & Lopez, 1992; Ditto, Munro, Apanovitch, Scepansky, & Lockhart, 2003; Ditto, Scepansky, Munro, Apanovich, & Lockhart, 1998). It is the (relatively rare) negative assessments that trigger deeper processing. The circumstances under which System 2 is activated and deeper analysis engaged, then, are not those that are likely to disabuse individuals of the notion that they have a considerable amount of ability or possess a positive trait in abundance.

Briefly, what Ditto and colleagues have found is that favorable or desirable information—"good news"—is processed effortlessly and mindlessly, whereas unfavorable or undesirable information—"bad news"—commands attention and more effortful processing (see also Dawson, Regan, & Gilovich, 2002; Gilovich, 1991; Schaller, 1992). In one noteworthy demonstration of this tendency, Ditto and Lopez (1992) gave undergraduates a test for a fictitious medical condition called "TAA deficiency" said to be associated with pancreatic disorders later in life. The test was straightforward: one simply puts one's saliva on a piece of yellow paper and observes whether it changes color within 20 seconds. In the *deficiency* condition, participants were told that if the paper remained the same color (yellow), they had the medical condition; in the *no deficiency* condition, participants were told that if the paper changed to a dark green, they had the condition. The paper remained yellow for all participants. Thus, those in the deficiency condition would be motivated to see the paper change color and they should be disturbed by the evidence with which they were confronted—that the paper remained yellow. Indeed, these participants gave the test almost 30 seconds longer to work than those who received more welcome evidence. Participants in the no deficiency condition took in the good news and moved on; those in the deficiency condition subjected the bad news to further scrutiny.

Thus, if the sort of automatic assessments we have discussed here produce a favorable result, they are unlikely to be examined further and hence unlikely to be corrected. Instead, it is the negative initial assessments that are likely to elicit deeper, corrective processing. The net effect is that further review may be more likely to feed the illusion of personal strength than to dampen it.

Adjustments Made from Initial Assessments Are Typically Insufficient

Sometimes, of course, an initial optimistic assessment will prompt further processing and lead to the conclusion that a revision is in order. "Things aren't that rosy." "Maybe I'm being too generous with myself." "I'm not always that magnanimous." On the rare occasions when our initial, positive self-assessments *are* corrected, how are they modified? How does the correction process work? A substantial body of research indicates that initial assessments such as these are modified through a conscious, effortful, and serial process of adjustment. This is particularly true when the "anchor"—in this case, the initial self-assessment—is self-generated (Epley, 2004; Epley & Gilovich, 2001; Gilovich, 2002). People typically know the proper direction in which to adjust and so this process nearly always results in assessments that are more accurate than they would otherwise be. But the adjustments people make nonetheless tend to be insufficient, leaving the final assessments off the mark (Epley & Gilovich, 2004; Tversky & Kahneman, 1974). In this case, although deeper processing may moderate the illusion of personal strength, it is unlikely to eliminate the illusion altogether.

A pair of studies that were designed to ameliorate optimistic self assessments support this contention. In one, half of the participants were primed with honesty before being asked to fill out the sort of trait-rating scales that have regularly produced an above average effect (Williams and Gilovich, 2005b). The other participants were subjected to neutral primes and served as controls. The manipulation was effective: Those for whom the concept of honesty had been primed rated themselves less favorably than the control participants. But they still exhibited the above average effect. Across all of the positive traits, the average percentile rating among control participants was 66%. The corresponding percentile among the "honest" participants was 60%. The pull for honesty lowered participants' estimates, but it did not lower them enough. McKenna and Myers (1997) examined whether accountability would diminish the above average effect. Specifically, they asked participants to rate their driving ability relative to that of the "average driver" on three global dimensions and 17 specific subskills. They found that accountable participants provided ratings of general ability and specific subskills that were lower than those provided by control participants. But here too the ratings of the targeted group were, except in a few cases, still above average.

The research by Kruger (1999) that we discussed earlier reinforces this point. He had participants rate their relative ability to perform a number of tasks, and he had them do so while they were either cognitively busy or unencumbered and could consider their strengths and weaknesses in greater depth. He found that the busy participants' ratings were more extreme than those provided by participants with ample cognitive resources: they rated themselves more above average on simple tasks and more below average on difficult tasks. His argument is that, typically, people seize right away on the difficulty of the task, assess their standing among their peers based on this assessment of ease or difficulty, and then adjust to take into account whether the task is likely to be easy or difficult for others as well. Individuals too preoccupied to adjust their initial assessments leave out this extra step and so their final judgments are more extreme. His data support this account but it is important to note that even participants who were not cognitively busy made rather extreme assessments. That is, these participants likewise rated themselves above average in their ability to perform simple tasks and below average in their ability to complete difficult ones. They adjusted, but their adjustments were insufficient.

Finally, consider one of daily life's more commonly encountered illusions of personal strength—the "planning fallacy," or the pervasive tendency for people to estimate that they will complete projects more quickly than they actually do (Buehler, Griffin, & Ross, 1994). From construction contractors to clerical workers, small tasks that seem like they should take only a few minutes consume the better part of a day, and week-long chores can balloon into month-long burdens. Frequent experience with this particular illusion of personal strength may enable people to recognize that their initial forecasts are likely to be overly optimistic, but eliminating this optimistic bias has proven to be extremely difficult. Indeed, even people's predictions of their completion times under a "worst-case scenario" still underestimate the time required, on average, to complete important projects (Buehler et al., 1994).

To see why the planning fallacy is so common and persistent, consider how a person typically goes about predicting when a project will be completed. First, at least some of the detailed components of the project must be considered, as well as one's estimated sustained desire to work on the project (likely to be overestimated), and maybe one or two obvious obstacles to successful completion. Frequent experience with the planning fallacy will likely lead a person to adjust an initial estimate of completion time to accommodate inevitable but unknown delays. This adjustment is likely to involve a step-by-step increase to one's initial estimate (one more day? three more days? seven more days?) until a plausible final estimate is reached. But because such adjustments stop as soon as one reaches the first plausible value, they tend to be insufficient, and the final forecasts too optimistic.

Evidence supporting the role of insufficient adjustment in the planning fallacy comes from an experiment in which college students were asked to predict how long it would take them to complete four academic projects that were due sometime during the following month (Epley & Gilovich, 2005). Participants in one condition were asked to make these estimates while nodding their heads up and down (a nonverbal "yes") and the other half were asked to shake their heads from side to side (a nonverbal "no"). Previous research has found that people are more inclined to believe a proposition if they consider it while nodding their heads up and down than while shaking their heads from side to side (Wells & Petty, 1980). If participants in this context were adjusting from an overly optimistic initial assessment, these head movements should influence the likelihood of accepting an estimate encountered early in the process of adjustment. Those nodding their heads up and down while predicting their completion times should therefore predict that they would be done sooner than those shaking their heads from side to side. That is exactly what happened. Those nodding their heads up and down thought they would complete their projects, on average, 5.1 days before they were due, whereas those shaking their heads from side to side thought they would finish only 2.9 days early.

More important, when participants were contacted at the end of the month and asked when they actually completed each project, those who had nodded their heads when making their estimates showed a stronger planning fallacy than those who had shaken their heads from side to side. Head nodders completed their tasks, on average, 6.2 days *after* their predicted completion date, compared to only 1.4 days after among the head shakers. Here as elsewhere, therefore, it is not that people are always unaware that their shallow thoughts are likely to be overly optimistic; it's that the adjustments they make to rein in their reflexive optimism tend to be insufficient.

AUTOMATIC SELF-ASSESSMENTS NOT OPTIMISTICALLY BIASED

Our account of the quick, relatively mindless sources of optimistic self-assessments also specifies when such assessments are less likely to be so optimistic. Recall that it is a person's implicit positive self-regard that creates an automatic association between the self and positively-valued traits and abilities. This association, in turn, leads to the reflexive search for information that one possesses the positive attributes in question.

This implies, of course, that people who lack this implicit positive self-regard should be less prone to the kind of illusion of personal strength we have examined throughout this chapter. Depressed individuals are the most obvious example. Individuals who suffer from depression have been shown to be less likely to exhibit the sort of optimistic self-assessments characteristic of the nondepressed population (Tabachnik, Crocker, & Alloy, 1983; Taylor & Brown, 1988). To be sure, many of the cognitions that accompany depression are of the elaborated, quite conscious sort that lead to destructive rumination (Nolen-Hoeksema, 2000) and are amenable to conscious intervention and retraining (Beck, 1970; 1991; Hollon, Haman, & Brown, 2002). But that is surely not all there is to depressive thought. A depressed individual's conscious self loathing may exist alongside negative self-assessments that arise automatically, and may be built up on top of such automatic self-assessments in the manner we have described here. The reflexive links between "me" and positively-valenced traits and "not me" and negatively-valenced traits that exist for the bulk of the population may be turned around in the depressed (Greenwald & Banaji, 1995). This would give rise to a shallow pessimism that parallels the shallow optimism we have examined throughout this chapter.

The present analysis also implies that the illusion of personal strength is likely to exhibit a different profile among members of collectivist cultures whose self-regard is structured differently. Members of collectivist cultures appear to have lower self-esteem, on average, than members of individualist cultures (Kitayama, Markus, Matsumoto, & Norasakkunkit, 1997), and so they may less readily form a unit between the self and positively valued traits and activities. This should lead, in turn, to self-assessments that are less optimistically biased, a pattern found with some regularity in the relevant literature (Heine, Lehman, Markus, & Kitayama, 1999; Markus & Kitayama, 1991). At the same time, members of collectivist cultures may be more likely to form a quick, reflexive unit between the groups to which they belong and various positively valued traits and abilities. This should lead to strong illusions, not of personal strength, but of in-group strength. Indeed, this exact pattern of group-enhancement in Asian cultures, compared to self-enhancement in European cultures, has been reported in the literature (Endo, Heine, & Lehman, 2000; Sedikides, Gaertner, & Toguchi, 2003).

CODA

People's insistence that they would not obey in the Milgram experiment, their conviction that they would intervene in the sorts of emergencies studied by Darley and Latane (1968), or their belief that, on average, they are very much above average, can all seem like the products of considered thought. A person takes in what seems to be the most pertinent evidence and arrives at a deliberate assessment. The attempt to explain the optimistic biases that plague such assessments thus boils down to identifying the biases, both cognitive and motivational, that plague our deliberate thoughts. What we have endeavored to explore here, however, is how optimistic self-assessments might arise from a set of more automatic mental operations. Many optimistic biases, we have tried to show, are the product of shallow thought, not reflective consideration. It is our hope, of course, that in trying to explicate the shallow thinking that underlies so many self assessments, we haven't been guilty of too much shallow thinking ourselves.

REFERENCES

Beck, A. T. (1970). *Depression: Causes and treatment.* Philadelphia: University of Pennsylvania Press.

Beck, A.T. (1991). Cognitive therapy: A 30-year retrospective. *American Psychologist, 46,* 368–375.

Bierbrauer, G. (1979). Why did he do it? Attribution of obedience and the phenomenon of dispositional bias. *European Journal of Social Psychology, 9,* 67–84.

Buehler, R., Griffin, D., & Ross, M. (1994). Exploring the "planning fallacy": Why people underestimate their task completion times. *Journal of Personality and Social Psychology, 67,* 366–381.

Chaiken, S., & Trope, Y. (1999). *Dual-process theories in social psychology.* New York: Guilford Press.

Crocker, J. (1982). Biased questions in judgment of covariation studies. *Personality and Social Psychology Bulletin, 8,* 214–220.

Csikszentmihalyi, M. (1990) *Flow: The psychology of optimal experience.* New York: Harper and Row.

Darley, J. M., & Latane, B. (1968). Bystander intervention in emergencies: Diffusion of responsibility. *Journal of Personality and Social Psychology, 8,* 377–383.

Dawson, E., Regan, D. T., & Gilovich, T. (2002). Motivated reasoning and the Wason selection task. *Personality and Social Psychology Bulletin, 28,* 1379–1387.

Ditto, P. H., & Boardman, A. F. (1995). Perceived accuracy of favorable and unfavorable psychological feedback. *Basic & Applied Social Psychology, 16,* 137–157.

Ditto, P. H., & Lopez, D. F. (1992). Motivated skepticism: Use of differential decision criteria for preferred and nonpreferred conclusions. *Journal of Personality and Social Psychology, 63,* 568–584.

Ditto, P. H., Munro, G. D., Apanovitch, A. M., Scepansky, J. A., & Lockhart, L. K. (2003). Spontaneous skepticism: The interplay of motivation and expectation in responses to favorable and unfavorable medical diagnoses. *Personality and Social Psychology Bulletin, 29,* 1120–1132.

Ditto, P. H., Scepansky, J. A., Munro, G. D., Apanovich, A. M., & Lockhart, L. K. (1998). Motivated sensitivity to preference-inconsistent information. *Journal of Personality and Social Psychology, 75,* 53–69.

Dunning, D., Meyerowitz, J. A., & Holzberg, A. (1989). Ambiguity and self evaluation: The role of idiosyncratic trait definitions in self-serving assessments of ability. *Journal of Personality and Social Psychology, 57,* 1082–1090.

Ehrlinger, J., & Dunning, D. (2003). How chronic self-views influence (and potentially mislead) estimates of performance. *Journal of Personality and Social Psychology, 84,* 5–17.

Ehrlinger, J., Gilovich, T., & Ross, L. (2005). Peering into the bias blindspot: People's assessments of bias in themselves and others. *Personality and Social Psychology Bulletin, 31,* 680–692.

Endo, Y., Heine, S. J., & Lehman, D. R. (2000). Culture and positive illusions in close relationships: How my relationships are better than yours. *Personality and Social Psychology Bulletin, 26,* 1571–1586.

Epley, N. (2004). A tale of tuned decks? Anchoring as adjustment and anchoring as accessibility. In J. K. Koehler & N. Harvey (Eds.), *The Blackwell handbook of judgment and decision making* (pp. 240–256). Oxford, UK: Blackwell Publishers.

Epley, N., & Dunning, D. (2000). Feeling "holier than thou": Are self-serving assessments produced by errors in self- or social prediction? *Journal of Personality and Social Psychology, 79,* 861–875.

Epley, N., & Gilovich, T. (2001). Putting adjustment back in the anchoring and adjustment heuristic: An examination of self-generated and experimenter-provided anchors. *Psychological Science, 12,* 391–396.

Epley, N., & Gilovich, T. (2004). Are adjustments insufficient? *Personality and Social Psychology Bulletin, 30,* 447–460.

Epley, N., & Gilovich, T. (2005). *Insufficient adjustment from best- and worst-case scenarios.* Unpublished manuscript, Harvard University.

Epley, N., & Gilovich, T. (in press). When effortful thinking influences judgmental anchoring: Differential effects of forewarning and incentives on self-generated and externally-provided anchors. *Journal of Behavioral Decision Making.*

Epstein, S. (1994). Integration of the cognitive and the psychodynamic unconscious. *American Psychologist, 49,* 709–724.

Fazio, R. H. (2001). On the automatic activation of associated evaluations: An overview. *Cognition & Emotion, 15,* 115–141.

Ferguson, M. J., & Bargh, J. A. (2004). How social perception automatically influences behavior. *Trends in Cognitive Sciences, 8*, 33-39.

Gilovich, T. (1991). *How we know what isn't so: The fallibility of human reason in everyday life.* New York: Free Press.

Gilovich, T. (2002). Anchoring in egocentric social judgment and beyond. In J. P. Forgas & K. D. Williams (Eds.), *The social self: Cognitive, interpersonal, and intergroup perspectives* (pp. 37–50). New York: Psychology Press.

Greenwald, A. G., & Banaji, M. R. (1995). Implicit social cognition: Attitudes, self-esteem, and stereotypes. *Psychological Review, 102*, 4–27.

Greenwald, A. G., Banaji, M. R., Rudman, L. A., Farnham, S. D., Nosek, B. A., & Mellott, D. S. (2002). A unified theory of implicit attitudes, stereotypes, self-esteem, and self-concept. *Psychological Review, 109*, 3–25.

Heider, F. (1958). *The psychology of interpersonal relations.* New York: Wiley.

Heine, S. J., Lehman, D. R., Markus, H. R., & Kitayama, S. (1999). Is there a universal need for positive self-regard? *Psychological Review, 106*, 766–794.

Hollon, S. D., Haman, K. L., & Brown, L. L. (2002). Cognitive-behavioral treatment of depression. In I. H. Gotlib & C. L. Hammen (Eds.), *Handbook of depression* (pp. 383–403). New York: Guilford Press.

Kahneman, D., & Frederick, S. (2002). Representativeness revisited: Attribute substitution in intuitive judgment. In T. Gilovich, D. W. Griffin, & D. Kahneman (Eds.), *Heuristics and biases: The psychology of intuitive judgment* (pp. 49–81). New York: Cambridge University Press.

Kitayama, S., Markus, H. R., Matsumoto, H., & Norasakkunkit, V. (1997). Individual and collective processes in the construction of the self: Self-enhancement in the United States and self-criticism in Japan. *Journal of Personality and Social Psychology, 72*, 1245–1267.

Klar, Y., & Giladi, E. (1999). Are most people happier than their peers, or are they just happy? *Personality and Social Psychology Bulletin, 25*, 586–595.

Klayman, J., & Ha, Y. W. (1987). Confirmation, disconfirmation, and information in hypotheses testing. *Psychological Review, 94*, 211–228.

Koehler, D. J., & Poon, C. S. K. (2005). *Self-prediction based on strength of intention.* Manuscript under editorial review.

Kruger, J. (1999). Lake Wobegon be gone! The 'below average effect' and the egocentric nature of comparative ability judgments. *Journal of Personality and Social Psychology, 77*, 221–232.

Kruger, J., & Burrus, J. (2004). Egocentrism and focalism in unrealistic optimism (and pessimism). *Journal of Experimental Social Psychology, 40*, 332–340.

Kruger, J., & Gilovich, T. (2004). Actions, intentions, and self assessment: The road to self-enhancement is paved with good intentions. *Personality and Social Psychology Bulletin, 30*, 328–339.

Lewin, K., Dembo, T., Festinger, L., & Sears, P. S. (1944). Level of aspiration In J. McV. Hunt (Ed.), *Personality and the behavior disorders* (pp. 333–378). New York: Ronald.

MacDonald, T. K., & Ross, M. (1999). Assessing the accuracy of predictions about dating relationships: How and why do lovers' predictions differ from those made by observers? *Personality and Social Psychology Bulletin, 25*, 1417–1429.

Markus, H. R., & Kitayama, S. (1991). Culture and the self: Implications for cognition, emotion, and motivation. *Psychological Review, 98*, 224–253.

McKenna, F. P., & Myers, L. B. (1997). Illusory self-assessments — Can they be reduced? *British Journal of Psychology, 88*, 39–51.

Moore, D. A., & Kim, T. G. (2003). Myopic social prediction and the solo comparison effect. *Journal of Personality and Social Psychology, 85*, 1121–1135.

Mussweiler, T. (2003). Comparison processes in social judgment: Mechanisms and consequences. *Psychological Review, 110*, 472–489.

Mussweiler, T., & Strack, F. (1999). Hypothesis-consistent testing and semantic priming in the anchoring paradigm: A selective accessibility model. *Journal of Experimental Social Psychology, 35*, 136–164.

Nolen-Hoeksema, S. (2000). The role of rumination in depressive disorders and mixed anxiety/depressive symptoms. *Journal of Abnormal Psychology, 109*, 504–511.

Pronin, E., Gilovich, T., & Ross, L. (2004). Objectivity in the eye of the beholder: Divergent perceptions of bias in self versus others. *Psychological Review, 111,* 781-799.

Rozin, P., & Royzman, E. B. (2001). Negativity bias, negativity dominance, and contagion. *Personality and Social Psychology Review,* 5, 296–320.

Rumelhart, D. E., & McClelland, J. L. (1986). *Parallel distributed processing.* Cambridge, MA: MIT Press.

Schaller, M. (1992). In-group favoritism and statistical reasoning in social inference: Implications for formation and maintenance of group stereotypes. *Journal of Personality and Social Psychology, 63,* 61–74.

Sedikides, C., Gaertner, L., & Toguchi, Y. (2003). Pancultural self-enhancement. *Journal of Personality and Social Psychology, 84,* 60–79.

Skov, R. B., & Sherman, S. J. (1986). Information gathering processes: Diagnosticity, hypothesis-confirmatory strategies, and perceived hypothesis confirmation. *Journal of Experimental Social Psychology, 22,* 93–121.

Sloman, S. A. (1996). The empirical case for two systems of reasoning. *Psychological Bulletin, 119,* 3–22.

Slowiaczek, L. M., Klayman, J., Sherman, S. J. & Skov, R. B. (1992). Information selection and use in hypothesis testing: What is a good question, and what is a good answer? *Memory and Cognition, 20,* 392–405.

Smith, E. R. (1996). What do connectionism and social psychology offer each other? *Journal of Personality and Social Psychology, 70,* 893–-912.

Strack, F., & Mussweiler, T. (1997). Explaining the enigmatic anchoring effect: Mechanisms of selective accessibility. *Journal of Personality and Social Psychology, 73,* 437–446.

Tabachnik, N., Crocker, J., & Alloy, L. B. (1983). Depression, social comparison, and the false-consensus effect. *Journal of Personality and Social Psychology, 45,* 688–699.

Taylor, S. E., & Brown, J. D. (1988). Illusion and well-being: A social psychological perspective on mental health. *Psychological Bulletin, 103,* 193–210.

Tetlock, P. E. (1992). The impact of accountability on judgment and choice: Toward a social contingency model. In M. P. Zanna (Ed.), *Advances in experimental social psychology* (vol. 25, pp. 331–376). New York: Academic Press.

Tversky, A., & Kahneman, D. (1974). Judgment under uncertainty: Heuristics and biases. *Science, 185,* 1124–1131.

Ward, W. C., & Jenkins, H. M. (1965). The display of information and the judgment of contingency. *Canadian Journal of Psychology, 19,* 231–241.

Wason, P. C., & Johnson-Laird, P. N. (1972). *Psychology of reasoning: Structure and content.* Cambridge, MA: Harvard University Press.

Wells, G. L., & Petty, R. E. (1980). The effects of overt head movements on persuasion: Compatibility and incompatibility of responses. *Basic and Applied Social Psychology, 1,* 219–230.

Williams, E., & Gilovich, T. (2005a). *The benefit of doubt: Motivated reasoning and the above average effect.* Unpublished data.

Williams, E., & Gilovich, T. (2005b). *Honestly, maybe I'm not so good: The effect of honesty primes on the above average effect.* Unpublished data.

Wilson, T. D., Houston, C., Etling, K. M., & Brekke, N. (1996). A new look at anchoring effects: Basic anchoring and its antecedents. *Journal of Experimental Psychology: General, 4,* 387–402.

Windschitl, P. D., Kruger, J., & Simms, E. N. (2003). The influence of egocentrism and focalism on people's optimism in competitions: What affects us equally affects me more. *Journal of Personality and Social Psychology, 85,* 389–408.

Zajonc, R. B. (1980). Feeling and thinking: Preferences need no inferences. *American Psychologist, 35,* 151–175.

5

The Better-Than-Average Effect

MARK D. ALICKE
Ohio University
OLESYA GOVORUN
Ohio State University

Most people are average but few people believe it. The tendency to evaluate oneself more favorably than an average peer is one of social psychology's chestnuts—a finding that will never let you down when running a class demonstration. This better-than-average effect has been obtained in numerous studies, with diverse populations, on multiple dimensions, and with various measurements techniques.

The better-than-average effect is a particular type of social comparison, one in which people compare their characteristics or behaviors against a norm or standard, which is usually the average standing of their peers on the characteristic. In this regard, the better-than-average effect falls outside the mainstream of traditional social comparison theory. Following Festinger (1954), social comparison theorists have emphasized the precursors and consequences of comparisons between people. Arguably, however, comparisons with normative standards are at least as prevalent as interpersonal comparisons. The self versus average peer judgments studied in better-than-average effect research are akin to social comparisons such as assessing whether one is meeting a group's moral standards or performance expectations.

The better-than-average effect is considered to be one of the most robust of all self-enhancement phenomena (Taylor & Brown, 1988; Sedikides & Gregg, 2003). The better-than-average effect shares this distinction with the optimistic bias—the tendency to overestimate one's chances of good fortune and to underestimate one's risk for misfortune. Whereas the better-than-average effect pertains to self versus average peer comparisons on behavior and trait dimensions, the optimistic bias involves comparisons about life events such as winning the lottery or getting divorced. Although we concentrate on the better-than-average effect in this chapter, many of the issues underlying better-than-average judgments apply as well to relative risk assessments. Connections and distinctions between these two research areas will be drawn throughout this chapter.

Various explanations have been proposed for the better-than-average effect (see Gilovich, Epley, & Hanko, this volume). These explanations encompass two broad issues. The first issue concerns the role of behavioral and interpersonal comparisons in the better-than-average effect . One prominent explanation for the effect is that when asked to compare themselves with an average peer, people select comparison targets who fare especially poorly on the judgment dimension (Perloff & Fetzer, 1986). Another possibility is that people think selectively about behaviors on which they fare better than others (Weinstein, 1980). In contrast to these views, Alicke et al. (2001) have argued that behavioral comparisons are unnecessary to account for the effect, and that people routinely employ a "better-than-average" heuristic which entails a compromise between existing self-knowledge and ideal trait conceptions.

A second main issue underlying better-than-average explanations is whether nonmotivational mechanisms can account for the effect. The four most prominent nonmotivational explanations center on whether people selectively recruit information or comparison targets that ensure their own superiority, whether the judgment task encourages people to focus on themselves rather than on the average peer (focalism), whether people's own behaviors or characteristics are considered more thoroughly and weighted more heavily (egocentrism), and whether the effect is due to differences between comparing a single entity (the self) with an aggregate (an average peer).

To anticipate our conclusion, we do not believe that nonmotivational mechanisms account sufficiently for the better-than-average effect, and we also believe that various lines of evidence indicate that self-enhancement motives contribute to the effect. Furthermore, many of the nonmotivational explanations that have been discussed are as readily interpretable in motivational terms. The fact that people concentrate unduly on their own characteristics in making comparisons (egocentrism), for example, could result from the tendency to believe that their own characteristics are better or more important than others'. At the same time, we hardly wish to argue that nonmotivational mechanisms are unimportant in explaining the better-than-average effect. Any satisfactory explanation of self-related effects must encompass both the why and the how of behavior. To argue that the better-than-average effect occurs because people wish to view themselves positively tells us nothing about how the effect occurs. Therefore, after a brief historical survey of the emergence of better-than-average effect research, and a consideration of factors that moderate the effect, we discuss the mechanisms that contribute to the better-than-average effect. After this, we review evidence that points to the role of self-enhancement motives in this research area and discuss avenues for future research.

EARLY STUDIES

Data collected in conjunction with the 1976 College Board Exams provide one of the earliest, most striking, and most frequently-cited demonstrations of the better-than-average effect. Of the approximately one million students who took the SAT that year, 70% placed themselves above the median in leadership ability, 60% above the median in athletic ability, and 85% rated themselves above the median in their ability to get along well with others. Amazingly, 25% of the students rated themselves in the 1st percentile on this latter characteristic. These data are noteworthy because in contrast to many subsequent better-than-average and optimistic bias studies, students were not asked to compare themselves to an average peer but simply to indicate where they stood in relation to the median. Thus, these results cannot be ascribed to negative connotations associated with the word "average." / discussion?

Around this time, Cross (1977) distributed a questionnaire to instructors at three branches of the University of Nebraska. This questionnaire was concerned primarily with undergraduate teaching issues, but included a question that asked professors to rate their teaching abilities. Results showed that 94% of the faculty considered themselves above average in teaching ability and 68% placed their teaching abilities in the top 25%. These data demonstrated at the outset that the better-than-average effect was not limited to college students.

Another frequently-cited study by Svenson (1981) showed that 88% of American college students, and 77% of Swedish college students, considered themselves to be above the 50th percentile on driving safety. Svenson's research was motivated by an earlier study in which Preston and Harris (1965) compared 50 drivers who had been hospitalized following car accidents (34 of whom had caused the accidents, according to police records) with 50 matched drivers without accident histories. Preston and Harris's results showed not only that both groups considered themselves to be above average in driving skills, but that the accident group's evaluation of their driving abilities did not differ from those who were uninvolved in accidents.

The first experimental research on the better-than-average effect was conducted in France where Codol (1975) studied what he called the "superior conformity of the self." Codol placed his research in the context of identifying with desirable norms. The hypothesis guiding these studies was that people believed they adhered to desirable norms more than others. Codol employed various self versus other measurements in his twenty studies, and so this research did not establish a basic paradigm for subsequent investigations. Furthermore, the context of norm identification obscured somewhat the general, social-comparative implications of the better-than-average effect. Nevertheless, Codol presciently raised issues that still resound in the better-than-average effect literature. His findings suggest, for example, that the better-than-average effect is larger when people compare themselves to others in general than to specific group members. Codol also conjectured that the tendency to view oneself as superior to others represents a desire to self-enhance rather than to denigrate others.

MODERATING FACTORS

Self researchers recognize that people are not indiscriminately self-serving (e.g., Baumeister, 1998; Schlenker, 1980; Sedikides & Gregg, 2003). Self-serving tendencies such as the better-than-average effect are pervasive but not inevitable. As previously noted, even the earliest better-than-average effect studies assessed moderating factors that alter the effect's strength. Four main classes of moderating factors have been identified: the scales on which the effect is measured, the nature of the judgment dimension, the nature of the comparison target, and characteristics of the judge.

Direct and Indirect Measurements

Research on the optimistic bias and better-than-average effect employs two basic methodologies. With the *direct* method, self is compared to an average peer on a single scale that uses "average" as the midpoint. At the low end, direct scales are usually anchored with wording such as "considerably below average" and on the high end at "considerably above average." The estimate of the better-than-average effect is straightforward: The higher the number circled, the greater the magnitude of the effect. With indirect ratings, participants rate the self and average peer on separate scales. The better-than-average effect is calculated by subtracting the average rating from the self rating so that higher scores indicate greater bias. Studies suggest that people are more self-serving when they use the direct rather than the indirect scale (Otten & van der Pligt, 1996). Direct scales provide a stronger comparative frame and may, therefore, elicit more pronounced tendencies to contrast the self upward from the average peer or to contrast the average peer downward from the self.

The direct method of assessing the better-than-average effect is used more often, although it is less informative. With the direct method, it is impossible to estimate whether the better-than-average effect results from people underestimating the average peer's standing, overestimating their own standing, or both. The one exception to this occurs when a person's standing on a dimension is objectively known and can be used as a reference point (Epley & Dunning, 2000). The indirect method, by contrast, is informative of the direction of contrast. Because the indirect method has been less frequently used, there is no solid basis yet for concluding whether the better-than-average effect represents self-inflation, average peer deflation, or some combination of both.

The Nature of the Judgment Dimension

People who claim positive characteristics that are easily refuted risk being ridiculed. Furthermore, the need to maintain coherent and believable self-images (Swann, Rentfrow, & Guinn, 2003) is threatened when people cling tenaciously to dubious abilities and characteristics. Self-serving tendencies, therefore, operate within reality bounds. As a general rule, we assume that people are most self-serving when they have the latitude to interpret events in a self-serving manner (Sedikides & Strube, 1997). Self-enhancement is accomplished with the least obvious distortion when the judgment dimension is subjective or abstract as opposed to objective or concrete. Self-enhancement is also facilitated when people believe they have the ability to alter their standing on the dimension. Each of these factors is discussed separately below.

Criteria for Assessing Traits

The criteria for assessing intellectual and physical abilities are generally more objective than those for evaluating social or moral ones (Reeder & Brewer, 1979; Rothbart & Park, 1986). The view that people are more self-serving when making subjective or ambiguous judgments than objective ones leads to the prediction that the better-than-average effect will be larger on ability than on social or moral judgment dimensions. ?

This expectation has been confirmed by Allison, Messick and Goethals (1989) who found that the tendency for people to believe that they performed more moral behaviors than their peers was greater than their tendency to believe they performed more intellectual behaviors, although the latter was still significant. Allison et al. termed this the "Muhammed Ali effect."

The ubiquitous Muhammed Ali also provides a fitting introduction to Dunning, Meyerowitz, and Holzberg's (1989) demonstration that ambiguity moderates the better-than-average effect. In an interview with Muhammed Ali after winning an early fight, sportscaster Howard Cosell suggested that Ali was mighty "truculent" that evening, to which Ali replied: "I don't know what truculent is, but if it's good, I'm it." Dunning et al. captured something like this reasoning in a more formal and less truculent manner. Their first two studies showed that the better-than-average effect was greater on dimensions that had been preclassified as ambiguous versus unambiguous. In the third study, trait ambiguity was manipulated by presenting some participants with specific criteria for assessing a trait, whereas others were free to define the traits for themselves. Results generally showed that the better-than-average effect was larger when participants provided their own trait definitions, although this effect was more consistent for positive than for negative trait dimensions.

Controllability

In addition to having the latitude to interpret a trait's meaning, self-enhancement is facilitated when people can construe their standing on a trait in a self-serving manner. Positive characteristics that people believe they control have greater self-serving value than characteristics they believe are less alterable, whereas negative uncontrollable characteristics are less deflating than controllable ones.

The first large-scale, systematic study of the better-than-average effect assessed the moderating influence of a trait characteristic's perceived controllability. Participants in this study examined self versus average ratings on separate scales for 171 trait dimensions (Alicke, 1985). These traits were prerated to represent four levels of desirability (high, moderately-high, moderately low, and low) and two levels of controllability (high and low). The larger set of desirability than controllability categories reflects the greater range in desirability preratings.

Although we assumed that people would evaluate themselves more favorably than they would an average peer, we expected this tendency to be moderated by controllability. The primary prediction was that participants would believe themselves to be characterized more by positive controllable than positive uncontrollable traits in relation to the average college student, and more by negative uncontrollable than negative controllable traits. These predictions can be summarized in the phrase: "I make me good, fate makes me bad."

As we anticipated, the tendency to evaluate oneself more favorably than the average college student on positive traits, and less unfavorably on negative traits, was pervasive. The predicted effects of controllability were also obtained such that participants rated themselves more favorably in relation to the average college student on positive controllable traits and more unfavorably on negative uncontrollable traits.

The Nature of the Comparison Target

A fundamental question surrounding better-than-average effect judgments concerns the nature of the comparison target. Whereas traditional social comparison studies include comparisons between individuals, better-than-average effect research entails comparisons between oneself and an hypothetical or statistical entity, namely, an average peer. Extensive attributional and decision-making research shows that people tend to deemphasize or misuse statistical information (Nisbett & Ross, 1980). The better-than-average effect, therefore, might disappear when comparisons are effected between real people rather than between a person and a statistic.

Alicke et al. (1995) conducted a series of studies to see if the better-than-average effect would be eliminated when people compared themselves to a real person rather than an average peer. In their first and simplest study, half the participants were brought to a large room and asked to look at the person sitting next to them. These participants then changed their seats and made 40 trait comparisons (20 positive, 20 negative) between themselves and the person they had sat next to. A second group of participants compared themselves on these same dimensions to the average college student. Results showed that the better-than-average effect was pervasive in both groups, but was significantly reduced in comparisons with real people.

This first study suggested that people adjust their evaluations when comparing with real versus hypothetical targets, but still view themselves more favorably in person-to-person comparisons. Six more studies were conducted to investigate in greater detail the differences between real and hypothetical comparison targets. These studies used a common paradigm in which an interviewer asked a series of predetermined questions of an interviewee (actually a confederate) who always gave the same stock answers. In the first study using this paradigm, a live observer watched the interaction in the same room, another group watched the interaction on videotape, a third read a written transcript of the interview, and a fourth made self versus average college student judgments. Ratings in the first study were made on the kinds of life events studied in optimistic bias research. Consistent with the first study's findings, the better-than-average effect (or optimistic bias in this case) was greater when participants compared themselves to the average college student than in any of the other conditions. The more novel finding of this study was that the better-than-average effect was greater in the transcript and video conditions than in the live observer or interviewer conditions. No differences were obtained between the live observer and interviewer conditions, suggesting that actual interaction with the target does not influence comparisons beyond experiencing the target's live presence.

This study, therefore, established two differences between real and hypothetical comparison targets. The first difference is individuation. Any specific target ostensibly reduces the better-than-average effect in relation to comparisons with an hypothetical entity such as an average peer. The second difference is live contact. The better-than-average effect is reduced when people are in the same room with the comparison target regardless of whether an actual interaction takes place.

Subsequent studies sought further refinements. Participants in the individuation condition of the previous study received some information from the target in the form of the target's answers to the interview questions. To create even more basic individuation conditions, participants in one group saw only a still image of the target, and in another, saw only the back of the target's head (to eliminate facial cues). We also created conditions in which participants thought they were watching a contemporaneous interview on a TV monitor, and conditions in which participants watched the interview from behind a one-way mirror with the belief that the interviewee could, or could not, see them. In the mirror conditions, participants stood almost the exact distance from the interviewee as in the live observer condition, and also saw the interviewee from the same angle. The results were clear: Every condition in which participants compared themselves to the interviewee produced a decreased better-than-average effect in relation to comparisons with an average college student, and an increased better-than-average effect in relation to live observer conditions.

These findings suggest that individuation per se reduces the better than average effect. The results of these studies also show that the features that differentiate live- from nonlive contact are quite subtle. Live contact did not increase feelings of similarity to the interviewee, nor did it require any type of interaction. Simply being in the same room with the target was sufficient to reduce the better-than-average effect, and this same reduction did not occur when participants believed they were watching the interaction live on a monitor, or even when they watched the interview through a mirror in the next room and knew that the interviewee could see them.

Another issue these studies investigated was whether participants perceived the "average" student pejoratively. One possible explanation for better-than-average effect findings is that people do not want to be considered average because of its negative connotation. To assess how participants viewed the average student, we had them create distributions for 16 different trait dimensions. For example, for the trait dimension dependable-undependable, participants listed the percentage of people they thought fell into nine categories between extremely dependable and extremely undependable, with the understanding that their percentages should total to 100%. The mean of each trait dimension was calculated, and this value was compared to where on the dimension participants placed themselves, the average college student, or a real person whom they had sat next to. As in the previous studies, participants evaluated themselves and the real person more favorably than the average college student, while consistently placing themselves above the real person. More germane for the purposes of this study, participants consistently placed the average college student above the distribution mean. In these data, therefore, the average college student was not viewed pejoratively, at least not in relation to the distribution mean. These findings suggest that even the average college student is perceived as a more individuated entity than the mean of a trait distribution.

Characteristics of the Judge

Relatively few better-than-average effect studies have examined individual difference factors. The one factor that has been routinely analyzed—gender—rarely produces significant effects. In this section, we briefly review the two characteristics that have received some attention, namely self-esteem and depression.

Self-Esteem

Not everyone believes they exceed the average by the same degree. Self-esteem is perhaps the first individual difference factor that comes to mind in considering variations in the better-than-average effect. In fact, self-esteem did come to mind very early in research on this topic. Brown (1986) found that the tendency to evaluate oneself more favorably than others was greater for high self-esteem than for low self-esteem participants, although this effect was obtained for positive and not for negative traits.

More recently, Suls, Lemos, and Stewart (2002, Study 1) assessed the self versus average peer comparisons of high and low self-esteem participants on traits varying in ambiguity. They found that whereas both high and low self-esteem individuals exhibited a greater better-than-average effect for ambiguous versus unambiguous traits on positive trait dimensions, low self-esteem individuals did not show this ambiguity effect on negative trait dimensions. Thus, only high self-esteem individuals took advantage of the interpretational latitude afforded by negative, ambiguous traits.

Depression

Tabachnik, Alloy, and Crocker (1983) compared the self versus average peer judgments made by students who scored relatively high or low on the Beck Depression Inventory. Their main hypothesis was that those who scored higher would view themselves as more similar to the average college student on depression-relevant items but not on irrelevant items. As it turned out, depressive participants viewed themselves as more similar to average on both depression-relevant and depression-irrelevant items. Because the depression-relevant items were all negative, and the depression-irrelevant items were predominantly positive, these findings suggest that depressives exhibit a diminished better-than-average effect across the board. In other words, depressives have a reduced tendency to evaluate themselves less negatively on negative characteristics relative to the average student as well as a reduced tendency to evaluate themselves more positively on positive characteristics.

EXPLAINING THE BETTER-THAN-AVERAGE EFFECT

Five primary mechanisms have been proposed to explain how the better-than-average effect operates. One prevalent idea is that people selectively recruit downward targets who make them look favorable by comparison, or relatedly, that they selectively recruit behavioral evidence that favors the self. A second prominent explanation is that people focus egocentrically on their own positive attributes and that the heightened availability of their own behaviors and propensities produces the better-than-average effect. Third, focusing explanations argue that the position of the self as the subject of judgment and the average person as the target produces the better-than-average effect. By this reasoning, reversing the position of subject and target should eradicate the effect. Fourth, the self versus aggregate position argues that individual entities, such as the self, are evaluated more favorably than group or aggregate estimates, such as an average peer. Finally, the better-than-average effect could be a heuristic that is applied automatically in social judgments and then modified for specific comparison targets or dimensions. Each of these explanations is discussed in turn below.

Selective Recruitment

Most explanations of the optimistic bias, and some of the better-than-average effect, involve the way people think about their characteristics in relation to others. In his early optimistic bias research, Weinstein (1980, 1984; Weinstein & Lachendro, 1982) proposed the most prevalent variant of this explanation, namely, that when people compare their characteristics to others, they think selectively about their own strengths or about others' weaknesses. Weinstein first tested the selective recruitment hypothesis in a study (1980, Study 2) in which participants listed behaviors that increased or decreased their chances of experiencing each of a series of life events. Some participants were then given the opportunity to read others' lists. Results showed a reduced optimistic bias in participants who read others' lists versus those who did not have access to this information. Importantly, access to other people's responses reduced, but did not eliminate, the optimistic bias. Weinstein and his colleagues showed similar reductions in the optimistic bias in studies that provided participants with specific information about others' risks for misfortune (Weinstein, 1984; Weinstein & Lachendro, 1982).

Perfloff and Fetzer (1986) considered another aspect of the selective recruitment hypothesis, namely, that when asked to compare themselves with an average peer, people select targets who compare unfavorably on the judgment dimension. People may think, for example, of an especially dishonest person, which casts their own honest behaviors in an especially favorable light. To test this downward comparison idea, Perloff and Fetzer had participants compare their vulnerabilities to misfortune with those of their closest friend, a close friend, and the average college student. Perloff and Fetzer assumed that identifying a specific, well-known comparison target (i.e., their closest friend) would prevent participants from selecting a target who was worse off than themselves on the comparison dimension or from recruiting specific behaviors or characteristics on which they fare better. Consistent with this assumption, they found that what they called "the illusion of invulnerability" was reduced when people compared themselves to their closest friend, relative to when they compared with a close friend or with an average college student.

As Perloff and Fetzer noted, however, there are competing explanations for these findings. The explanation they favored was that people possess more information about their closest friends, which enables them to conclude that these friends are no more susceptible to misfortune than themselves. Another plausible explanation, however, is that people like their closest friend more than a close friend or an average peer and evaluate their closest friend more favorably on this basis. These studies, therefore, provide less clear evidence about the moderating role of behavioral information than Weinstein and his colleagues' research (1980 1984; Weinstein & Lachendro, 1982). What Perloff and Fetzer's results do suggest is that the better-than-average effect is reduced when positive self-evaluations are extended to others, such as close friends.

Egocentrism

Egocentrism is the probably the most prevalent nonmotivational explanation for better-than-average and optimistic bias effects. Egocentrism as applied to the better-than-average effect is the tendency to place undue weight on one's own characteristics, beliefs and experiences in making self versus average comparisons. In contrast to the selective recruitment hypothesis, egocentrism does not necessarily entail a self-serving review of behavioral evidence. In judging their relative honesty, for example, people may consider the same honest behaviors for themselves and the target but still place greater weight on their own honest behavior. Furthermore, selective recruitment can entail thinking about the other's negative characteristics without focusing unduly on one's own.

One source of support for the egocentrism view comes from studies showing that self versus average peer comparisons are predicted better by absolute self ratings (that is, self ratings alone, without ratings of the average) than by absolute peer ratings (that is, peer ratings alone, without ratings of the self). Klar and Giladi (1999), for example, had participants make absolute ratings of their own contentment, absolute ratings of their peers' contentment, and also comparative ratings of their own contentment relative to their peers. The main finding in their two studies was that absolute self-ratings predicted the comparative contentment ratings better than did absolute peer ratings. In fact, the relationship between absolute peer ratings and the comparative ratings were low and nonsignificant in both studies. Although these studies examined only one trait dimension, other studies have obtained analogous results with different judgment tasks (e.g., Eiser, Pahl, & Prins, 2001; Chambers, Windshitl, & Suls, 2003).

One of the most compelling demonstrations of the egocentrism position is Kruger's (1999) finding that people consider themselves *worse* than average on difficult tasks. Kruger reasoned that if concentrating egocentrically on their positive attributes leads people to think that they are better than average, then concentrating on their negative attributes should lead them to believe that they are worse than average. This prediction can also be viewed from an anchoring and adjustment perspective: In the case of tasks for which people believe that they have high ability, anchoring on their own characteristics should lead to relatively extreme positive self-judgments, with insufficient upward adjustments for their peers, whereas for tasks on which people believe that they have low ability, anchoring should produce extreme negative self-judgments, with insufficient downward adjustments for their peers.

Based on pretesting, Kruger classified activities as easy (e.g., driving, using a mouse) or difficult (telling jokes, juggling) and then had participants estimate their percentile ranking for each of the activities. In accord with the egocentrism position, participants consistently placed themselves above the 50th percentile for easy activities, and below the 50th percentile for difficult ones. These findings are consistent, therefore, with the assumption that people concentrate egocentrically on their own attributes in comparative judgments and that emphasis on their negative characteristics leads them to overestimate their shortcomings.

The tendency to concentrate egocentrically on personal prospects and characteristics has important implications for self-other comparisons. In general, if people think egocentrically about their own prospects, then factors that increase their chances of success at the task should induce overconfidence about their prospects (because people focus egocentrically on their own advantage without realizing others have the same advantage), whereas factors that augur equally unfavorably for themselves and others should lead to pessimistic predictions. Chambers, Windschitl, and Suls (2003) tested this hypothesis by asking participants to predict the likelihood that they versus an average peer would purchase their dream home within a short time frame (next 6 years) or a long one (next 32 years). Because the probability is higher that the event will occur in the longer time frame, egocentrism predicts that people will be overly optimistic about their chances in the long than in the short time frame. The results confirmed this prediction.

Focalism

Focalism is the tendency to place greater weight on whatever hypothesis or outcome is currently the focus of attention (Schkade & Kahneman, 1998). In contrast to egocentrism, which explicitly involves self-reference, focalism involves concentrating on an object due to the way a judgment task is structured. By asking people to compare their characteristics to those of an average peer, studies on the better-than-average effect tend to place the self in the focal position and the average peer in the referent position. Because self-representations contain a greater number of unique qualities than other representations (Karylowski, 1990; Karylowski & Skarzynaka, 1992), focusing on the self highlights these unique features and leads people to perceive themselves as less similar to the average.

By making the self the focal object, therefore, the better-than-average effect methodology increases the perceived differences between self and other. According to this reasoning, when people compare the average other to themselves, these differences should be attenuated. In other words, if the positions of self and average are switched, such that the average peer is made the focal object and the self is made the referent, the better-than-average effect should be reversed or at least diminished.

The main support for this focalism prediction comes from studies using the optimistic bias paradigm. Otten and van der Pligt (1996) and Eiser, Pahl, and Prins (2001) both manipulated whether participants were asked to estimate how they would fare relative to their peers on various life events (self-other focus), or how their peers would fare relative to themselves (other-self focus). These studies showed a reduced optimistic bias in the latter condition, that is, when the average peer was the focal object and the self was the referent.

Other studies have compared focalism and egocentrism predictions, although not with average peer comparisons. In two similar lines of research, Windschitl, Kruger, and Simms (2003) and Moore and Kim (2003) placed participants in a competitive situation and asked them to estimate their chances of success. These studies assessed egocentrism by varying whether participants believed the task facilitated or discouraged success (e.g., playing an easy or hard trivia game). Because the task was equally difficult for themselves and their opponent, there was no rational reason for them to alter their estimates based on this information. But from the egocentrism standpoint, concentrating disproportionately on one's own prospects should lead to overestimation in the case of an easy task and underestimation in the case of a difficult one, which is what these studies demonstrated. Focalism was independently manipulated by asking participants to estimate their own or their opponent's chances of winning. Although the results varied somewhat across experiments, both focalism and egocentrism influenced participants' estimates of success.

Self Versus Aggregate Comparisons

In the better-than-average and optimistic bias paradigms, a single entity, the self, is compared to an aggregate, the average peer. The fact that the self is routinely evaluated more favorably than average is generally believed to manifest self-esteem enhancement. However, Klar and Giladi's demonstration of "non-selective superiority and inferiority" biases (Klar, 2002; Klar & Giladi, 2002) calls into question whether self-enhancement assumptions are needed to explain the better-than-average effect. What Klar and Giladi have demonstrated in numerous experiments is that any member of a positively-evaluated group is rated more favorably than the group average (Klar, 2000; Klar & Giladi, 1997). Randomly-selected students at one's university, for example, are evaluated more favorably than the average student at the university. This finding obtains even when comparing an individual group member to other distinct individuals, such as comparing a single police officer to the average of other police officers in the room. Giladi and Klar (2002) have demonstrated this same effect with impersonal comparisons, such as soap fragrances and musical selections.

Klar and Giladi's (1997, 2002) findings suggest that the greater positivity people claim for themselves may be subsumed by a more general tendency to place greater weight on single entities than on aggregates. The generality of their view is extended by their consistent findings of inferiority biases, that is, the tendency for members of disliked groups to be evaluated less favorably than the group as a whole.

Klar and Giladi's findings are consistent with those of Alicke et al. (1995) in showing that the better-than-average effect is reduced by comparisons with individuated entities versus an average peer. Klar and Giladi's results suggest further that part of the tendency to evaluate oneself more favorably than an average peer is due to the greater weight people place on any individuated entity versus an aggregate such as an average peer. On the other hand, Alicke et al.'s research show that compared to other individuated entities, the self has a privileged role in that the better-than-average effect is greater when the self is compared to any other individuated entity. Thus, while Klar and Giladi's model provides a cogent and general account of individual-group comparisons, an additional factor appears to be operating when the self is plugged into the comparison.

Klar and Giladi have recently expanded their view in what they call the LOGE model (local comparisons-general standards model, 2002). According to this model, the task of estimating, for example, a group member's politeness relative to the average student, requires comparing the individual's politeness to a local standard, namely, the average level of politeness in the immediate peer group (for example, students at this university). When people make this comparison, however, they are unable to avoid applying a more general standard, which might include all other people. To the extent that the local standard is more favorable than the general one (i.e., this group is more polite than people in general), superiority biases should emerge such that any person in the group will be evaluated more favorably than the group average. This occurs because people inadvertently take into account the superiority of the local standard to the general one, rather than simply recognizing that the person is an average member of a superior group. By this same reasoning, evaluations of any individual who belongs to an inferior group (relative to the general standard) should be less favorable than the group average. The LOGE model, therefore, provides a useful and general account of comparisons between specific entities and group averages. The model's limitation as applied to the better-than-average effect is that it does not contain mechanisms to explain the enhanced favorableness that is generally accorded to the self versus other entities.

Better-Than-Average Heuristic

Research on selective recruitment leaves little doubt that the optimistic bias is altered by providing people with access to others' beliefs about their prospects in life. We question, however, whether careful thinking about one's behavior is a necessary, or even a typical component, of self versus other comparisons. The assumption that people think carefully about specific behaviors is less tenable in the better-than-average effect paradigm than in optimistic bias research. In better-than-average effect research, participants typically judge abstract traits rather than concrete behaviors. Furthermore, the better-than-average effect has been obtained in settings in which participants make hundreds of trait comparisons, and it seems unlikely that they engage in careful behavior analyses for each comparison.

Alicke et al. (1995; 2001) have suggested that the better-than-average effect is attributable to people applying a better-than-average heuristic. This heuristic entails an automatic tendency to assimilate positively-evaluated social objects toward ideal trait conceptions, and does not assume that people routinely review their behaviors to make self-other judgments. The assumption that people apply a better-than-average heuristic is consistent with Sears' (1983) notion of a person positivity bias, and with the general positivity bias that pervades social judgment (Matlin & Stang, 1978). The degree of assimilation varies for social objects of different value. Family members and friends are accorded a great deal of positivity, and concrete individuals are accorded more than an average or hypothetical peer. At the apex of the positivity ladder resides the self.

The extent to which people assimilate toward ideal trait conceptions depends on the ambiguity of the judgment dimension and on the strength of prior self-conceptions. As noted previously, people are not indiscriminately self-serving and tend to avoid easily-refutable claims. Nevertheless, trait comparisons are especially susceptible to the better-than-average heuristic because trait conceptions can become independent of behavioral exemplars (Klein & Loftus, 1993; Klein, Loftus, & Burton, 1989; Klein, Loftus, Trafton, & Fuhrman, 1992). Research by Klein and Loftus shows that people require the same amount of time to recall an instance in which they displayed a trait regardless of whether they first judge whether that trait is self-descriptive or simply define the trait. If people accessed specific behaviors to answer trait questions, then judging whether a trait was self-descriptive would facilitate recalling an instance in which the trait was displayed. Based on numerous failures to find such facilitation effects, Klein and Loftus argue that trait and behavioral information are stored in separate memory systems.

The better-than-average heuristic entails three main assumptions. First, when people are asked, for example, to judge their "kindness" in relation to an average peer, the default is to assimilate their self-ratings toward their ideal conceptions of kindness. These ideal trait constructs do not necessarily translate into the highest available scale point. People who are too cooperative, for example, can be taken for patsies, and extreme honesty can slide into rudeness.

The second assumption is that people make automatic adjustments based on past self-conceptions. Those who have frequently been criticized for their unhelpfulness will still associate with ideal conceptions of helpfulness but will assimilate less to accommodate reality. The final assumption is that average peers, rather than being assimilated toward idea standards, are evaluated in relation to oneself. Because the self typically represents a relatively high scale point, average peers are assimilated toward oneself, while still being rated less favorably.

Although better-than-average heuristic assumptions have not been tested directly, there is strong evidence to suggest that behavior recruitment is not a necessary component of the better-than-average effect. One source of support for this assertion comes from the fact that the better-than-average effect emerges even under extreme cognitive load conditions (Alicke et al., 1995, Study 7).

Another source of support for the nonbehavioral assumption comes from research on what we have called the "better-than-myself" effect (Alicke et al., 2001).

In our first study on this topic, participants in a pretesting session estimated the percentage of times they exhibited behaviors relevant to various trait dimensions. For example, participants were asked to estimate the percentage of times they were cooperative or uncooperative when the opportunities to display that trait arose. This behavior percentage methodology was modeled on the act-frequency approach to personality (Buss & Craik, 1983) which assumes that people define their traits by estimating the frequency with which they engage in trait-relevant behaviors. Participants in Study 1 were told to use their percentage estimates to rate themselves on each corresponding trait dimension.

In the main session conducted approximately six weeks later, participants received what they believed were the average behavior percentage estimates obtained during the academic quarter. What participants actually received were the identical estimates they had provided in the pretesting session. Thus, if participants estimated that they were cooperative 86% of the time and uncooperative 14% of the time, they were led to believe that the average student was cooperative 86% of the time and uncooperative 14% of the time. Participants were asked to use these estimates to evaluate where they and the average college student fell on the trait dimension.

Results were consistent across the board: Despite looking at the exact behavior estimates they had provided in pretesting, participants evaluated themselves more favorably than the average college student on almost every dimension. These findings were replicated in a second study in which participants received what they believed were the behavior estimates made by a randomly-selected peer rather than the average college student. Although the magnitude of the effect was reduced, participants still placed themselves significantly above their peers based on identical behavior estimates.

A third study assessed whether participants might want to change their behavior estimates once they saw the estimates of an average person or a peer. A possible explanation for the previous studies' results is that participants believed they had underestimated the frequency with which they engaged in positive behaviors after seeing others' estimates. To test this, we gave participants the opportunity to change their frequencies after seeing others' estimates. In general, participants made relatively few changes. Furthermore, changes that were made did not correlate with comparative ratings.

The better-than-myself paradigm used in these studies has one notable limitation, namely, that while participants might readily acknowledge that their behavior frequencies are similar to others', they could still conclude that their own trait-relevant behaviors are more exemplary. For example, people might accept that they and another person are cooperative 85% of the time but believe that their own cooperative behaviors are *more* cooperative than someone else's. We used a different methodology to circumvent this problem in a fourth study. This time, we asked participants to list every behavior they could think of that reflected where they stood on one of four trait dimensions (kind-unkind, intelligent-unintelligent, honest-dishonest, and creative-uncreative). After listing the relevant behaviors, participants received a list made by another student and then compared themselves to the student on the trait dimension. On average, the lists participants received from others should have been just as positive as the ones they produced themselves. Nevertheless, with a peer's trait-relevant behaviors in front of them, they continued to evaluate themselves more favorably than the peer. We believe that this study provides reasonably strong evidence that differences in behavior recruitment are not a necessary component of the better-than-average effect.

THE MOTIVATION-NONMOTIVATION BOGEY

Selective recruitment, focalism, and egocentrism have all been shown to moderate the better-than-average effect. These judgment features have been proposed as alternatives to self-enhancement assumptions (Chambers & Windshitl, 2004). The credibility of the nonmotivational position would be heightened if it could be shown that these factors, either in isolation or combination, eliminate the better-than-average effect. But as a general rule, variations in these judgment facets alter, but do not eliminate, the better-than-average effect. For example, for focalism to provide a sufficient explanation of the better-than-average effect, people must evaluate average peers more favorably than themselves when the average peer is the focal object and the self is this referent. This is not what happens. In studies on focalism, reversing the position of self and average attenuates but does not eliminate the effect. The same is true for effects attributable to egocentrism or selective recruitment. Thus, the specific information people focus on, and the kinds of comparisons they make, while important moderators of the better-than-average effect, do not suffice to explain it.

This failure of these various mechanisms to account completely for the better-than-average effect does not, of course, establish the role of self-enhancement. But various other findings do suggest a role for self-enhancement. The finding in our early study (Alicke, 1985) that the better-than-average effect increases with positive controllable traits and decreases with negative uncontrollable traits, provides one source of support for the self-enhancement motive. This result shows that people are most self-aggrandizing when they feel responsible for their positive characteristics, and least self-aggrandizing when they believe that fate accounts for their negative characteristics.

That the tendency to evaluate oneself more favorably than others increases with the desirability of the judgment dimensions provides even more basic support for the self-enhancement motive (Weinstein, 1980; Hayes & Dunning, 1996). Another aspect of the better-than-average effect that is difficult to account for without reference to self-enhancement is the consistent finding that the effect is stronger on ambiguous or subjectively-defined dimensions (Allison, Messick, & Goethals, 1989; Dunning, Meyerowitz, & Holzberg, 1989). Apparently, people are most self-serving when they have the latitude to construe comparisons in a manner that emphasizes their superiority.

Egocentrism and selective recruitment, the two most prominent and general nonmotivational explanations of the better-than-average effect, assume that the effect involves the type of behaviors or comparison targets people think about, or the relative emphasis they place on their own actions and characteristics. Research on the better-than-myself effect, however, shows that the tendency to evaluate oneself more favorably than others perseveres even when behavioral evidence is equated for self and other. Furthermore, the tendencies to emphasize one's own actions and characteristics, and to recruit selectively information that casts oneself in the most favorable light, are readily interpretable as serving the need to self-enhance.

The idea that people automatically identify with ideal trait conceptions is seemingly contradicted by Kruger's findings of a worse-than-average effect and Klar and Giladi's findings of inferiority biases. This apparent discrepancy can be readily resolved, however, by expanding the better-than-average heuristic view to include the possibility for contrast as well as assimilation effects. Contrast effects are likely to occur when the object of judgment is obviously unfavorable, such as a behavioral weakness or a disliked individual. Kruger, for example, obtained his worse-than-average effects with behaviors such as juggling and playing chess– behaviors for which the majority of people readily recognize their shortcomings. Instead of automatic assimilation to ideal trait conceptions, we assume that people automatically contrast themselves from the ideal under such circumstances.

SUMMARY AND CONCLUSIONS

People like to think favorably of themselves, and for good reason. Positive self-views promote harmonious personal relationships and successful goal-striving. Those who feel good about themselves are less prone to negative moods and depression (Taylor et al., 2003). The ways in which people strive to maintain favorable self-images are legion, including taking credit for positive outcomes and denying responsibility for negative ones (Bradley, 1978; Zuckerman, 1979), selectively recalling favorable information about themselves (Sedikides & Gregg, 2003), exaggerating the ability of people who outperform them and who they outperform (Alicke et al., 1997), searching selectively for information that confirms a positive self-image, evaluating others in a way that reflects favorably on one's own performance (Dunning & Cohen, 1992), and affirming threatened aspects of self (Steele, 1978). Each of these behavior tendencies, either strategically or inadvertently, serves to promote favorable self-views.

The better-than-average effect is difficult to locate in this "zoo" (Tesser, 2000) of self-enhancement mechanisms. For one thing, it is unclear whether the better-than-average effect reflects an already favorable self-image, or is constructed spontaneously. In other words, the better-than-average effect could be a consequence of the aforementioned self-enhancement mechanisms, or it could be a distinct mechanism in it own right. Although numerous better-than-average effect studies have been conducted, we still do not know precisely what kind of effect it is. Does the better-than-average effect, for example, primarily reflect a tendency to contrast oneself upward from the average, to contrast the average downward from the self, or as the better-than-average heuristic implies, upward assimilation of both self and average toward an ideal trait concept, with greater assimilation for the self. To answer this basic question requires a design in which different groups of participants make either absolute self-judgments or absolute average-peer judgments, followed by comparative self versus average judgments. This design would make it possible to analyze precisely assimilation and/or contrast effects in self versus average peer ratings.

The better-than-average effect would be less important if it were due solely to the vague and amorphous nature of comparisons with an "average peer." But numerous studies have shown that people also evaluate themselves more favorably than specific peers, although the effect is attenuated in such comparisons. An interesting offshoot of better-than-average effect research concerns the nature of the difference between comparisons with specific and average peers. One possible difference is that people confer "personhood" on real human beings and evaluate them more favorably than statistical entities on this basis (Sears, 1983). A related possibility is that people are more modest in comparisons with real individuals and therefore inhibit self-serving tendencies.

One important direction for future research is, as noted above, to compare conditions in which people make comparative self versus average peer ratings to those in which they rate self and average individually. This design would answer a fundamental question regarding the better-than-average effect, namely, whether self or average ratings are altered when made comparatively, and if so, in which direction this alteration occurs. Most researchers, including us, assume that the self is an anchor point against which average peer ratings are referred, but this assumption has not been tested directly in previous research. If the self-anchoring assumption is correct, then self-ratings should not change when they are made individually versus when they are made in comparison to the average peer. A downward contrast of the average peer from the self would indicate that the effect involves downplaying others' characteristics relative to one's own. A different possibility is that people anchor on the average peer, and contrast the self upward from that point, suggesting self-inflation relative to the average standard. A third possibility, one that the better-than-average heuristic predicts, is that self ratings represent a stable (and high) anchor based on immediate associations with an ideal standard, and that comparisons with the high self standard lead to upward assimilation of the average peer, but an assimilation that falls short of the self.

Another direction for future research is to introduce manipulations designed to alter the better-than-average effect. An obvious possibility is to introduce threats to one's perceived standing on a trait dimension. Self-enhancement perspectives predict that the better-than-average effect should be increased when people confront a threat to an important aspect of their identities. Again, this fundamental assumption has yet to be tested explicitly.

As noted at the outset, the better-than-average effect is a type of social comparison in which people are asked to evaluate themselves with reference to a normative standard, namely, an average peer or the midpoint of a distribution. Research on this topic has shown consistently that people place themselves above this standard, and also above specific peers. The better-than-average effect tells us that people evaluate themselves more favorably than others, and this effect is not due solely to the weight they place on their own characteristics in comparative judgments, their tendencies to focus on themselves as the judgment object, or on the tendency to recruit favorable information about themselves. In fact, one can reasonably argue that both egocentrism and selective recruitment serve self-enhancement needs. In other words, thinking egocentrically about one's own positive qualities, or selecting downward comparison targets, may represent motivated propensities to reach favorable conclusions about one's standing relative to others. Thus, various findings suggest that the better-than-average effect is due, at least in part, to a desire to view oneself in a favorable light relative to one's peers. The task in future investigations is to evaluate which kinds of self-threats influence self versus average judgments, and to assess whether such alterations entail changes in self ratings, average ratings, or both.

REFERENCES

Alicke, M. D. (1985). Global self-evaluation as determined by the desirability and controllability of trait adjectives. *Journal of Personality and Social Psychology, 49*, 1621–1630.

Alicke, M. D., Klotz, M. L., Breitenbecher, D. L., Yurak, T. J., & Vredenburg, D. S. (1995). Personal contact, individuation, and the better-than-average effect. *Journal of Personality and Social Psychology, 68*, 804–825.

Alicke, M. D., LoSchiavo, F. M., Zerbst, J., & Zhang, S. (1997). The person who outperforms me is a genius: Maintaining perceived competence in upward social comparison. *Journal of Personality and Social Psychology, 72*, 781–789.

Alicke, M. D., Vredenburg, D. S., Hiatt, M., & Govorun, O. (2001). The "better than myself" effect. *Motivation and Emotion, 25*, 7–22.

Allison, S. T., Messick, D. M., & Goethals, G. R. (1989). On being better but not smarter than others: The Muhammad Ali effect. *Social Cognition, 7*, 275–296.

Baumeister, R. F. (1998). The self. In D. T. Gilbert, S. T. Fiske, & G. Lindzey (Eds.), *The handbook of social psychology* (4th ed., pp. 680–740). Boston: McGraw-Hill.

Bradley, G. W. (1978). Self-serving bias in the attribution process: A reexamination of the fact or fiction question. *Journal of Personality and Social Psychology, 36*, 56–71.

Brown, J. D. (1986). Evaluations of self and others: Self-enhancement biases in social judgments. *Social Cognition, 4*, 353–376.

Buss, D. M., & Craik, K. H. (1983). The act frequency approach to personality. *Psychological Review, 90*, 105–126.

Chambers, J.R., Windschitl, P.D. Biases in comparative judgments: The role of nonmotivated factors in above-average and comparative-optimism effects. *Psychological Bulletin, 130*, 813–838.

Chambers, J. R., Windschitl, P. D., & Suls, J. (2003). Egocentrism, event frequency, and comparative optimism: When what happens frequently is "more likely to happen to me." *Personality and Social Psychology Bulletin, 29*, 1343–1356.

Codol, J. P. (1975). On the so-called "superior conformity of the self" behavior: Twenty experimental investigations. *European Journal of Social Psychology, 5*, 457–501.

College Board. (1976–1977). Student descriptive questionnaire. Princeton, NJ: Educational Testing Service.

Cross, P. (1977). Not can but will college teachers be improved? *New Directions for Higher Education, 17*, 1–15.

Dunning, D., & Cohen, G.L. (1992). Egocentric definitions of traits and abilities in social judgment. *Journal of Personality and Social Psychology, 63*, 341–355.

Dunning, D., & Hayes, A. F. (1996). Evidence for egocentric comparison in social judgment. *Journal of Personality and Social Psychology, 71*, 213–229.

Dunning, D., Meyerowitz, J. A., & Holzberg, A. D. (1989). Ambiguity and self-evaluation: The role of idiosyncratic trait definitions in self-serving assessments of ability. *Journal of Personality and Social Psychology, 57*, 1082–1090.

Epley, N., & Dunning, D. (2000). Feeling "holier than though": Are self-serving assessments produced by errors in self or social prediction? *Journal of Personality and Social Psychology, 79*, 861–875.

Eiser, J. R., Pahl, S., & Prins, Y. R. A. (2001). Optimism, pessimism, and the direction of self-other comparisons. *Journal of Experimental Social Psychology, 37*, 77–84.

Festinger, L. (1954). A theory of social comparison processes. *Human Relations, 7*, 117–140.

Giladi, E. G., & Klar, Y. (2002). When standards are wide of the mark: Nonselective superiority and inferiority biases in comparative judgments of objects and concepts. *Journal of Experimental Psychology: General, 131*, 538–551.

Karylowski, J. J. (1990). Social reference points and accessibility of trait-related information in self-other similarity judgments. *Journal of Personality and Social Psychology, 58*, 975–983.

Karylowski, J. J., & Skarzynska, K. (1992). Asymmetric self-other similarity judgments depend on priming self-knowledge. *Social Cognition, 10*, 235–254.

Klar, Y. (2002). Way beyond compare: Nonselective superiority and inferiority biases in judging randomly assigned group members relative to their peers. *Journal of Experimental Social Psychology, 38*, 331–351.

Klar, Y., & Giladi, E. E. (1997). No one in my group can be below the group's average: A robust positivity bias in favor of anonymous peers. *Journal of Personality and Social Psychology, 73*, 885–901.

Klein, S. B., & Loftus, J. (1993). The mental representation of trait and autobiographical knowledge about the self. In T. K. Srull & R. S. Wyer (Eds.), *Advances in social cognition* (Vol. 5, pp. 1–49). Hillsdale, NJ: Erlbaum.

Klein, S. B., Loftus, J., & Burton, H. A. (1989). Two self-reference effects: The importance of distinguishing between self-descriptiveness judgments and autobiographical retrieval in self-referent encoding. *Journal of Personality and Social Psychology, 56*, 853–865.

Klein, S. B., Loftus, J., Trafton, J. G., & Fuhrman, R. W. (1992). Use of exemplars and abstractions in trait judgments: A model of trait knowledge about the self and others. *Journal of Personality and Social Psychology, 63*, 739–753.

Kruger, J. (1999). Lake Woebegon be gone! The "below-average effect" and the egocentric nature of comparative ability judgments. *Journal of Personality and Social Psychology, 77*, 221–232,

Matlin, M., & Stang, D. (1978). *The Pollyanna principle: Selectivity of language, memory, and thought.* Cambridge, MA: Schenkman.

Moore, D. A., & Kim, T.G. (2003). Myopic social prediction and the solo comparison effect. *Journal of Personality and Social Psychology, 85*, 1121–1135.

Nisbett, R. E., & Ross, L. (1980). *Human inference: Strategies and shortcomings of social judgment.* Englewood Cliffs, NJ: Prentice-Hall.

Otten, W., & Van der Pligt, J. (1966). Context effects in the measurement of comparative optimism in probability judgments. *Journal of Social and Clinical Psychology, 15*, 80–101.

Perloff, L. S., & Fetzer, B. K. (1986). Self-other judgments and perceived vulnerability to victimization. *Journal of Personality and Social Psychology, 50,* 502–510.

Preston, C. E., & Harris, S. (1965). Psychology of drivers in traffic accidents. *Journal of Applied Psychology, 49,* 284–288.

Reeder, G. D., & Brewer, M. B. (1979). A schematic model of dispositional attribution in interpersonal perception. *Psychological Review, 86,* 61–79.

Rothbart, M., & Park, B. (1986). On the confirmability and disconfirmability of trait concepts. *Journal of Personality and Social Psychology, 50,* 131–142.

Schlenker, B. R. (1980). *Impression management: The self-concept, social identity, and interpersonal relations.* Monterey, CA: Brooks/Cole.

Schkade, D. A., & Kahneman, D. (1998). Does living in California make people happy? A focusing illusion in judgments of life satisfaction. *Psychological Science, 9,* 340–346.

Sears, D. O. (1983). The person-positivity bias. *Journal of Personality and Social Psychology, 44,* 233–250.

Sedikides, C., & Gregg, A.P. (2003). Portraits of the self. In M. A. Hogg & J. Cooper (Eds.), *Sage handbook of social psychology* (pp. 110–138). London: Sage.

Sedikides, C., & Strube, M. J. (1997). Self-evaluation: To thine own self be good, to tine own self be sure, to thine own self be true, and to thine own self be better. In M. P. Zanna (Ed.), *Advances in experimental social psychology* (Vol 29, pp. 209–269). New York: Academic Press.

Steele, C. M. (1988). The psychology of self-affirmation: Sustaining the integrity of the self. In L. Berkowitz (Ed.), *Advances in experimental social psychology* (Vol. 21, pp. 261–302). New York: Academic Press.

Suls, J., Lemos, K., & Stewart, H. L. (2002). Self-esteem, construal, and comparisons with the self, friends, and peers. *Journal of Personality and Social Psychology, 82,* 252–261.

Svenson, O. (1981). Are we all less risky and more skillful than our fellow drivers? *Acta Psychologica, 47,* 143-148.

Swann, W. B. Jr., Rentfrow, P. J., & Guinn, J. S. (2003). Self-verification: The search for coherence. In M. R. Leary and J. P. Tangney (Eds.), *Handbook of Self and Identity* (pp. 367–383). New York: Guilford Press.

Tabachnik, N., Crocker, J., & Alloy, L. B. (1983). Depression, social comparison, and the false-consensus effect. *Journal of Personality and Social Psychology, 45,* 688–699.

Taylor, S. E., & Brown, J. D. (1988). Illusion and well-being: A social psychological perspective on mental health. *Psychological Bulletin, 103,* 193–210.

Taylor, S. E., Lerner, J. S., Sherman, D. K., Sage, R. M., & McDowell, N. K. (2003). Are self-enhancing cognitions associated with healthy or unhealthy biological profiles? *Journal of Personality and Social Psychology, 85,* 605–615.

Tesser, A. (2000). On the confluence of self-esteem maintenance mechanisms. *Personality and Social Psychology Review, 4,* 290–299.

Weinstein, N. D. (1983). Reducing unrealistic optimism about illness susceptibility. *Health Psychology, 2,* 11–20.

Weinstein, N. D. (1980). Unrealistic optimism about future life events. *Journal of Personality and Social Psychology, 39,* 806–820.

Weinstein, N. D. (1984). Why it won't happen to me: Perceptions of risk factors and susceptibility. *Health Psychology, 3,* 431–457.

Weinstein, N. D., & Lachendro, E. (1982). Egocentrism as a source of unrealistic optimism. *Personality and Social Psychology Bulletin, 8,* 195–200.

Windschitl, P. D., Kruger, J., & Sims, E. N. (2003). The influence of egocentrism and focalism on people's optimism in competition: When what affects us equally affects me more. *Journal of Personality and Social Psychology, 85,* 389–408.

Zuckerman, M. (1979). Attribution of success and failure revisited, or: The motivational bias is alive and well in attribution theory. *Journal of Personality, 47,* 245–287.

PART *III*

SELF AND OTHERS COMPARED

6

The Knife That Cuts Both Ways
Comparison Processes in Social Perception

THOMAS MUSSWEILER
University of Cologne
KAI EPSTUDE
KATJA RÜTER
University of Würzburg

*H*ow people see themselves is inextricably intertwined with how they see others. Self-evaluation does not take place in isolation. Rather the activities from which people infer information about the self are situated in a social context in which the self relates to other objects in the world (Kant 1787; see Baumeister, 1998, for a discussion). As a consequence, the self can only be perceived and its attributes can only be inferred in a relative manner. Such a "relational" perspective is at the core of a number of classic psychological approaches to the self. Lewin (1951), for example, suggested that one's performances are evaluated in comparison to a particular frame of reference. Similarly, Festinger (1954) claimed that there is a drive in the human organism to evaluate one's opinions and abilities and that people use salient comparison standards to do so.

These different perspectives on the self converge on the assumption that the self is not an absolute entity. Rather, it is perceived, constructed, and evaluated in relation to salient standards, with social standards presuming a particularly important role (Klein, 1997). How people see themselves thus critically depends on how they perceive others. And vice versa—how people see others critically depends on how they see themselves. As is true for the self, the people and actions we evaluate are set in a rich social context. Given the prominent role the self plays in our lives and minds (Kihlstrom & Cantor, 1984), the self constitutes a particularly salient part of this evaluative context. In this respect, evaluations of the self and others mutually influence one another. People are egocentric in their assessments of others—they use the self as a standard when evaluating others. And, people are sociocentric in their assessments of self—they use social others as standards when evaluating the self.

SELF-OTHER COMPARISON

In fact, abundant research attests this mutual influence. How people evaluate and feel about themselves strongly depends on those who surround them. How competent people perceive themselves, for example, depends on whether self-evaluation takes place in the context of a competent or an incompetent other (e.g., Morse & Gergen, 1970). Similarly, how content people are with a particular performance depends on whether this performance is made in the context of a salient other who performed better or worse (e.g., Gilbert, Giesler, & Morris, 1995).

In much the same way, how people evaluate the attitudes (Sherif & Hovland, 1961) and abilities (Dunning & Cohen, 1992) of others is critically shaped by the evaluative context that is set by their own attitudes and abilities. And, how they predict the reactions of others is influenced by their own reactions (Ross, Greene, & House, 1977). In fact, social judgments are often egocentric in that judges use information about the self as a basis for judgments about others (e.g., Gilovich, Savitsky, & Medvec, 1998; Gilovich, Medvec, & Savitsky, 2000). As is true for any judgment (Brown, 1953; Helson, 1964), evaluations of self and others thus depend on the context in which they are made, with others forming a particularly salient context for self evaluation and the self forming a particularly salient context for the evaluation of others.

But how do these respective contexts influence the critical target evaluations? A salient context can only influence a target judgment, if a relation between context and target is established (Brown, 1953). To use a specific context as a basis for target evaluation, it has to be related to this target. To use the performance of a salient other to evaluate one's own performance, for example, one has to relate both performances to one another. Similarly, to use one's own behavior as a basis for evaluating the behaviors of others (Dunning & Cohen, 1992) one has to relate both behaviors to one another. Comparisons are a primary way to establish these relations, so that comparisons form a crucial link in the mutual evaluative influence of self and others. We evaluate others by comparing them to ourselves and we evaluate ourselves by comparing us to others. In this respect, egocentrism and sociocentrism operate via comparison.

This reasoning suggests that self-other comparisons may be at the heart of social judgment and social perception. Notably, such comparisons occur spontaneously, even if they are not explicitly asked for. When evaluating another person, people spontaneously activate comparison-relevant information about the self. For example, in evaluating the mathematical abilities of a target person, people appear to spontaneously think about their abilities in this domain. In one study demonstrating this spontaneous activation of comparison-relevant self-knowledge (Dunning & Hayes, 1996), participants were exposed to a brief description of a target person which involved some information about this person's mathematical abilities (i.e., the SAT score). After evaluating this person's mathematical abilities, participants were asked a series of questions regarding themselves, including a question about their SAT score. Those participants who had previously judged the target person, were faster in reporting their own SAT score. This facilitation effect indicates that these participants had previously thought about their own SAT while evaluating the target's score.

Similarly, people spontaneously activate comparison-relevant information about a comparison other when evaluating the self. A series of our own studies (Mussweiler & Rüter, 2003; Rüter & Mussweiler, 2005) demonstrates this spontaneous activation of standard knowledge during self-evaluation. More specifically, we demonstrated that after self-evaluation, participants are faster in making a lexical decision about the name of their best friend—a standard that is routinely used for comparison by our undergraduate participants. Furthermore—paralleling the findings of Dunning and Hayes (1996)—participants are faster in evaluating their best friend along a dimension on which they previously judged themselves (Mussweiler & Rüter, 2003). Thus, self-other comparisons are spontaneously engaged when the self or another person are evaluated.

In fact, self-other comparisons appear to happen so naturally that they are even engaged with standards that are hardly present. Under specific conditions, even standards to which judges have only been exposed rather fleetingly—so fleetingly that they are not even aware of it—are used for evaluative comparisons. In a series of our own studies (Mussweiler, Rüter, & Epstude, 2004a), for example, judges who were subliminally presented with potential comparison standards while reflecting on their own abilities, used these standards for self-evaluative comparisons. Judges' self-evaluations of athletic ability, for example, depended on whether they were subliminally exposed to the name of Michael Jordan or Pope John Paul while thinking about their athletic abilities. The fact that even such briefly presented standards are used for self-evaluation suggests that self-other comparisons are a truly ubiquitous process.

COMPARISON CONSEQUENCES

These comparisons reliably influence the outcome of the evaluation process. In fact, using the self as a comparison standard reliably influences how a target other is evaluated. Oftentimes, evaluations of the target are contrasted away from the self. For example, the physical height of a target person is often judged to be taller by people who are relatively short themselves than by people who are tall themselves (Hinckley & Rethlingshafer, 1951). At times, similar contrastive influences of the self can be found for psychological traits and abilities. Students who are highly punctual, for example, judge fellow students that are sometimes a little late for class to be less punctual than do those students who are frequently late themselves (Dunning & Cohen, 1992).

Using the self as a comparison standard for evaluations of others, however, does not invariably lead to contrast. Sometimes, evaluations of others can also be assimilated toward the self. Research on the false consensus effect (Ross et al., 1977)—people's tendency to overestimate the consistency between their own reactions and those of others—provides ample examples for this possibility (for a review see Krueger, 1998). In a classic study (Ross et al., 1977), for example, college students overestimated the extent to which their fellow students would be willing to walk around campus with a sign exclaiming "Repent" after they had done so themselves. Presumably, this was the case because they used the self as a comparison standard in deriving their prediction about the behavior of their fellow students. In this case, using the self as a comparison standard thus led to assimilation rather than contrast. Similar assimilative influences can be found in other instances of egocentric social judgment. Using one's privileged access to one's own internal states as a basis to assess others' ability to read these states, for example, leads people to overestimate these abilities (Gilovich et al., 1998). Egocentrism can thus lead to assimilation or contrast in evaluations of others.

Using an other as a standard in evaluations of the self yields similarly diverse judgmental consequences. Oftentimes, self-evaluations are contrasted away from the comparison other (e.g., Cash, Cash, & Butters, 1983; Gilbert et al., 1995; Morse & Gergen, 1970). For example, it has been found that job candidates who were asked to wait in the company of an impeccable rival who displayed a super-competent appearance saw themselves as less confident (Morse & Gergen, 1970). Similarly, being confronted with a very attractive person can lead one to doubt one's own attractiveness (Cash et al., 1983). At other times, however, self-evaluations are assimilated toward a comparison other (e.g., Brewer & Weber, 1994; Lockwood & Kunda, 1997; Mussweiler & Strack, 2000a; Pelham & Wachsmuth, 1995). The self may thus be evaluated as more competent after a comparison with a competent rather than an incompetent standard. Sociocentrism can thus lead to assimilation or contrast in self-evaluation.

In this way, self-other comparisons influence evaluations of the self and others in similar ways. No matter whether the judgmental target is the self or an other, target evaluations are sometimes assimilated toward and sometimes contrasted away from the standard. In fact, self-other comparisons do not only influence evaluations of the self and others in similar ways. This mutual influence may also result from the same comparison, so that one comparison simultaneously influences the self and a social other. Consistent with this assumption, it has been demonstrated that similar judgmental tasks can be used to examine influences on evaluations of the self and others. Forming an impression of a briefly described target person and thereby using the self as a comparison standard, for example, subsequently influences evaluations of this target person (Dunning & Hayes, 1996). In much the same way, forming an impression of a similarly described target influences evaluations of the self (Mussweiler & Bodenhausen, 2002). Using the self as a standard in evaluating an other person not only influences how we see this other person but also how we see ourselves. By the same token, using an other person as a standard for self-evaluation, not only influences how we see ourselves, but also how we see this other person. Self-other comparisons thus appear to be a knife that cuts both ways.

Evidence for such evaluative consequences of self-other comparison is abundant. At the same time, the exact psychological mechanisms that underlie these comparisons and that produce their various evaluative consequences remain unclear. How is the self used as comparison standard in evaluations of others and how are others used in evaluations of the self? What are the psychological mechanisms that underlie such self-other comparisons? And how do these mechanisms relate to the evaluative consequences of self-other comparisons? Furthermore, why do such comparisons sometimes lead to assimilation and sometimes to contrast, and why are these consequences equally apparent on evaluations of self and others? In the present chapter, we will examine these questions. We will first describe the psychological mechanisms that lead to assimilation and contrast in self-other comparisons. We will then detail how these mechanisms can be used to explain and integrate the literature on the diverse consequences of self-other comparisons.

COMPARISON MECHANISMS: SIMILARITY AND DISSIMILARITY TESTING

To understand these variable consequences, we propose, one has to examine their informational underpinnings (Mussweiler, 2003a). As any judgment, postcomparison target evaluations are based on the implications of the judgment-relevant knowledge that is accessible at the time the judgment is made (for an overview, see Higgins, 1996). Thus, self-other comparisons may affect self-evaluations because they influence what knowledge is rendered accessible and is consequently used as a basis for target evaluation. From this perspective, understanding what knowledge is activated during the comparison process is crucial to understand their evaluative consequences.

To carry out a comparison, judges have to obtain specific judgment-relevant information about the target and the standard which allows them to evaluate both elements relative to one another. This specific knowledge is best obtained by an active search for judgment-relevant information through processes of hypothesis-testing in which judges relate their stored knowledge regarding the target to the judgmental task at hand (Trope & Liberman, 1996). Such hypothesis-testing processes are often selective in that they focus on one single hypothesis that is then evaluated against a specific criterion (Sanbonmatsu, Posavac, Kardes, & Mantel, 1998; see also, Klayman & Ha, 1987; Trope & Lieberman, 1996). Rather than engaging in an exhaustive comparative test of all plausible hypotheses, judges often limit themselves to the test of a single focal hypothesis. In light of this tendency toward selective hypothesis-testing, the critical question is which concrete hypothesis will be tested.

In principle, two hypotheses can be distinguished. Judges can either test the possibility that the target is similar to the standard or they can test the possibility that the target is dissimilar from the standard. Which of these hypotheses is tested depends on the overall perceived similarity of the target and the standard. As an initial step in the selective accessibility mechanism, judges engage in a quick holistic assessment of target and standard (Smith, Shoben, & Rips, 1974) in which they briefly consider a small number of salient features (e.g., category membership, salient characteristics) to determine whether both are generally similar or dissimilar. The outcome of this screening is a broad assessment of similarity. Although such an assessment is by itself too general to be used as the basis for target evaluation, it is sufficient to determine the specific nature of the hypothesis that is then tested. The hypothesis-testing mechanism thus focuses on the possibility that is suggested by the initial holistic assessment. If this assessment indicates that the target is generally similar to the standard, judges will engage in a process of similarity testing and test the hypothesis that the target is similar to the standard on the comparison dimension. If the initial assessment indicates that the target is dissimilar from the standard, however, judges will engage in a process of dissimilarity testing and test the hypothesis that the target is dissimilar from the standard.

Notably, because judges typically select standards that are similar to a given target (Festinger, 1954) and because they initially establish a common ground on which they compare target and standard (Gentner & Markman, 1994), similarity testing constitutes the default comparison mechanism. In fact, comparisons are often characterized by an initial focus on similarities (Chapman & Johnson, 1999; Lockwood & Kunda, 1997) so that dissimilarity testing is more of an exception that is primarily carried out when salient characteristics clearly indicate target-standard dissimilarity.

We conceptualize the critical initial assessment of target-standard similarity as a quick holistic screening of features that are salient, easy to process, and have immediate implications for target-standard similarity. Two features which fulfill these criteria are category membership and standard extremity. Similarity testing, for example is more likely to be engaged for standards that belong to the same category as the standard (Mussweiler & Bodenhausen, 2002) and whose standing on the judgmental dimension is moderate rather than extreme (Mussweiler et al., 2004a, 2004b). In addition, the motivational underpinnings of the comparison situation may influence the outcome of this initial assessment. For example, if judges are motivated to preserve a positive self-image when confronted with a low standard they may focus more on the ways in which they are different from this standard and consequently engage in dissimilarity testing.

The literature on hypothesis-testing further suggests that once a hypothesis is selected, it is often tested by focusing on hypothesis-consistent evidence (Klayman

& Ha, 1987; Snyder & Swann, 1978; Trope & Bassok, 1982; Trope & Liberman, 1996). Applied to the case of hypothesis-testing in comparative judgment, this suggests that judges selectively generate information that is consistent with the focal hypothesis of the comparison. If judges test the hypothesis that the target is similar to the standard, for example, they will do so by selectively searching for standard-consistent target knowledge—evidence indicating that the target's standing on the judgmental dimension is indeed similar to that of the standard. By the same token, if judges test the hypothesis that the target is dissimilar from the standard, they do so by selectively searching for standard-inconsistent target knowledge—evidence indicating that the target's standing differs from that of the standard. This selectivity in the acquisition of judgment-relevant knowledge about the target has clear informational consequences. The mechanism of similarity testing selectively increases the accessibility of standard-consistent target knowledge, whereas dissimilarity testing selectively increases the accessibility of standard-inconsistent target knowledge. This selective accessibility effect constitutes the core informational consequence of comparison (see Figure 6.1).

The described selective accessibility mechanism is likely to be a two-edged sword that changes the accessibility of knowledge about the comparison target and knowledge about the comparison standard in similar ways. To test either of the two core hypotheses, judges have to seek and activate knowledge about the target as well as about the standard. As a consequence, the accessibility of knowledge about both comparison elements is likely to be changed. Similarity testing would thus not only move the representation of the target toward the standard but rather move both representations toward one another. By the same token, dissimilarity testing may move the representations of the target and the standard away from each other. Selective accessibility is a knife that cuts both ways.

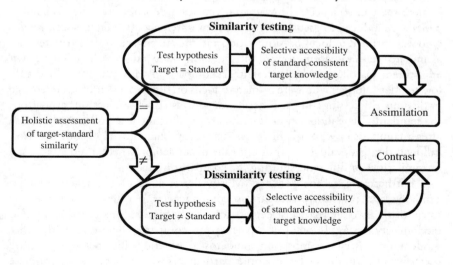

FIGURE 6.1

To the extent that judges use the target-knowledge that became accessible during the comparison as a basis for target evaluations, their subsequent judgment will reflect the implications of this knowledge. Basing target evaluations on the implications of standard-consistent knowledge, indicating that the target's standing on the judgmental dimension is similar to that of the standard, will thus move evaluations closer to the standard. Basing target evaluations on the implications of standard-inconsistent knowledge indicating that the target's standing on the judgmental dimension is dissimilar from that of the standard, on the other hand, will move evaluations further away from the standard. This suggests that the default consequence of similarity testing is assimilation, whereas dissimilarity testing typically leads to contrast.

From this perspective, whether judges engage in the alternative comparison processes of similarity or dissimilarity testing critically determines the evaluative consequences of self-other comparisons. The informational focus judges take during the comparison—whether they focus on similarities or differences—determines whether target evaluations are assimilated toward or contrasted away from the standard.

Direct support for the critical effect judges' informational focus on similarities versus differences has on the direction of comparison consequences stems from a social comparison study in which we directly manipulated participants' informational focus. In particular, using a procedural priming task (Smith, 1994) we induced our participants to either focus on similarities or differences during a social comparison in which they compared themselves with a social standard who was either high or low on the critical dimension of adjustment to college (Mussweiler, 2001a). Subsequent to this comparison, participants evaluated their own adjustment to college. Consistent with a selective accessibility perspective on comparison consequences, self-evaluations critically depended on whether participants were induced to focus on similarities or differences (see Figure 6.2). Judges who were primed to focus on similarities, and thus to engage in similarity testing, assimilated self-evaluations toward the standard. These judges evaluated their own adjustment to college to be better after a comparison with a high rather than a low standard. Judges who were primed to focus on differences and thus to engage in dissimilarity testing, on the other hand, contrasted self-evaluations away from the standard. These judges evaluated their own adjustment to college to be worse after a comparison with a high rather than a low standard. How a comparison influenced target evaluations thus critically depended on whether judges focused on similarities or differences during the comparison process.

Furthermore, recent evidence (Mussweiler et al., 2004b) suggests that assimilative and contrastive comparison consequences are often accompanied by traces of the two alternative selective accessibility mechanisms of similarity and dissimilarity testing. In one study, participants compared themselves with either moderate or extreme comparison standards of athletic ability before evaluating their own athletic ability. For example, participants were either asked to compare

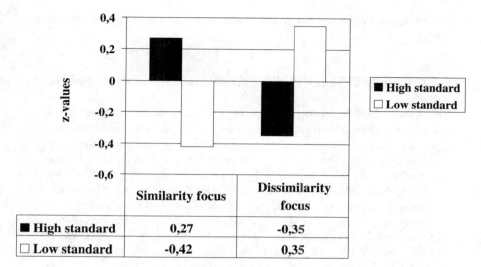

	Similarity focus	Dissimilarity focus
■ High standard	0,27	-0,35
□ Low standard	-0,42	0,35

FIGURE 6.2

their athletic ability with the moderately low standard Bill Clinton or with the extremely low standard pope John Paul. They then evaluated a number of core athletic abilities, such as the number of sit-ups they can perform and the time they need to run 100 meters. Consistent with evidence in the social judgment literature (Herr, 1986), participants assimilated their self-evaluations to the moderate standards and contrasted them away from the extreme standards. Subsequent to these assimilative and contrastive comparisons, we assessed participants' focus on similarities versus dissimilarities. Specifically, participants were asked to compare two pictures that were unrelated to the social comparison and to indicate how similar these pictures are. If assimilative comparison consequences are indeed produced by an informational focus on similarities and contrastive consequences result from a focus on dissimilarities, then these respective foci should carry over to the picture comparison. Participants who assimilated self-evaluations toward the moderate standards, because they selectively focused on similarities to these standards, should also focus on similarities between the two pictures. Participants who contrasted self-evaluations away from extreme standards, because they selectively focused on dissimilarities, should also focus on dissimilarities between the two pictures. Consistent with these expectations, our results demonstrate that participants rated both pictures to be more similar after comparing themselves with a moderate rather than an extreme social comparison standard. This finding suggests that the alternative informational foci on similarities versus dissimilarities do indeed underlie assimilative and contrastive comparison consequences.

In combination, these theoretical considerations and empirical findings suggest that the assimilative and contrastive consequences of self-other comparisons are produced by the two alternative mechanisms of similarity and dissimilarity testing.

EXPLAINING SELF-OTHER COMPARISON CONSEQUENCES

The described selective accessibility perspective may help to integrate the diverse consequences that self-other comparisons have been demonstrated to have. As we have described before, such comparisons influence target evaluations in multiple and variable ways. Sometimes comparisons lead to assimilation of target and standard (e.g., Buunk, Collins, Taylor, VanYperen, & Dakof, 1990; Gilovich et al., 1998, 2000; Mussweiler & Strack, 2000a; Ross et al., 1977) at other times they lead to contrast (e.g., Dunning & Cohen, 1992; Morse & Gergen, 1970). Furthermore, a variety of moderators have been demonstrated to determine which of these alternative consequences prevail (e.g., Brewer & Weber, 1994; Brown, Novick, Lord, & Richards, 1992; Herr, 1986; Lockwood & Kunda, 1997; Mussweiler & Bodenhausen, 2002; Pelham & Wachsmuth, 1995; Tesser, 1988). To date, this body of evidence stands as a disintegrated puzzle. A selective accessibility perspective, however, allows us to explain assimilative and contrastive consequences of self-other comparison and to relate many of the established moderators to the two comparison mechanisms of similarity and dissimilarity testing.

Methodological and Conceptual Clarifications

Before the existing evidence on self-other comparisons can be related to mechanisms of selective accessibility, two conceptual clarifications have to be made.

The first clarification has to do with differential influences of different stages in the process of comparative evaluation. Any instance of comparative evaluation consists of at least three stages: standard selection, comparison, and evaluation (Mussweiler, 2003a). First, judges have to select a standard that can then be compared to the judgmental target. The target knowledge that is obtained during this comparison is then integrated into the final judgment. As a consequence of the existence of these multiple stages, variations in the final outcome of self-other comparison can be attributed to influences on either one of these stages. For example, variations in the extent to which judges assimilate their assessment of others to themselves (e.g., Gilovich et al., 2000), may be attributed to changes in which standard is selected for comparison, how the comparison is carried out, and how the obtained knowledge is integrated into the final judgment. If evaluations of others are less strongly assimilated toward the self, for instance, this may be the case either because the self is not selected as a comparison standard, or because the comparison process does not focus on knowledge indicating self-other similarity, or because this knowledge is excluded from or not used for the final judgment. This distinction may be important to understand some of the moderators of egocentric and sociocentric effects. The fact that egocentric assimilation is reduced by a delay between the time at which participants experienced their own reaction and the target persons' reaction (Gilovich et al., 2000), for example, is likely to result because this delay reduces participants' tendency to use the self as a comparison standard, not because the comparison or evaluation process is changed. In this respect, similar moderating effects may be due to quite distinct psychological mechanisms.

The second clarification has to do with the existence of two parallel comparison influences. The first influence is captured by the selective accessibility mechanism: A self-other comparison increases the accessibility of a specific subset of target knowledge. In addition, a self-other comparison provides a reference point against which the implications of this accessible knowledge can be evaluated. For example, comparing oneself to a high social standard of athletic ability may not only lead oneself to consider the ways in which one is athletic (similarity testing), it also suggests a reference point against which to evaluate the implications of this knowledge. Research in psychophysics (Brown, 1953; Helson, 1964) and social judgment (Ostrom & Upshaw, 1968) has repeatedly demonstrated that the latter mechanism typically produces contrast effects (for a detailed discussion, see Wyer & Srull, 1989). For example, a target stimulus is typically judged to be lighter in the context of a heavy stimulus than in the context of a light stimulus (e.g., Helson, 1964). Applied to the context of self-other comparison, this suggests that one would judge the target to be lower on the critical dimension after a comparison with a high standard than after a comparison with a low standard. In fact, such contrast effects have been found in a host of studies (e.g., Brown et al., 1992; Cash et al., 1983; Morse & Gergen, 1970).

Notably, both comparison consequences have differential effects on different types of target judgments. It has been suggested (Biernat, Manis, & Nelson, 1991; Biernat, Manis, & Kobrynowicz, 1997) that the contrast effects that result from reference point use are primarily apparent on subjective judgments for which participants may use a reference point to interpret the endpoint of the given scale. For example, in order to indicate how large a person's drug consumption is on a scale from "1" ("not at all large") to "9" ("very large") one first has to interpret the given scale labels (Mussweiler & Strack, 2000a). That is, one has to determine what a drug consumption of "9" is supposed to stand for. In this situation, judges are likely to use salient standards to "anchor" the response scale. Doing so typically yields a contrast effect (see Wyer & Srull, 1989, for a more elaborate discussion). For example, using an upward standard (e.g., the musician Frank Zappa) to anchor the response scale may lead judges to assume that this upward standard represents the upper end of the response scale (e.g., "9" is equivalent to Zappa's drug consumption). Compared to this high standard, the target's standing is likely to appear fairly low, so that judges will ascribe a low value to this target. In contrast, using a low standard (e.g., the tennis professional Steffi Graf) to anchor the response scale (e.g., "1" is equivalent to Graf's drug consumption) may lead them to ascribe a high value to the target. Thus, differential response scale anchoring is likely to produce a contrast effect (Upshaw, 1969).

Such response scale anchoring, however, is unlikely to influence objective judgments (e.g., "How often do you use drugs per week?"). Because these judgments pertain to objective numeric quantities, the underlying response scale does not have to be interpreted by the judge. As a consequence, absolute judgments do not have to be anchored and are thus more directly based on the implications of accessible knowledge. Consistent with this assumption, our research has demonstrated that objective judgments typically reflect the implications of accessible target knowledge (e.g., Mussweiler & Strack, 2000a; see Mussweiler, 2003a, for an overview).

Notably, much of the evidence on the consequences of comparison has been obtained with subjective judgments for target evaluation. Because these subjective judgments are the joint product of selective accessibility and reference point use, they depend on the relative strength of these two influences. This perspective on subjective judgments as the product of two independently operating mechanisms is supported by ample evidence on the judgmental consequences of priming (for overviews, see Stapel & Koomen, 2001; Wyer & Srull, 1989). The net outcome that a comparison has on subjective judgments thus depends on the relative strength of the selective accessibility and the reference point mechanism. If the default assimilative selective accessibility effect is stronger than the contrastive reference point effect, then assimilation will be the net outcome. If the reverse is true, however, contrast is likely to ensue. For data that were obtained on subjective judgments, it is thus difficult to identify the exact mechanism that is responsible for the effect.

In evaluating the relative strength and importance of both mechanisms, it is crucial to keep in mind that selective accessibility captures the informational consequences of comparisons and thus represents actual changes in target representation that have robust (e.g. Wilson, Houston, Etling, & Brekke, 1996) and long lasting (Mussweiler, 2001c; Srull & Wyer, 1979) evaluative effects. Reference point effects, on the other hand, are more transient and partly communicational in nature. In fact, our research has demonstrated that selective accessibility effects are, indeed, more robust then reference point effects (Mussweiler & Strack, 2000a). Because reference point effects result in part from changes in response language use, they are communicational rather than representational in nature (Biernat et al., 1991; Upshaw, 1978). In this respect, the reference point effect may be seen as a contrastive influence that superimposes the actual representational consequence of selective accessibility. This contrastive layer has to be removed to make apparent the actual representational consequences of self-other comparisons.

Thus, at least two ambiguities exist concerning the accumulated evidence on the consequences of self-other comparisons. First, these effects can be attributed to different stages in the comparative evaluation process. Second—at least for effects on subjective judgments—they may be the product of two independent mechanisms that potentially influence the final judgment in opposite directions.

Keeping these ambiguities in mind, most of the factors that are associated with the occurrence of assimilation versus contrast in self-other comparison can be related to the basic distinction of similarity and dissimilarity testing. The established moderators of comparison consequences may thus yield their effects by inducing judges to either test for similarity or dissimilarity. Because the nature of the tested hypothesis depends on the outcome of the initial assessment of similarity, any factor that affects the perceived similarity of the target and the standard may influence whether a comparison yields assimilation or contrast. The consequences self-other comparisons have for evaluations of the self and the consequences they have for evaluations of others can be related to this basic distinction between similarity and dissimilarity testing.

EXPLAINING SOCIOCENTRIC ASSIMILATION AND CONTRAST

A multitude of moderators of assimilative versus contrastive comparison consequences on self-evaluation has been identified in the realm of social comparison (for related discussions, see Collins, 1996; Mussweiler, 2003a; Mussweiler & Strack, 2000b). The factor most directly linked to the focal hypothesis and tested during a comparison (i.e., similarity versus dissimilarity testing) is the perceived similarity to the standard. Conceivably, judges are more likely to test for similarity to the standard, if they initially see themselves as similar to it. As a consequence, assimilation is more likely to occur if judges see themselves as similar rather than dissimilar to the standard. A recent study demonstrates this dependency (Mussweiler, 2001b). Here, the perceived similarity to the same standard was manipulated by varying the direction of the comparison (i.e., whether participants compared themselves to the standard or the standard to themselves). Based on Tversky's (1977) feature matching model of similarity, it has been demonstrated that the self is generally seen as more similar to a target other if the other is compared to the self rather than the self to the other (Holyoak & Gordon, 1983; Srull & Gaelick, 1983). Consequently, assimilation should be more likely to occur if participants compared the standard to themselves (i.e., when perceived similarity was higher), whereas contrast should ensue if the self is compared to the standard (i.e., when perceived similarity was lower). This pattern was obtained in two studies. These findings attest that perceived similarity between the target and the standard critically determines the direction of comparison consequences.

Other factors that are more indirectly related to target-standard similarity may influence comparison outcomes in much the same way. Most factors that have been established as moderators of the self-evaluative consequences of comparisons with others are related to the psychological closeness between the self and the standard. As a series of studies attests, judges are likely to assimilate self-evaluations to the standard, if they feel psychologically close to him or her. If experienced closeness is low, however, contrast is likely to occur (e.g., Brewer & Weber, 1994; Brown et al., 1992; Pelham & Wachsmuth, 1995). This may be the case because judges are more likely to test the hypothesis that they are similar to the standard when the other seems close to the self.

The effects that other factors related to psychological closeness have on the self-evaluative consequences of social comparison can be explained along similar lines. The attainability of the standard's standing is one further case in point. A series of studies has demonstrated that the self-evaluative consequences of comparison differ for standards whose performance seems attainable from those who seem unattainable (e.g., Buunk et al., 1990; Lockwood & Kunda, 1997; Taylor, Wayment & Carrilo, 1996). For example, exposure to an upward comparison standard who is highly competent on a valued dimension may be inspiring for those who assume that they can still attain a similar degree of excellence. Consequently, they may assimilate their self-evaluations to the high performance of the standard. Such inspiration, however, is unlikely to result for those who perceive themselves as unable to reach the standard, in which case the comparison is likely to yield contrast (Lockwood & Kunda, 1997).

Similarly, a comparison with a downward standard may produce adverse affective consequences if the comparison target assumes that he or she may reach the inferior state of the standard (Taylor et al., 1996). This seems especially likely, if the critical dimension is uncontrollable. Consistent with this assumption, Buunk et al. (1990) demonstrated that for these conditions, negative reactions to downward comparisons prevail. From the current perspective, assimilation may occur for attainable standards, because judges are likely to test for similarity if the standard's level of performance is attainable. If the standard is not attainable, however, they are likely to test for dissimilarity.

Relative group membership of the self and the standard, is another important determinant of the evaluative consequences of social comparison. Similarity testing is more likely to be engaged if the self and the standard belong to the same group than if they belong to different groups. Our own research has supported this assumption (Mussweiler & Bodenhausen, 2002). In our study, participants assimilated self-evaluations toward an in-group standard and contrasted away from an out-group standard. For example, male participants, who had spontaneously compared with a highly caring other, assimilated self-evaluations of their own interpersonal caring towards the other, if this person was also male and thus belonged to the same gender category. If the highly caring person was female, and, thus, belonged to the opposite gender category, however, our male participants contrasted self-evaluations away from the other.

Another factor influencing whether target evaluations are assimilated toward the standard is the ambiguity or mutability of target information. Whereas evaluations of ambiguous targets are likely to be assimilated towards a standard, evaluations of unambiguous targets are likely to be contrasted away from the standard (e.g., Herr, Sherman, & Fazio, 1983). Similarly, self-evaluations are more likely to be assimilated towards a social comparison standard if people see themselves as mutable (Stapel & Koomen, 2000). If people see themselves as immutable, however, they are more likely to contrast self-evaluations away from a standard. This may be the case because similarity to the standard is easier to assume with an ambiguous or mutable target. Because an ambiguous target offers a lot of interpretational leeway, it is easier to construe it as similar to any given standard. An unambiguous target, on the other hand, is too restrictively defined to allow for such a flexible construal, so that here judges may be more likely to test for dissimilarity.

From this perspective, many of the factors that have been found to determine whether the self is assimilated toward or contrasted away from a social standard may be linked to the same mechanism, namely similarity versus dissimilarity testing. The same appears to be true for the assimilative and contrastive consequences self-other comparisons have for evaluations of other people.

EXPLAINING EGOCENTRIC ASSIMILATION AND CONTRAST

As is true for the findings on sociocentric evaluation of the self, a first riddle in the evidence on egocentric social judgment that has to be solved is that sometimes evaluations of others are assimilated to the self (e.g., Gilovich et al., 1998, 2000; Ross et al., 1977) and sometimes they are contrasted away from the self (e.g., Dunning & Cohen, 1992; Dunning & Hayes, 1996).

A first factor, that is likely to contribute to this divergence in the direction of self-other comparison effects, is that assimilation is often obtained on objective judgments (e.g., Gilovich et al., 2000), whereas contrast is often observed on subjective judgments (Dunning & Hayes, 1996). Egocentric assimilation, for example, was apparent when participants estimated others' ability to detect a celebrity depicted on an embarrassing t-shirt along an objective percentage scale (Gilovich et al., 2000). Egocentric contrast, however, was apparent when participants evaluated others' athletic abilities on a subjective 7-point scale (Dunning & Hayes, 1996). Because the objective percentage estimates are less easily influenced by shifting scale labels, they are more likely to show assimilative comparison consequences. For subjective scale ratings, on the other hand, such assimilation may be superimposed by the contrastive influences of using the self as a reference point for scale anchoring.

A second factor that may contribute to the occurrence of egocentric assimilation versus contrast has to do with different levels of ambiguity that are associated with the critical dimension, as well as the target other to which the judgment pertains. Egocentric assimilation often results if target ambiguity is high. For example, Lambert and Wedell (1991) demonstrated that judgments about ambiguous others are typically assimilated toward participants' own position. Thus, assimilation is more likely to result if target ambiguity is high because judges have little information available about the critical behavior or ability and about the target other. These criteria seem to be fulfilled in the original false-consensus studies where participants judge, for example, the likelihood that a target other will perform a rare behavior—such as carrying around a "Repent" sign (Ross et al., 1977)—about which they have little information. In these studies, egocentric assimilation thus appears to result for judgments about uncommon behaviors. Egocentric contrast, on the other hand, is often obtained for judgments about behaviors and abilities that are more typical and about which judges thus have more information—such as athletic abilities (Dunning & Hayes, 1996).

More important, egocentric assimilation is often obtained for judgments about vaguely defined targets, such as judges' peers (Ross et al., 1977) or a random array of people (Gilovich et al., 2000). Egocentric contrast, however, is often found for judgments about concrete others about whom judges receive at least some concrete information. In the research by Dunning and Hayes (1996), for example, participants judged the abilities of one concrete person who was described to them in a brief paragraph. As we have suggested in the preceding discussion of the self-evaluative effects of self-other comparison, the more ambiguous a given target or dimension, the more leeway judges have in construing this target as sufficiently similar to the standard to pursue the default comparison route of similarity testing (e.g., Herr, 1986; Stapel & Koomen, 2000). Judges who are asked to evaluate a vaguely defined other or group of others on an unusual dimension are thus more likely to engage in similarity testing and consequently assimilate target-evaluations toward the self. Under these conditions of ambiguity, this assimilative influence may at times even be sufficiently strong to compensate for the contrastive reference-point mechanism so that assimilation may result even on subjective judgments. Judges who are asked to evaluate a clearly defined specific other on a common dimension, however, are less likely to engage in similarity testing, so that assimilative influences may not result at all, or be too weak to compensate for the contrastive influences of reference point use.

In addition to the influence of target ambiguity, that may help explain variations in egocentric assimilation and contrast across different studies, other moderators are also related to the selective accessibility mechanism. Research on the false consensus effect (Ross et al., 1977) is a first case in point. This basic tendency to overestimate the consistency between the reactions of self and others is less prevalent when the self is perceived as distinct from the target other (e.g., Sarason et al., 1991). This finding is clearly consistent with the present perspective. Similarity testing appears to be the default process so that, in the absence of factors indicating that the self differs from the target other, judges will test for similarity and consequently predict the target other to behave consistent with the self. If, however, factors indicate that the self is distinct from the target, then dissimilarity testing will be engaged so that no false consensus results.

The false consensus effect has also been found to depend on the order in which judgments about self and other are made (Fabrigar & Krosnick, 1995). This dependency can be explained along similar lines. Meta-analyses of the false consensus effect have found that judges are more likely to show false consensus if the other is judged before the self (Fabrigar & Krosnick, 1995; Mullen et al., 1985; Mullen & Hu, 1988). This may be the case, because whether the other is judged before or after the self influences the perceived similarity of self and other and is consequently likely to determine whether a self-other comparison will involve similarity or dissimilarity testing. The self is generally seen as more similar to a target other if the other is compared to the self rather than the self to the other (Holyoak & Gordon, 1983; Srull & Gaelick, 1983). This dependency of perceived similarity on the direction of comparison (i.e., other => self versus self => other) suggests that similarity testing is more likely to be engaged if the other is evaluated before the self so that the comparison direction is from other to self. Our own research demonstrates this dependency in the realm of social comparison (Mussweiler, 2001b). False consensus may thus be more pronounced if the other is judged before the self because this order increases perceived similarity and consequently renders the assimilative comparison mechanism of similarity testing more likely.

Finally, the finding that false consensus is reduced in domains of high personal relevance (described in Karniol, 2003) can also be related to the basic comparison mechanisms of similarity and dissimilarity testing. In self-relevant domains predictions that differ for the self and a target other may be more frequent, because in these important domains people are motivated to see themselves as special and unique (Bosveld, Koomen, & van der Pligt, 1996). As a consequence, they are more likely to engage in dissimilarity testing. In domains of limited self-relevance, however, the motivation to be distinct from others is less pronounced (Bosveld et al., 1996), so that the default process of similarity testing is engaged, leading to consistent predictions for self and other.

Similar motivational influences on the initial assessment of target-standard similarity may be responsible for a related finding on the magnitude of egocentric contrast in social judgment. Here, it has been demonstrated that judges whose self-esteem has been threatened by negative feedback, show more egocentric contrast in evaluating the intelligence of a target person than those whose self-esteem has been bolstered by positive feedback (Beauregard & Dunning, 1998). Specifically, self-threatened judges with high levels of academic aptitude judge a moderately intelligent target person in particularly negative ways (i.e., show a strong contrast effect). This may be the case, because the motivational benefits of seeing themselves as better than this target person guides the initial assessment of target-standard similarity and thus gears judges towards dissimilarity testing.

The diverse findings on how self-other comparisons influence evaluations of others can thus be integrated with the selective accessibility perspective. Egocentric assimilation can in principle be conceptualized as the consequence of similarity testing whereas egocentric contrast can at times be attributed to dissimilarity testing. Furthermore those factors that influence the occurrence and magnitude of both effects can be related to the factors that influence mechanisms of selective accessibility on the one hand, and reference point use on the other hand.

CONCLUSION

We have suggested that the assimilative and contrastive consequences of self-other comparisons may be produced by mechanisms of selective accessibility. Our previous research (for overviews, see Mussweiler 2003a, 2003c) has demonstrated that similarity testing produces assimilation whereas dissimilarity testing produces contrast (Mussweiler, 2001a; Mussweiler & Bodenhausen, 2002; Mussweiler et al., 2004b). Consequently, any factor that influences which of these alternative selective accessibility mechanisms is engaged is likely to influence whether self-other comparisons lead to assimilation or contrast. The empirical evidence we have gathered to examine the role similarity and dissimilarity testing play in the genesis of assimilation and contrast focused on the self-evaluative consequences of comparison. Here we have demonstrated that inducing judges to focus on similarities versus dissimilarities in social comparison yields the predicted assimilative versus contrastive consequences (Mussweiler, 2001a). Furthermore, such sociocentric assimilation versus contrast is typically accompanied by traces of similarity versus dissimilarity testing (Mussweiler et al., 2004b). This evidence provides a save haven from which the selective accessibility mechanism can be used as a conceptual tool to integrate the diverse findings on self-evaluative consequences of comparisons with others. In principle, moderators that have been found to determine whether sociocentric assimilation or contrast is found can be related to the alternative mechanisms of similarity and dissimilarity testing. Selective accessibility may thus serve as an integrative theoretical framework for sociocentric comparisons.

This perspective can also be extended to the realm of egocentric comparisons (Mussweiler, 2003b). As we have suggested in this chapter, egocentric assimilation and contrast may be conceptualized as comparison consequences that are produced by the same mechanisms that we have shown to operate in sociocentric assimilation and contrast. Clearly, this possibility remains somewhat speculative, as no empirical evidence directly demonstrating that selective accessibility mechanisms also operate in this paradigm exists. On a conceptual level, however, core moderators of egocentric assimilation and contrast effects can be related to those factors that are likely to influence selective accessibility mechanisms. Direct empirical support for this possibility remains to be provided by future research.

This selective accessibility perspective on egocentric and sociocentric assimilation and contrast is based on a general model of comparison processes. In fact, the described mechanisms of selective accessibility are not limited to self-other comparisons. They equally operate in paradigms that—on the surface—have little resemblance with the classic phenomena of social comparison, false consensus, and egocentric contrast that we have focused on in this chapter. In this respect, paradigms and phenomena that are quite distinct can be discussed in terms of the same psychological mechanisms. Conceptualizing egocentric and sociocentric assimilation and contrast as instances of selective accessibility thus has considerable integrative potential.

Finally, this perspective is consistent with the possibility that self-other comparisons influence evaluations of self and others in similar ways. Selective accessibility may thus explain why and how self-other comparisons become a knife that cuts both ways.

ACKNOWLEDGEMENTS

Our research described in this chapter was supported by a grant from the German Research Foundation (DFG). We would like to thank the members of the Würzburg Social Cognition Group for stimulating discussions of this work. Correspondence concerning this chapter should be send to Thomas Mussweiler, Institut für Psychologie, Erziehungswissenschaftliche Fakultät, Universität zu Köln, Gronewaldstrasse 2, 50931 Köln, Germany, email: thomas.mussweiler@uni-koeln.de.

REFERENCES

Baumeister, R. F. (1998). The self. In D. T. Gilbert, S. T. Fiske, & G. Lindzey (Eds.), *The handbook of social psychology* (Vol. 1, pp. 680- 740). New York: McGraw-Hill.

Beauregard, K. S., & Dunning, D. (1998). Turning up the contrast: Self-enhancement motives prompt egocentric contrast effects in social judgment. *Journal of Personality and Social Psychology, 74,* 606–621.

Biernat, M., Manis, M., & Kobrynowicz, D. (1997). Simultaneous assimilation and contrast effects in judgments of self and others. *Journal of Personality and Social Psychology, 73,* 254–269.

Biernat, M., Manis, M., & Nelson, T. E. (1991). Stereotypes and standards of judgment. *Journal of Personality and Social Psychology, 60,* 485–499.

Bosveld, W., Koomen, W., & Van der Pligt, J. (1996). Estimating group size: Effects of category membership, differential encoding and selective exposure. *European Journal of Social Psychology, 33,* 457–466.

Brewer, M. B., & Weber, J. G. (1994). Self-evaluation effects of interpersonal versus intergroup social comparison. *Journal of Personality and Social Psychology, 66,* 268–275.

Brown, D. R. (1953). Stimulus-similarity and the anchoring of subjective scales. *American Journal of Psychology, 66,* 199–214.

Brown, J. D., Novick, N. J., Lord, K. A., & Richards, J. M. (1992). When Gulliver travels: Social context, psychological closeness, and self-appraisals. *Journal of Personality and Social Psychology, 62*(5), 717–727.

Buunk, B. P., Collins, R. L., Taylor, S. E., VanYperen, N. W., & Dakof, G. A. (1990). The affective consequences of social comparison: Either direction has its ups and downs. *Journal of Personality and Social Psychology, 59*(6), 1238–1249.

Cash, T. F., Cash, D., & Butters, J. W. (1983). "Mirror, mirror, on the wall ...?": Contrast effects and self-evaluations of physical attractiveness. *Personality and Social Psychology Bulletin, 9*(3), 351–358.

Chapman, G. B., & Johnson, E. J. (1999). Anchoring, activation, and the construction of values. *Organizational Behavior and Human Decision Processes, 79,* 1–39.

Collins, R. L. (1996). For better or worse: The impact of upward social comparison on self-evaluations. *Psychological Bulletin, 119*(1), 51–69.

Dunning, D., & Cohen, G.L. (1992). Egocentric definitions of traits and abilities in social judgment. *Journal of Personality and Social Psychology, 63,* 341–355.

Dunning, D., & Hayes, A. F. (1996). Evidence of egocentric comparison in social judgment. *Journal of Personality and Social Psychology, 71,* 213–229.

Fabrigar, L. R., & Krosnick, J. A. (1995) Attitude importance and the false consensus effect. *Personality and Social Psychology Bulletin, 21,* 468–479.

Festinger, L. (1954). A theory of social comparison processes. *Human Relations, 7,* 117–140.

Gentner, D., & Markman, A. B. (1994). Structural alignment in comparison: No difference without similarity. *Psychological Science, 5,* 152–158.

Gilbert, D. T., Giesler, R. B., & Morris, K. A. (1995). When comparisons arise. *Journal of Personality and Social Psychology, 69,* 227–236.

Gilovich, T., Savitsky, K., & Medvec, V. H. (1998). The illusion of transparency: Biased assessments of others ability to read one's emotional states. *Journal of Personality and Social Psychology, 75,* 332–346.

Gilovich, T., Medvec, V. H., & Savitsky, K. (2000). The spotlight effect: An egocentric bias in estimates of the salience of one's own actions and appearances. *Journal of Personality and Social Psychology, 78,* 211–222.

Helson, H. (1964). *Adaptation level theory: An experimental and systematic approach to behavior.* New York: Harper.

Herr, P. M. (1986). Consequences of priming: Judgment and behavior. *Journal of Personality and Social Psychology, 51,* 1106–1115.

Herr, P. M., Sherman, S. J., & Fazio, R. H. (1983). On the consequences of priming: Assimilation and contrast effects. *Journal of Experimental Social Psychology, 19,* 323–340.

Higgins, E. T. (1996). Knowledge activation: Accessibility, applicability, and salience. In E. T. Higgins & A. W. Kruglanski (Eds.), *Social psychology: Handbook of basic principles* (pp. 133–168). New York: Guilford Press.

Hinckley, E., & Rethlingshafer, D. (1951). Value judgments of heights of men by college students. *Journal of Personality, 31,* 257–296.

Holyoak, K. J., & Gordon, P. C. (1983). Social reference points. *Journal of Personality and Social Psychology, 44,* 881–887.

Kant, I. (1956/1787). *Kritik der reinen Vernunft* [Critique of pure reason]. Frankfurt, Germany. (Original work published 1787).

Karniol, R. (2003). Egocentrism versus protocentrism: The status of self in social prediction. *Psychological Review, 110,* 564–580.

Kihlstrom, J. F., & Cantor, N. (1984). Mental representation of the self. In L. Berkowitz (Ed.), *Advances in experimental social psychology* (Vol. 17, pp. 145–180). New York: Academic Press.

Klayman, J., & Ha, Y.-W. (1987). Confirmation, disconfirmation, and information in hypotheses testing. *Psychological Review, 94,* 211–228.

Klein, W. M. (1997). Objective standards are not enough: Affective, self-evaluative, and behavioral responses to social cognition information. *Journal of Personality and Social Psychology, 72,* 763–774.

Krueger, J. (1998) On the perception of social consensus. *Advances in Experimental Social Psychology, 30,* 164–240.

Lambert, A. J., & Wedell, D. H. (1991). The self and social judgment: Effects of affective reaction and "own position" on judgments of unambiguous and ambiguous information about others. *Journal of Personality and Social Psychology, 61,* 884–897.

Lewin, K. (1951). *Field theory in social science.* New York: Harper.

Lockwood, P., & Kunda, Z. (1997). Superstars and me: Predicting the impact of role models on the self. *Journal of Personality and Social Psychology, 73*(1), 91–103.

Morse, S., & Gergen, K. J. (1970). Social comparison, self-consistency, and the concept of self. *Journal of Personality and Social Psychology, 16*(1), 148–156.

Mullen, B., Atkins, J. L., Champion, D. S, Edwards, C., Hardy, D., Stroy, J. E., & Vanderklok, M. (1985) The false consensus effect: A meta analysis of 115 hypothesis tests. *Journal of Experimental Social Psychology, 21,* 262–283.

Mullen, B., & Hu, L-T. (1988) Social projection as a function of cognitive mechanisms: Two meta-analytic integrations. *British Journal of Social Psychology, 27,* 333–356.

Mussweiler, T. (2001a). "Seek and Ye shall find": Antecedents of assimilation and contrast in social comparison. *European Journal of Social Psychology, 31,* 499–509.

Mussweiler, T. (2001b). Focus of comparison as a determinant of assimilation versus contrast in social comparison. *Personality and Social Psychology Bulletin, 27,* 38–47.

Mussweiler, T. (2001c). The durability of anchoring effects. *European Journal of Social Psychology, 31*, 431–442.

Mussweiler, T. (2003a). Comparison processes in social judgment: Mechanisms and consequences. *Psychological Review, 110*, 472–489.

Mussweiler, T. (2003b). When egocentrism breeds distinctness: Comparison processes in social prediction. *Psychologcial Review, 110*, 581–584.

Mussweiler, T. (2003c). "Everything is relative". Comparison processes in social judgment. *European Journal of Social Psychology, 33*, 719–733.

Mussweiler, T., & Bodenhausen, G. (2002). I know you are but what am I? Self-evaluative consequences of judging ingroup and outgroup members. *Journal of Personality and Social Psychology, 82*, 19–32.

Mussweiler, T., & Rüter, K. (2003). What friends are for! The use of routine standards in social comparison. *Journal of Personality and Social Psychology, 85*, 467–481.

Mussweiler, T., Rüter, K., & Epstude, K. (2004a). The man who wasn't there: Subliminal social comparison standards influence self-evaluation. *Journal of Experimental Social Psychology, 40*, 689-696.

Mussweiler, T., Rüter, K., & Epstude, K. (2004b). The ups and downs of social comparison: Mechanisms of assimilation and contrast. *Journal of Personality and Social Psychology, 87*, 832-844.

Mussweiler, T., & Strack, F. (2000a). The "relative self": Informational and judgmental consequences of comparative self-evaluation. *Journal of Personality and Social Psychology, 79*, 23–38.

Mussweiler, T., & Strack, F. (2000b). Consequences of social comparison: Selective accessibility, assimilation, and contrast. In J. Suls & L. Wheeler (Eds.), *Handbook of social comparison: Theory and research* (pp. 253–270). New York: Plenum.

Ostrom, T. M., & Upshaw, H. S. (1968). Psychological perspectives and attitude change. In A. G. Greenwald, T. C. Brock, & T. M. Ostrom (Eds.), *Psychological foundations of attitudes* (pp. 217–242). New York: Academic Press.

Pelham, B. W., & Wachsmuth, J. O. (1995). The waxing and waning of the social self: Assimilation and contrast in social comparison. *Journal of Personality and Social Psychology, 69*(5), 825–838.

Ross, L., Greene, D., & House, P. (1977) The false consensus phenomenon: An attributional bias in self-perception and social-perception processes. *Journal of Experimental Social Psychology, 13*, 279–301.

Rüter, K., & Mussweiler, T. (2005). Bonds of friendship—comparative self-evaluations evoke the use of routine standards. *Social Cognition, 23*, 137–160.

Sanbonmatsu, D. M., Posavac, S. S., Kardes, F. R., & Mantel, S P. (1998). Selective hypothesis testing. *Psychonomic Bulletin and Review, 5*, 197–220.

Sarason, B. R., Pierce, G. R., Shearin, E. N., Sarason, I. G., Waltz, J. A., Poppe, L. (1991). Perceived social support and working models of self and actual others. *Journal of Personality and Social Psychology, 60*, 273–287.

Sherif, M., & Hovland, C. I. (1961). *Social judgment: Assimilation and contrast effects in communication and attitude change.* New Haven, CT: Yale University Press.

Smith, E. E., Shoben, E. J, & Rips, L. J. (1974). Structure and process in semantic memory: A featural model for semantic decisions. *Psychological Review, 81*, 214–241.

Smith, E. R. (1994). Procedural knowledge and processing strategies in social cognition. In R. S. Wyer & T. K. Srull (Eds.), *Handbook of social cognition* (2nd ed., Vol. 1, pp. 99–152). Hillsdale, NJ: Erlbaum.

Snyder, M., & Swann, W. B. (1978). Hypothesis-testing processes in social interaction. *Journal of Personality and Social Psychology, 36*, 1202–1212.

Srull, T. K., & Gaelick, L. (1983). General principles and individual differences in the self as a habitual reference point: An examination of self-other judgments of similarity. *Social Cognition, 2*, 108–121.

Srull, T. K., & Wyer, R. S. (1979). The role of category accessibility in the Interpretation of information about persons: Some determinants and implications. *Journal of Personality and Social Psychology, 37*, 1660–1672.

Stapel, D., & Koomen, W. (2000). Distinctness of others, mutability of selves: Their impact on self-evaluation. *Journal of Personality and Social Psychology, 79*, 1068-1087.

Stapel, D., & Koomen, W. (2001). Let's not forget the past when we go to the future: On our knowledge of knowledge accessibility effects. In G. Moswoitz (Ed.), *Cognitive social psychology: The Princeton symposium on the legacy and future of social cognition* (pp. 229–246). Mahwah, NJ: Erlbaum.

Taylor, S. E., Wayment, H. A., & Carrillo, M. (1996). Social comparison, self-regulation, and motivation. In R. M. Sorrentino & E. T. Higgins (Eds.), *Handbook of motivation and cognition* (pp. 3–27). New York: Guilford Press.

Tesser, A. (1988). Toward a self-evaluation maintenance model of social behavior. In L. Berkowitz (Ed.), *Advances in experimental social psychology* (Vol. 20, pp. 181–227). New York: Academic Press.

Trope, Y., & Bassok, M. (1982). Confirmatory and diagnostic strategies in social information gathering. *Journal of Personality and Social Psychology, 43,* 22–34.

Trope, Y., & Liberman, A. (1996). Social hypothesis testing: Cognitive and motivational factors. In E. T. Higgins & A. W. Kruglanski (Eds.), *Social psychology: Handbook of basic principles* (pp. 239–270). New York: Guilford Press.

Tversky, A. (1977). Features of similarity. *Psychological Review, 84,* 327–352.

Tversky, A., & Kahneman, D. (1974). Judgment under uncertainty: Heuristics and biases. *Science, 185,* 1124–1130.

Upshaw, H. S. (1978). Social influences on attitudes and on anchoring of congeneric attitude scales. *Journal of Experimental Social Psychology, 14,* 327–339.

Upshaw, H. S. (1969). The personal reference scale: An approach to social judgment. In L. Berkowitz (Ed.), *Advances in experimental social psychology* (Vol. 4, pp. 316–371). New York: Academic Press.

Wilson, T. D., Houston, C., Etling, K. M., & Brekke, N. (1996). A new look at anchoring effects: Basic anchoring and its antecedents. *Journal of Experimental Psychology: General, 4,* 387–402.

Wyer, R. S., & Srull, T. K. (1989). *Memory and cognition in its social context.* Hillsdale, NJ: Erlbaum.

7

A Feature-Based
Model of Self-Other
Comparisons

SARA D. HODGES
University of Oregon

"Well, don't you look just like your daddy?" "Is my resume stronger than hers?" "Is he as nice as the piano tuner?" "Which would be better for dinner, tamales or tofu?" People make comparisons all day long, attempting to make decisions that will bring them maximum utility and satisfaction. People also use comparisons to increase their understanding (e.g., "Is the war in Iraq more like Vietnam or World War II?") and as a means of explanation (e.g., "She's been like a sister to me"). These latter functions of comparison are particularly relevant when the comparison involves the self and another person.

This chapter takes feature matching, a general cognitive model of how people make comparisons, and examines how well this model fits self-other comparisons. In many cases, the model fits very nicely, suggesting that self-other comparisons are just like any other kind of comparison. Under other circumstances, at first glance, outcomes for self-other comparisons appear to differ from those predicted by the general model. However, with closer examination, these apparent deviations can be mostly accounted for by considering special qualities associated with the self, such as familiarity, accessibility, and a motivation to maintain a positive view of the self. The qualities may constitute specific examples of variables known to moderate general feature matching outcomes.

The chapter starts by introducing the feature matching model. It will then cover two "hallmarks" of feature matching, direction of comparison effects and cancellation effects, introducing each one's role in comparisons in general and then exploring the evidence for these effects in self-other comparisons.

FEATURE MATCHING IN SIMILARITY
AND COMPARATIVE JUDGMENTS: SAME DIFFERENCE?

Tversky (1977) originally outlined a featured-based model of comparisons for similarity judgments. His initial model has since been extended to comparative judgments (see for example Hodges, 1997; 1998; Hodges, Bruininks, & Ivy, 2002; Houston, Sherman, & Baker, 1989; 1991), a term used throughout this chapter to designate comparisons that involve ordering two or more items along some continuous dimension (e.g., deciding which of two menus is healthier). The basic idea behind feature matching is that when two items are compared, people match up the features shared by the two items, distinguishing these features from unique (unshared) features. This core process of feature matching is thought to be the same for both similarity judgments (e.g., "How similar are you and your brother?") and comparative judgments (e.g., "Can you sing better than your brother?"). At first blush, the mechanisms for making similarity judgments and comparative judgments may seem very different, even opposite, from each other: In similarity judgments, people are judging how alike two things are; whereas in comparative judgments, they are judging the difference between two things, in order to determine which of the two is higher on some dimension. However, at their core, these two kinds of judgments are more similar than they may initially appear to be (Medin, Goldstone, & Markman, 1995). Both share a fundamental first step of aligning the qualities of both items in such a way that a comparison can be made.

According to the feature matching model, the number of features shared by two items serves as an initial estimate of their similarity (Tversky, 1977). This estimate is then adjusted depending on the number of "leftover" unique features: A greater number of unique features reduces similarity. Thus, when considering the following resorts:

Resort A:	Resort B:
Stunning views	Stunning views
Excellent restaurants	Excellent restaurants
By the sea	In the mountains
Beautiful golf course	Specializes in spa treatments

the initial estimate of similarity based on the stunning views and excellent restaurants would then be adjusted downward to account for the different locations and the fact that Resort A has golf and Resort B has a spa.

In comparative judgments (e.g., preference judgments or judgments that rank order items along some dimension), shared features, by definition, do not distinguish between the two options. Once shared features are matched up, it is the features that are unique to one option or the other that allow people to decide which option is better (or scarier, or more liberal, or whatever the relevant comparative judgment being made is). In the resort example, people would have to decide whether they prefer a seaside vacation with golf, or a spa holiday in the mountains.

Thus, matching up shared features is a common element in both similarity and comparative judgments. In order to say how two things are different or similar, we first have to establish the dimension (or dimensions) on which they could possibly (but do not necessarily) share qualities. Of course, when we know exactly where two items stand on a numerical dimension that corresponds to the judgment at hand (e.g., when we are comparing the lengths of two pieces of ribbon and we have measurements of both), this part of comparison seems obvious, automatic, and barely worth discussing, especially when it comes to self-other comparisons: Very few studies of self-other comparison deal with people comparing themselves with others on height!

However, this first step in comparisons (including self-other comparisons) often involves integrating information about multiple features, some of which may be viewed as points along a continuous scale, and others of which are discrete categorical qualities. For example, when asked which piece of ribbon is *best*, we may need to integrate information about length, color, and whether the ribbon is washable. When asked whether one is as smart as one's brother, SAT scores, past verbal sparring matches, and other people's opinions may be called to mind.

This "determination of correspondences between representations" (Gentner & Markman, 1994, p. 157) constitutes a fundamental component of comparison and forms the basis of "alignability." This concept has notably refined Tversky's original comparison model. In Gentner and Markman's words, there is "no difference without similarity" (1994, p. 152). When the representation of one item in a comparison has elements that correspond to the representation of the other item in the comparison (whether those elements are features, points on the same continuum, or relationships), the comparison is said to be alignable. For example, when assessing which of two actresses is more popular, one could align the two actresses' respective standings on features such as average salary per film, whether each has been nominated for an Oscar, and frequency of appearance in the Hollywood tabloids. With the addition of alignability, feature matching can serve as a model for comparisons of items whose features include different scores on the same continuum, as well as items whose features are categorical in nature (Zhang & Markman, 2001).

Although alignability serves as a common basis for making comparisons (Gentner & Markman, 1997), it does not necessarily imply similarity between the items that are compared; it only provides the dimension on which similarity (or dissimilarity, for comparative judgments) will be assessed. In fact, Markman and Gentner (1996) have found that, paradoxically, the presence of alignable differences decreases similarity judgments more than that of nonalignable differences. This explains why the common English expression "that's like apples and oranges" is used to describe things that are very different, rather than using an expression such as, for example, "that's like apples and chairs." The former compares two items that have a number of alignable differences (e.g., color and skin texture) but that are actually quite similar to each other in many regards (e.g., both are fruits commonly used for snacks and to make juice), whereas the latter compares two items with few commonalities, but also few alignable differences.

DIRECTION OF COMPARISON

Thus, aligning features is the first step in feature matching, and it allows us to see which features are unique to one option or the other. These unique features play a critical role in both similarity and comparative judgments. Furthermore, some unique features are even more important than others, because the two items in a comparison are not interchangeable. Comparisons are generally anchored at one end with a *referent* that serves as a contextual frame. The referent can be thought of as a baseline to which the other object in the comparison, known as the *target* (or subject[1]) of comparison, is compared. Designating the referent sets the context of the comparison and determines the backdrop against which the target of comparison will be seen. Thus, when someone says to a woman, "You look just like your mother," the mother serves as the referent, and the woman being spoken to (the daughter) is the target of comparison.

The dimension (or dimensions) on which a comparison is to be made may be explicitly specified (e.g., "Are you more talkative than your mother?"), but sometimes the comparison dimension has to be extracted from contextual cues (as is the case for metaphors). In the latter case, specifying which item is the referent plays an even greater role in shaping the comparison, by suggesting on which dimensions the target will be compared to the referent (Medin, Goldstone, & Gentner, 1993). For example, when someone says, "The city lights are like stars," it is the sparkly aspect of stars that is relevant in the comparison, but when someone says, "She's shooting for the stars," the distance of the stars forms the base of the metaphor.

Because the features of the target are compared to those of the referent, and because features cannot be distinguished as shared or unique until both options have been experienced, the unique features of the target play a disproportionate weight in judgments. These unique features of the target are "leftover" after the target's shared features have been matched up with the corresponding features of the referent. Thus, these features play the primary role in determining the "distance" of the target from the referent. Because of this asymmetry, an important premise of Tversky's feature-based model of comparison is that comparisons have a specified direction, and furthermore, reversing that direction can have major consequences: Borrowing from the earlier vacation locale example, comparing Resort A to Resort B can often mean something quite different from comparing Resort B to Resort A.

The significance of the direction of comparison (and by extension, the assignment of target and referent roles) emerges most vividly in concrete examples. Consider Medin et al.'s (1993) example of the butcher who is compared *to* a surgeon. With the surgeon serving as the referent, defining qualities of surgeons are associated with the butcher, conjuring up images of a butcher who does meticulous work and has a spotlessly clean shop. Now, consider the surgeon who is compared to a butcher. When the defining qualities of a butcher (perhaps a bloody apron and aggressive knife work come to mind) are used as a referent for describing a surgeon, the comparison is definitely no longer as complimentary. If comparisons were symmetric, it would not make a difference what got compared to what, but clearly, direction of comparison matters.

DETERMINING DIRECTION OF COMPARISON

The direction of a comparison is determined in a number of ways. First and perhaps most simply, explicit verbal instructions can provide a direction of comparison. If someone asks, "Is Fiona as musical as Seth?" Seth's abilities serve as a benchmark and frame the comparison. Because Seth is referent, the questioner is expecting an answer framed in terms of his talents, e.g., "Almost, but she doesn't have perfect pitch like he does." Thus, by linguistically designating one object as the referent, notable aspects of the referent may determine the dimensions on which the comparison is made, if they are not otherwise explicitly stated (see Aguilar & Medin, 1999).

Direction of comparison may also be determined when one option in the comparison has inherent status as a reference point and thus functions as a referent. When graduate programs publish a composite profile of the successful applicant to their program, this profile serves as a referent for assessing the likelihood that a prospective applicant will get in. Other options become referent points in particular contexts. For example, a student applying for a scholarship may compare her application to that of someone who received the scholarship in the past, rather than comparing the past recipient's file to her own. The previously successful applicant serves as a marker of performance that is at least "good enough." Note how this second example also demonstrates how an individual's status as a target of comparison or referent is often not permanent. If the student applying for the scholarship ultimately receives it, then her own application may likely become the referent for the *next* person applying for the scholarship.

More standard or prototypical options also tend to be designated referents. For example, for those of us in North America at least, horses are much more common than zebras, and thus we are more likely to describe a zebra as "like a striped horse" than to describe a horse as a "like a zebra, but without the stripes" (Bowdle & Medin, in press). Salespeople try to sell the "deluxe" version of a product by comparing it to the "standard" version. More familiar or more prominent options also tend be designated as the referent (Karylowski, 1990; Tversky & Gati, 1978), as do more frequently encountered options (Polk, Behensky, Gonzalez, & Smith, 2002).

Finally, when there is no clear *a priori* reason why one option in a comparison should serve as the referent, people tend to use the first option they encounter as a referent (Agostinelli, Sherman, Fazio, & Hearst, 1986; Bruine de Bruin & Keren, 2003; Hodges, 1998; Houston et al., 1989). As Beike and Sherman (1998) point out, we tend to say children look like their parents (who precede them chronologically), rather than saying that parents look like their children. Temporal order is particularly likely to determine referent status in contexts where standards are relative. For example, in a figure skating competition, the winning performance might be very good some nights and not so good other nights; there is no absolute referent. In such cases, the first competitor becomes the de facto referent: "Yes indeed, Kristy Yamaguchi has set a VERY high standard tonight as the first performer in this competition, but she may have left a tiny gap for one of tonight's hungry young competitors to take the medal away from her."

Thus, an item in a comparison becomes the referent when it is designated as such with explicit verbal instructions, or in the absence of such instructions, it functions as the referent because it serves as a standard, because it is more prototypical, or because it is encountered first. Changing the direction of the comparison can markedly change perceptions and evaluations of the items in the comparison. This chapter next addresses direction of comparison effects, introducing them with studies of nonsocial comparisons and then exploring them in self-other comparisons, which largely parallel the results from studies of nonsocial comparisons, as well as demonstrating special qualities of the self that make it disproportionately likely to serve as the referent in self-other comparisons.

DIRECTION OF COMPARISON IN SIMILARITY JUDGMENTS

A study by Tversky and Gati (1978) provided an early and classic example of the importance of direction of comparison in similarity judgments. Participants in their study were asked how similar pairs of countries were. Specifically some subjects were asked how similar the more prominent country was to the less prominent country (i.e., the more prominent country was the target of comparison; the less prominent country was the referent, e.g., "How similar is China to North Korea?"). For other participants, the question was rephrased so that the less prominent country was the target of comparison (e.g., "How similar is North Korea to China?"). Relative to this latter condition, when the more prominent country was compared to the less prominent country, similarity ratings dropped (thus, China was less like North Korea than North Korea was like China). Tversky and Gati explained this finding as resulting from mapping the features of the target country on to those of the referent country. Because subjects knew more about the more prominent countries, they could call to mind more features of these countries. After matching up all the shared features of the two countries, subjects had many "leftover" features of the more prominent countries. Because the unique features of the target drive the judgments in directional comparisons, subjects downgraded their similarity judgments in accordance with the number of unique (leftover) features of the target.

When the *less* prominent country was the target of comparison, subjects had fewer leftover features because they knew less about these countries to begin with. Aguilar and Medin (1999) later identified an important condition that was necessary for this asymmetry in similarity judgments to occur: The same common features must come to mind for both items in the pair, regardless of the direction of comparison.

Tversky and Gati's (1978) results were soon tested and extended to the realm of self-other similarity judgments. Consistent with the idea that the self is more "prominent" than others, Srull and Gaelick (1983) found that college students rated other people in general as being more similar to themselves than they rated themselves as being similar to others. In a study conducted about the same time as Srull and Gaelick's, Holyoak and Gordon (1983, Study 1) used a specific comparison other—in this case, a friend of the participant—rather than collective "others" and found similar results (that is, comparing a specific other to the self produced higher similarity ratings than comparing the self to a specific other).

These initial studies only addressed direction of comparison effects in judgments of *global* similarity between the self and other, but the effect is seen for self-other similarity judgments on specific dimensions as well. For example, Mussweiler (2001) asked participants to rate the similarity of the self and the description of a stimulus person in terms of assertiveness. He found results consistent with the studies measuring global similarity: Self-other similarity ratings were lower when the self was compared to the other and higher when the other was compared to the self. Karylowski (1989) also used specific personality dimensions (such as stubbornness and self-confidence) and found that self-other similarity ratings were higher when the others were compared to self than when the self was compared to others.

Both Srull and Gaelick (1983) and Holyoak and Gordon (1983) conducted follow-up studies testing Tversky and Gati's (1978) theory that direction of comparison makes a greater difference when asymmetry in knowledge about the two items (or people) in the comparison is greater. Changing the direction of comparison should have less of an effect if equal amounts of information are known about the self and other. In their second study, Srull and Gaelick demonstrated that the direction of comparison asymmetry was more pronounced for unfamiliar others than it was for familiar others. With less knowledge about the unfamiliar others, participants were left with many leftover unique self features when they compared the self to the unfamiliar other, which resulted in lower similarity ratings. When comparing themselves to familiar others, however, the information asymmetry was less pronounced and direction of comparison had less of an effect on similarity judgments. Thus, reversing direction of comparison had a much greater effect when comparing Barbara Walters and the self than it did when comparing one's mother and the self.

Holyoak and Gordon chose to vary familiarity by using stereotypes of groups, rather than specific others. Participants were asked to evaluate the similarity between the self and the average members of various stereotyped groups. When the group stereotype was less familiar to participants, it was harder for them to generate attributes of the average member of the group, and thus, direction of comparison effects in similarity judgments were highly pronounced. However, when the stereotyped others were members of highly familiar groups (in this particular study, "jocks" and "preppies") and it was easy for participants to generate attributes for the stereotyped groups (just as it was easy for them to generate attributes about the self), the direction of comparison effect disappeared so that comparing the self to a member of a stereotyped group actually resulted in (nonsignificantly) higher similarity ratings than comparing the member of the stereotyped group to self. In two studies, Karylowski (1989; 1990) used specific comparison others who were probably quite familiar to participants (the "others" in the comparison were names of people provided idiographically by the participants themselves), and this familiarity appeared to dampen the asymmetry effect as well, just as self comparisons with more familiar stereotyped groups had in Holyoak and Gordon's study. Consistent with Tversky's (1977) original idea of "prominence," direction of comparison appears to have its greatest effect on self-other similarity judgments when it is hard to call to mind relevant information about the other person (something which would never be true about the readily-accessible self).

CHANGING DIRECTION IS NOT ALWAYS THAT EASY

As discussed earlier, explicit verbal instructions are just one of many factors that influence direction of comparison. In some cases, such instructions may not be the dominant factor, and thus, they may not successfully produce the intended direction of comparison. The self holds special status in self-other comparisons (at least in Western cultures)—not just because of motivated self favoring biases (e.g., Alicke, Klotz, Breitenbecher, Yurak, & Vredenburg, 1995; Taylor & Brown, 1988; Weinstein, 1980), but also because of cognitive factors. The self forms a readily available framework or schema for processing incoming social information (Clement & Krueger, 2000; Rogers, Kuiper, & Kirker, 1977). Although representations of other highly familiar and important people in our lives (for example, significant others and parents) also appear to shape person perception (e.g., Andersen, Glassman, Chen, & Cole, 1995), the self provides the most highly elaborated and accessible social representation. The pervasiveness of projective phenomena—that is, transferring aspects of the self to others (e.g., Dunning & Hayes, 1996; Hodges, Johnsen & Scott, 2002; Krueger, 2000; Marks & Miller, 1987; Nickerson, 1999) and the over-perception of the self as the focus of social interactions (Gilovich & Savitsky, 1999; Vorauer, 2001) vividly illustrate how the self is never far from our thoughts.

This accessibility has led researchers to categorize the self as a "habitual referent" (Catrambone, Beike, & Niedenthal, 1996; Karylowski, 1990). Thus, in the absence of other relevant prototypes or standards (e.g., explicit criteria, such as listing the minimum GPA and test scores required for a scholarship), the self can be thought of as a multi-purpose default reference point when evaluating people. Catrambone et al. (1996) cleverly demonstrated the self's habitual referent status by manipulating whether or not direction of comparison was provided with explicit verbal instructions. They either provided participants with instructions to compare "How similar are you to X?" or "How similar is X to you?", where "X" was a typical member of one of the stereotyped groups used in Holyoak and Gordon's 1983 study, or they provided no explicit cues, simply listing the self and the name of one of the stereotyped groups vertically on the screen (in a counterbalanced order) and asking participants to judge how similar the two were.

When no explicit cues were provided, self-other similarity judgments resembled those in the self as referent condition ("compare other to self" instructions); specifically, they were higher than the similarity ratings of participants who were instructed to "compare self to other," leading Catrambone et al. (1996) to conclude that in the absence of any explicit instructions about direction of comparison, the self is used as referent. Catrambone et al. obtained the same pattern of results when a highly familiar country took the place of the self and a less familiar country took the place of the stereotyped group member in the comparisons: Once again, when no explicit direction of comparison was provided, similarity ratings resembled those provided by participants who were explicitly instructed to compare the less familiar country to the more familiar country, suggesting that the more familiar country was serving as the referent. These parallel findings for familiar countries and for the self suggest that the self's "privileged" place as a referent may be due to familiarity.

The self may also be resistant to inducements to reverse the default direction of comparison (and thus less likely to yield its role as referent). In a study of self-other similarity comparisons by Karylowski (1990), participants were asked to provide personality traits that were highly characteristic of the self (self-relevant traits) as well as personality traits that were highly characteristic of people they knew well (other-relevant traits). When making similarity judgments for self-relevant traits between the self and the well-known others, the self would be expected to serve as the default referent, resulting in participants comparing other to self. For other-relevant traits, the well-known other should serve as a standard, and thus be the default referent, causing participants to compare self to other. Karylowski then provided explicit direction of comparison instructions that were either consistent with the expected default direction of comparison, or inconsistent with it (e.g., in self-relevant domains, asking participants to compare the self to the other person—in essence, to use the other person as the referent when the self would be the default referent).

The results showed that when the other person was the default referent, consistent explicit direction of comparison instructions facilitated self-other similarity judgments (judgments were made more quickly), while inconsistent instructions impeded self-other similarity judgments. However, when the self was a default referent in the domain of interest, explicit direction of comparison instructions had no effect on the speed of similarity judgments. These results suggest that the self is more resistant to attempts to dislodge it from its referent status than are other social entities (e.g., well-known others).

However, conditions have been identified under which the self may be more inclined to serve as the target of a comparison. The self is unique in that it can be viewed as a subject (the "I" self, as in the agent who is deciding where to go on vacation) or as an object (the "me" self, as in "What do other people think of me?"), whereas other items in comparisons are always objects. Considering the self in its object role appears to facilitate the use of the self as a target of comparison. Work by Karylowski and Skarzynksa (1992) suggests that priming self-knowledge (an exercise that would make participants objectively self-aware) is necessary in order to find the direction of comparison effects on self-other similarity reported by Srull and Gaelick (1983) and by Holyoak and Gordon (1983). Without self-priming, similarity judgments were either unchanged by direction of comparison, or even reversed slightly in the opposite direction (i.e., greater similarity was reported when the self was compared to the other).

DIRECTION OF COMPARISON IN COMPARATIVE JUDGMENTS

Direction of comparison influences not only similarity ratings of the two items in a comparison, but it also affects their relative standing on other dimensions. Changing the direction of comparison has been repeatedly demonstrated to cause reversals in how two items are ranked on the dimension on which they are being compared (e.g., comparing A to B may result in a preference for A, whereas comparing B to A results in a preference for B). Once again, the model developed to predict the outcome of nonsocial comparative judgments does a good job predicting results for self-other comparisons, as long as the special nature of the self as a habitual referent and as a favored (and protected) entity are taken into account.

To introduce the rating reversals produced by changing the direction of comparison, we turn first to a set of compelling studies performed by Houston, Sherman, and Baker (1989; 1991) outside of the realm of self-other judgments. In these studies, the comparison dimension was relative evaluation; in other words, people were asked which of two options they preferred. Houston et al. (1989) constructed descriptions of pairs of objects (for example, cars or college courses) or people (potential blind dates or work partners) that had equal numbers of comparable positive features and negative features, and all of the descriptions received equivalent overall ratings. However, the pairs varied as to which type of features (positive or negative) was shared and which was unique. For example (see Table 7.1), a pair of blind date candidates might both be described as sloppy and jealous (shared negative features) but one might also be creative and honest, whereas the other could be considerate and witty (unique positive features). Conversely, in a pair that shared positive features but had unique negative features, the two blind dates might both be creative and honest, but one would be sloppy and jealous, while the other was lazy and vain. Participants were presented first with the description

TABLE 7.1 Schematic of Houston, Sherman, & Baker's (1989)
Design, Using Comparisons of Potential Blind Dates.

Condition	Description of Potential Blind Date #1 (Referent)	Description of Potential Blind Date #2 (Target)	Which Date Preferred?
Shared negative features/ Unique positive features	Creative (+) Honest (+) *Sloppy* (−) *Jealous* (−)	CONSIDERATE (+) WITTY (+) *Sloppy* (−) *Jealous* (−)	#2 (Target), due to attraction to unique features of target, which are positive
Shared positive features/ Unique negative features	*Creative* (+) *Honest* (+) Sloppy (−) Jealous (−)	*Creative* (+) *Honest* (+) LAZY (−) VAIN (−)	#1 (Referent), due to avoidance of unique features of target, which are negative

Note. The shared features in a particular condition are italicized; capitalized unique features reflect the relatively greater amount of attention paid to these features, and the valence of each feature is in parentheses.

of one option, and then the other (with the order of the particular descriptions counterbalanced). They were then asked to compare the second description to the first, and to indicate which of the two options they preferred.

When participants saw pairs that had shared negative features and unique positive features (top half of Table 7.1), they had a noted preference for the target of comparison, which in the absence of explicit verbal instructions or other markers indicating referent status was the second option in a comparison. This preference was driven by the disproportionate attention placed on the unique features of the target of comparison. As participants encountered the second option, they mapped its shared features on to those of the referent, leaving the target's unique features, which happened to be positive in this case, to stand out.

When the valence of the shared and unique features was reversed, the preferences reversed as well (bottom half of Table 7.1). Participants who saw pairs that had shared positive features but unique negative features mapped the positive features of the target of comparison on to those same shared positive features of the referent and were left with the unique negative features of the target of comparison (lazy and vain, in this case). Avoidance of these salient unique negative features made choosers prefer the referent. Several studies have replicated Houston et al.'s (1989) basic findings (e.g., Hodges, 1998; Houston & Sherman, 1995; Houston et al., 1991; Sanbonmatsu, Kardes, & Gibson, 1991).

Note that the same description of an option could be used in both the shared negative/unique positive condition *and* the shared positive/unique negative condition (e.g., the same description appears as the referent for both conditions in Table 7.1). Furthermore, all of the descriptions were viewed as equally desirable when rated in isolation. Thus, unlike other "context effects" where, for example, baked chicken sounds deliciously gourmet after eating peanut butter crackers for a week, the context in Houston et al.'s (1989) study was not determined by the *overall* rating of the other option in the pair, but by the valence of features that the other option either shared or did not share.

Preference judgments require people to decide which of the available options is superior on an overall evaluative dimension, but preference judgments are not the only kind of comparative judgments people make. Sometimes, we are interested in picking the option that is superlative on a specific dimension, just as American high school yearbooks name the student who is the "Most Athletic," or "Most Likely to Succeed," in addition to identifying who is "Best All-Around." In fact, when trying to apply feature matching models to self-other comparisons, "preference" judgments do not really make sense. We are rarely asked to specify a preference between ourselves and another person, and if we were (and we answered honestly), the answer seems a foregone conclusion, given the pervasiveness of self-favoring biases. Comparative judgments of the self and other on specific dimensions, such as intelligence, electability, or fitness, are much more common. And, not surprisingly, designating the self or the other as the referent in these comparisons has important consequences. Think how different the implied meaning of, "You're no wiser than I" is from the meaning of, "I'm no wiser than you," even though both statements could be described as suggesting that the self and other possess similar levels of wisdom.

Hoorens (1995) directly addressed the question of direction of comparison effects in self-other judgments made on some dimension other than similarity by examining whether direction of comparison affected the magnitude of "self-favoring biases" (the tendency to see the self as better off than others; see Alicke, this volume). Hoorens' study manipulated direction of comparison explicitly, by asking student participants to compare themselves to the average student, or to compare the average student to themselves. First and foremost, but not surprisingly, Hoorens' participants revealed a strong overall self-favoring bias. More interestingly, direction of comparison significantly moderated the size of the self-favoring bias only when judgments were about positive domains. Relative to when participants compared the average student to themselves, participants rated themselves as higher on positive traits and thought good things were more likely to happen to them than other people when they compared themselves to the average student (see also Wänke, Schwarz, & Noelle-Neumann, 1995, for similar results). In fact, when making likelihood estimates for positive events, the direction of comparison effect erased the usual self-favoring bias: When asked to compare others to the self in terms of the likelihood of good future events occurring, participants' estimates for the self and other were essentially equal.

However, there was no effect of direction of comparison on the negative side: Participants generally thought that negative events were less likely to happen to the self than to others and also thought that negative traits were less attributable to themselves than to others, and the size of these biases was not significantly affected by varying whether participants were asked to compare themselves to the average student or to compare the average student to themselves. Hoorens (1995) raises an interesting possible explanation for the asymmetry between negative and positive domains. If the self functions as a habitual reference point, then instructing people to compare the average other to the self is "as it should be." If, however, people are asked to compare the self to the average other, then the self's position as reference point on that dimension is questioned, potentially challenging the self's status on that dimension. This threat to the self may prompt compensatory self-bolstering, which exacerbates the self-favoring bias. The fact that direction of comparison effects were found in positive domains and not negative ones fits nicely with Hoorens' speculation: There is no self threat involved in questioning the self's status as referent for *negative* outcomes or traits, and thus no need to boost self superiority. In fact, other work suggests that the self's habitual referent status may be limited to nonnegative domains (de la Haye & Penvern, 2002) assuming the usual self-protective biases are working. For most people, the self does not readily come to mind when considering standards for "jealousy" or "slothfulness."

What if the trait on which a self-other comparison is made is neutral, a quality people neither aspire to nor avoid? Hodges, Bruininks, and Ivy (2002) examined this question, using religiousness as the comparative dimension. This trait was rated as neither positive nor negative by the college student population used in this study. Hodges et al.'s work also demonstrates how feature matching effects operate when people make comparisons with individuated others rather than "average" others (see Alicke et al., 1995, for the importance of this distinction). In Study 1, participants first completed a checklist of religious behaviors (taken from Biernat, Manis, & Kobrynowicz, 1997) in a pretesting session. The scale included items such as "Prayed before or after meals" or "Refused to date a person of a different religion." Using a participant's own responses, an individuated comparison other was idiographically constructed for each participant. This comparison other always reported doing the same number of religious behaviors as the participant, and the behaviors the comparison other reported doing were matched on importance to those reported by the participant (whether these behaviors were the *same* behaviors or the *same number of equally important but different* behaviors was also varied, a variable that will be discussed in more depth in the section on cancellation effects).

Participants were told that the idiographically constructed comparison other was a previous participant in the study. Direction of comparison in Study 1 was manipulated with explicit instructions: Participants were told either to compare themselves to the comparison other in terms of religiousness, or to compare the comparison other to themselves. Results revealed an overall main effect of self versus other: The other was seen as more religious than the self. However, this main effect was modified by a direction of comparison effect. The self was seen as relatively more religious when the self was compared to the other, whereas the other was seen as relatively more religious when the other was compared to self. This effect was visible whether the ratings of the self were made on separate scales (e.g., assigning the self and other some score on a scale from 1 to 7, where 7 was "very religious"), or the ratings were made on a scale measuring the relative standing of the self and other (anchored at one end with "self is much more religious" and at the other end with "other is much more religious").

Like Catrambone et al.'s (1996) work, Hodges, Bruininks, and Ivy's (2002) second study provided results that were consistent with the idea that the self functions as the habitual referent in the absence of explicit instructions. When direction of comparison was manipulated in Study 2 by changing the order in which participants saw the religious behavior checklists (e.g., either self checklist last or the other's checklist last) instead of providing explicit verbal instructions (as in Study 1), the order manipulation had no effect. Apparently, the more subtle order manipulation was not strong enough to dislodge the self from its spot as habitual referent. This left the comparison other as the target of comparison, regardless of order of presentation. With the self as referent and the other person as target of the comparison, disproportionate attention was given to the religious behaviors of the comparison other, resulting in higher ratings of religiousness for the other than for the self.

DIRECTION OF COMPARISON EFFECTS IN SELF-OTHER COMPARISONS—SUMMARY AND FUTURE QUESTIONS

Direction of comparison effects appear to occur in self-other similarity judgments and in self-other comparative judgments in much the same way as they do for nonsocial comparisons, particularly comparisons for which there is asymmetric accessibility of knowledge about the two items being compared (often the case with the self and other). Direction of comparison makes a difference for self-other global similarity judgments, for similarity judgments on specific dimensions, and for comparative judgments on specific dimensions. The effects can occur whether the other is an "average other" or an individuated other. When self-other direction of comparison effects are not found, the cause can generally be traced back to the special nature of the self: When left to their own devices and in the absence of strong contextual cues that some other person should serve as the referent, people have a tendency to use the self as a default referent. In some cases, only powerful explicit instructions can reverse the direction of comparison. Furthermore, even with explicit linguistic instructions providing the direction of comparison, in the absence of either self priming or when self-favoring biases resist attempts to frame the self as a negative referent, direction of comparison effects in self-other comparisons may fail to appear.

Future interesting avenues of exploration might examine whether other variables that have been found to moderate direction of comparison effects could be applied to self-other comparisons. For example, Sanbonmatsu et al. (1991) found that when people were asked to form global evaluations of items in a preference judgment, direction of comparison effects were reduced. Contexts where global or summary evaluations of the self or other are available for the dimension on which the comparison is being made should thus result in the reduction of direction of comparison effects. Future research should also address *which* direction of comparison people naturally choose (i.e., other to self, or self to other) in various comparison contexts: How do people decide between casting themselves as either the referent or the target of comparison, and do these choices reflect possible self-protection strategies or individual differences in self perceptions?

CANCELLATION EFFECTS

Direction of comparison effects are one of the hallmarks of feature matching, and as previously discussed, they are common to both similarity and comparative judgments. However, the other "signature" pattern of feature matching, cancellation, emerges only in comparative judgments. After first defining these cancellation effects, we will next see how they operate in the judgment context where they were first identified—preference judgments—before considering the question of whether they also occur in self and other comparisons.

Tversky's (1977) model posited that when making similarity judgments, the number of shared features provided an initial estimate of the similarity between two items. However, shared features are useless in distinguishing between options in a comparative judgment: If I am trying to decide between a resort in the mountains and a resort at the seaside, and both locations offer excellent restaurants and stunning views, focusing on the views and restaurants will not facilitate my decision. It seems that I could safely ignore these shared features altogether in making my decision. And in fact, there is evidence that people do indeed "toss" these shared features—or at least cancel them out—possibly as a way of clearing away some more room on their mental "workbench" which can then be devoted to consideration of the unique features that *do* distinguish between the two options (Hodges, 1997). In Medin et al.'s (1995) terms, the shared features get "backgrounded," in the sense that they cease being "figure" and start being "ground." This might be an efficient strategy when choosing one option or the other (i.e., making a *relative* judgment), but cancellation effects appear to carry over to *absolute* evaluations of individual items as well. Whereas direction of comparison effects describe the asymmetrical focus on features that are unique to the target of comparison and are reflected in judgments of how the target is seen relative to the referent, cancellation effects describe what people do with the features shared by both items in the comparison, and how this treatment affects absolute judgments of both items.

What are the consequences of cancellation? Canceling out shared positive features can make the choice between two objectively good options feel like a no-win situation. Hodges (1997) asked college students to imagine that they were looking for a place to live. The students were first shown descriptions of two possible apartments. In the shared features condition, these two apartments shared positive features (e.g., they had big windows and laundry facilities on the premises), but had unique negative features (one of them had ants and torn screens; the other was drafty and had no deadbolt locks). When rated in isolation,[2] these apartments were seen as roughly equal and as more positive than negative. However, when participants evaluated these two apartments that shared positive features, the shared features did not distinguish between the two apartments and participants appeared to "cancel" them out. With the shared positive features out of the picture, and just the unique negative features to focus on, participants' ratings of the two apartments were downgraded. A choice that had initially been between two slightly positive apartments instead got framed as the choice between two apartments defined mainly by their unique bad features.

Furthermore, this cancellation of shared positive features appeared to carry over to subsequent evaluations. Participants in the shared features condition were later shown a third apartment that had all unique features, but that was mediocre overall due to the fact that its positive features were less positive (e.g., "separate dining room") and its negative features were more negative (e.g., "nosy neighbors") than those in the shared features apartments. Participants rated the mediocre apartment more positively when it was seen after the two shared features apartments had been "impoverished" by the cancellation of their shared positive features. People who viewed the earlier round of choice between the two shared positive/unique negative features apartments appeared to be defining the choice as one between the lesser of two evils. Contrasted against this dreary backdrop, the mediocre (but all unique) newcomer got a boost.

Other researchers have found a variety of ways to demonstrate the cancellation of shared features. For example, Houston et al. (1991) found that people deciding between options with shared positive features and unique negative features took longer to make the decisions and changed their minds more often before arriving at a final choice than people deciding between options that had shared negative features and unique positive features. Because people choosing between unique negative pairs had cancelled out the shared positive features, the decision seemed like a no-win situation that was going to result in ending up with a bad option regardless, and thus the participants were in no hurry to commit. On the other hand, when participants viewed options with shared negative features and unique positive features, the shared negative features cancelled out and the decision became an approach-approach conflict: Without the negative features, participants were eager to select one of the options that were now defined only by their unique positive features.

This perception that the decision was between "good" pairs or "bad" pairs was all the result of feature matching: As mentioned previously, all the options presented in the Houston et al. (1991) study, regardless of condition, had been created so that if seen in isolation, they were rated quite similarly. Thus, participants in the unique negative/shared positive features condition were not actually getting a substandard pair of options; it only seemed that way to them because they had cancelled out the shared positive features.

Dhar and Sherman (1995) demonstrated another effect of cancellation by giving people the option of choosing "none of the above." They gave participants a choice between two options that had either shared positive features and unique negative features, or shared negative features and unique positive features. However, participants were also informed that they had a third choice as well: to opt out and pick neither of the options. When choosing between shared positive/unique negative options, more people "opted out," as compared with people who were choosing between shared negative/unique positive options. In the former condition, canceling out the shared features and leaving just the unique negatives made "nothing" look better than "something" to many of the participants.

It is important to note that these cancelled shared features may be gone but not forgotten. Their influence may get cancelled out in terms of determining people's judgments, but when people are later asked to recall the features of the options they saw, shared features tend to be recalled at a greater rate than unique ones, probably because shared features are encountered twice as often (Hodges, 1997; Hodges & Hollenstein, 2001; Houston et al., 1989). Furthermore, if people recall one of the shared features for one of the options, there is a good chance they will recall that same shared feature for the other option too, suggesting that the shared features have been processed together (Hodges, 1997).

CANCELLATION EFFECTS IN SELF-OTHER COMPARISONS?

The cancellation effects of feature matching have received less attention than direction of comparison effects (perhaps because they are a bit more elusive; see Hodges & Hollenstein, 2001), and studies exploring cancellation in self-other comparisons are particularly rare. However, the Hodges, Bruininks, and Ivy (2002) paper that examined comparisons of religiousness suggests that there may be an interesting self-other asymmetry when it comes to cancellation of shared features. Remember, the participants in this study were given a checklist of religious behaviors customized by the researchers, supposedly completed by another research participant, who served as the comparison other. Sometimes this comparison other reported performing basically the *same* behaviors as the participant, but sometimes this comparison other reported performing a different set of equally important religious behaviors.[3] When participants saw a comparison other who had performed many of the same religious behaviors as the self, cancellation was clear in the ratings of the comparison other: Religiousness ratings of the other person dropped, relative to ratings given to a comparison other who did not perform overlapping behaviors (see Figure 7.1). However, ratings of the self showed no cancellation effects. In fact, Hodges et al.'s (2002) Study 1 showed that the self was actually rated as *more* religious when the self and other performed the same religious behaviors, relative to ratings of the self when the self and other performed equal numbers of equally important, but different, religious behaviors. Shared features appeared to be cancelled out for the comparison other (regardless of direction of comparison). That is, even though relative differences between the ratings of self and other revealed the effects of explicit direction of comparison instructions in Study 1, the

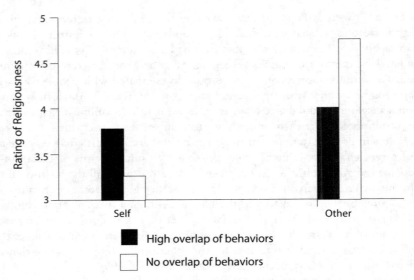

FIGURE 7.1 Cancellation results from Hodges, Bruininks, and Ivy, 2002.

effects of cancellation were evident in the form of lower religiousness ratings for the comparison other.

Thus, shared features were cancelled out when making judgments of others, but not when making judgments of the self. One possibility is that the self-other asymmetry in cancellation is another example of self-favoring bias: By canceling out the shared features for the others, but not the self, participants were stacking the deck in such a way to make the self appear more religious. Such a strategy would certainly make sense if the comparison was being made on a dimension that was clearly positive (e.g., intelligence or social skill). However, it is less clear that participants in the Hodges, Bruininks, and Ivy (2002) study would want self-superiority in terms of religiousness. A separate sample of research participants ($N = 310$; Hodges, 2004), similar to those that participated in the initial study, viewed religiousness as a generally neutral trait (or perhaps had little opinion about it at all). When asked whether saying someone was religious was a positive thing on a 5-point scale, where 5 was "very positive" and 1 was "very negative," participants' mean response was 3.41, and the modal response was clearly the midpoint (3.0) of the scale. Furthermore, people with higher self-esteem in the Hodges et al. (2002) study rated everyone (both self and other) lower on religiousness. Thus, it is hard to make a strong case that the asymmetry in cancellation seen in the Hodges et al. (2002) was self-favoring, although it might serve that purpose in other contexts.

Would the self-other asymmetry in cancellation hold for unambiguously positive or negative traits? Trait valence may moderate the effect. In the interest of self-serving goals, the tendency to cancel for the other person and not the self might be increased when the characteristics in question were positive: If Fiona and Seth are both on the dean's list and both have perfect scores on the SAT, then Fiona can still see herself as smarter if she cancels out these shared features for Seth, but not for herself. On the other hand, self-serving goals would predict that the asymmetry found in the Hodges, Bruininks, and Ivy's (2002) study would be reduced or possibly even reversed when the shared features were negative. For example, people may cancel out their pack-a-day smoking habit and high cholesterol diet that they share with others when assessing their risk of heart attack. Under these circumstances, the asymmetry in cancellation might flip-flop, with people canceling out shared negative features for themselves, but not for the other person.

Past studies outside the realm of self-other comparisons suggest another possibility. At least one published study of preference judgments (Hodges, 1998) and several unpublished ones suggest greater cancellation effects for shared positive features than shared negative features, perhaps due to the greater vigilance accorded negative information (Pratto & John, 1991). Thus, the asymmetry in self-other cancellation might disappear when shared features are negative, not for self-serving reasons, but because negative features, of the self or other, command more attention.

Finally, it must be kept in mind that cognitive processing concerns as well as motivational ones may moderate cancellation effects in self-other comparisons. Although matching up features and canceling them requires cognitive work, the matching appears to be an essential part of comparison (Gentner & Markman, 1994), and the cancellation may ultimately make the process of comparison clearer, especially when a lot of information needs to be integrated. Matching up shared features and setting them aside helps organize the features used in making judgments. However, when making judgments about the self, other organizational schemas may be available.

Indirect evidence that cancellation is the result of using the self as a means for processing information about the other comes from a particular group of subjects in the Hodges, Bruininks, and Ivy (2002) study who showed less evidence of cancellation. In Study 2, participants completed a measure of "religious schematicity," i.e., questions about how important being religious was to them and how much time they spent engaged in religious activities. Participants who scored high on a measure of religious schematicity—and thus might be thought of as "experts" in making judgments in this domain—were less affected by degree of overlap between the self and other. In other words, they did not cancel for the other *or* the self, suggesting that perhaps they were using some referent other than the self—perhaps a stored standard—to process the features of the other. This pattern is analogous to the difference between regular people who dine out and a restaurant critic. The restaurant critic's ratings of a particular restaurant are not relative to the last restaurant she ate at, but instead reflect a comparison to a set of learned criteria, that the critic, as an expert, can bring to mind.

Further evidence that the religious schematics processed the information differently comes from recall data in the Hodges, Bruininks, and Ivy (2002) Study 2. There was a general tendency for participants to recall more of the comparison other's religious behaviors in the high overlap condition than in the low overlap condition, which is consistent both with work demonstrating a memory advantage for self-referenced information, and with past feature matching studies showing a memory advantage for shared features (e.g., Hodges 1997; Hodges & Hollenstein, 2001; Houston et al., 1989). However, this memory advantage was much greater for low schematics than high schematics.[4] Again, this suggests that the high schematics may use some framework other than the self for processing the features of the comparison other.

SELF-OTHER COMPARISONS IN THE REAL WORLD AND CONCLUDING COMMENTS

The studies reviewed in this chapter—both those for self-other comparisons and other kinds of comparisons—place participants in a context where comparison is the central task at hand and there is little to distract research participants from doing their job. However, much of the everyday social comparison that people engage in occurs in the context of ongoing social interactions, which may distract or even override feature matching strategies. For example, imagine meeting your boyfriend's ex at a social gathering where you have to make small talk while simultaneously attempting to figure out why he quit dating her and now dates you instead. Or, imagine working on a group project, while at the same time assessing whether you or another team member would be better at making the final oral presentation.

Very few studies of social comparison have been conducted in the context of an actual social interaction, but at least one showed virtually no evidence that people processed the features that were available to them in ways predicted by feature matching models (Hodges, Johnsen, & Scott, 2002). Instead, in this study, conversational concerns (such as finding common ground) appeared to play a big role in people's judgments of themselves and the other person. Furthermore, in most research studies of social comparison, the comparison other is someone with whom research participants were previously unacquainted. However, outside the lab, many social comparisons involve known others, and people may rely on stored evaluations or summary judgments of themselves and these other people, perhaps adjusting or updating these judgments to incorporate new information but rarely returning to the "raw data." Add biased informational processing and motivational concerns, and the sum result is that "real" self-other comparisons are a great deal more complex than the comparisons that have been studied in past feature matching studies. However, as this chapter has attempted to demonstrate, there is still a lot to be learned by aligning self-other comparisons with their nonsocial counterparts.

ACKNOWLEDGMENTS

The author would like to thank Holly Arrow, Stephan Dickert, Andy Kohnen, Brian Ooi, and Josephine Casey Witte for comments on an earlier draft of this chapter.

NOTES

1. Tversky's (1977) original terminology referred to "subjects" of comparison. However, this term has proved confusing, both because the subject of comparison is often not the grammatical subject of the comparative question being asked, and because of the fact that psychologists often refer to research participants as "subjects." Thus, "target" of comparison will be used throughout this paper, which has the additional benefit of connoting something that can vary in distance (and similarity) from the referent, or "home" reference point.
2. Of course, even when rating one item in isolation, people still might compare it to some implicit referent; in this case, an ideal apartment or one's current living quarters.
3. According to pilot testing of the behaviors.
4. This result was not reported in the Hodges, Bruininks, and Ivy (2002) paper.

REFERENCES

Agostinelli, G., Sherman, S. J., Fazio, R. H., & Hearst, E. S. (1986). Detecting and identifying change: Addictions versus deletions. *Journal of Experimental Psychology: Human Perception and Performance, 12,* 445–454.
Aguilar, C. M., & Medin, D. L. (1999). Asymmetries of comparison. *Psychonomic Bulletin and Review, 6,* 328–337.
Alicke, M. D., Klotz, M. L., Breitenbecher, D. L., Yurak, T. J., & Vredenburg, D. S. (1995). Personal contact, individuation, and the better-than-average effect. *Journal of Personality and Social Psychology, 68,* 804–825.
Andersen, S. M., Glassman, N. S., Chen, S., & Cole, S. W. (1995). Transference in social perception: The role of chronic accessibility in significant-other representations. *Journal of Personality and Social Psychology, 69,* 41–57.
Beike, D. R., & Sherman, S. J. (1998). Framing of comparisons in research and practice. *Applied and Preventive Psychology, 7,* 161–180.
Biernat, M., Manis, M., & Kobrynowicz, D. (1997). Simultaneous assimilation and contrast effects in judgments of self and others. *Journal of Personality and Social Psychology, 73,* 254–269.
Bowdle, B. F., & Medin. D. L. (in press). Reference point reasoning in similarity and difference comparisons. *Journal of Experimental Psychology: General.*
Bruine de Bruin, W., & Keren, G. (2003). Order effects in sequentially judged options due to the direction of comparison. *Organizational Behavior and Human Decision Processes, 92,* 91–101.
Catrambone, R., Beike, D., & Niedenthal, P. (1996). Is the self-concept a habitual referent in judgments of similarity? *Psychological Science, 7,* 158–163.
Clement, R. W., & Krueger, J. (2000). The primacy of self-referent information in perceptions of social consensus. *British Journal of Social Psychology, 39,* 279–299.
de la Haye, A. M., & Penvern, S. (2002). On the special function of the self-concept in judgements of similarity between persons. *Swiss Journal of Psychology, 61,* 59–72.
Dhar, R., & Sherman, S. J. (1996). The effect of common and unique features in consumer choice. *Journal of Consumer Research, 23,* 193–203.
Dunning, D., & Hayes, A. F. (1996). Evidence for egocentric comparison in social judgment. *Journal of Personality and Social Psychology, 71,* 213–229.

Gentner, D., & Markman, A. B. (1994). Structural alignment in comparison: No difference without similarity. *Psychological Science, 5,* 152–158.

Gentner, D., & Markman, A. B. (1997). Structure mapping in analogy and similarity. *American Psychologist, 52,* 45–56.

Gilovich, T., & Savitsky, K. (1999). The spotlight effect and the illusion of transparency: Egocentric assessments of how we are seen by others. *Current Directions in Psychological Science, 8,* 165–168.

Hodges, S. D. (1997). When matching up features messes up decisions: The role of feature matching in successive choices. *Journal of Personality and Social Psychology, 72,* 1310–1321.

Hodges, S. D. (1998). Reasons for the referent: Reducing direction of comparison effects. *Social Cognition, 16,* 367–390.

Hodges, S. D. (2004). Unpublished data. University of Oregon.

Hodges, S. D., Bruininks, P., & Ivy, L. (2002). It's different when I do it: Feature matching in self-other comparisons. *Personality and Social Psychology Bulletin, 28,* 40–53.

Hodges, S. D., & Hollenstein, T. (2001). Direction of comparison in typicality judgments. *Social Cognition, 19,* 601–624.

Hodges, S. D., Johnsen, A. T., & Scott, N. S. (2002). You're like me, no matter what you say. *Psychologica Belgica, 42,* 107–112.

Holyoak, K. J., & Gordon, P. C. (1983). Social reference points. *Journal of Personality and Social Psychology, 44,* 881–887.

Hoorens, V. (1995). Self-favoring biases, self-presentation, and the self-other asymmetry in social comparison. *Journal of Personality, 63,* 793–817.

Houston, D. A., & Sherman, S. J. (1995). Cancellation and focus: The role of shared and unique features in the choice process. *Journal of Experimental Social Psychology, 31,* 357–378.

Houston, D. A., Sherman, S. J., & Baker, S. M. (1989). The influence of unique features and direction of comparison on preferences. *Journal of Experimental Social Psychology, 25,* 121–141.

Houston, D. A., Sherman, S. J., & Baker, S. M. (1991). Feature matching, unique features and the dynamics of the choice process: Predecision conflict and postdecision satisfaction. *Journal of Experimental Social Psychology, 27,* 411–430.

Karylowski, J. L. (1989). Trait prototypicality and the asymmetry effect in self-other similarity judgments. *Journal of Social Behavior and Personality, 4,* 581–586.

Karylowski, J. L. (1990). Social reference points and accessibility of trait-related information in self-other similarity judgments. *Journal of Personality and Social Psychology, 58,* 975–983.

Karylowski, J. L., & Skarzynska, K. (1992). Asymmetric self-other similarity judgments depend on priming of self-knowledge. *Social Cognition, 10,* 235–254.

Krueger, J. (2000). The projective perception of the social world: A building block of social comparison processes. In J. Suls & L. Wheeler (Eds.), *Handbook of social comparison: Theory and research* (pp. 323–351). New York: Kluwer Academic.

Markman, A. B., & Gentner, D. (1996). Commonalities and differences in similarity comparisons. *Memory and Cognition, 24,* 235–249.

Marks, G., & Miller, N. (1987). Ten years of research on the false-consensus effect: An empirical and theoretical review. *Psychological Bulletin, 102,* 72–90.

Medin, D. L., Goldstone, R. L., & Gentner, D. (1993). Respects for similarity. *Psychological Review, 100,* 254–278.

Medin, D. L., Goldstone,, R. L., & Markman, A. B. (1995). Comparison and choice: Relations between similarity processes and decision processes. *Psychonomic Bulletin and Review, 2,* 1–19.

Mussweiler, T. (2001). Focus of comparison as a determinant of assimilation versus contrast in social comparison. *Personality and Social Psychology Bulletin, 27,* 38–47.

Nickerson, R. S. (1999). How we know—and sometimes misjudge—what others know: Imputing one's own knowledge to others. *Psychological Bulletin, 125,* 737–759.

Polk, T. A., Behensky, C., & Gonzalez, R., & Smith, E. E. (2002). Rating the similarity of simple perceptual stimuli: Asymmetries induced by manipulating exposure frequency. *Cognition, 82,* B75–B88.

Pratto, F., & John, O. P. (1991). Automatic vigilance: The attention-grabbing power of negative social information. *Journal of Personality and Social Psychology, 61,* 380–391.

Rogers, T. B., Kuiper, N. A., & Kirker, W. S. (1977). Self-reference and the encoding of personal information. *Journal of Personality and Social Psychology, 35,* 677–688.

Sanbonmatsu, D. M., Kardes, F. R., & Gibson, B. D. (1991). The role of attribute knowledge and overall evaluations in comparative judgment. *Organizational Behavior and Human Decisions Processes, 48,* 131–146.

Srull, T. K., & Gaelick, L. (1983). General principles and individual differences in the self as a habitual reference point: An examination of self-other judgments of similarity. *Social Cognition, 2,* 108–121.

Taylor. S. E., & Brown, J. D. (1988). Illusion and well-being: A social psychological perspective on mental health. *Psychological Bulletin, 103,* 193–210.

Tversky, A. (1977). Features of similarity. *Psychological Review, 84,* 327–352.

Tversky, A., & Gati, I. (1978). Studies of similarity. In E. Rosch & B. Lloyd (Eds.), *Cognition and categorization* (pp. 81–98). Hillsdale, NJ: Erlbaum.

Vorauer, J. D. (2001). The other side of the story: Transparency estimation in social interaction. In G. Moskowitz (Ed.), *Cognitive social psychology: The Princeton Symposium on the legacy and future of social cognition* (pp. 261–276). Mahwah, NJ: Erlbaum.

Wänke, M., Schwarz, N., & Noelle-Neumann, E. (1995). Asking comparative questions: The impact of the direction of comparison. *Public Opinion Quarterly, 59,* 347–372.

Weinstein, N. D. (1980). Unrealistic optimism about future life events. *Journal of Personality and Social Psychology, 39,* 806–820.

Zhang, S., & Markman, A. B. (2001). Processing product unique features: Alignability and invovlement in preference construction. *Journal of Consumer Psychology, 11,* 13–27.

8

Self-Other Asymmetries in Behavior Explanations
Myth and Reality

BERTRAM F. MALLE
University of Oregon

A moment's thought suggests that people explain their own behavior quite differently from the way they explain other people's behavior. People know more (or different things) about their own behavior, they have different goals when explaining it, and they probably express their explanations differently in language. That the self differs from others as a target of explanation is a straightforward hypothesis, seemingly an obvious truth. But this chapter describes how the straightforward becomes complicated and the obvious unforeseen when we carefully examine a psychological phenomenon rather than take at face value what is generally claimed in textbook psychology.

So explanations of behavior performed by self and other differ. But exactly how? And why?

There are classic answers to this pair of questions (Jones, 1976; Jones & Nisbett, 1972; Watson, 1982). First, explanations for self and other differ in terms of dispositional and situation causes—people explain, in the "actor" role, their own behavior using situation causes and, in the "observer" role, other people's behavior using dispositions. Second, this classic "actor-observer asymmetry" holds because people know more about their own experiences, intentions, and history and because, as actors, they attend to the situation and, as observers, they attend to the other person's behavior (Jones & Nisbett, 1972).

In this chapter I examine the viability of these answers, both theoretically and in light of the existing evidence, and then discuss a pair of alternative answers. This alternative, to give a brief preview, suggests that explanations for self and other do not diverge in the use of person and situation causes but in other, more important aspects of explanation—for example, whether the explanation concerns intentional or unintentional behavior and whether it refers to reasons or causal histories, beliefs or desires. Furthermore, I will suggest that these self-other asymmetries exist primarily because people explain their own versus another person's behavior on the basis of different information and with different pragmatic goals in mind.

SELF-OTHER ASYMMETRIES: A MAP

Before examining self-other asymmetries in behavior explanations, I should locate these specific kinds of asymmetries within a map of the broader landscape of self- and other-cognition.

Many comparisons have been made between self and other as the two major targets of cognition. Research has shown generally better memory for self-related information (Rogers, Kuiper, & Kirker, 1977), greater enhancement in self-descriptions and evaluations (Greenwald, 1980; Locke, 2002; Taylor & Brown, 1988), and considerable influence of one's own preferences and knowledge on the predictions about others' preferences and knowledge (Krueger, 1998; L. Ross, Greene, & House, 1977; Nickerson, 1999). Moreover, attention in social interaction is unevenly distributed such that people (as actors) routinely attend more to their own mental states and (as observers) more to the other person' observable actions (Malle & Pearce, 2001; Sheldon & Johnson, 1993).

All these patterns reflect differences in general processes such as memory, attention, evaluation, and judgment. Explanations of behavior should be considered a category in their own right, because they serve unique purposes, even though they rely on each of these general processes. In particular, behavior explanations have two main functions in social life: They are a cognitive tool with which people create meaning, and they are a social tool with which they manage social interactions (Malle, 2004). This dual function subjects behavior explanations to a variety of processes that can generate self-other asymmetries, such as knowledge structures, attention, and impression management. Self-other asymmetries in behavior explanation thus reflect important cognitive and motivational differences in self- and other-cognition but implement these differences in unique ways, owing to the specific social functions that behavior explanations serve.

An important landmark on the map of self-other cognition and explanation is the distinction between *which* behaviors actors and observers explain and *how* they explain them. If we don't assume with Kelley (1967) that all explained events are essentially the same, we can ask what *types* of events people are interested in explaining, and what we find are robust self-other differences (Malle & Knobe, 1997b). People try to explain more of their own *unintentional* than intentional events and more of their own *unobservable* than observable events. Events that are both unintentional and unobservable (which we can label *experiences*) are thus the single most frequently explained event type for oneself. By contrast, people try to explain more of others' *intentional* than unintentional events and more of their *observable* than unobservable events. Events that are both intentional and observable (which we can label *actions*) are thus the single most frequently explained event type for others. To the extent that different event types elicit different kinds of explanations, self-other asymmetries will also emerge in the *kinds* of explanations used. Such explanation patterns triggered by differing event choices are intriguing and may even account for some of the classic actor-observer findings, but they are a topic treated elsewhere (Malle, 2004; Malle & Knobe, 1997b).

The focus of this chapter is on a different question: that of *how* actors' and observers' explanations differ for the same event—such as a particular action, a particular experience. I first explore the classic answer to this question and then propose a new approach.

THE CLASSIC POSITION: JONES AND NISBETT (1972)

In a famous paper, Jones and Nisbett (1972) formulated the hypothesis that "actors tend to attribute the causes of their behavior to stimuli inherent in the situation, while observers tend to attribute behavior to stable dispositions of the actor" (p. 93). For example, a senator might explain her vote against going to war by saying, "Preemptive wars are unjustified" whereas a political observer might explain the senator's vote by saying, "She is a soft-hearted liberal."

Three features of the Jones-Nisbett thesis are noteworthy. First, the thesis is meant to apply to all behaviors—whether intentional or unintentional, observable or unobservable, positive or negative. Second, the thesis assumes that relevant attributions are of only two types: situational or dispositional. Third, however, attributions to *dispositions* turn out to be ambiguous (M. Ross & Fletcher, 1985), as they can refer either to any factor that lies within the person (including emotions, traits, beliefs, sensations) or specifically to stable traits. Though most discussions of the Jones-Nisbett thesis focused on the latter, the stable-trait meaning, strictly speaking we should consider two classic actor-observer asymmetries—one regarding person attributions in general, the other regarding stable trait attributions in particular. I return to this ambiguity later.

These are then the parameters of the classic actor-observer thesis: Attributions of any behavior can refer to either the situation or the actor's dispositions, and actors tend to explain their behavior by referring to the situation whereas observers tend to explain the same behavior by referring to the actor's dispositions.

What is the Evidence for the Classic Actor-Observer Thesis?

In the secondary literature on attribution research, the classic actor-observer asymmetry has been described as "firmly established" (Watson, 1982, p. 698), "robust and quite general" (Jones, 1976, p. 304), and "an entrenched part of scientific psychology" (Robins et al., 1996, p. 376). We learn that "evidence for the actor-observer effect is plentiful" (Fiske & Taylor, 1991, p. 73) and that there is "considerable evidence that the actor-observer bias is pervasive" (Aronson, 2002, p.

168). But there is, in fact, no thorough review available of the 30 years of research into the actor-observer asymmetry.[1] I therefore decided to conduct a meta-analysis on the primary literature of published actor-observer studies (Malle, 2005).

To survey the research literature on the actor-observer asymmetry in behavior explanation, I searched two databases (PsycINFO and Web of Science) for articles since 1973 that either contained relevant keywords (*attribution, actor, observer*) or cited the Jones and Nisbett (1972) paper. From this pool of about 1,500 articles, I selected those that (a) reported empirical data, (b) assessed explanations ("causal attributions") instead of mere trait inferences from behavior, and (c) measured both genuine actor and genuine observer explanations (excluding studies, for example, that compare observer explanations with or without empathy instructions). Foreign-language articles were acceptable as long as I was able to conduct or obtain a translation into English. I then studied the results sections for reported data from which effect sizes could be computed (i.e., means, standard deviations, F or t values), in particular effect sizes for three dependent measures: (a) an overall difference score of person/disposition minus situation, (b) a separate person/disposition score, and (c) a separate situation score. In addition, where available, overall scores were computed separately for negative and positive events/behaviors.[2] Ninety-five articles with a total of 137 studies and 12,000 participants were examined.

As the effect size measure for each study, Cohen's d was chosen, corrected for sampling bias following Hunter and Schmidt (1990, p. 281). The effect size averages in Table 8.1 were computed as weighted means, adjusted for differences in sample size across studies. The results are remarkable. Across all studies, we see a small overall effect of $d = 0.073$ (Unweighted means show the same pattern of results, with slightly higher numbers.)

These results hardly support the Jones-Nisbett hypothesis. For one thing, the overall effect is vanishingly small, corresponding to a correlation coefficient of less than .04. More important, the asymmetry obtains only for negative events ($r = .11$) and reverses for positive events ($r = -.13$). This pattern is consistent with a mild self-serving bias according to which actors, compared to observers, are more reluctant to explain negative events by reference to their own characteristics. The general claim, however, that actors explain their behavior with external causes and observers explain it in internal causes is not supported by 30 years of research.

TABLE 8.1 Meta-Analysis Results of the Traditional Actor-Observer Asymmetry for Causal Attributions, Based on 137 Studies

	Average Effect Size
Overall score[*]	0.073
Internal score only	0.045
External score only	0.000
Negative events/outcomes only (overall score)	0.221
Positive events/outcomes only (overall score)	−0.258

[*]Internal-external difference score or interaction term for perspective (actor, observer) by locus (internal, external)

At this point we should take note that the hypothesized actor-observer asymmetry is neither pervasive nor robust, and certainly not firmly established, as textbooks of psychology would make us believe. But we need not necessarily conclude that actor-observer differences in behavior explanations are a myth; reality may just be more complex than past studies were able to reveal. One reason for the highly fluctuating results in testing the classic thesis may be that all studies relied on the dichotomy between personal/dispositional and situational attributions. This theoretical distinction has several drawbacks. First, the two categories are extremely vague in that the "person" category could be taken to indicate a behavior's intentionality, the agent's moral responsibility, or the agent's conscious reason for acting, to name just a few. Likewise, the "situation" category could be taken to indicate a behavior's unintentionality, the agent's impunity, or an actual cause in the environment. Second, the person-situation dichotomy oversimplifies the way people explain behavior, forcing them to translate their potentially complex thoughts about the event in question into a crude bipolar language. It should be no wonder that enormous variations occur in such a translation, resulting in substantial error variance across studies. Perhaps actor-observer asymmetries in explanation really do exist, but to document them we need to do justice to people's own concepts of behavior and explanation and to let them express those concepts in unfettered, natural ways. This would require giving up the simple person-situation dichotomy, and this is the approach I propose.

AN ALTERNATIVE APPROACH

Theoretical Framework

When people interpret human behavior, they sharply distinguish between intentional and unintentional behavior (Malle & Knobe, 1997a). The intentionality concept begins to form in infancy and helps the child perceive order and structure in the streams of human behavior (Baldwin, Baird, Saylor, & Clark, 2001), and it is a basic building block for human communication (Bretherton, 1991). With progressing age, the intentionality concept becomes more refined and is used to make moral judgments and plays a key role in promises, reciprocity, and other social contracts (e.g., Greenberg & Frisch, 1972; Kugelmass & Breznitz, 1968; Malle & Nelson, 2003). What is so important about the distinction of intentionality for behavior explanations is that people use different modes of explanation for each type of behavior (Malle, 1999, 2001, 2004).

As shown in Figure 8.1, when explaining *unintentional* behavioral events people use only one mode: that of causes. Cause explanations depict the factors that "mechanically" brought about the unintentional event—that is, without the agent's control and often without the agent's awareness. Consider these examples of cause explanations:

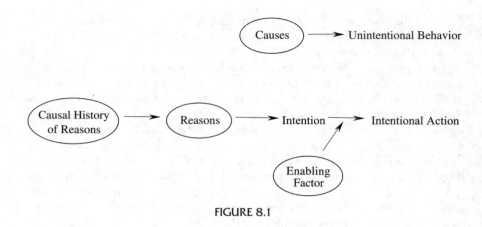

FIGURE 8.1

I almost failed my exams. *Why?* Oh, 'cause I didn't really prepare for them. A friend cried on the phone. *Why?* She felt that no one loved her.

When explaining *intentional* behavioral events, by contrast, people have to make a number of choices. The primary mode of explanation refers to the *reasons* the agent had for acting (Buss, 1978; Davidson, 1963; Locke & Pennington, 1978; Malle, 1999; Read, 1987). Reasons are seen as mental states (desires, beliefs, valuings) that the agent combines in a (sometimes rudimentary) process of reasoning, which then leads up to an intention and, if all goes well, to the intended action. So when people give reason explanations they really try to cite what was on the agent's mind when deciding to act—the reasons *in light of which* and *on the grounds of which* the agent acted. Suppose someone asks, "Why did Gina work 70 hours last week?" The conversation partner's explanation will likely cite one (or several) of Gina's reasons, such as "she wanted to impress her new boss," "to get overtime pay," "she knew that the project was due," or "she was going on vacation the week after." In all these explanations the explainer assumes two things: that the agent was subjectively aware of her reasons (she acted in light of them) and that these reasons rationally favored her course of action (she acted on the grounds of them). These two assumptions of *subjectivity* and *rationality* are the defining characteristics of reason explanations and differentiate them from all other modes of explanation. (For further discussion and evidence, see Malle, 1999; Malle et al., 2000; Mele, 1992; Searle, 1983.)

Under some conditions people cannot or do not want to offer reason explanations and therefore use one of two alternate modes of explaining intentional behavior. The first alternate mode refers to the *causal history of reasons,* which are factors that lie in the background of reason and clarify how these reasons came about. Consider again Gina's working 70 hours a week. If the explainer wanted to offer a causal history explanation, he might say, "she is driven to achieve," or "that's the company norm." Note that in the first of these causal history explanations, a disposition of the agent is mentioned (driven to achieve), whereas in the second, a situational factor is mentioned (company norm). It is important to keep in mind that the nature of causal history explanations has nothing to do with the person-situation dichotomy. Some causal history factors lie in the agent, others lie in the situation. What makes them causal history explanations is not their "causal locus" but the fact that they explain what brought about an intentional action and that they do so by referring to factors preceding the agent's reasons. Because they precede reasons but are not themselves reasons, causal history factors neither meet the subjectivity assumption (the agent does not act in light of the factor) nor the rationality assumption (the agent does not regard the factor as grounds for acting).

To illustrate the distinction between reasons and causal histories, Table 8.2 contains two behaviors with contrasting reason explanations and causal history of reason (CHR) explanations.

The second alternate mode of explaining intentional action refers to factors that enabled the action to succeed. What these *enabling factor explanations* clarify is not what motivated the agent to act (which is explained by reasons or causal histories); rather, they clarify *how it was possible* that the agent's intention turned into a successful action (McClure & Hilton, 1997; Turnbull, 1986). This "How possible?" question comes up for achievements (such as in academics, arts, or sports) but rarely for social actions (Malle et al., 2000), and as a result, enabling factors do not figure prominently in tests of actor-observer asymmetries.

Predictions

On the basis of this theoretical framework, what kinds of actor-observer asymmetries should we expect? Because, as previously mentioned, actors are generally concerned with explaining their own unintentional behaviors whereas observers

TABLE 8.2 Causal History of Reason (CHR) Explanations and Reason Explanations for the Same Behaviors

Behavior	Reason explanation	CHR explanation
Kim chose not to vote in the last election.	None of the candidates appealed to her.	She is lazy.
	She didn't want to support the system.	She doesn't realize that every vote counts.
Brian used heavy drugs last Sunday at the party.	He was curious what it would feel like.	He is a junkie.
	He thought it would be cool.	He grew up in a drug-dealing home.

Note. From Malle (1999, p. 35, Table 2).

are more concerned with explaining others' intentional behaviors (Malle & Knobe, 1997b), it follows that actors use more causes than observers do, since causes are the only mode of explanation for unintentional behaviors. This effect, however, is solely due to a choice of *which* behaviors one explains rather than a choice of *how* one explains them, that is, with what kinds of explanations. Far more interesting is the possibility that, for example, when explaining the same intentional behavior, actors use more reasons (and fewer causal histories) than observers do. This pattern constitutes a first actor-observer hypothesis, the reason asymmetry.

Hypothesis 1: Reason Asymmetry

Reasons are the default explanation mode of intentional action. They refer to the actual mental states that figured in the agent's reasoning that underlies the intention to act. Explainers—both actors and observers—will normally strive to offer reason explanations. In fact, on average, reasons make up about 70 percent of intentional action explanations. However, an explainer may offer a CHR explanation when either (1) information access is limited or (2) pragmatic goals favor causal history factors over reasons. A case of limited information access occurs when the explainer does not know the agent's reason and cannot easily infer it (O'Laughlin & Malle, 2002). A case of pragmatic goals favoring CHR explanations occurs when the explainer downplays the agent's awareness and deliberate decision process and instead points to the "objective" causal determinants of those reasons.

From these two conditions, we can derive an actor-observer asymmetry for reasons versus causal histories. For actors, limited information access will be rare. Actors normally know (or at least believe they know) their reasons for acting and are therefore apt to report them in their explanations (Buss, 1978; Locke & Pennington, 1982). Moreover, since an agent's reasons actually figured in her decision to act, reasons should be highly salient and accessible in the agent's explicit memory (Cowan, 1995; Russell & D'Hollosy, 1992). Observers, by contrast, often do not know the agent's reasons. As a result, they more frequently resort to causal history explanations, citing, for example, a general feature of the action context, a cultural norm, or a personality trait. The information access condition therefore predicts that observers offer a greater number of causal histories (and fewer reasons) than actors do.

Pragmatic goals that favor causal histories can in principle be pursued by either actors or observers. However, more often than not, actors will want to appear as rational decision makers and will therefore prefer reason explanations (Malle et al., 2000) whereas observers don't have a similar impression-management motivation, especially if they have no relationship with the agent. Consequently, pragmatic goals, too, predict that observers offer a greater number of causal histories (and fewer reasons) than do actors.

In addition to delineating multiple modes of explanation, the alternative approach I am proposing also specifies particular features of each mode, and some of those reflect additional actor-observer asymmetries. For three of the modes—causes, causal history factors, and enabling factors—the features are relatively simple because we are dealing with causal factors that can be classified along traditional attribution dimensions (e.g., internal-external, stable-unstable), allowing a further test of the classic actor-observer hypothesis. More interesting, however, are the specific features of reason explanations, because this mode represents a major departure from classic attribution models.

Reasons have the most complex features of all explanation modes because they are based on the unique conceptual assumptions about how intentional action is generated—namely, by subjective, rational consideration of desires and beliefs and a subsequent decision to act. Two features of reasons stand out (Malle, 1999).

First, any reason appears as one of three mental state types: a desire ("because she wanted more money"), a belief ("because she thought it would help"), or a valuing ("because she found it interesting"). We call this feature *reason type*. Second, explainers either linguistically mark a reason as a subjective mental state by using a mental state verb (such as "I wanted," "she thought," "he liked") or else they leave the reason unmarked. This feature captures the presence or absence of *mental state markers*. One additional feature, the *reason content* (i.e., *what* is desired, believed, or valued), can be classified in the traditional way as being about the agent or the situation. However, this classification appears to have little predictive power (for either actor-observer asymmetries or other phenomena we have examined; Nelson & Malle, 2005; O'Laughlin & Malle, 2002), so I will set it aside in this discussion.

With regard to the two features of reason type and mental state markers, we can derive two further predictions—the belief-desire hypothesis and the unmarked belief hypothesis—regarding actor-observer asymmetries in behavior explanations.

Hypothesis 2: Belief-Desire Asymmetry

This hypothesis posits that actors use more belief reasons and fewer desire reasons than observers do. The principle of information access is critical here as well. When observers try to infer an agent's reasons, they should have particular difficulties inferring belief reasons, because beliefs often represent idiosyncratic, context-specific information, such as perceived circumstances, anticipated outcomes, and considered alternative paths of acting, which are difficult to know for most observers. Desire reasons, by contrast, can be more easily inferred from general social rules and cultural practices (Bruner, 1990), which is also why children learn to attribute desires before they learn to attribute beliefs (e.g., Nelson-LeGall, 1985; Wellman & Woolley, 1990) and explain actions with desires before they explain them with beliefs (Bartsch & Wellman, 1989). A second psychological process that leads to the belief-desire asymmetry is impression management, which refers to attempts at influencing an audience's impression of the behavior or agent in question. Beliefs, but not desires, portray the agent as rational and deliberate (Malle et al., 2000), and actors are normally more concerned than observers with presenting such an image.

Hypothesis 3: Belief Marker Asymmetry

This hypothesis posits that actors, more than observers, leave their belief reasons unmarked (i.e., do not formulate the reason with a mental state verb such as *think, believe,* or *know*). Two converging processes suggest this prediction. First, actors' information access to their belief reasons is such that in their minds they directly represent the *content* of their belief—e.g., REPRESENT→[the plants are dry]. They do not normally represent their own belief qua mental state; that is, they usually do not REPRESENT→[*I believe* the plants are dry]. When formulating their belief reasons in language, actors will often express simply what they represented, and so they usually leave their belief reasons unmarked: "Why did you turn on the sprinkler?"—"Because the plants were dry." Observers, by contrast, often represent the agent's thinking *qua* mental state—e.g., REPRESENT→[*she thought* the plants were dry]—and are therefore more likely to formulate a belief reason marked by a mental state verb: "Perhaps *she thought* the plants were dry."

The second process suggesting a belief marker asymmetry results from the explainer's pragmatic goal of conveying an evaluative attitude toward the agent's reason (Malle, 1999; Malle et al., 2000). Specifically, omitting a belief marker indicates an endorsement of that belief whereas using a marker indicates distance from the belief. For example, if an explainer says, "She turned on the sprinkler because the plants were dry," he himself seems to believe that the plants were actually dry. By contrast, if he says, "She turned on the sprinkler because *she thought* the plants were dry," he distances himself from her belief. By explicitly stating that the agent thought the plants were dry, the explainer suggests that there is some doubt as to the truth of the agent's belief. Actors can use this same linguistic device to distance themselves from their own past reasons ("I locked the door because I thought you had already left"), but this is a less frequent case. On the whole, observers are more likely than actors to use belief markers as a distancing device.

I should note that this same logic does not hold for desire reasons because, at least in English, the grammatical form of desires renders marked and unmarked expressions similar to one another ("Why is she running?"—"She wants to be on time" vs. "To be on time"). Because they are so similar, they fail to carry an attitude implication of either distancing or endorsement (Malle et al., 2000).

We now have derived three hypotheses from our alternative theory of explanation:

H1 Actors offer more reasons (and fewer causal history explanations) than observers do.

H2 Actors offer more belief reasons (and fewer desire reasons) than observers do.

H3 Actors offer more unmarked belief reasons than observers do.

What evidence is there in support of these hypotheses?

Evidence for Alternative Predictions

In an extensive series of studies, my colleagues and I have examined actor and observer explanations of behavior in a variety of contexts, including memory protocols, natural interactions, and interviews (Knobe & Malle, 2002; Malle, 2002; Malle, Knobe, & Nelson, 2005). Some studies asked people to recall why-questions and their corresponding explanations, others identified spontaneous explanations in conversation. Some studies let people choose the behaviors they explained, others predetermined those behaviors. In all of them, we let people explain behaviors in their own words and then carefully coded those explanations into conceptual and linguistic categories (Malle, 2003). In total, we examined over 700 participants and over 6,000 explanations.

Hypothesis 1, postulating a reason/CHR asymmetry, received consistent support. Averaged across five studies, actors offered 80% reasons (and 20% CHRs) per intentional behavior explained, whereas observers offered 60% reasons (and 40% CHRs), for a total effect size of $d = 0.69$. Sample reason explanations by actors and sample causal history explanations by observers illustrate this asymmetry:

Reason explanations by actors:

Why did you plan to buy your brother a video game?—'Cause it was his **birthday** [reason] and **I wanted to have him get something that he would actually use** [reason].

Why did you decide to go hiking up the peak?—**Just to kind of get a change of scenery** [reason]. **I was getting sick of what everyone else was doing, kind of** [reason].

Causal history of reason explanations by observers:

Her family like had these family get-togethers all the time 'cause they had **quite a few aunt and uncles in the family** [CHR].

Sometimes he [divorced father] would break in and put gifts all around the house, **because for a long time he was torn between still loving her and hating what she'd done** [CHR].

Hypothesis 2, postulating a belief asymmetry, received consistent support as well. On average, actors offered 65% belief reasons whereas observers offered 45% belief reasons, for an effect size of $d = .52$. Sample belief reasons by actors and sample desire reasons by observers again put this asymmetry into relief.

Belief reasons by actors:
I wanted to pick up a friend 'cause he was just at home doing nothing [belief].
And I looked in this pack and got out this little band-aide case in this pack or something like that, 'cause I thought it would have something that I needed in it [belief].

Desire reasons by observers:
Dad refused to move out for two months after [wife/mother] filed for divorce just because he wanted to be with his kids [desire] and he didn't want to leave the house we had in West Linn [desire].
So she put the knives under her bed to protect herself [desire].

Finally, hypothesis 3 received support as well. On average, actors offered 81% unmarked belief reasons whereas observers offered 60% unmarked belief reasons, $d = 0.58$.

Unmarked belief reasons by actors:
I'm probably taking next fall off because my boyfriend lives in Florida and that in itself is a very difficult situation [unmarked beliefs]

Marked belief reasons by observers:
I'm guessing that he waited [to die] till I left 'cause he knew that I was leaving [marked belief].

All three hypotheses that were derived from our alternative theory of explanation received considerable support across multiple studies and multiple methodologies. In those same studies we were also able to test the two versions of the classic actor-observer asymmetry—one for the general person-situation dichotomy and one for trait explanations. In order to make the two tests independent, we formed two statistical contrasts: the first comparing all person factors to all situation factors, the second comparing traits to nontraits among person factors.

Across these studies, there was no evidence for a person-situation asymmetry among cause explanations of unintentional behavior (actors = 64% person causes, observers = 62% person causes) or among causal history explanations of intentional behavior (actors = 65% person CHRs, observers = 78% person CHRs), with only one out of ten comparisons statistically significant in the predicted direction. Classifying the contents of reason explanations provided no evidence either, as actors mentioned 48% and observers mentioned 50% person content in their reasons.

The trait asymmetry faired only slightly better. Across causal history and cause explanations observers used slightly more traits (38%) than actors did (28%). However, the trait asymmetry held only when the observer knew the agent well (cf. Hampson, 1983).

Why Do Explanations for Self and Other Differ?

We have considered three novel actor-observer hypotheses and found reliable evidence for each of them. Now the question becomes why these asymmetries exist. Our hypotheses generally drew on two psychological principles—information access and pragmatic goals. I now analyze in more detail what these principles entail and hope to clarify what might be special, if anything, about the way the "self" explains behavior.

Hypothesis 1: Reason Asymmetry

If information access is driving the reason asymmetry, there are at least two versions of access we need to consider. The first concerns a direct path of information activation that allows actors to recall the very reasons for which they acted (Brewer, 1994; Malle, 2004). Especially when the actor had engaged in active deliberation, her representation of the action will be intimately tied in memory to her representations of the reason contents in light of which and on the grounds of which she acted.[3] For the observer, no such direct connection normally exists (unless the actor shared her deliberations with the observer). Observers rely on a second kind of information access, namely, knowledge structures that contain representations of the circumstances (if the observer was copresent) as well as general knowledge about the actor and the given type of action. These representations can form the basis of reason explanations (e.g., in the case of inferring the actor's desires and beliefs in the particular circumstances) but will often form the basis of causal history explanations (e.g., in the case of general knowledge about actor or action). The result should be a tendency for observers to use more causal history explanations.

The second process that may be driving the reason asymmetry concerns the explainer's pragmatic goals, particularly impression management goals, which are often more pronounced for actors than for observers. From previous research we know that reasons help an actor portray herself in a rational light (Malle et al., 2000) whereas CHR explanations keep a "distance" from the agent (Nelson & Malle, 2005), so unless an observer wants to explicitly bridge this distance and make the agent look socially desirable, we would expect actors to offer more reasons than observers do.

A study we conducted recently provide direct evidence for the impression management influence on the reason asymmetry. We found that observers who are explicitly instructed to make the agent look good substantially increased the number of reasons and decreased the number of causal histories in their explanations, with the result that the actor-observer asymmetry was virtually eliminated (Malle et al., 2005). We also have evidence that merely better general knowledge about the agent does not affect the reason asymmetry (Malle et al., 2005). One might suspect that it is primarily the "direct access" difference between actors and observers that influences the asymmetry, but no empirical evidence is currently available for this hypothesis. One method of testing it is to vary the actor's amount of explicit deliberation before acting or the time passed between action deliberation and explanation, which should decrease the actor's direct memory access to reasons but leave an observer's information basis unchanged. Another method is to make the observer privy to the actor's deliberations, such as by having actors deliberate their action decisions out loud in the laboratory.

Hypothesis 2: Belief-Desire Asymmetry

The two processes of information access and pragmatic goals influence actors and observers differently when it comes to offering belief reasons versus desire reasons. Observers will tend to offer more desire reasons both because desires are easier to infer from the action itself, from its context, and from cultural scripts (Bruner, 1990) and because observers are rarely concerned with presenting the agent in a rational, reasonable light, for which belief reasons are most suitable. If actors, by contrast, know their reasons at all, they know both beliefs and desires, so the choice between belief reasons and desire reasons is solely one of pragmatic goals. Specifically, actors will engage in impression management, which in most situations is better accomplished by beliefs than by desires (Malle et al., 2000). Moreover, they may sometimes engage in "audience design," which is the tailoring of a communicative message—an explanation in this case—to what the audience presumably does not know (e.g., Slugoski, Lalljee, Lamb, & Ginsburg, 1993). Audiences are always in the observer role, and if observers often know (or can infer) desire reasons, then an actor would be more likely to offer belief reasons when explaining her action to an audience.

Recent studies provide initial support for these considerations, though questions linger. In one study we were able to eliminate the established belief-desire asymmetry by comparing actors' explanations to explanations given by observers who knew the agent well (Malle et al., 2005). However, a follow-up study that more closely compared observers' explanations for two groups of agents—strangers and intimates—did not replicate the expected difference in belief reasons. A feature that may account for the inconsistency is that in the study where the actor-observer asymmetry was eliminated, observers were not only very familiar with the agent but were also copresent when the agent performed his or her action. In the second study, by contrast, the intimate observer was not copresent in a good proportion of the cases. We are currently exploring the possible role of copresence as a mediator of observers' access to belief reason information.

The impression management process was tested in one study that specifically instructed observers "to create a positive impression" of the agent. On this instruction, observers increased their use of belief reasons to a rate that was almost as high as actors' rate. However, they also increased their use of desire reasons, which casts doubt on the role of impression management in the *differential* use of belief reasons. Additional studies will have to create a more realistic context for observers to portray an agent in a positive light, such as making the explainer a spokesperson for the agent and having the audience assess the explainer's successful (vicarious) impression management.

Hypothesis 3: Belief Marker Asymmetry

Actors, I said earlier, tend to represent the contents of their beliefs directly ("It's going to rain.") and may add mental state markers only if they are needed in communication ("Well, I *thought* it would rain."). Observers, by contrast, will normally represent the agent's beliefs *as* mental states ("She thinks it's going to rain.") and therefore readily include a mental state verb. This may be a difficult hypothesis to test, but one way is to have actors explain out loud a number of actions as they are deciding on them, in which case they should report directly the unmarked belief reasons they have on their minds. Observers, by contrast, who watch those same actors decide and are later asked to explain their actions are more likely to provide beliefs with mental state markers.

Probably the more powerful influence on the belief marker asymmetry is the now familiar self-other difference in impression management motivation. An actor will often leave her belief reasons unmarked because that way they sound like statements of fact (e.g., "I watered the azaleas because *the soil was dry!*"), whereas observers normally don't have that kind of impression management motivation. On the contrary, they may sometimes be actively motivated to distance themselves from the agent's beliefs and therefore use a mental state marker to highlight that distance ("She watered the azaleas because *she thought* the soil was dry.").

Traits Versus Nontraits

The only traditional actor-observer asymmetry for which we have found some evidence in our studies is the greater use of traits by observers than actors. However, the pattern we found lent only partial support to classic claims about trait explanations. First off, there is no evidence for "rampant dispositionism" (L. Ross & Nisbett, 1991) among observers, as they use far fewer trait explanations than nontrait explanations. Expressed as a proportion of all their explanations, observers use traits in less than 10% of cases (and actors in around 5%). Second, the trait asymmetry tended to be more reliable for explanations of unintentional behavior than for explanations of intentional behavior. When accounting for intentional behaviors with causal history explanations, even actors offered a fair number of traits among their person causal history factors ($M = 30\%$), no fewer than observers did ($M = 29\%$). That was especially true in the case of socially undesirable actions, for which both actors and observers normally increase causal history explanations (Nelson and Malle, 2005).

When we turn to the processes that may underlie the trait asymmetry (for unintentional behavior), we must consider Jones and Nisbett's (1972) widely cited postulate of attention differences. However, there is virtually no evidence that attentional salience leads to more trait explanations (e.g., Bierbrauer, 1976; Enzle & Hansen, 1976; Martin & Huang, 1984; McArthur & Post, 1977; Taylor & Fiske, 1975; Uleman, Miller, Henken, Riley, & Tsemberis, 1981), nor is there any psychological mechanism that would automatically translate attention to an agent's *behavior* into explanations using the agent's *traits* (Knobe & Malle, 2002). Beyond that, Jones and Nisbett suggested that observers use traits because they have less information available than actors do. But when observers have increased knowledge of the agent, they do not use fewer but *more* traits (Hampson, 1983; Kerber & Singleton, 1984; Malle et al., 2005). In fact, observers barely use traits at all unless they know the person well.

To explain the full pattern of data we have available, we must turn Jones and Nisbett's proposal around and posit that reasonable information about the agent's personality or past behavior is a *prerequisite* for observers' trait explanations. Normally observers will, just as actors, try to provide the specific causal trigger of the unintentional behavior in question. When that trigger is unknown, observers who have personality information available can offer traits in place of it. For example:

Why is she in such a good mood today?—**She is always enthusiastic**.

The observer knows the agent and even saw her that day; nonetheless, he doesn't exactly know why she is in such a good mood, and he therefore confines himself to a trait explanation. Actors, by contrast, usually have a pretty good idea what triggered their unintentional behaviors, and they cite those presumed triggers in the form of nontrait cause explanations.

Why are you in such a good mood today?—**Because I had a good interview this morning**.

The considerations must differ in the case of causal history explanations, where actors appear to offer no fewer traits than observers do. Actors, we might suspect, will choose an occasional trait CHR if it helps their impression management. In fact, qualitative inspection of our data suggests that actors may use those traits primarily when they explain actions that lie far in the past and were undesirable, putting their past self down in the service of managing impressions of the current self (e.g., "I was immature and stupid"). This hypothesis can be put to a more direct test by asking actors and observers to explain actions that vary in desirability and in the amount of time passed since performing them.

CONCLUSIONS AND IMPLICATIONS

This chapter has examined two fundamental questions about self-other asymmetries in behavior explanation: What asymmetries are there, and why do they exist? I surveyed the 30-year evidence for the traditional hypothesis of a person-situation asymmetry and the results were surprising: The meta-analytic average of published studies is very small and the effect is limited to negative events. However, this does not mean that no general self-other asymmetries exist at all; they are just not tracked by the person-situation distinction. An alternative approach to the study of self-other asymmetries relies on what I have called the "folk-conceptual theory of behavior explanation" (Malle, 1999, 2001, 2004). This theory identifies people's own (i.e., folk-conceptual) assumptions about behaviors and their explanations and postulates two central psychological processes—information access and pragmatic goals—that guide people's choice of explanations. Three actor-observer hypotheses can be derived from this model: Compared to observers, actors (a) use more reasons and fewer causal histories; (b) more belief reasons and fewer desire reasons; and (c) more unmarked than marked belief reasons. The evidence for these asymmetries is new but consistent across multiple studies (Malle et al., 2005). Evidence for the specific psychological processes that account for each of these asymmetries is as yet incomplete, but the emerging data suggest that all three asymmetries are driven by differences both in information access and impression management. Table 8.3 provides a summary contrast between the traditional and the folk-conceptual view on explanations.

Two questions linger. First, is the traditional actor-observer asymmetry just a myth? Second, what are the implications of the proposed alternative view on self-other asymmetries in explanation?

Is the Traditional Asymmetry a Myth?

Even though the average effect size of the traditional Jones-Nisbett hypothesis amounted to an r of less than .04, it is reasonable to assume that several past studies that found an effect captured real psychological phenomena. One such phenomenon is, of course, the self-serving bias in people's accounts of negative and positive outcomes, which at times was measured explicitly (and yielded a positive effect size) and at times was confounded with the purportedly tested general actor-observer asymmetry. But my proposal goes further in suggesting that many past studies that found an effect—either the one predicted by Jones and Nisbett or its reversal—may have unwittingly tapped into one or more of the actor-observer asymmetries that the folk-conceptual theory describes and therefore only appeared to demonstrate an actor-observer difference on their person-situation measures.

For example, some studies that found a reverse person-situation difference in explanations of admirable actions (e.g., Mitchell, 1985; Newman, 1978; Schlenker, Hallam, & McCown, 1983) may actually have tapped into the reason asymmetry. Actors who perform an admirable action normally offer reason explanations (Nelson & Malle, 2000), but being faced with "person" and "situation" rating scales they would likely favor the person scale because it better expresses the intentionality and "ownership" they will want to indicate about an admirable action.

TABLE 8.3 Contrast Between Traditional and Folk-Conceptual Views on Actor-Observer Asymmetries in Behavior Explanation

	Traditional Attribution View	Folk-Conceptual View
Events Explained	All events are explained the same way.	Intentional events are explained differently from unintentional events.
Relevant Parameters of Explanation	All explanations are classified into either person/disposition causes or situation causes.	For unintentional behaviors: Causes (person-trait, person-nontrait, situation, interaction). For intentional behaviors: Reasons (belief marked or unmarked; desire marked or unmarked; valuings); Causal Histories (person-trait, person-nontrait, situation, interaction).
Asymmetries	Actors, compared to observers, use more situation causes and fewer disposition causes.	Actors, compared to observers, use (a) more reasons than causal histories, (b) more belief reasons than desire reasons, and (c) more unmarked than marked belief reasons.
Processes Underlying Asymmetries	Information availability, attention focus, sense of freedom.	Information access (direct recall, knowledge structures); pragmatic goals (audience design, impression management)

Other studies coded free-response explanations into person/situation categories and found supportive evidence for the classic thesis because they may have capitalized on the belief asymmetry and belief marker asymmetry identified earlier. How so? Researchers appeared to classify explanations as "about the person" or "about the situation" merely on the basis of the explanation's *linguistic surface* (Antaki, 1994; Malle, 1999; Miller, Smith, & Uleman, 1981; Monson & Snyder, 1977; L. Ross, 1977). For example, Nisbett, Caputo, Legant, & Mareček's (1973) illustration of a person attribution for a choice of major was "because I want to make a lot of money" (p. 158) and McGill's (1989) example was "I like jobs that are challenging" (p. 191). Both of these "person attributions" are marked reasons that mention the agent in the mental state verb. Nisbett et al.'s (1973) illustration of a situation attribution was "because chemistry is a high-paying field" and McGill's (1989, p. 191) example was "because finance is very challenging." Both of these "situation attributions" are unmarked beliefs that mention the reason's situation content. Extrapolating from these examples, we can assume that the category of person attributions picked up on marked reasons (which are often desires; Malle et al., 2000), whereas the category of situation attributions picked up on unmarked reasons with situation content (which are often beliefs; Malle et al., 2000).

Now, we know that when observers offer reasons, they more often cite desire reasons, which, for grammatical reasons, are often marked (Malle, 1999), leading primarily to "person attribution" codes for observer explanations. We also know that actors use many belief reasons, especially unmarked beliefs (which often have situation content; Malle, 1999), and all that results in a good number of "situation attribution" codes for actor explanations. Thus, if free-response behavior explanations are coded for their linguistic surface, a spurious person-situation asymmetry can emerge, not because of any true self-other asymmetry in person/situation "causes" but because of the confluence of two asymmetries described by the folk-conceptual approach, that of belief reasons and that of belief markers. (For empirical support of these considerations, see Malle, 1999; Malle et al., 2000.)

There may then be some evidence for genuine self-other asymmetries hidden in the bulk of traditional studies (both those that contradicted and those that supported Jones and Nisbett), but it is quite probably evidence for the multitude of folk-conceptual asymmetries I have discussed, not for the broad formulation of a single person-situation difference.

Implications of the Alternative Approach

The alternative view on actor-observer asymmetries stresses the sophisticated conceptual framework that people bring to the task of explaining behavior. Distinctions between types of behavior, modes of explanations, and features of each of mode create a complex set of choices for the explainer. Multiple psychological processes guide those choices, and they can be grouped into two main categories: information access (including direct recall, knowledge structures, representational form) and pragmatic goals (including audience design, impression management, self-distancing). If one acknowledges that this folk-conceptual approach makes more theoretical sense and better fits the data than the classic person-situation model, there is still the question how far the folk-conceptual theory can be pushed. What implications does it have for phenomena such as relationships, perspective taking, or conflict resolution?

Attribution theory has played a notable role in the study of relationships (e.g., Bradbury & Fincham, 1990; Fincham, Bradbury, & Grych, 1990). However, because of the limited predictive power of traditional attribution concepts researchers tended to add more and more "attribution dimensions" to their studies, ranging from locus, stability, and globality to intentionality and responsibility (e.g., Fincham, Beach, & Nelson, 1987). Even so, evidence for the classic actor-observer asymmetries has remained inconsistent (e.g., Fincham, Beach, & Baucom, 1987). A folk-conceptual approach to explanations in relationships would examine naturally occurring behavior explanations that people give for their own and their partner's behavior and track the various actor-observer asymmetries (for reasons, beliefs, etc.) as indexes of how wide the gap is between self and other in a given relationship. The underlying processes of information access and pragmatic goals could also be independently assessed or manipulated to determine whether self-other gaps are a matter of epistemic, communicative, or motivational problems, and this host of variables could be related to measures of relationship quality and stability.

In romantic as well as political relationships, bridging the self-other gap is a major goal of conflict resolution, and perspective taking is one promising tool with which to achieve this goal. But how do we know when conflict partners do or do not take each other's perspective? Explanations of each other's behaviors could be used as indicators of perspective taking (Nelson, 2003), and changes in actor-observer asymmetries could specifically indicate progress in perspective taking. By monitoring the explanations conflict partners give for their own and the other's behavior before and after conflict-resolution interventions, the effectiveness of such interventions could be assessed. Moreover, the shaping of explanations as having "actor style" or "observer style" may itself serve as a conflict resolution intervention. If actors were encouraged to offer causal history explanations they might gain more distance from their subjective (self-enhancing) point of view, and if observers were encouraged to offer reason explanations they might better see the actor's point of view. Perhaps explaining behavior in the style of the other perspective can help not only take that perspective but also sway the associated evaluations, introducing self-criticalness to the actor perspective and lessening blame from the observer perspective.

The folk-conceptual theory's rich set of parameters also invites studying the developmental dynamics of self-other asymmetries in explanation. With very few exceptions, these asymmetries have not been studied among age groups other than young adults. We might wonder, for example, whether preschool children show any such asymmetries. Some theorists have argued that, at this age, there is no difference in cognition of self and other (Gopnik, 1993), so there should be no cognitively mediated differences in explanations as well. Others maintain that even preschoolers have privileged access to their own mental states (Goldman, 1993), and if so, this privilege should foster both a reason asymmetry and a belief asymmetry in behavior explanations for self and other. Furthermore, we might wonder whether adolescents have renewed difficulties with connecting to other minds, which would amplify certain self-other asymmetries in behavior explanation. Finally, does old age come with the wisdom of greater balance between explanations for one's own and other people's behavior? Questions such as these can be readily studied within the folk-conceptual framework by analyzing naturally occurring explanations and assessing their fundamental parameters at the conceptual, cognitive, and linguistic level.

The search for universals and cultural differences can also be conducted with more acuity by examining parameters of folk explanation at both the linguistic and the conceptual level. Current cross-cultural research on behavior explanations uses the simple person–situation dichotomy for an undoubtedly complex phenomenon (e.g., Choi, Dalal, Kim-Prieto, & Park, 2003; Morris & Peng 1994), and it seems likely that a framework with finer distinctions will be more sensitive to those complexities. For example, claims about a lesser gap between self and other in Eastern cultures can be put to a better test when we distinguish the separate contributions of information access and impression management on a variety of explanation parameters, such as the choice of events explained (intentional vs.

unintentional), the modes of explanation (e.g., reasons vs. causal histories), and the features of each mode (e.g., marked vs. unmarked reasons). Current models depict Eastern explainers as using more "situational attributions," but the vagueness of this theoretical category allows too many ways in which such findings can come about. For example, the results would be much less impressive if they stemmed from Eastern explainers applying, for pragmatic reasons, fewer mental state markers than if they reflected a cognitive shift toward using more causal history explanations from the self perspective.

In conclusion, the folk-conceptual approach to self-other asymmetries in behavior explanation is not only a tool for critical analysis of past attribution research but also opens numerous avenues for future research. Some of this research will refine the proposed theoretical model of explanation, some will make adjustments to the empirical claims voiced in this chapter. All of it, I hope, will help revise and expand our knowledge of self-other asymmetries in explanation, distancing ourselves from the myths, and bringing us closer to reality.

ACKNOWLEDGMENT

Many thanks for Joshua Knobe and the volume editors for their insightful comments on an earlier draft of this chapter.

NOTES

1. Watson's (1982) review was published long ago, and even at its time the article covered only a limited proportion of the relevant studies.
2. Analyses of other potential moderator variables and details of the various effect size computations can be found in Malle (2005).
3. Some readers might ask whether Nisbett and Wilson (1975) have not shown that people normally lack access to the reasons of their actions. But these researchers have shown no such thing (nor has recent research on automaticity). By folk definition, reasons are on the agent's mind at the time of acting, and if the agent does not forget, she can later report on them. Whether there are other, perhaps unconscious processes that helped bring about the action is a separate issue. These additional processes can be cited, of course, in causal history of reason explanations, which are what Nisbett and Wilson offered for their participants' behavior. Their famous studies showed that agents can be unaware of some factors in the causal history of their reasons (hence, their actions), and this corresponds to our position that CHR explanations do not presuppose the agent's subjectivity or awareness.

REFERENCES

Antaki, C. (1994). *Explaining and arguing: The social organization of accounts*. Thousand Oaks, CA: Sage Publications.
Aronson, E. (2002). *The social animal* (8th ed.). New York: Worth Publishers.
Baldwin, D. A., Baird, J. A., Saylor, M. M., & Clark, M. A. (2001). Infants parse dynamic action. *Child Development, 72,* 708–717.
Bartsch, K., & Wellman, H. M. (1995). *Children talk about the mind*. New York: Oxford University Press.
Bierbrauer, G. (1979). Why did he do it? Attribution of obedience and the phenomenon of dispositional bias. *European Journal of Social Psychology, 9,* 67–84.

Bradbury, T. M., & Fincham, F. D. (1990). Attributions in marriage: Review and critique. *Psychological Bulletin, 107,* 3–33.

Bretherton, I. (1991). Intentional communication and the development of an understanding of mind. In D. Frye & C. Moore (Eds.), *Children's theories of mind* (pp. 49–75). Hillsdale, NJ: Erlbaum.

Brewer, W. F. (1994). Autobiographical memory and survey research. In N. Schwarz & S. Sudman (Ed.), *Autobiographical memory and the validity of retrospective reports* (pp. 11–20). New York: Springer.

Bruner, J. (1990). Acts of meaning. Cambridge, MA: Harvard University Press.

Buss, A. R. (1978). Causes and reasons in attribution theory: A conceptual critique. *Journal of Personality and Social Psychology, 36,* 1311–1321.

Choi, I., Dalal, R., Kim-Prieto, C., & Park, H. (2003). Culture and judgment of causal relevance. *Journal of Personality and Social Psychology, 84,* 46–59.

Cowan, N. (1995). *Attention and memory: An integrated framework.* New York: Oxford University Press.

Davidson, D. (1963). Actions, reasons, and causes. *Journal of Philosophy, 60,* 685–700.

Enzle, M. E., & Hansen, R. D. (1976). Effects of video-mediated visual contact on observers' attributions of causality and reciprocal game behavior. *Simulation and Games, 7,* 281–294.

Fincham, F. D., Beach, S. R., & Baucom, D. H. (1987). Attribution processes in distressed and nondistressed couples: 4. Self-partner attribution differences. *Journal of Personality and Social Psychology, 52,* 739–748

Fincham, F. D., Beach, S. R., & Nelson, G. (1987). Attribution processes in distressed and nondistressed couples: III. Causal and responsibility attributions for spouse behavior. *Cognitive Therapy and Research, 11,* 71-86.

Fincham, F. D., Bradbury, T. N., & Grych, J. H. (1990). Conflict in close relationships: The role of intrapersonal phenomena. In S. Graham & V. S. Folkes (Eds.), *Attribution theory: Applications to achievement, mental health, and interpersonal conflict* (pp. 161-184). Hillsdale, NJ: Erlbaum.

Fiske, S. T., & Taylor, S. E. (1991). *Social cognition* (second ed.). New York: McGraw-Hill.

Goldman, A. I. (1993). The psychology of folk psychology. *Behavioral and Brain Sciences, 16,* 15–28.

Gopnik, A. (1993). How we know our minds: The illusion of first-person knowledge of intentionality. *Behavioral and Brain Sciences, 16,* 1–14.

Greenberg, M. S., & Frisch, D. M. (1972). Effect of intentionality on willingness to reciprocate a favor. *Journal of Experimental Social Psychology, 8,* 99–111.

Greenwald, A. G. (1980). The totalitarian ego: Fabrication and revision of personal history. *American Psychologist, 35,* 603–618.

Hampson, S. E. (1983). Trait ascription and depth of acquaintance: The preference for traits in personality descriptions and its relation to target familiarity. *Journal of Research in Personality, 17,* 398–411.

Hunter, J. E., & Schmidt, F. L. (1990). *Methods of meta-analysis: Correcting error and bias in research findings.* Newbury Park, CA: Sage.

Jones, E. E. (1976). How do people perceive the causes of behavior? *American Scientist, 64,* 300–305.

Jones, E. E., & Nisbett, R. E. (1972). The actor and the observer: Divergent perceptions of the causes of behavior. In E. E. Jones, D. Kanouse, H. H. Kelley, R. E. Nisbett, S. Valins, & B. Weiner (Eds.), *Attribution: Perceiving the causes of behavior* (pp. 79–94). Morristown, NJ: General Learning Press.

Kelley, H. H. (1967). Attribution theory in social psychology. In D. Levine (Ed.), *Nebraska Symposium on Motivation* (Vol. 15, pp. 129-238). Lincoln: University of Nebraska Press.

Kerber, K. W., & Singleton, R. (1984). Trait and situational attributions in a naturalistic setting: Familiarity, liking, and attribution validity. *Journal of Personality, 52,* 205–219.

Knobe, J., & Malle, B. F. (2002). Self and other in the explanation of behavior: 30 years later. Special issue on self-other asymmetries: *Psychologica Belgica, 42,* 113–130.

Krueger, J. (1998). On the perception of social consensus. *Advances in Experimental Social Psychology, 30,* 163–240.

Kugelmass, S., & Breznitz, S. (1968). Intentionality in moral judgment: Adolescent development. *Child Development, 39,* 249–256.

Locke, D., & Pennington, D. (1982). Reasons and other causes: Their role in attribution processes. *Journal of Personality and Social Psychology, 42,* 212–223.

Locke, K. D. (2002). Are descriptions of the self more complex than descriptions of others? *Personality and Social Psychology Bulletin, 28*, 1094–1105.

Malle (2005). The actor-observer asymmetry in causal attribution: A (surprising) meta-analysis. Manuscript submitted for publication.

Malle, B. F. (1999). How people explain behavior: A new theoretical framework. *Personality and Social Psychology Review, 3*, 23–48.

Malle, B. F. (2001). Folk explanations of intentional action. In B. F. Malle, L. J. Moses, & D. A. Baldwin (Eds.), *Intentions and intentionality: Foundations of social cognition* (pp. 265–286). Cambridge, MA: MIT Press.

Malle, B. F. (2002). The social self and the social other. Actor-observer asymmetries in making sense of behavior. In J. P. Forgas & K. D. Williams (Eds.), *The social self: Cognitive, interpersonal, and intergroup perspectives* (pp. 189–204). Philadelphia, PA: Psychology Press.

Malle, B. F. (2003). *F.Ex: Coding scheme for people's folk explanations of behavior.* University of Oregon. Retrieved from http://darkwing.uoregon.edu/~bfmalle/fex.html on July 1, 2004.

Malle, B. F. (2004). *How the mind explains behavior: Folk explanations, meaning, and social interaction.* Cambridge, MA: MIT Press.

Malle, B. F., & Knobe, J. (1997a). The folk concept of intentionality. *Journal of Experimental Social Psychology, 33*, 101-121.

Malle, B. F., & Knobe, J. (1997b). Which behaviors do people explain? A basic actor-observer asymmetry. *Journal of Personality and Social Psychology, 72*, 288-304.

Malle, B. F., & Nelson, S. E. (2003). Judging mens rea: The tension between folk concepts and legal concepts of intentionality. *Behavioral Sciences and the Law, 21*, 1-18.

Malle, B. F., & Pearce, G. E. (2001). Attention to behavioral events during social interaction: Two actor-observer gaps and three attempts to close them. *Journal of Personality and Social Psychology, 81*, 278-294.

Malle, B. F., Knobe, J., & Nelson, S. (2005). *Actor-observer asymmetries in folk explanations of behavior: New answers to an old question.* Manuscript in preparation, University of Oregon.

Malle, B. F., Knobe, J., O'Laughlin, M., Pearce, G. E., & Nelson, S. E. (2000). Conceptual structure and social functions of behavior explanations: Beyond person–situation attributions. *Journal of Personality and Social Psychology, 79*, 309–326.

Martin, D. S., & Huang, M. (1984). Effects of time and perceptual orientation on actors' and observers' attributions. *Perceptual and Motor Skills, 58*, 23–30.

McArthur, L. Z., & Post, D. L. (1977). Figural emphasis and person perception. *Journal of Experimental Social Psychology, 13*, 520–535.

McClure, J., & Hilton, D. (1997). For you can't always get what you want: When preconditions are better explanations than goals. *British Journal of Social Psychology, 36*, 223–240.

McGill, A. L. (1989). Context effects in judgments of causation. *Journal of Personality and Social Psychology, 57*, 189–200.

Mele, A. R. (1992). *Springs of action: Understanding intentional behavior.* New York: Oxford University Press.

Miller, F. D., Smith, E. R., & Uleman, J. (1981). Measurement and interpretation of situational and dispositional attributions. *Journal of Experimental Social Psychology, 17*, 80–95.

Mitchell, T. E. (1985). Actor-observer differences in attributions to morality. *Journal of Social Psychology, 125*, 475–477.

Monson, T. C., & Snyder, M. (1976). Actors, observers, and the attribution process: Toward a reconceptualization. *Journal of Experimental Social Psychology, 13*, 89–111.

Morris, M. W., & Peng, K. (1994). Culture and cause: American and Chinese attributions for social and physical events. *Journal of Personality and Social Psychology, 67*, 949–971.

Nelson, S. E. (2003). *Setting the story straight: A study of discrepant accounts of conflict and their convergence.* Unpublished Doctoral Dissertation, University of Oregon

Nelson, S. E., & Malle, B. F. (2000, April). *Explaining intentional actions: Explanations as modifiers of social perception and judgment.* Poster presented at the Annual Meeting of the Western Psychological Association, Portland, Oregon.

Nelson, S., & Malle, B. F. (2005). Self-serving biases in explanations of intentional behavior. Manuscript in preparation, University of Oregon.

Nelson-LeGall, S. A. (1985). Motive-outcome matching and outcome foreseeability: Effects on attribution of intentionality and moral judgments. *Developmental Psychology, 21,* 323–337.

Newman, A. (1978). Actor-observer differences in perception of self-control. *Journal of Social Psychology, 105,* 199–204.

Nickerson, R. S. (1999). How we know—and sometimes misjudge—what others know: Imputing one's own knowledge to others. *Psychological Bulletin, 125,* 737–759.

Nisbett, R. E., & Wilson, T. D. (1977). Telling more than we know: Verbal reports on mental processes. *Psychological Review, 84,* 231–259.

Nisbett, R. E., Caputo, C., Legant, P., & Marecek, J. (1973). Behavior as seen by the actor and as seen by the observer. *Journal of Personality and Social Psychology, 27,* 154–164.

O'Laughlin, M. J., & Malle, B. F. (2002). How people explain actions performed by groups and individuals. *Journal of Personality and Social Psychology, 82,* 33–48.

Read, S. J. (1987). Constructing causal scenarios: A knowledge structure approach to causal reasoning. *Journal of Personality and Social Psychology, 52,* 288–302.

Robins, R. W., Spranca, M. D., & Mendelsohn, G. A. (1996). The actor-observer effect revisited: Effects of individual differences and repeated social interactions on actor and observer attributions. *Journal of Personality and Social Psychology, 71,* 375–389.

Rogers, T. B., Kuiper, N. A., & Kirker, W. S. (1977). Self-reference and the encoding of personal information. *Journal of Personality and Social Psychology, 35,* 677–688.

Ross, L. (1977). The intuitive psychologist and his shortcomings: Distortions in the attribution process. In L. Berkowitz (Ed.), *Advances in experimental social psychology* (Vol. 10, pp. 174–221). New York: Academic Press.

Ross, L., & Nisbett, R. E. (1991). *The person and the situation: Perspectives of social psychology.* New York: McGraw-Hill.

Ross, L., Greene, D., & House, P. (1977). The "false-consensus effect:" An egocentric bias in social perception and attribution processes. *Journal of Experimental Social Psychology, 13,* 279–301.

Ross, M., & Fletcher, G. J. O. (1985). Attribution and social perception. In G. Lindsey & E. Aronson (Eds.), *The Handbook of Social Psychology* (Vol. 2, pp. 73–114). New York: Random House.

Russell, E. W., & D'Hollosy, M. E. (1992). Memory and attention. *Journal of Clinical Psychology, 48,* 530–538.

Schlenker, B. R., Hallam, J. R., & McCown, N. E. (1983). Motives and social evaluation: Actor-observer differences in the delineation of motives for a beneficial act. *Journal of Experimental Social Psychology, 19,* 254–273.

Searle, J. R. (1983). *Intentionality: An essay in the philosophy of mind.* Cambridge: Cambridge University Press.

Sheldon, K. M., & Johnson, J. T. (1993). Forms of social awareness: Their frequency and correlates. *Personality and Social Psychology Bulletin, 19,* 320–30.

Slugoski, B. R., Lalljee, M., Lamb, R., & Ginsburg, G. P. (1993). Attribution in conversational context: Effect of mutual knowledge on explanation-giving. *European Journal of Social Psychology, 23,* 219–238.

Taylor, S. E., & Brown, J. D. (1988). Illusion and well-being: A social psychological perspective on mental health. *Psychological Bulletin, 103,* 193–210.

Taylor, S. E., & Fiske, S. T. (1975). Point-of-view and perceptions of causality. *Journal of Personality and Social Psychology, 32,* 439–445.

Turnbull, W. (1986). Everyday explanation: The pragmatics of puzzle resolution. *Journal for the Theory of Social Behavior, 16,* 141–160.

Uleman, J. S., Miller, F. D., Henken, V., Riley, E., & Tsemberis, S. (1981). Visual perspective or social perspective?: Two failures to replicate Storms' rehearsal, and support for Monson and Snyder on actor–observer divergence. *Replications in Social Psychology, 1,* 54–58.

Watson, D. (1982). The actor and the observer: How are their perceptions of causality divergent? *Psychological Bulletin, 92,* 682–700.

Wellman, H. M., & Woolley, J. D. (1990). From simple desires to ordinary beliefs: The early development of everyday psychology. *Cognition, 35,* 245–275.

PART IV

INTEGRATED
APPROACHES

9

Judging for Two
Some Connectionist Proposals for How the Self Informs and Constrains Social Judgment

EMILY BALCETIS
DAVID A. DUNNING
Cornell University

*T*he task of judging other people presents an inherent difficulty. For the most part, any single action by another person is ambiguous in its implications, in that a variety of conclusions can be reached about that person's talents, personality, and potential. For example, suppose that Clay excitedly buys a fancy new personal digital assistant, one that sends and receives email. Does this mean that Clay is a little bit of a geek—entranced with the latest gadgets flaunted by Radio Shack? Or, instead, does it mean that he is a show-off, buying the newest and most extravagant device to one up his friends and acquaintances? Or, does it mean that Clay is so outgoing and people-oriented that he hates being out of email contact with the world even for one moment?

To disambiguate such pieces of social information, people must call upon whatever knowledge they might happen to have about the social world: Do many people they know own such an elaborate PDA? Who tends to buy such gadgets? Among their friends who own PDAs, what has motivated them to buy them? A common theme within social psychology over the past few decades has been to determine how people incorporate what they already know about the social world, or at least suspect they know, to inform and constrain the judgments they make about others (e.g., Fiske & Taylor, 1991; Kunda, 1999).

In this chapter, we discuss one specific and prominent constraint people apply to their judgments of others. That constraint is the self. What people believe about themselves plays a leading role in the theater of social judgment, in that people tend to reach judgments of others that affirm, or at least do not contradict, beliefs people hold about themselves. Kelly, for example, might label her friend, the one whose stacks of journals and textbooks prevent any sighting of the color of the carpet, as an *intellectual*—but Kelly will do so only to the extent that she sees herself as an intellectual and displays the same sort of behavior. Similarly, Reuben might describe the Williams sisters' agile and spirited performance on the tennis courts as astonishingly *nimble,* a conclusion harmonious with his belief that his own sprightly jumps toward the latté line provide at least a modicum of evidence that he deserves the trait, too.

Decades of research have revealed just how pervasively the self-concept informs and constrains social judgment (for a review, see Dunning, 2002a). For example, people tend to exaggerate how common their own attitudes and actions are in the general population, a phenomenon typically known as the false consensus effect (Krueger, 1998; Ross, Greene, & House, 1977). Justin, overestimating how much other people share his passion for Kenny G, may quickly be ousted from his position of aspiring DJ by a crowd of jazz aficionados who would accept nothing less than Miles Davis. Similarly, fans of music from the 1960s actually do overestimate the extent to which others concur on its value when comparing it to music of the 1980s (Gilovich, 1990). Those wearing a religious symbol or regularly attending religious services are more likely than their less religious complements to overestimate the percentage of others that perform those actions as well (Biernat, Manis, & Kobrynowicz, 1997).

In addition, people tend to use themselves as the "norm" or "benchmark" against which others are judged. In judgments of competence and character, people give significant weight to whether other people possess the same skills and strengths as the self (Carpenter, 1988; Lewicki, 1983). Indeed, people tend to color their definitions of important interpersonal traits, like *leadership* and *intelligence*, with much of their own personality. For instance, a person who considers herself *tactful, extroverted,* and *friendly* will view those characteristics as more central to *leadership* than someone who denies having those attributes. A person who is *mathematically adept* will consider that competence more central to her notion of *intelligence* than will a person not so mathematically skilled (Dunning, Perie, & Story, 1991). In short, abstract traits are defined egocentrically and then become the metric by which others are judged.

Demonstrations that the self influences and constrains social judgment are varied and numerous. That said, in the current psychological literature, there is a healthy ongoing debate about how specifically the self interjects itself into social judgment. Some agree that the self has a powerful influence over social judgment, although they propose varying explanations for how it is accomplished, and whether that influence is direct (Krueger, 2003; Mussweiler, 2003; Mussweiler, Epstude, & Rüter, this volume; Sedikides, 2003); whereas some argue instead that the impact of the self is indirect or spurious (Karniol, 2003). Given this state of affairs, it is clear that a good number of unanswered questions still remain about *how* the self influences judgments, attributions, and predictions about others.

TWO PRINCIPLES GUIDING THE INFLUENCE
OF SELF ON SOCIAL JUDGMENT

In this chapter, we describe one potential approach for explaining how the self sculpts judgments of others. That approach rests on a *connectionist* framework, in which we suggest that beliefs about others must enter and remain consistent with a whole host of other beliefs that a person happens to hold and that are connected to each other via a network of associations (Read & Miller, 1998; Smith, 1996).

However, before describing how a connectionist approach might account for the links between self and social judgment, we must stipulate two preliminary principles, both heavily supported by social psychological data, that establish a link between self and social judgment. The first principle is that observing the attributes or actions of others prompts people spontaneously to bring their own characteristics, behaviors, and related self-beliefs to mind. The second principle is that any judgment made of that other person must be rendered compatible or harmonious with such self-information. With these two principles in place, one can explain many of the patterns found in past research in which the judgments people make of others are crafted around beliefs about the self.

JUDGING OTHER PEOPLE EVOKES SELF-INFORMATION

The first principle is that judging others' achievement or action often involves bringing to mind one's own. When making judgments of others, people appear to rely upon reference points (Higgins & Lurie, 1983; Higgins & Stangor, 1988). One does not know, for example, whether Clay's new PDA is expensive until one compares it to others in a catalogue, or perhaps compares Clay's gadget to one's own.

Although there are many types of information that assist social judgment, the need for reference points suggests that one particularly powerful type of information people use is social comparison information (Suls & Wheeler, 2000). In appraising another person, people seek out others to compare this person with. Many considerations go into the selection of comparison others. Comparison others can be selected based on relevant similarities to the person being judged (Wheeler, Martin, & Suls, 1997). For example, to establish Rick as a beer buff, one might compare Rick's expertise to the proprietor of the local Chapter House Pub who offers and can extol the virtues of approximately 50 fine brews on tap.

Importantly, social judgments can commonly be influenced by comparison others who just simply happen to be around or cognitively accessible (Herr, 1986; Herr, Sherman, & Fazio, 1983; Higgins & Lurie, 1983; Higgins & Stangor, 1988). Consider a case when the target of judgment is the self. In the case of self-judgment, Mussweiler and Rüter (2003) found that people tend to bring to mind, or to activate, the behavior of people they think about frequently, namely their friends and acquaintances. As a consequence of this frequency of activation, friends became "routine" comparison points, people whose behaviors are thought of whenever a social comparison is called for. Consistent with this proposal, participants more quickly identified the names of their friends after judging themselves along a series of personality dimensions. They also more quickly described the personality characteristics of their friends after judging themselves. This evidence from Mussweiler and Rüter suggests that the selection of comparison others can become quite an efficient process. Instead of effortfully deliberating over the choice of comparisons, people instead rely on routine comparison standards that are quickly evoked without much effort.

If people rely on such routine comparison points as they reach social judgments, there is every reason to believe that the self would be one of those points. When judging other people, the self is an exemplar that is easily evoked. In addition, because people link so many beliefs and cognitions to the self (Catrambone, Beike, & Niedenthal, 1996; Holyoak & Gordon, 1983; Prentice, 1991), there are many indirect routes to self-activation. The frequency, consistency, and ease with which the self can be brought to mind, then, can prompt the self to be a routine standard.

Direct evidence suggests that people spontaneously think of themselves as they judge another person's behavior (Dunning & Beauregard, 2000; Dunning & Cohen, 1992; Lambert & Wedell, 1991; Sherif & Hovland, 1961). For example, when asked if a set of traits described people in general, participants responded in ways that matched what they thought of themselves. In fact, personal opinions were used more heavily than were endorsements or rejections made by another individual, even though that other person's choices are just as informative as are the self's (Clement & Krueger, 2000). Similarly, Dunning and Hayes (1996) presented participants with bits of information about another person, such as a score of 620 on the math SAT, and then asked them to judge that person along a relevant trait (e.g., math skill). When questioned about how they had gone about reaching these judgments, 39% of participants spontaneously reported that they compared their own behavior and achievements with those of the other person before reaching an evaluation. When specifically prompted in another question to reflect on whether they had used any comparison points in their judgments, another 42% of participants admitted using themselves (for a total of 71%). Other comparison points were mentioned (e.g., what acquaintances did, what the population norm was), but none were mentioned nearly as frequently as the self.

Follow-up studies provided further evidence that people recruit thoughts about themselves as they judge others. Participants again were asked to judge another person's skills and characteristics, such as whether this person had good math skills when provided with that same math SAT score. They were next asked to rank their own behavior in relation to the other person's. Relative to a control group, participants who had evaluated another person's behavior subsequently took less time to report their own behavior. In essence, because judging another person had prompted them to use their own behavior as a comparison point, they could more quickly answer questions about that behavior when asked (Dunning & Hayes, 1996, Studies 2 & 3).

Although the self frequently intrudes on judgment and categorization tasks, the particular self-knowledge brought to mind changes, depending on the specific nature of the judgment to be made. Information about the self that makes the comparison most efficient is brought to the judgment table. For example, a man asked to rate how caring a woman is need not engage in point-by-point comparisons between himself and the woman. Instead, he could simply use gender category information to make such a judgment. Consistent with this assertion, data show that people more quickly indicate their gender (a category level trait) after rating a member of the opposite as opposed to the same sex (Mussweiler & Bodenhausen, 2002). However, when making judgments about in-group members, such as a man judging another man, individuating knowledge about the self and the target, rather than simple gender category information is required. Indeed, data show that after judging a same-sex individual, people show evidence of thinking about their individual attributes and skills, rather than the category label *male*, suggesting instead that judging an ingroup member causes people to activate different sets of self-information than they would for judgments of an outgroup member (Mussweiler & Bodenhausen, 2002). This suggests that social comparisons can be based on two types of self-relevant knowledge: (1) knowledge about one's social category (i.e. gender), and (2) individuating information about the self. In both cases, it is evident then that the self is used in comparison, but the specific types of self-information called upon depends on the target. In particular, when the target and the self belong to distinct social groups, category level information is all that is required to produce a judgment. However, when the target and self belong to the same group, more individuating information is called into use.

BRINGING JUDGMENTS OF OTHERS INTO HARMONY WITH BELIEFS ABOUT THE SELF

The second principle is that once some portion of self-information is activated, the judgments that people make of others are brought into harmony with that information. Evaluations of others require integrating new information into what is already known about the world, and harmonious integration means that what an individual makes of this new information must remain compatible and avoid contradictions with currently held beliefs. Of course, those beliefs include opinions about the self. For example, suppose an aspiring lawyer encounters two established lawyers on the train. This aspiring lawyer has a firm belief that he has a brilliant mind that will undoubtedly bring success, yet he realizes he does not handle details very well. One of the lawyers he meets, Tina, is a smart, "big picture"

type who focuses on broad strategy. The other, Richard, is a detailed-oriented individual who sweats out every comma on a contract. It is likely that the aspiring
lawyer will think of Tina as a terrific lawyer and Richard as a more mediocre one
because those conclusions fit into his own self-beliefs more harmoniously than
other assessments.

An increasing body of evidence suggests that people align their judgments of
others to remain compatible with the web of beliefs they hold about themselves
(Dunning, 1999, 2002a, 2002b). Usually, but not always, people apply positive
traits to themselves and avoid attaching negative ones—at times even much more
than they really can justify (Alicke, 1985, this volume; Brown, 1986; Dunning,
Meyerowitz, & Holzberg, 1989; Weinstein, 1980). They view themselves to be
people of fine moral worth, imbued with many valuable skills and enviable talents.
Thus, when people judge others, the conclusions they reach must remain consistent with the largely favorable beliefs that people hold about themselves however
inflated they may be.

SUMMARY

In short, we argue that the act of judging another person is never about that
person alone. Whatever conclusions people reach about that other person must
remain consistent with the particular concoction of self-beliefs that arise during
the judgment process. Because the self looms so large in social judgment, when
people assess the skills, traits, and abilities of others, they are really "judging
for two." Their evaluations of others contain a statement not only about their
beliefs about another person, but are importantly statements about themselves.
Prior beliefs about the self must be "honored," in that any inference made about
another person must navigate around the knowledge and opinions people hold
about themselves.

Self as Constraint: A Connectionist Approach

With these two principles in place, the complicated dance between self-image
and social judgment becomes more ordered and predictable. In addition, these
principles directly suggest one framework that can profitably be exploited to describe the link between self and social judgment. That framework is based on the
connectionist approach to social cognition (Read & Miller, 1998; Smith, 1996).
Connectionist approaches to social cognitive phenomena have over the last few
years become increasingly popular and theoretically valuable, particularly for their
ability to describe complex patterns of interacting information and integration in
cognitive and evaluative judgment processes.

In particular, one variant of connectionist models, parallel constraint satisfaction models, have proven quite useful for researchers focused on social psycho-

logical issues. People construct judgments to fit with the available or preexisting information. Constraint satisfaction models presume that people strive to satisfy or optimally piece together existing information and incorporate new information in a way that does not upset the harmonious structure that has already been formed. Constraint satisfaction models have been successfully applied to a number of situations in social cognition in which people must take in new information and make sense of it given what they already know. Constraint satisfaction models have described, for example, the situational determinants of preference for parsimony or breadth in explanations of behavior (Read & Marcus-Newhall, 1993). Another model has proposed a computational unifying theory for cognitive dissonance reduction (Shultz & Lepper, 1996). Additionally, connectionist models have been developed to describe the many known influences on person perception, such as accessibility of exemplars (Smith & DeCoster, 1998), stereotypes (Kunda & Thagard, 1996), discounting trait attributions when given situational information, as well as primacy, recency, assimilation and contrast effects in priming (Van Overwalle & Labiouse, 2004).

In this chapter, we provide a brief introduction to parallel constraint satisfaction models and demonstrate how such models might account for the constraints that self-beliefs impose upon assessments of others—thus showing how judgments of others really involve judging for two. We hope to provide a conceptual basis for the general structure of a connectionist model that might synthesize these observations of self and social judgments. In particular, we describe how a connectionist approach would depict when people (1) overperceive similarity with others, (2) provide extreme evaluations of peers versus more muted ones, (3) overperceive differences, and (4) infer additional personality attributes of another person given very little information.

We should note that a multitude of theoretical accounts have been proposed to explain how the self is related to social judgment, such as the Self-As-Distinct model (Karniol, 2003), as well as various egocentric comparison theories (Dunning & Hayes, 1996; Mussweiler, 2003; Sedikides, 2003). However, we believe that a connectionist approach may offer a framework that more comprehensively describes the process by which self-views encroach upon social judgments.

One key feature that distinguishes a connectionist approach from previous accounts has to do with the serial versus parallel nature of the process. Traditional models suggest a serial process in which social information is acquired, and then people perform a sequential series of systematic steps to determine what judgment to deduce from the new information they have been given. By using a connectionist framework, we suggest instead that attitudes, beliefs, and behaviors related to the self and others are all processed and altered simultaneously, concurrently serving to influence one another. By proposing such a parallel processing system, we can model how judgment tasks simultaneously activate information about the self and incorporate such details into estimates of others' skills, traits, and abilities. This type of parallel processing system can describe how apparently deliberate and motivated social judgments might be less intentionally created than originally described in the literature (see Gilovich, Epley, & Hanko, this volume, for thoughts that echo this assertion).

The Framework

This perspective of social judgment assumes that information about the self and others including traits, behaviors, and attitudes can be represented as interconnected nodes in a web. This web can take on many different architectures, but the general characterization is a pattern of interconnected nodes with each receiving activation from other nodes, then spreading its own activation to other nodes depending on whether it receives enough input to surpass a certain threshold. The assimilation of input from other nodes and generation of its own output to other nodes takes place concurrently instead of sequentially, until the entire web settles into a pattern of activation that leaves it in harmonious stasis.

To illustrate, bits of information such as beliefs about personal levels of athleticism, the number of hours spent at the gym, and opinions about what it takes to be considered *brawny* can be modeled as nodes in this net. Figure 9.1 is a schematic illustration that depicts the relationship among related associations in a network involving a person's beliefs about his athleticism. In this and the following figures, circles exemplify nodes representing traits (e.g., weak), beliefs (e.g., I am athletic), and behaviors (e.g., time spent exercising).[1] Lines connecting these nodes depict the nature of the connections among them. Solid lines indicate positive correlations or connections while broken, dotted lines describe negative connections. Thus, the passing of information or spread of activation between nodes is constrained by excitatory (positive) and inhibitory (negative) associations.

For example, as the number of hours logged at cardio kickboxing classes increases (positive, excitatory activation) and the number of hours spent flipping through the Food Network, QVC: the Home Shopping Club, or daytime soaps decreases (negative, inhibitory activation), the more likely it is that this budding bruiser will consider himself *athletic*. As information or activation in one particular node changes (i.e., as the number of hours spent on a stair-stepper increases or decreases), activation levels in other nodes also change within this interdependent system of associations. The result of these interactions is an increased likelihood of believing that the self is *athletic*. Such is the nature of a spreading activation type model.[2]

In this vein, we propose that attributions about the self and others occur by a spread of activation. However, we add that the social judgment process arises by parallel constraint satisfaction. Given that perceptions of personal traits, skills, and abilities are relatively fixed in generally a positive, flattering manner, the incorporation of information or any judgments about others must occur in a way that respects this relatively stable network representing the self. Thus, the manner in which incoming information or input is incorporated into this network is constrained by the previously formed web of self-associations. A self-proclaimed

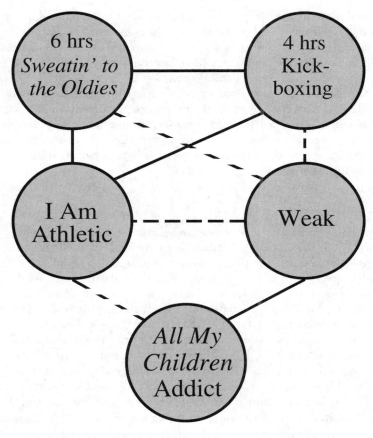

FIGURE 9.1

muscle man will most likely evaluate others' dedication to the gym in comparison to his own attendance and commitment formulating an opinion that allows him to continue thinking of himself as athletic. The resultant judgment is an artifact of this self-description but one that also honors this established belief. In other words, associated units of information are activated and deactivated simultaneously, jointly constraining impressions, while honoring complex relationships between traits, beliefs, and behaviors that define the self.

Unlike earlier simple spreading activation models (e.g., Collins & Loftus, 1975; Quillian, 1968) which assumed that all associations are positive and capable of boundless activation, we assume that nodes activate and inhibit one another in addition to refusing participation in particular activation patterns. Again, the muscle man, when considering his athletic ability, will most likely suppress the memory or inhibit activation of the incident last week when the 10-pound bar bell proved too hefty after only one set. And if this incident is recalled, most likely the memory will die quickly, its activation decaying rapidly because it will be inhibited by many of the other nodes in the network. As such, this model draws considerable inspiration from network architectures proposed by connectionist theorists (Rumelhart & McClelland, 1986).

The following is a *conceptual sketch* of such a perspective, in the form of loosely defined networks that bear the properties just described. Although the model is not fully realized in mathematical, computational formulae, the following discussion is intended to lay the conceptual groundwork for models that would account for influences of self on social judgment already documented in the psychological literature.

Projection

People tend to project their own personal attitudes and attributes onto others (Holmes, 1968, 1978). Happy individuals are more likely to rate photographed others as happy compared to their downcast counterparts (Goldings, 1954). Students playing a game are likely to assume that their playing partner will choose the same cooperative or selfish moves as they do themselves (Messé & Sivacek, 1979). When people are asked to describe friends and acquaintances in their own words, the terms they use tend to be those that they use to describe themselves (Dornbusch, Hastorf, Richardson, Muzzy, & Vreeland, 1965; Lemon & Warren, 1974; Park, Kraus, & Ryan, 1997; Shrauger & Patterson, 1974).

Importantly, projection can be a useful aid in making accurate social judgments (e.g., Dawes, 1989). If Simon, for example, does not like cheese on pickles, he is probably safe in assuming that Paula will not either. However, people can project their attitudes and attributions onto others too much, perceiving much more similarity than is actually the case (Krueger, 1998). When deciding if Randy would enjoy driving a Chevy Nova, Simon most likely would be wrong if he bases his inference on his own preference for that car. Given that the majority of people would not find a Nova to provide an adequate level of driving excitement, Simon's reliance upon his own opinion would lead to errors in prediction and judgment.

A connectionist model can illustrate how and why people project their own attributes onto others, as well as when they will be more versus less likely to do so. Consider the model depicted in Figure 9.2 that illustrates a situation in which someone has to decide whether another person is *athletic*. The left-most node depicts the self-belief that one is athletic. This node activates a "hidden unit" (depicted as donut shaped circles) that filters or computationally mediates activations between nodes that represent traits, their valence, self-belief, and behavioral information. Because of the excitatory link between the hidden node 1 and the node representing beliefs about others' trait possession, this hidden unit then activates the belief that the other person is *athletic* the more the self is thought to be *athletic*.

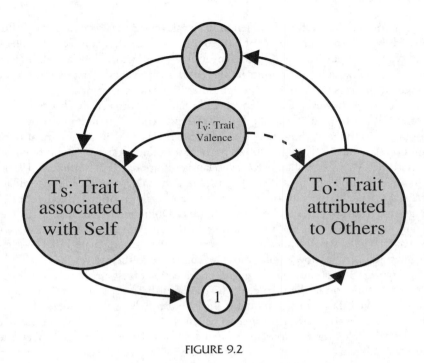

FIGURE 9.2

Figure 9.2 also contains another feature, represented by another node showing that *athletic* is considered to be a positive attribute. A wealth of past research shows that people attribute positive attributes to themselves more than they do to other people (e.g., Alicke, 1985; Brown, 1986; Weinstein, 1980; Kunda & Sanitioso, 1989). This phenomenon is illustrated by the fact that as a trait becomes more positive, the node responsible for documenting valence activates attribution of the trait to the self and inhibits it for other people. Depicted in this way, the model illustrated in Figure 9.2 shows how thoughts about target's abilities are constrained by beliefs about one's own athletic abilities. Specifically, the valence of *athletic* suggests people will frequently ascribe this trait to themselves. However, in doing so, it becomes increasingly unlikely to see others as *athletic*. That said, the fact that one possesses the belief that one is *athletic* will cause that trait to be applied to others.

Two notes must be mentioned about this model. First, if a person does not believe himself or herself to be athletic, then the node representing self-belief will be comparatively less activated. As a result, there is less activation to spread to other nodes in the system; this makes it less likely that others will be judged as athletic.

Second, the inclusion of hidden units in this model may seem to be superfluous. However, we retain the use of hidden units because they can receive, collect, and compare input from many different sources, not just the self (as will be seen later). As such, these hidden units imply that the self may not directly impact the judgment process but proceed through other filters or constraints.

There are, however, exceptions to and nuances of projection. People do not project all the time to all people. Instead, people tend to attribute their own attributes selectively to those they like, particularly those who are a part of one's ingroup (Clement & Krueger, 2002), or those they find attractive (Brent & Granberg, 1982; Marks & Miller, 1982; Moreland & Zajonc, 1982; Mashman, 1978). On an intimate level, members of satisfying and stable relationships assimilate their partners' interpersonal qualities, values, and daily emotional fluctuations to their own (Murray, Holmes, Bellavia, Griffin, & Dolderman, 2002). For example, couples expect that they and their partner are matched on dimensions of *warmth, dominance, importance of equality*, and *general happiness*, among many others—overestimating in reality how similar those intimates are to themselves.

Figure 9.3 illustrates that the degree of projection of self-attributes onto others varies as a function of the valence of the trait and the degree to which the target person is liked. Fixed in this model is the extent to which the evaluator feels he or she possesses the trait, the degree to which the target is liked, and the valence of the trait. Take, for example, the case of a self-proclaimed comic who feels she possesses a fine talent for humor. Certainly the ability to evoke laughter (without, of course, the use of props) is a desirable quality. The node representing self-beliefs the comic holds about her humor (T_s) supplies activation to hidden node 1.[3] The trait valence node (T_v) is excited, yet it is negatively related to T_o. However, the amount of inhibition it provides is minimal in comparison with that received from hidden node 1. If the situation asks the rising comic to judge whether her best friend (who also knows to avoid props) possess a keen wit, the likeability node (L) will also be activated and excite hidden node 1. The hidden node, then, receives positive activation from T_s, V, and L, which it will pass on to the node representing the level of humor attributed to her friend (T_o). Having received positive input, T_o will be activated and the friend dubbed a terrific comic.

However, say the rising comic is asked to determine whether a disliked rival is entertaining. L will feed negative activation to hidden node 1. T_v remains positively active but inversely related to T_o. Although T_s still excites the hidden node, the amount of activation T_o receives is qualitatively less. In such an instance, it is less probable that T_o will receive the positive input necessary to be activated and thus the trait less likely to be attributed to the rival.

Without necessitating changes, this model can also illustrate one interesting and unexpected wrinkle within the attributive projection literature—people are more likely to project *negative* traits onto people they like than they are to people they dislike (Bramel, 1963; Secord, Backman, & Eachus, 1964). For example, when Sherwood (1979) convinced a group of nurses that they possessed a high

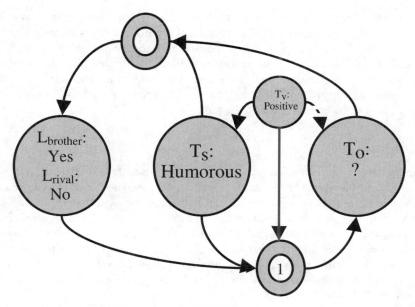

FIGURE 9.3

level of *neuroticism* (a negative trait), those nurses were more likely to tag other nurses they admired as neurotic than they were to tag nurses they disliked.

To illustrate how the model handles this surprising set of results, consider a circumstance in which the evaluator believes he or she possesses a negative trait and must evaluate whether a friend also possesses it. Excitation will be passed from T_s and L and aggregated in hidden unit 1. Although neuroticism would produce negative activation in T_v, T_o receives the inverse of the input as suggested by their negative relationship or weight, and so T_v will further excite T_o. Thus the aggregation of the input received from T_v, L, and T_o (by way of hidden unit 1) produces maximum activation of T_o. A friend is then labeled neurotic. However, when the target is disliked, T_o by way of hidden unit 1 is comparatively less active as L is now sending negative activation. T_o may not receive enough input in this instance to pass threshold. That is, a supposedly neurotic nurse is less likely to label disliked others similarly.

This model also handles further results of the Sherwood (1979) study. When nurses were not convinced of their neuroticism, they frequently attributed neuroticism to nurses they disliked more than they did to nurses they liked. Specifically, when the self is considered *not neurotic,* the system still functions in the same way. However, the current trait (*not neurotic*) is a positive one. When the target is liked, hidden unit 1 is excited by L and T_s. This activation is then passed along to T_o. Although the trait is positive, T_o considers the inverse of its activation, yet the impact is nominal. The conclusion then is that a friend is *not neurotic* as well. However, when the target is disliked, the *likeability* node inhibits activation of T_o. *Not neurotic*, a positive state, produces positive activation within T_v which in turn inhibits the activation of T_o. In such a situation, T_o is inhibited by T_v and receives less activation from hidden unit 1 compared to times when the target is liked. Accordingly, a target held in low regard is less likely to be labeled *not neurotic*, and more likely to be seen as neurotic, instead.

Polarization

Parallel constraint models can account for other self-related phenomena as well. For example, people who believe that they posses a positive trait provide more extreme, or polarized, judgments of others' along that trait dimension than do those who fail to claim the trait. Take, for instance, that those who consider themselves to be *sociable*, are far more likely to proclaim that another person who goes to several parties a week is an outgoing person than those who do not think of themselves as sociable. These same social bugs also more adamantly declare a wallflower avoiding all parties to be unsociable than those who do not see themselves as sociable (Lambert & Wedell, 1991).

Figure 9.4 depicts a connectionist model that can account for such polarization effects in social judgment, specifically describing the way in which beliefs about the self and actual behaviors can be incorporated into judgments about others. Suppose people who consider themselves *bold* were asked to judge the courage of a person who has just volunteered to bungee jump off a bridge into a gorge. Being bold themselves, they are more likely to think that they would volunteer to take the plunge.

From Figure 9.4, one can see that the node responsible for attributing boldness to this other person (T_o) would receive a great deal of activation from three sources. First, the behavior of the other person (B_o) directly activates the trait attribution of boldness as well as the hidden node. The second source of activation comes from the projection of self-beliefs of boldness (represented in T_s) onto the hidden node, which then excites attribution to the other person. Finally, a node representing the belief that self-behavior matches the other person's behavior ($B_s = B_o$) also produces activation in the hidden node. In addition, (T_s) maintains a recursive relationship with the $B_s = B_o$ node, leading to further activation of this particular behavior node and subsequently the hidden node, which collects all this activation and passes it along to T_o. The net effect of this activation is a strong inference of *boldness* to the other person.

However, suppose that the other person acts more timidly, refusing a chance to bungee jump. B_o will now inhibit the attribution of boldness. The $B_s = B_o$ node also provides negative activation, given that self-behavior is now the opposite of the other person's. Thus, the amount of activation needed to see the other person as bold is far from what is necessary to activate the node responsible for labeling the other as bold.

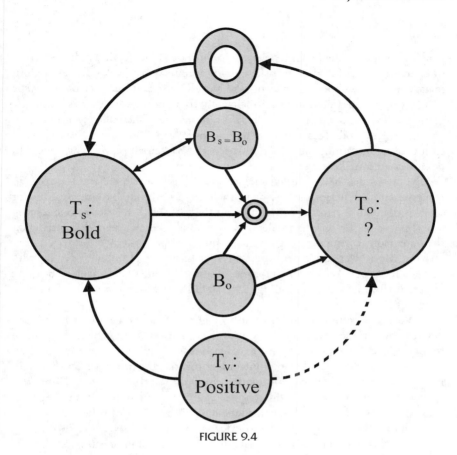

FIGURE 9.4

The model in Figure 9.4 also depicts why people denying boldness in themselves will not make such extreme judgments of others. Suppose such a person judged another who wanted to bungee jump. Again, B_o activates trait attribution of boldness. However, because self-behavior is not similar to the behavior of others (people who do not consider themselves to be bold are likely not to assume they would bungee jump), the $B_s = B_o$ fails to positively activate this system. In addition, because people do not think of themselves as bold, the T_s node refuses participation providing little activation that would support an attribution of boldness, either to the hidden unit or to the $B_s = B_o$ node.

In contrast, consider how a nonbold person would judge another person who forgoes an opportunity to bungee jump. The B_o node negatively activates attributions of boldness. The $B_s = B_o$ node will excite some activation, because self-behavior is once again similar to the other person's behavior, but this activation will not be promoted by a strong activation from the T_s node. Thus, again, attributions to the other person are muted.

Contrast

People also judge other people's behavior in contrast to their own. Finding out that someone else plays intramural basketball for 3 hours every week is not enough to make conclusions about another. Instead, deciding that another person is *athletic* depends on a consideration of self-behavior. To a person who exercises only by getting up from the couch to reach for the remote, the basketball player may seem like an athletic god. To a varsity athlete who devotes 20 hours a week to wind sprints, weight training, and team practice, the basketball player may appear to be more of a casual couch potato.

Many studies have revealed such contrast effects in which people appear to compare another person's behavior to their own, with notable implications for social judgment. A person scoring high on the math SAT, relative to one scoring low, thinks a person scoring moderately as less skilled in math and less intelligent than a person scoring low. A perpetually punctual person will consider another arriving late to class once per week as rather untimely, although a person who makes a habit of never arriving on time will consider the same person to be quite punctual (Beauregard & Dunning, 1998; Dunning & Cohen, 1992; Dunning & Hayes, 1996).

With only minimal modification to Figure 9.5, a connectionist model can describe how these contrast effects arise. See Figure 9.5, in which the general framework of the previous figure remains intact, with nodes representing trait attribution to self (T_s), behavioral information about the other person (B_o), and, most importantly, behavioral information about the self (B_s) activated. Within this model, we propose that the hidden node assumes a comparative process. Specifically, thoughts about personal behaviors and those actions of others are filtered through this hidden unit. Likewise, the degree to which the self possesses this trait feeds into this central hidden unit. The ultimate impression of this person's traits will depend on the relative strengths of the direct positive and negative associations of the observed behaviors, their indirect associations to another by way of the comparative hidden node, and beliefs about personal trait possession. A trivia buff, for example, who believes in her abilities and who outperforms the competition will be less likely to attribute superstar status to her competitors; however that trivia buff might be more inclined to assign superstar status to someone who outperforms her.

Suppose that we hear again about our 3-hour-a-week basketball player. That piece of information causes B_o to excite T_o. This piece of information also excites the hidden unit in the model. However, the hidden unit receives input from B_s as well; in particular, activation of the hidden unit is inhibited as B_s increases in strength. By linking the B_o node in an excitatory way, and B_s in an inhibitory way, we can capture the comparison processes central to the contrast effect described above. To the extent that the target shows a good deal of athletic activity (e.g., pursues athletic activities for a number of hours each week), the B_o node will excite the hidden unit and, thus, produce more trait attribution. However, to the extent

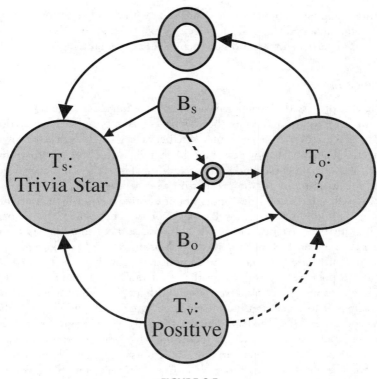

FIGURE 9.5

that the self engages in a good deal of athletic activity, the B_s node will inhibit the hidden unit and dampen any trait attribution. Thus, when self-performance is high, B_s will provide a large amount of inhibition and prevent trait attribution. When self-performance is low, B_s will provide less inhibition, thus permitting the activation flowing from B_o to further excite trait attribution.

This comparative aspect of this model also explains another phenomenon that has been revealed in social judgment: people tend to praise the brilliance of anybody who outperforms them on an intellectual task, a phenomenon termed the *genius effect* (Alicke, LoSchiavo, Zerbst, & Zhang, 1997). As the model in Figure 9.5 depicts, when someone outperforms us, their behavior (B_o) will directly and generously excite trait attributions of intelligence. Such trait attributions will also be boosted by the fact that B_o excites the hidden unit involved in the comparison process, whereas one's self behavior (B_s) is not inhibiting that unit to a great degree. Of key interest, once trait attributions of intelligence to the other person are activated (T_o), they will tend to excite attributions of intelligence to the self, leading people to view themselves as more intellectually capable than they would be without judging the other person. Consistent with this observation, Alicke et al. (1997) found that evaluating the intelligence of another person who outperformed them caused participants to also rate themselves as more intelligent.

Inference Effects

After having processed trait and behavioral information about others, people often make further attributions about others' skills. For example, once Ned has decided that Stacey is extroverted, he can infer whether Stacey would be a good coworker, intelligent, generally a happy person, or likely to be successful in future life. Past research shows that people tend to make additional inferences if they believe they possess the attribute in question. A person who believes himself or herself to be outgoing will infer a good deal more about another person if they decide that this other person is outgoing as well. If a person does not believe that he or she is outgoing, further inferences are avoided, or at least made in a more circumspect manner (Carpenter, 1988; Catrambone & Markus, 1987; Lewicki, 1983).

Hill, Smith, and Lewicki (1989) demonstrated that it is specifically the belief that the self possesses a positive trait that moderates this inference process. Students in a computer skills class were asked both at the beginning and at the end of the semester to make trait judgments about others who either did or did not possess computer skills. Those students consistently receiving grades of As and Bs in their computer skills course were increasingly likely as the semester progressed to report that other computer masterminds possessed exemplary social skills, had a good sense of humor, and were rather intelligent among a host of other positive traits. However, those computer students in doubt of their skill, after having received Cs and Ds throughout the term, were less likely to indicate that computer skills were indicative of other qualities. Instead, they claimed, through their ratings of others, that computer skills would not provide much insight even into traits seemingly closely associated with computer skills, such as memory and mathematical abilities.

Figure 9.6 provides a pictorial description of this trait inference process. Again notice there are nodes representing an individual's belief in their possession of a particular trait (T_s), an individual's belief that this trait is shared by another (T_o), and one describing the valence of the trait in question (T_v). Activation and information from these three nodes feed into a hidden unit which transforms this input and subsequently triggers the trait inference process. The rectangular node depicts the host of related traits that one may attribute to target individual. Note that the arrow or connection in Figure 9.6 from trait valence to the hidden unit is thicker. This heavier line is meant to imply that the weight between these two nodes would be stronger than the weight between either of the other two nodes and the hidden unit. The hidden unit is receiving proportionally more input from T_v than the other two nodes. However, once activated, the hidden unit can feed back to T_s and T_o. This recursive function suggests that activation of T_s and T_o can be updated based on the current activations of any of the other nodes. As Figure 9.6 depicts, high-flying computer students, aware of their talents through course feedback, have activated T_s. As Hill and colleagues (1989) simply told participants that they were judging other talented computer students, T_o is activated. Finally, it can be argued that those students in a computer course felt it desirable to possess such a skill, hence their choice of study. As a result, T_v provides positive activation to the hidden unit. The additive total output then would activate the *additional attributions* node.

However, for those computer students left to believe that their skills were a bit lacking, activation of T_s would be close to zero. Although making judgments about a skilled target on such a positive trait would suggest activation of these other nodes, the cumulative activation received by the hidden unit would be significantly less. The downstream consequence of this is decreased input to omnibus *additional attributions* node. The result then might be reluctance to describe the target along any other dimension.

This model in particular appears quite localistic and modular in how it functions. Obviously vague, we mean to imply that sets of traits housed in the *additional*

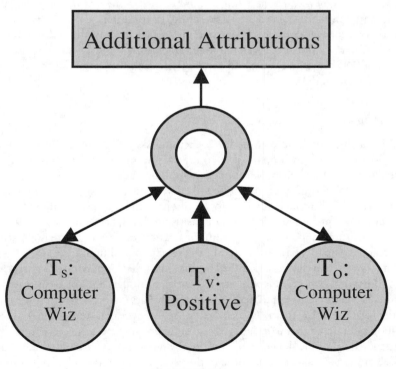

FIGURE 9.6

attributions node are themselves a product of a web of beliefs constructed under the logic of additional parallel constraint satisfaction models. The particular constellation of traits that will be attributed to the target other is individualized. For each individual, there is a particular pattern of correlated traits or descriptions that might be inferred about the target. Behavioral and other situational information, as well as semantic relations, assist in determining which traits will be included in this additional attributions node. Thus, we leave a description of the mechanism behind the activation and implementation of the additional attributions node vague in this particular description but suggest that it too is the result of a learned series of associations that develops over time. We are merely suggesting a framework for consideration of the types of information that assist in such an attribution process. We certainly advocate for and have earlier suggested how the contents of each of these nodes are additional distributed, parallel processing systems.

ADVANTAGES OF A CONNECTIONIST FRAMEWORK

In sum, connectionist models that focus on parallel constraint satisfaction networks can go a long way toward modeling a number of self-effects that have long been documented in the social judgment literature. Beyond that, such models can also provide other advantages for researchers interested in how the self is linked to and presumably influences social judgment. Revealing those advantages, however, involves discussing some issues and concerns often and appropriately raised about those types of models.

Falsifiability

In this chapter, we have provided a conceptual sketch of connectionist models that can account for the impact of self on social judgment. The models allow us to formally specify how self-beliefs, liking or disliking of the target, other cognitions, and judgments about others might be linked in a coherent and systematic way. By their nature, such models force us to specify how the self might influence social judgment in a precise and internally consistent manner. In our efforts, we have shown how such models might account for a variety of actual judgmental patterns that real participants have exhibited in the psychological literature.

However, one can raise skeptical points about the connectionist approach we have illustrated here. One could argue that such models are not falsifiable: One just takes judgmental patterns already in the literature and constructs a *post hoc* model to account for them. As a consequence, even if such models fully account for judgmental patterns in a rigorous and coherent way, because these models are constructed to mimic data already out there, there is no way to test whether these models are actually a truthful account of the psychology behind those data or merely an aesthetically-pleasing yet false fiction. There is no independent test that these models actually depict the processes by which people make judgments of others.

In this chapter, we have focused exclusively on how such models can account for past data, and so do not take issues about falsifiability dead-on. However, it is possible to test whether such models truthfully reflect how people go about making social judgments. Namely, such models can be tested by seeing if they predict judgmental patterns not yet seen in the literature. That is, models can be used to generate new hypotheses of how people reach judgments, at which point researchers can return to the laboratory to see if people act in accord with these new hypotheses. Indeed, one can argue that one of the strengths of connectionist models is that their very nature often suggests new ways of thinking about old phenomena, and can generate many new hypotheses to test.

In the models we have described, one sees how a variety of different cognitions (e.g., beliefs about the self, liking for another individual, trait attributions toward that other individual) are linked together. Our focus has been on how all these linkages work together to influence judgments of another person, but it is clear from these models that judgments of that other person can, in turn, influence the cognitions such judgments are linked to. Our models, as is true of most connectionist models, allow all nodes in the model to influence one another—a trait that is known as *full connectivity*. Because of this, such models expand the types of issues this chapter and other research in the area of self and social judgment have considered.

For example, Figure 9.3 depicts a case in which liking for a target person can influence whether the person will be ascribed traits similar or dissimilar to the self. Although this model describes the judgments and decisions made by nurses about friends and foes, it suggests an interesting turn of events not investigated within Sherwood's (1979) initial inquiry. In particular, one might surmise that if a trait describes both oneself and another person, liking toward the other person could be altered—and this, in fact, is the case. People expect that their liking for another person will be affected by their similarity to that person (Chapdelaine, Kenny, & LaFontana, 1994) and they are generally right (see Wakimoto & Fujihara, 2004 for a recent example). These notions suggest several new avenues for future work on the relationship between self and social judgment.

Self-Concept Changes

Connectionist perspectives, and parallel-distributed processing more generally, have gained advocates within and outside psychology (e.g., Adeli & Hung, 1995; Todd & Loy, 1991). The variety of models we have sketched here share many features with the types described by other researchers. In particular, although the networks we have presented here are, in a sense, organized around the self, it is not the case that the *self* comprises an omnipresent singular node spreading activation through the entire system. Instead, the self arises out of a connected series of beliefs and opinions that refer to it and its environment (as depicted in Figure 9.1). This property has important implications for how one could view the interaction between self-belief and social judgment.

Perhaps the most important implication is that our approach to self and social judgment does not hold the self "constant." Instead, it is possible to look at changes to "self" over time and with the addition of new types of information about other people. The self may influence how people view others—but the behavior and attributes of those other people may importantly change how people view themselves, and connectionist models allow for that revision. If a student's roommate—the one with the lower LSAT score—is accepted into Harvard Law, then that student's self-beliefs about their potential to get into a good law school may very well change.

Thus, this framework here suggests how vast complexes of interacting social information systems quite frequently include that the "interjection" of information pertinent to the self can produce changes in self-concept. For example, Figure 9.3 was designed to model how beliefs about the self might inform the trait evaluations that people make of others. However, this model could also be used to describe how impressions of others might, in turn, modify evaluations of the self. Dunning and Cohen (1992, Study 4) demonstrated that when considering lackluster performances of others, the self is used to modify impressions of them. However, it might be the case that when a target's behavior is extremely positive, views of the self are instead modified. For example, consider how reading a biography of Einstein might produce more changes in the reader's self-beliefs about intelligence than self-beliefs influence evaluations of Einstein's intellect. It is precisely the full connectivity that provides enough flexibility to suggest and describe such interactions.

Of course, the next research step would be to use such a model to predict when and which particular nodes will be subject to the most change. When will cognitions about the self most influence assessments of others? When will assessments of others most influence opinions of the self?

The Role of Self-Esteem

Carrying this line of thinking further, the impact of self on social judgment versus social judgment on the self may very well depend on a person's self-esteem. Self-esteem is commonly described as personal evaluations of worth and competence (Baumeister, Campbell, Krueger, & Vohs, 2003). Those who have high self-esteem possess a strong sense of belonging, competence, and purpose. Those without it are painted as withdrawn, unenthusiastic, insecure souls. These differences in self-esteem also extend to assessments of others. High self-esteem individuals tend to describe friends or randomly selected others on positive traits less favorably than themselves. That is, they display the highest degree of thinking themselves as unique and special—in a positive direction. Conversely, those low on self-esteem are less likely to assert superiority over friends or others on positive traits, and do not rate themselves any differently than the same groups on negative traits (Brown, 1986; Martin, Abramson, & Alloy, 1984; Suls, Lemos, & Stewart, 2002; Taylor & Brown, 1988).

More intriguing, the major difference in self-concepts between high and low self-esteem individuals involves the clarity of the self-concept (Baumgardner, 1990; Campbell, 1990). Low esteem is associated with uncertainty in assessments of the self (Baumgardner, 1990). Those low in esteem also provide less extreme and confident self-ratings about their skills and talents. Those assessments tend to be less internally consistent and show less stability over a 2-month interval. Low self-esteem individuals are also slower in reaction time studies to describe their personal characteristics (Campbell, 1990). Such evidence suggests that low self-esteem individuals possess a less solid and coherent concept about the self. Those high in self-esteem seem to have established a clearer picture of their personal traits, skills, and actions than those low in self-esteem.

This definition suggests that the self associated with a low self-esteem individual would influence social judgment much less than the self associated with a high self-esteem person. And, indeed, data do suggest this. Low self-esteem individuals are less likely to project their talents and attributes onto their definitions of social traits, and less likely to have their judgments of others biased by what they believe about themselves (Beauregard & Dunning, 2001; Campbell, 1986). People with low self-views are also less likely to use their behavior as a benchmark against which others are judged—instead paying attention more directly to the specific behavior the other person has displayed (Dunning & Beauregard, 2000).

Given this conception of esteem—one that is moderated by self-clarity—one might rightly assume that the literature to which we refer and on which we base our models describes more specifically those with high self-esteem. However, the differential consequences for social judgments between those high and low self-esteem can be modeled quite easily within a connectionist framework in any of three ways. First, attributions by low self-esteem individuals may not employ nodes representing personal trait ascriptions. If it is unclear to a person low in esteem whether he or she can be considered *athletic*, then models would not need to even include a node representing personal possession of that trait. Second, those low in esteem may think of themselves as athletic, but because they have less of a concrete idea of all the beliefs that represent the self, a node representing this belief may not be connected within the network to many other nodes involving self-information. Finally, a person may believe herself to be athletic and use this belief in assessments of others and the self. However, the weights or connections between nodes may in fact be quite weak or easy to change. The impact of this particular bit of information within the network might then be minimal.

Thus, there are several mechanisms or models that might be behind the comparative lack of reliance on self-information for those low in esteem—and little work has been attempted to dissociate these possibilities. That said, what seems clear is that those high in esteem utilize more strongly their own beliefs and behaviors as a comparative basis within the social judgment process, but explaining why that exploitation occurs would involve untangling why low self-esteem individuals fail to follow the same steps. Perhaps, though, the answer lies within the issue of self-clarity.

Intrapersonal versus Interpersonal Selves

Casting self and social judgment in connectionist networks suggests new ways of exploring other ways in which people are connected. We have emphasized instances where assessments of others are biased by the infusion of self-information in the judgment process. However, a cursory glance at this chapter would suggest that we have been focusing primarily on how the *intrapersonal* self—one defined by personal, internal dispositions, abilities, attitudes, and behaviors—constrains and interacts with the social judgment process. In particular, the intrapersonal self calls for personal success, separateness from others, and uniqueness (see Sedikides, Gaertner, & Toguchi, 2003 for a discussion). Such a self-construal could cloud innumerable considerations. Opinions of others' skills, traits, and abilities, we argue, are often the product of egocentric comparisons (Alicke, 1993; Dunning & Cohen, 1992) or the concurrent activation of information about the self (Dunning & Hayes, 1996). The results, then, are judgments of others that are biased by inflated, overly optimistic personal behavioral predictions and attitudinal and trait assessments about the self.

Such egocentric comparisons and self-enhancing consequences may not be universal in magnitude but ones that are exacerbated by an intrapersonal self-construal. Specifically, the drive toward uniqueness and the demand to excel above expectations, the status quo, or a comparison group is strongly tied to individualistic contexts (Heine et al., 1999; Markus & Kitayama, 1991). In contrast, many collectivist cultures emphasize interconnectedness, building a sense of self through the development of relationships with others, and adopting a realization that behavior is determined by the thoughts, feelings, motivations, and actions of others within a social unit—giving rise to an *interpersonal self,* one that defines the self more in terms of interpersonal relationships and social roles. These cultures emphasize the pursuit of maximum collective welfare obtained by adjusting oneself to the group. The goal of conformity requires accurate perceptions of the expectations and behaviors of the group (see Markus & Kitayama, 1991 for a review). It seems improbable that these same egocentric and self-serving predictions would appear within a collectivist culture that encourages a drive toward group unity and whose members admit (more so than do individualists) that their behavior is guided by social norms (Heine, Lehman, Okugawa, & Campbell, 1992).

Here, we have done little to specifically address the impact of the interpersonal self for social judgment. An interpersonal self-construal, as opposed to one that advocates for independence, would likely contribute to perceptions of the similarity between self and friend (Cross, Morris, & Gore, 2002, Studies 5 & 6). Because of this, investigations of people maintaining relational self-construals or interpersonal selves may produce comparatively scant evidence for self-serving evaluations of others and the infusion of the self into social judgments. However, that would not be to say that the self fails to influence social judgment: People's views of others might need to remain harmonious with beliefs about one's interpersonal self, and constraint satisfaction models might reveal themselves to be a useful way to account for such a process. Those who define themselves through their relationships to others would still require a web of beliefs that align in some degree of accord. Future research could explore this possibility.

Self as an Automatic and Not Deliberate Self-Serving Influence

In addition, modeling self and social judgment phenomena through parallel constraint satisfaction network gives a different flavor to the role played by the self in social judgment from that usually portrayed in the social psychological literature. Usually, the impact of self on social judgment is depicted as an active and intentional process. People wish to maintain positive images of self, and so they deliberately tailor their evaluations to bolster such images. However, according to a connectionist approach, the impact of self on social judgment might be more automatic and mechanical. People just need to activate some sort of background information to judge others, and information about the self usually happens to be available.

Thus, we might take a step back and ask how self-relevant information comes to be immediately included in social judgment processes. It could be that the interjection of the self into social judgments is so common and occurs so frequently that eventually it becomes automatic. Just as with increased experience we can successfully ride a bike to work without having to consciously consider every left turn or each landmark along the way, the inclusion of self-relevant information may be a process that functions on auto-pilot the more frequently we find ourselves in a social judgment task (see Gilovich et al., this volume, for similar speculations).

These models, and this theoretical push in general, allow for the activation of self-relevant information without a motivational agenda. Patterns defining the self might be activated automatically, or at minimum concurrently, within the social judgment process. People may not inject the self into social judgment primarily as a means toward self-enhancement, but rather may insert the self in the judgmental process simply as an artifact of the manner in which social information is routinely represented internally and judgments are reached. Judgments of others may turn out to be self-enhancing, then, not because of deliberate intent, but rather because the self-beliefs people impose upon on their understanding of social information just happen to be positive ones. Thus, instead of accepting models that suppose information about the self is consciously, intentionally, and purposefully called upon in the judgment process, this perspective suggests that the imposition of the self occurs automatically. Future research could examine whether the impact of self-information does proceed in such an automatic manner.

However, motivational accounts for the reliance upon the self are not at odds with this automatic, connectionist approach to the social judgment process. Although a timeline has not yet been investigated, it might be the case that self-relevant information is activated immediately at the start of an attribution task, an automatic process. However, motivated needs to affirm the self may still come into play as a more deliberative and conscious process, particularly when self-esteem is under pressure (e.g., Beauregard & Dunning, 1998; Dunning, Leuenberger, & Sherman, 1995), leading to social judgments that are even more biased in favor of the self. In such a system, the integration of self-relevant information into judgment processes may be immediate but still modified at times by higher order, effortful, and conscious reports of comparisons (see Alicke & Govorun, this volume; Gilovich et al., this volume, for related discussions).

Alternatively, it could be the case that motivation influences the rather positive beliefs that people have about themselves, especially as people spend a lifetime mulling over their abilities and evaluating the content of their character. Once in place, these distorted beliefs (a product of motivation) then have an automatic (and not "deliberately" motivated) impact on judgments of others. In short, the judgment made today of another person may not in of itself be an active and deliberate act of distortion designed to enhance one's self-esteem. However, the judgment may still be motivationally biased in the sense that it is based on a number of distorted self-beliefs that have been put into place in the person's past.

SUMMARY

Thus, connectionist models are often used as springboards for theorizing about interesting interactions among components of social judgment. Such models expand the conceptual horizon. By adding or focusing on different variables in a connectionist web, it is possible to account for a greater proportion of either statistical variance or observed behavior. That is, we can see which component of the model produces the biggest differences to the end product or is most changed as a result of the process. A model is capable of suggesting relationships among variables that perhaps were left unconsidered in original studies and can be tested against novel behavioral observations. In this way, the flexibility that modeling offers is not a weakness but one of its foremost strengths (Siegle & Hasselmo, 2002).

Concluding Remarks

It has long been observed that the self is related to and presumably influences social judgment (for reviews, see Dunning, 2002a). However, although that observation has a longstanding status, there is still much work to be done to explain why that link between the self-beliefs and social beliefs arises. In this chapter, we have sketched one possible approach to the interrelationships between self and social judgment, and described how that approach might explain some specific phenomenon known in the field, as well as describe how judgments of other people are really *de facto* judgments of two.

However, a close reading of this chapter, as well as of this entire volume (and, indeed, the current psychological literature), suggests just how much more work must be done to understand why judgments of others seem so pervasively tied to opinions about the self. We believe that, although a connectionist approach might not be the only one available to study self and social judgment, it is a particularly promising one.

ACKNOWLEDGMENTS

Preparation of this chapter was facilitated financially by NIMH Grant RO1 56072, awarded to David Dunning. We thank Rick Dale for his wise guidance around the terrain of connectionist modeling.

NOTES

1. Our coding strategy for traits in this network is usually referred to as a *localist* scheme, in that each trait stands for one local node in the network. Another strategy, often thought theoretically key to connectionism, is the distributed encoding strategy. This sees traits not as individual nodes, but complex patterns of nodes that fire together. Even when connectionist modelers of cognition use the localist scheme, there is often an assumption that it is a convenient idealization (Elman, 2001). We adopt this assumption here. We describe traits and beliefs about the self as individual nodes although we presume that the underlying structure of such nodes is too a function of more complex social processes.
2. Although not displayed in these models, weights (i.e., the markers of the strength of the connections) indicate the relative importance of the information being passed amongst nodes. Weights, combined with each node's level of activity or activation, are important computationally if these models were to be implemented. The activation of each node is calculated after the model settles on a pattern of activation that takes into consideration all of the relative inputs from other nodes. Weights would need to be specified when the model is put through repeated, parallel cycles of activation, adjustment, and updating.
3. If this model were to be implemented, most likely this hidden layer would contain multiple hidden units to allow for full connectivity; Figure 9.2, though, means to simply provide a theoretical framework in which to consider how the self could function in such a network.

REFERENCES

Adeli, H., & Hung, S. L. (1995). *Machine learning: Neural networks, genetic algorithms, and fuzzy systems.* New York: Wiley.

Alicke, M. D. (1985). Global self-evaluation as determined by the desirability and controllability of trait adjectives. *Journal of Personality and Social Psychology, 49,* 1621–1630

Alicke, M. D. (1993). Egocentric standards of conduct evaluation. *Basic and Applied Social Psychology, 14,* 171–192.

Alicke, M. D., LoSchiavo, F. M., Zerbst, J., & Zhang, S. (1997). The person who outperforms me is a genius: Maintaining perceived competence in upward social comparison. *Journal of Personality and Social Psychology, 72,* 781–789.

Baumeister, R. F., Campbell, J. D., Krueger, J. I., & Vohs, K. D. (2003). Does high self-esteem cause better performance, interpersonal success, happiness, or healthier lifestyles? *Psychological Science in the Public Interest, 4,* 1–44.

Baumgardner, A. H. (1990). To know oneself is to like oneself: Self-certainty and self-affect. *Journal of Personality & Social Psychology, 58,* 1062–1072.

Beauregard, K. S., & Dunning, D. (1998) Turning up the contrast: Self-enhancement motives prompt egocentric contrast effects in social judgments. *Journal of Personality and Social Psychology, 74,* 606–621.

Beauregard, K. S., & Dunning, D. (2001). Defining self worth: Trait self-esteem moderates the use of self-serving trait definitions in social judgment. *Motivation and Emotion, 25,* 135–162.

Biernat, M., Manis, M., & Kobrynowicz, D. (1997). Simultaneous assimilation and contrast effects in judgments of self and others. *Journal of Personality and Social Psychology, 73,* 254–269.

Bramel, D. A. (1963). Selection of a target for defensive projection. *Journal of Abnormal and Social Psychology, 66,* 318-324.

Brent, E. E., & Granberg, D. (1982) Subjective agreement with the presidential candidates of 1976 and 1980. *Journal of Personality and Social Psychology, 42,* 393–403.

Brown, J. D. (1986). Evaluations of self and others: Self-enhancement biases in social judgments. *Social Cognition, 4,* 353–376.

Campbell, J. D. (1986). Similarity and uniqueness: The effects of attribute type, relevance, and individual differences in self-esteem and depression. *Journal of Personality and Social Psychology, 50,* 281–294.

Campbell, J. D. (1990). Self-esteem and clarity of the self-concept. *Journal of Personality & Social Psychology, 59,* 538–549.

Carpenter, S. (1988). Self-relevance and goal-directed processing in the recall and weighting of information about others. *Journal of Experimental Social Psychology, 24,* 310–332.

Catrambone, R., & Markus, H. (1987). The role of self-schemas in going beyond the information given. *Social Cognition, 5,* 349–368.

Catrambone, R., Beike, D., & Niedenthal, P. (1996). In the self-concept a habitual referent in judgments of similarity? *Psychological Science, 7,* 158–163.

Chapdelaine, A., Kenny, D. A., & LaFontana, K. (1994). Matchmaker, matchmaker, can you make me a match?: Predicting liking between two unacquainted persons. *Journal of Personality and Social Psychology, 67,* 83–91.

Clement, R. W., & Krueger, J. (2000). The primacy of self-referent information in perceptions of social consensus. *British Journal of Social Psychology, 39,* 279–299.

Clement, R. W., & Krueger, J. (2002). Social categorization moderates social projection. *Journal of Experimental Social Psychology, 38,* 219–231.

Collins, A. M., & Loftus, E. F. (1975). A spreading-activation theory of semantic processing. *Psychological Review, 82,* 407–428.

Cross, S. E., Morris, M. L., & Gore, J. (2002). Thinking about oneself and others: The relational-interdependent self-construal and social cognition. *Journal of Personality and Social Psychology, 82,* 399–418.

Dornbusch, S. M., Hastorf, A. H., Richardson, S. A., Muzzy, R. E., & Vreeland, R. S. (1965). The perceiver and the perceived: Their relative influence on the categories of interpersonal cognition. *Journal of Personality and Social Psychology, 1,* 434–440.

Dunning, D. (1999). A newer look: Motivated social cognition and the schematic representation of social concepts. *Psychological Inquiry, 10,* 1–11.

Dunning, D. (2002a). *The relation of self to social perception.* In M. Leary and J. Tangney (Eds.), Handbook of self and identity (pp. 421–441). New York: Guilford Press.

Dunning, D. (2002b). The zealous self-affirmer: How and why the self lurks so pervasively behind social judgment. In S. Fein & S. Spencer (Eds.) *Motivated social perception: The Ontario symposium* (Vol. 9, pp. 45–72), Mahwah, NJ: Erlbaum.

Dunning, D., & Beauregard, K. S. (2000). Regulating impressions of others to affirm images of the self. *Social Cognition, 18,* 198–222.

Dunning, D., & Cohen, G. L. (1992). Egocentric definitions of traits and abilities in social judgment. *Journal of Personality and Social Psychology, 63,* 341–355.

Dunning, D., & Hayes, A. F. (1996). Evidence for egocentric comparison in social judgment. *Journal of Personality and Social Psychology, 71,* 213–229.

Dunning, D., Leuenberger, A., & Sherman, D. A. (1995). A new look at motivated inference: Are self-serving theories of success a product of motivational forces? *Journal of Personality and Social Psychology, 69,* 58–68.

Dunning, D., Meyerowitz, J. A., & Holzberg, A. D. (1989). Ambiguity and self-evaluation: The role of idiosyncratic trait definitions in self-serving assessments of ability. *Journal of Personality and Social Psychology, 57,* 1082–1090.

Dunning, D., Perie, M., & Story, A. L. (1991). Self-serving prototypes of social categories. *Journal of Personality and Social Psychology, 61*, 957–968.

Elman, J. L., Bates, E. A., Johnson, M. H., Karmiloff-Smith, A. et al. (1996). Rethinking innateness: A connectionist perspective on development. *Neural network modeling and connectionism, No. 10*. Cambridge, MA: The MIT Press.

Fiske, S. T., & Taylor, S. E. (1991). *Social cognition* (2nd edition). New York: McGraw-Hill.

Goldings, H. J. (1954). On the avowal and projection of happiness. *Journal of Personality, 23*, 30–47.

Gilovich, T. (1990). Differential construal and the false consensus effect. *Journal of Personality and Social Psychology, 59*, 623–634.

Heine, S. J., Lehman, D. R., Markus, H. R., & Kitayama, S. (1999). Is there a universal need for positive self-regard? *Psychological Review, 106*, 766–794.

Heine, S. J., Lehman, D. R., Okugawa, O., & Campbell, J. D. (1992). The effects of culture on self-implicated processes: A comparison of Canadians and Japanese. *Ritsumeikan Social Sciences Review, 28*, 29–39.

Herr, P. M. (1986). Consequences of priming: Judgments and behavior. *Journal of Personality and Social Psychology, 51*, 1106–1115.

Herr, P. M., Sherman, S. J., & Fazio, R. H. (1983). On the consequences of priming: Assimilation and contrast effects. *Journal of Experimental Social Psychology, 19*, 323–340.

Higgins, E. T. (1996). Knowledge activation: Accessibility, applicability, and salience. In E. T. Higgins & A. W. Kruglanski (Eds.), *Social psychology: Handbook of basic principles* (pp. 133–168). New York: Guilford Press.

Higgins, E. T., & Lurie, E. T. (1983). Context, categorization, and memory: The "change-of-standard" effect. *Cognitive Psychology, 15*, 525–547.

Higgins, E. T., & Stangor, C. (1988). A "change-of-standard" perspective on the relations among context, judgment, and memory. *Journal of Personality and Social Psychology, 54*, 181–192.

Hill, T., Smith, N., & Lewicki, P. (1989). The development of self-image bias: A real-world demonstration. *Personality and Social Psychology Bulletin, 15*, 205–211.

Holmes, D. S. (1968). Dimensions of projection. *Psychological Bulletin, 69*, 248–268.

Holmes, D. S. (1978). Projection as a defense mechanism. *Psychological Bulletin, 83*, 677–688.

Holyoak, K. J., & Gordon, P. C. (1983). Social reference points. *Journal of Personality and Social Psychology, 44*, 881–887.

Karniol, R. (2003). Egocentrism versus protocentrism: The status of self in social predication. *Psychological Review, 110*, 564–580.

Krueger, J. (1998). On the perception of social consensus. *Advances in Experimental Social Psychology, 30*, 163–240.

Krueger, J. I. (2003). Return of the ego—self-referent information as a filter for social prediction: Comment on Karniol (2003). *Psychological Review, 110*, 585–590

Kunda, Z. (1999). *Social cognition: Making sense of people*. Cambridge, MA: MIT Press.

Kunda, Z., & Sanitioso, R. (1989). Motivated changes in the self-concept. *Journal of Experimental Social Psychology, 25*, 272–285.

Kunda, Z., & Thagard, P. (1996). Forming impressions from stereotypes, traits, and behaviors: A parallel-constraint-satisfaction theory. *Psychological Review, 103*, 284–308.

Lambert, A. J., & Wedell, D. H. (1991). The self and social judgment: Effects of affective reaction and "own position" on judgments of unambiguous and ambiguous information about others. *Journal of Personality and Social Psychology, 61*, 884–897.

Lemon, N., & Warren, N. (1974) Salience, centrality and self-relevance of traits in construing others. *British Journal of Social and Clinical Psychology, 13*, 119–124.

Lewicki, P. (1983). Self-image bias in person perception. *Journal of Personality and Social Psychology, 45*, 384–393.

Marks, G., & Miller, N. (1982). Target attractiveness as a mediator of assumed attitude similarity. *Personality and Social Psychology Bulletin, 8*, 728–735

Marks, G., & Miller, N. (1987). Ten years of research on the false-consensus effect: An empirical and theoretical review. *Psychological Bulletin, 102*, 72–90.

Markus, H., & Kitayama, S. (1991). Culture and the self: Implications for cognition, emotion, and motivation. *Psychological Review, 98,* 224–253.

Martin, D. J., Abramson, L. Y., & Alloy, L. B. (1984). Illusion of control for self and others in depressed and nondepressed college students. *Journal of Personality and Social Psychology, 46,* 125–136.

Mashman, R. C. (1978). The effect of physical attractiveness on the perception of attitude similarity. *Journal of Social Psychology, 106,* 103–110.

Messé, L. A., & Sivacek, J. M. (1979). Predictions of others' responses in a mixed-motive game: Self-justification or false consensus? *Journal of Personality and Social Psychology, 37,* 602–607.

Moreland, R. L., & Zajonc, R. B. (1982). Exposure effects in person perception: Familiarity, similarity, and attraction. *Journal of Experimental Social Psychology, 18,* 395–415.

Murray, S. L., Holmes, J. G., Bellavia, G., Griffin, D. W., Dolderman, D. (2002). Kindred spirits? The benefits of egocentrism in close relationships. *Journal of Personality and Social Psychology, 82,* 563–581.

Mussweiler, T. (2003). When egocentrism breeds distinctness: Comparison processes in social prediction. *Psychological Review, 110,* 581–584.

Mussweiler, T., & Bodenhausen, G. V. (2002). I know you are but what am I? Self-evaluative consequences of judging ingroup and outgroup members. *Journal of Personality and Social Psychology, 82,* 19–32.

Mussweiler, T. & Rüter, K. (2003). What friends are for — The use of routine standards in social comparison. *Journal of Personality and Social Psychology, 85,* 467–481.

Quillian R. M, (1968) Semantic memory. In Minsky, M. (Ed.) *Semantic information processing.* (pp. 227–270). Cambridge, MA: MIT Press.

Park, B., Kraus, S., & Ryan, C. S. (1997). Longitudinal changes in consensus as a function of acquaintance and agreement in liking. *Journal of Personality and Social Psychology, 72,* 604-616.

Prentice, D. (1990). Familiarity and differences in self-and other-representations. *Journal of Personality and Social Psychology, 59,* 369–383.

Read, S. J., & Marcus-Newhall, A. (1993). Explanatory coherence in social explanations: A parallel distributed processing account. *Journal of Personality and Social Psychology, 65,* 429–47.

Read, S. J., & Miller, L. C. (Eds.) (1998). *Connectionist models of social reasoning and social behavior.* Mahwah, NJ: Erlbaum.

Ross, L., Greene, D., & House, P. (1977). The false consensus phenomenon: An attributional bias in self-perception and social perception processes. *Journal of Experimental Social Psychology, 13,* 279–301.

Rumelhart, D. E., & McClelland, J. L. (1986). On learning the past tenses of English verbs. In J. L. McClelland, D. E. Rumelhart, and the PDP Research Group (eds.), *Parallel distributed processing: Explorations in the microstructure of cognition* (Vol. 2, pp. 216–271).

Secord, P. F., Backman, C. W., & Eachus, H. T. (1964). Effects of imbalance in the self concept on the perception of persons. *Journal of Abnormal and Social Psychology, 68,* 442–446.

Sedikides, C. (2003). On the status of self in social prediction: Comment on Karniol (2003). *Psychological Review, 110,* 591–594.

Sedikides, C., Gaertner, L., Toguchi, Y. (2003). Pancultural self-enhancement. *Journal of Personality and Social Psychology, 84,* 60–79

Sherif, M., & Hovland, C. I. (1961). *Social judgment: Assimilation and contrast effects in communication and attitude change.* New Haven, CT: Yale University Press.

Sherwood, G. G. (1979). Classical and attributive projection: Some new evidence. *Journal of Abnormal Psychology, 88,* 635–640.

Shrauger, J. S., & Patterson, M. B. (1974). Self-evaluation and the selection of dimensions for evaluating others. *Journal of Personality, 42,* 569–585.

Shultz, T. R., & Lepper, M. R. (1996). Cognitive dissonance reduction as constraint satisfaction. *Psychological Review, 103,* 219–240.

Siegle, G. J., & Hasselmo, M. E. (2002). Using connectionist models to guide assessment of psychological disorder. *Psychological Assessment, 14,* 263–278.

Smith, E. R. (1996). What do connectionism and social psychology offer each other? *Journal of Personality and Social Psychology, 70,* 893–912.

Smith, E. R, & DeCoster, J. (1998). Knowledge acquisition, accessibility, and use in person perception and stereotyping: Simulation with a recurrent connectionist network. *Journal of Personality and Social Psychology, 74*, 21–35.

Suls, J., Lemos, K., & Stewart, H. (2002). Self-esteem, construal and comparisons with self, friends and peers. *Journal of Personality and Social Psychology, 82*, 252–261.

Suls, J., & Wheeler, L. (Eds.). (2000). *Handbook of social comparison: Theory and research*. New York: Kluwer Academic/Plenum Publishers.

Taylor, S. E., Brown, J. D. Illusion and well-being: A social psychological perspective on mental health. *Psychological Bulletin, 103*, 193–210.

Todd, P. M., & Loy, D. G. (Eds.). (1991). *Music and connectionism*. Cambridge, MA: MIT Press.

Van Overwalle, F., & Labiouse, C. (2004). A recurrent connectionist model of person impression formation. *Personality and Social Psychology Review, 8*, 28–61.

Wakimoto, S., & Fujihara, T. (2004). The correlation between intimacy and objective similarity in interpersonal relations. *Social Behavior and Personality, 32*, 95–102.

Weinstein, N. D. (1980). Unrealistic optimism about future life events. *Journal of Personality and Social Psychology, 39*, 806–820.

Wheeler, L., Martin, R., & Suls, J. (1997). The proxy model of social comparison for self-assessment of ability. *Personality and Social Psychology Review, 1*, 54–61.

10

A Hierarchy Within
On the Motivational and Emotional Primacy of the Individual Self

LOWELL GAERTNER
University of Tennessee
CONSTANTINE SEDIKIDES
University of Southampton

*E*xtend to someone the seemingly straightforward invitation "So, tell me about yourself," and prepare for a narrative barrage of traits, interests, roles, and relationships. To say the least, the self-concept is a complex collection of diverse representations, definitions, or motivationally- and emotionally-laden personality aspects. Of particular relevance to the current chapter are two general forms of self: the individual and collective. The individual self represents unique aspects that distinguish a person from others. The collective self represents aspects shared with ingroup members that assimilate a person with others. In other words, people conceptualize themselves both as unique or independent entities and as undifferentiated or interconnected group members. The coexistence of these different (and sometimes antagonistic) forms of self raises an interesting and important question regarding the essence of the self-concept: Does either self deserve the status of "primary?"

In this chapter, we review a program of research that addresses empirically the issue of self-definitional primacy from a motivational and emotional framework. According to this framework, the more primary self is the one that reacts most intensely to threat and enhancement. Metaphorically speaking, the more primary self is the one that screams the loudest when harmed and smiles the brightest when praised. Capitalizing on the fact that this framework is more textured than an "either/or" argument, our research program addresses three competing hypotheses.

THREE HYPOTHESES OF MOTIVATIONAL AND EMOTIONAL PRIMACY

The Individual-Self-Primacy Hypothesis

According to this hypothesis, the individual self is primary and provides the motivational and emotional essence of the self-concept. This hypothesis is supported, in part, by research on: (1) self-stability, (2) self-enhancement, and (3) the role of the individual in natural selection.

Stability of the Individual Self

The core individual self consists of self-schemas that are held with high certainty and regarded as important. These self-schemas remain relatively stable across time (Pelham, 1991; Pelham & Wachsmuth, 1995) and situations (Bem & Allen, 1974; Roberts & DelVecchio, 2000). Being resistant to internal (e.g., mood; Sedikides, 1995) and external (e.g., feedback; Sedikides, Campbell, Reeder, & Elliot, 1998) changes, self-schemas perpetuate by incorporating affirming information (Sedikides, 1993) and facilitating memorial and behavioral confirmation (Swann, Pentfrow, & Guinn, 2003). The self-schemas further promote stable self-perceptions by guiding the processing of information about self (Markus, 1977) and others (Sedikides, 2003) as well as projecting onto meta-perceptions of self (Kenny & DePaulo, 1993). Attesting to the self-schemas' tenacity, stability, and deflection of undesirable information, Greenwald (1980) likened them to a totalitarian regime.

Enhancement of the Individual Self

Research reveals a strong motivation to protect and to enhance the individual self (for reviews, see Baumeister, 1998; Sedikides & Gregg, 2003). For example, people are more likely to make internal attributions for favorable than unfavorable outcomes (Campbell & Sedikides, 1999), avoid social comparison following poor personal performance in self-relevant domains (Gibbons, Persson Benbow, & Gerrard, 1994), perceive their own attributes as more positive than those of the average person (Alicke, 1985; Alicke & Govorun, this volume), and have better memory for positive than negative self-relevant attributes (Sedikides & Green, 2004; Walker, Skowronski, & Thompson, 2003). In group settings, members take individual credit for the group's success and deny individual blame for the group's failure (Mullen & Riordan, 1988; Schlenker & Miller, 1977). The motive to protect and enhance the individual self is not only pervasive but also functional: Taylor, Lerner, Sherman, Sage, and McDowell (2003a, b; but see Kwan, John, Kenny, Bond, & Robbins, 2004) have documented a relation between enhancement of the individual self and psychological / biological health.

The Individual in Natural Selection

Classic evolutionary theory argues that natural selection operates on the individual of a given species (Dawkins & Krebs, 1978; Wiley, 1983; Wallace, 1973). More recent theory construes the individual self as a human trait that evolved in response to ecological and social forces and, consequently, affords the human organism with several advantages such as social-information processing, affect regulation, and goal-pursuit (Sedikides & Skowronski, 1997, 2000, 2003; Sedikides, Skowronski, & Gaertner, 2004). This perspective suggests that the primacy of the individual self is a consequence of selection pressures that favored the welfare of the individual.

The Collective Self Primacy Hypothesis

According to this hypothesis, the collective self is primary and provides the motivational and emotional essence of the self-concept. This hypothesis is supported by (1) theories involving social groups in natural selection and (2) the perspective that the collective self is the optimal self.

Social Groups in Natural Selection

Despite periods of waxing-and-waning popularity, theories of group selection suggest that natural selection operates on groups of a given species and selection pressures favor, at times, traits and behavioral tendencies that promote the welfare of the collective (Bulmer, 1978; Wilson & Sober, 1994). A somewhat different view on human evolution regards the social group as the primary environment for individual-level selection (Caporael & Brewer, 1991; Caporael & Baron, 1997). This view, however, also suggests that selection pressures favor traits and behaviors that promote the welfare of the group: individuals less fit for a group environment (e.g., unwilling or unable to cooperate and display loyalty) were less likely to be accepted in the group and, consequently, less likely to reap the survival advantages of group living (e.g., shared resources, cooperative child-rearing). In summary, these perspectives suggest that the primacy of the collective self is a consequence of selection pressures that favored the welfare of the group.

The Collective Self as the Optimal Self-Definition

Optimal distinctiveness theory (ODT; Brewer, 1991; Brewer & Roccas, 2001) states that fluctuations in self-definition arise in response to competing needs for assimilation and differentiation. Definition in terms of the individual self maximizes differentiation but at the expense of assimilation. Definition in terms of the collective self, however, enables the simultaneous satisfaction of assimilation and differentiation via intragroup and intergroup comparison, respectively. Given its ability to provide an optimal level of self-definition, the collective self arguably has a privileged status within the self-concept.

THE CONTEXTUAL-PRIMACY HYPOTHESIS

According to the contextual-primacy hypothesis, neither self is inherently primary. Instead, contextual factors that influence the relative accessibility of the individual and collective self determine *momentary* primacy. Perspectives that emphasize the context dependent nature of self-definition support this hypothesis.

The construct of a working self-concept (Markus & Kunda, 1986; Markus & Wurf, 1987), for example, accounts for the stability and malleability of self-definition. The working self-concept consists of the subset of self-aspects that are currently accessible, with accessibility influenced by the chronic activation of a self-aspect as well as situational factors that render self-aspects immediately salient. Likewise, self-categorization theory (SCT; Onorato & Turner, 2004; Turner, Hogg, Oakes, Reicher, & Wetherell, 1987; Turner, Oakes, Haslam, & McGarty, 1994) suggests that fluctuations in self-definition arise from contrasts afforded by the social context. Based on SCT's principle of meta-contrast (i.e., social categories become salient to the extent to which the degree of difference perceived between aggregates of stimuli outweigh the degree of difference perceived within aggregates of stimuli), the collective self becomes increasingly salient in intergroup contexts and the individual self becomes increasingly salient in intragroup contexts.

In summary, three equally plausible hypotheses offer rival accounts of the essence of the self-concept. Each hypothesis is reasonable in its own right and draws from a body of psychological theory for support. Nonetheless, these hypotheses are not mutually compatible, and, likely one hypothesis is more empirically plausible and tenable than the others. So, which self provides the essence of the self-concept? Is the individual-self primary? Is the collective-self primary? Does primacy depend on contextual factors?

To discern the most empirically tenable hypothesis, we designed a program of research that pitted the hypotheses head-to-head in an empirical competition—a sort of self-Olympics. We hosted the initial competitions in the domain of threat.

PRIMACY IN THE DOMAIN OF THREAT

In three studies, we compared relative reactions to threats against the individual versus collective self with the rationale being that threatening stimuli are experienced more negatively and reacted to more forcefully when directed to the more primary self. Of course, careful methodological control was of crucial importance to maintain the validity of our comparisons. We directed threatening information at one self without simultaneously threatening the other self to provide an accurate assessment of the unique motivational or emotional potential of each self. We varied across studies the dimension on which the selves were threatened and held constant the particular dimension of threat within a study to prevent confounding the target of threat (individual, collective) with a particular dimension of threat. We assessed varied reactions to threat across studies to rule out the possibility that any conclusion regarding primacy is unique to a particular reaction. Finally, across studies we implemented different procedures of controlling the relative accessibility of the individual and collective self in order to be able to carry out a valid assessment of the contextual-primacy hypothesis.

Threat and Concurrent Accessibility

In an initial study (Gaertner, Sedikides, & Graetz, 1999, Investigation 1), we first rendered cognitively accessible both the individual self and the collective self and then threatened one of those selves. Participants were female undergraduates at the University of North Carolina at Chapel Hill (UNC-CH). We operationalized the collective self in regard to membership in the group UNC-CH women. Computerized instructions informed participants that the Department of Psychology was assessing the characteristics of female undergraduates on behalf of the (fabricated) Office of Student Affairs (OSA).

We imbedded in the instructions phrases intended to prime both the individual and collective self. For example, to prime the individual self, instructions indicated that the student body at UNC-CH is "extremely diverse; after all, each one of you is an individual with your own unique background, personality traits, skills, abilities, and hobbies." To prime the collective self, instructions also informed participants that "you also share membership with other students in various social groups... [O]ne of the most important social groups to which people belong is gender... you are female, and you share membership in the social group UNC-CH women."

Participants completed the "highly reliable and valid" Berkeley Personality Inventory (BPI). For the first half of the BPI, participants responded to 30 statements vaguely related to emotional states (e.g., "Sad movies touch me deeply"). For the second half of the BPI, participants indicated how frequently during the previous month they experienced each of 30 emotions (e.g., cheerful, afraid). Instructions subsequently informed participants that the computer was in the process of scoring their responses to the BPI. During this time, we initiated our manipulation of threat directed either at the individual or collective self.

To instigate threat, we provided feedback regarding the trait "moodiness," a trait that a pilot sample of female UNC-CH students considered negative and stereotypic of women. Instructions explained that the BPI assesses the trait moodiness, which refers to "an inability to control one's mood state. People who are moody experience frequent and inconsistent shifts in their feelings in response to various situational cues. Moodiness creates potential problems in social interactions, because others are unable to anticipate one's mood state and behavior."

Additional information indicated that moodiness "is a very important personality trait. High levels of moodiness have been found to be related to poor adjustment to college life, pessimism, poor mental health, unsatisfactory social relationships, low academic success, and even low success after college." The computer then informed participants that the scoring of the BPI was complete.

To threaten the individual self, we provided computerized feedback indicating that "participant #53191 is excessively moody." The feedback reiterated the previously presented information regarding the trait moodiness and its negative consequences in the second person (i.e., "Moodiness refers to an inability to control your mood state ... ").

We provided similar feedback when threatening the collective self. However, instructions indicated that the OSA would not allow the presentation of personalized feedback. Instead, participants would receive feedback concerning the average score of the 1,500 UNC-CH women tested, excluding their own score. Feedback indicated that "UNC-CH women are excessively moody" and reiterated the previously presented information regarding the trait moodiness and its negative consequences in reference to UNC-CH women (i.e., "Moodiness refers to an inability for UNC-CH women to control their mood state ... ").

So, which self, if either, metaphorically screamed louder? Participants' reactions were consistent with the individual-self-primacy hypothesis. Participants considered the threatening feedback to be more negative and reported feeling more displeased when the feedback threatened the individual than collective self.

Despite support for the individual-self-primacy hypothesis, it is possible that the methodology of this initial study was inadequately refined and, indeed, biased against the other hypotheses. In particular, participants may have responded more passively to a threat of their collective self because the group that comprised the collective self (i.e., UNC-CH women) was of minimal importance. Research suggests that high group identifiers are more apt to protect their group's identity under conditions of threat than nonthreat (e.g., Branscombe & Wann, 1994; Spears, Doojse, & Ellemers, 1997). Consequently, we decided to "raise the bar" in our second round of empirical tests and differentiate between low and high group identifiers. The contextual-primacy hypothesis suggests that the individual self is primary among low group identifiers, whereas the collective self is primary among high group identifiers.

Threat and Group Identification

In the second study (Gaertner et al., 1999, Investigation 2), we informed male and female undergraduates at UNC-CH that we were conducting a project on behalf of a national testing agency that gathered data on the creativity of college students. An experimenter explained that the students would complete a highly valid creativity test, but first they would answer a demographics questionnaire. We embedded in the questionnaire three items that assessed identification with UNC-CH: "How important is your university to you?", "To what extent does being a member of your university reflect an important aspect of who you are?", and "How much do you identify with your university?"

To control for the possibility that the dimension of threat (i.e., creativity) was of differential importance to the individual and collective self, we administered a prethreat measure of importance. Participants rated how important creativity is to "you" or "UNC-CH students" depending on whether they would receive a threat to their individual or collective self, respectively. Both low and high group identifiers considered creativity more important to the individual than collective self. Consequently, we included this prerating of importance as a covariate in all statistical comparisons to adjust for the differential importance of the dimension of feedback.

Participants subsequently completed a 10 minute creativity test in which they listed as many uses as possible for a brick and then for a candle. The experimenter scored the test and provided participants with written feedback.

The threat to the individual self-informed participants "Your total score... was calculated to be at the 31st percentile. This means that your score is worse than 69% of the creativity scores in the normative reference sample." A histogram providing a graphic depiction of the student's performance accompanied the written feedback.

The threat to the collective self-informed participants that, for ethical reasons, we could not provide personalized feedback, but we could provide feedback about the average performance of UNC-CH students, excluding their own score. Written feedback indicated "UNC-CH's total score... was calculated to be at the 31st percentile. This means that UNC-CH's score is worse than 69% of the creativity scores in the normative reference sample." A graphic depiction of UNC-CH's performance accompanied the written feedback.

We measured two reactions to the threatening feedback: feedback derogation and mood state. To assess derogation, we asked participants to rate the importance of the outcome of the test for either "you" or "UNC-CH students," depending on whether the feedback pertained to the individual or collective self, respectively. Participants subsequently rated the extent to which 14 unpleasant-mood adjectives (e.g., upset, miserable, threatened) described their feelings. Research indicates that the tactic to disparage threatening-feedback serves a self-protective function (e.g., "sour grapes;" Wyer & Frey, 1983). Consequently, a threat to the more primary self should result in a more negative mood and a stronger derogation of the feedback.

The results conceptually replicated the previous study and were fully consistent with the individual-self-primacy hypothesis. Regardless of group identification, participants experienced more emotional-distress and disparaged the threat more vociferously when the threat pertained to the individual than collective self. In particular, group identification did not moderate reactions to the threatening feedback. Both low and high identifiers reported a more negative mood state and considered creativity less important when they personally were characterized as relatively uncreative as opposed to when UNC-CH students were characterized as relatively uncreative. After two rounds of competitive hypothesis testing, the individual-self-primacy hypothesis best accounts for the available data and is ahead in the Olympics.

Threat and Alternating Accessibility

We approached the accessibility issue in the previous studies either by making both selves accessible or differentiating participants in regard to their level of group identification. In a third study (Gaertner et al, 1999, Investigation 3), we varied a contextual factor that influences the relative accessibility of the selves. In particular, the meta-contrast principle of self-categorization theory suggests that the individual self becomes increasingly salient in interpersonal contexts and the collective self becomes increasingly salient in intergroup contexts (Hogg & Turner, 1987; Turner et al., 1987). Following such a principle, we directed either threatening or nonthreatening information to the individual self in an interpersonal context or to the collective self in an intergroup context. In other words, we maximized the accessibility of one self and minimized the accessibility of the other self—a practice that enabled us to compare the relative reaction of the individual and collective self in contexts in which each self is maximally accessible. The reaction that we assessed was self-reported anger.

Six UNC-CH undergraduate students participated per session. In the individual-self condition, we randomly divided participants into three 2-person dyads and each participant sat in a separate cubicle. Participants anticipated interacting with their partner on a Prisoner's Dilemma Game (PDG) and subsequently received either insulting or noninsulting feedback from their partner. In the collective-self condition, we randomly divided participants into two 3-person groups and each group sat in a separate cubicle. Each group anticipated interacting with the other group on a PDG and subsequently received insulting or noninsulting feedback from the other group.

Each person or group received instructions on how to read a 3-choice PDG and completed a brief comprehension exercise. To ostensibly save time, the experimenter distributed evaluation forms and suggested that each person (or group) check the accuracy of the other person's (group's) comprehension exercise. Participants received their opponent's answers (actually a standardized form), rated the answers, and, if desired, provided written comments. The experimenter returned the original exercises along with bogus performance feedback.

Participants in the noninsult condition received a high rating and a written comment indicating, "This group (person) did well. They (he or she) really seem(s) to know what's going on." Participants in the insult condition received a low rating and a written comment indicating, "This group (person) did not do well. They (he or she) must be a little slow." Participants subsequently indicated how much anger they felt at the moment.

The individual-self-primacy hypothesis suggest that an insult will arouse more anger when directed to the individual than to the collective self, but noninsulting information will be equally (non)arousing to the individual and collective self. However, the collective-self-primacy hypothesis suggests that an insult will arouse more anger when directed to the collective than individual self, but noninsulting information will be equally (non)arousing to the individual and collective self. Finally, the contextual-primacy hypothesis suggests that an insult will arouse equivalent anger in the two selves and both selves will express stronger anger in response to insulting than noninsulting information.

The results, once again, were consistent with the individual-self-primacy hypothesis. Noninsulting information aroused equally low levels of anger when directed to the individual versus collective self. Insulting information, on the other hand, aroused more anger when directed to the individual than collective self. Even in contexts that maximize the accessibility of the relevant selves, threat to the individual self elicited a stronger reaction than did threat to the collective self.

Prior to our competitive hypothesis tests in the domain of threat, three rival-hypotheses offered equally plausible accounts of self-primacy. In the aftermath of those empirical competitions, only one hypothesis remained unscathed and capable of accounting for the data. The empirical competitions controlled contextually relevant variables (e.g., level of group identification, accessibility of the selves) and potential confounding variables (e.g., relative importance of the threat dimension). Even with those methodological controls, participants considered a threat more severe, experienced a more negative mood state, felt more angry, and more vigorously derogated the source of the threat when the threat pertained to the individual self. These findings suggest that the individual self is motivationally and emotionally primary (Sedikides & Gaertner, 2001a, b).

A META-ANALYTIC SYNTHESIS

Encouraged by the consistent results of our laboratory experiments, we engaged an alternative method of testing the three hypotheses (Gaertner, Sedikides, Vevea, & Iuzzini, 2002). That alternative method was a meta-analysis (Johnson & Eagly, 2000). We approached the meta-analysis with two objectives: to test the hypotheses in the domains of enhancement and threat, and to address a potential criticism endemic to our laboratory studies.

We achieved our first objective by identifying existing studies that empirically compared reactions of the individual and collective self to threat and enhancement, respectively. Of course, the vast majority of those studies were designed with a purpose other than examining the primacy issue. Nonetheless, a meta-analysis would enable us to integrate the results of those studies and empirically compare which of the three hypotheses best accounts for the existing data. Concerning our second objective, the potential criticism of our laboratory studies is that the results are limited to the particular procedures, threats, and social groups that we used. The meta-analysis is particularly appealing because it enables the application of a random-effects analysis, which tests whether inference generalizes to other *possible* studies varying in particular procedures and characteristics (Hedges & Vevea, 1998; National Research Council, 1992).

Literature Search

We began our meta-analysis with a search of the literature for data relevant to the primacy issue. We searched the database of PsychINFO between the years of 1970 and April 2000 using the broad search terms "individual" and "group," as well as the focused terms "individual self," "individual identity," and "personal identity" for the individual self and "collective self," "collective identity," and "social identity" for the collective self. We subsequently searched the Social Sciences Citation Index for articles citing authors who, according to our PsychINFO search, published research relevant to the primacy issue. Furthermore, we browsed the social and personality psychology journals between January 1970 and April 2000. Our search identified 37 effects that met our inclusion criteria.

Inclusion Criteria

Because the majority of the studies were not designed to test the primacy issue, we included studies only if they met explicit criteria that enabled a meaningful comparison of the competing hypotheses. The independent variable separately threatened the individual and collective self or separately enhanced the individual and collective self. Likewise, the dependent variable assessed comparable responses of the individual and collective self, such as mood state, perceived valence of feedback, and trait ratings of the individual and collective self. Gaertner et al. (2002) list the included and excluded studies and offer a description of the inclusion criteria.

Studies included in the domain of threat, for example, provided unfavorable information about the performance or characteristics of the individual and collective self, respectively, or used a within-subjects format in which participants rated the individual and collective self, respectively, on unfavorable traits. Likewise, studies included in the domain of enhancement provided favorable information about the performance or characteristics of the individual and collective self, respectively, or used a within-subjects format in which participants rated the individual and collective self, respectively, on favorable traits.

Quantifying the Primacy Hypotheses

We calculated an effect size from each study by standardizing the mean difference between the response of the individual versus collective self to threat or enhancement. In other words, the effect-sizes assessed the extent to which the individual self reacted to a threat (or enhancement) relative to the extent to which the collective self reacted to a threat (or enhancement). The competing hypotheses offer unique predictions regarding the pattern of aggregated effect-sizes.

The individual-self-primacy hypothesis predicts that persons will (1) react more vigorously to threat or enhancement of the individual than collective self and will (2) more willingly deny threatening information or accept enhancing information when the information pertains to the individual than collective self. On the other hand, the collective-self-primacy hypothesis predicts the opposite pattern. Persons will (1) react more vigorously to threat or enhancement of the collective than individual self and will (2) more willingly deny threatening information or accept enhancing information when the information pertains to the collective than individual self.

The contextual-primacy hypothesis predicts that contextual factors will moderate the relative reaction of the individual and collective selves to threat and enhancement. We coded the effect sizes for two contextual variables relevant to the primacy issue: identification and type of group. Identification reflects the extent to which the social group momentarily provides self-definition (Abrams, 1994; Branscombe & Wann, 1994). We coded each effect size as reflecting high or low group identification. For some effect sizes, the primary study directly assessed whether identification was high or low. For other effect sizes, we inferred level of identification based on a meta-contrast criterion derived from self-categorization theory: We coded effects from intergroup contexts as high-identification and effects from intragroup contexts as low identification. Whether identification was determined by the primary study or by the meta-contrast criterion did not influence the results of the meta-analysis.

We coded as a second contextual moderator the type of group on which the collective self was based. Some studies used natural groups (e.g., fraternity or sorority affiliation, gender, political party membership, university affiliation). Other studies established novel groups using the minimal-group paradigm (Tajfel, 1970). Minimal and natural groups differ in several respects (Ostrom & Sedikides, 1992) that could influence the relative primacy of the collective self. Minimal groups, by definition, are novel. Members have negligible familiarity and experience with such groups and are less committed and invested in them (compared to natural groups).

The contextual-primacy hypothesis anticipates that identification and type of group moderates the relative reaction of the individual versus collective self to threat and enhancement. In particular, a pattern of individual-self-primacy should emerge when persons identify weakly with the social group or when a minimal group provides the basis of the collective self. On the other hand, a pattern of collective-self-primacy should emerge when persons identify strongly with the social group or when a natural group provides the basis of the collective self.

Which Hypothesis Best Accounts for the Existing Data?

The pattern of the effect-sizes was uncomplicated and consistent with only the individual-self-primacy hypothesis. Neither identification nor type of group moderated the relative reaction of the individual versus collective self to threat or enhancement. Persons reacted more strongly to both threatening and enhancing information when the information was directed to the individual self than to the collective self.

In terms of the estimated effect sizes, persons responded 5/10ths of a standard deviation more strongly ($g = 0.546$) when a threat was directed to the individual self than to the collective self, and they responded approximately 4/10ths of a standard deviation more strongly ($g = .383$) when enhancement was directed to the individual self than to the collective self. Furthermore, the random-effects analysis broadens our scope of inference beyond the specifics of the studies included in the analysis and allows for the probability that the strong tendency toward individual-self-primacy generalizes across forms of enhancement and threat, modes of reaction, and groups upon which a collective-self is based.

PANCULTURAL VITALITY OF THE INDIVIDUAL SELF

Our laboratory studies and meta-analysis provide a remarkably consistent and sizeable pattern of effects suggesting the presence of a basic social psychological phenomenon: the motivational and emotional primacy of the individual self. Challenging such an assertion, however, is what some might consider the ultimate contextual moderator of social functioning: culture.

The cultural-self perspective is based on Triandis' (1989) conceptualization of self in cultural context and is exemplified by Markus and Kitayama's (1991a, b) theory of independent versus interdependent self-construal. The core tenet of this perspective is that the cognitive, emotional, and motivational elements of the self-system are culturally constructed. Social institutions, teachings, proverbs, and symbols transmit cultural norms and ideals that articulate standards of behavior and social values. Those norms and ideals define the essence of what it means to be a good person and, when internalized as a self-construal, shape the self-system such that cognitive processes, emotional experiences, and motivational strivings are orchestrated in accordance with cultural standards and values.

The cultural-self perspective distinguishes between the self-construals fostered by Western versus Eastern culture. Western culture (e.g., North America, North and Western Europe, Australia) emphasizes independence, uniqueness, and personal success (Bellah, Madsen, Sullivan, Swidler, & Tipton, 1985; Cahoone, 1996; Spindler & Spindler, 1990). That is, the normative imperative of Western culture is to "become independent from others and to discover and express one's unique attributes" (Markus & Kitayama, 1991a, p. 226). Internalizing the Western mandate fosters an independent (i.e., idiocentric, separate, individualistic) self-construal (Markus & Kitayama, 1991ab; Triandis, 1989).

Eastern culture, in contrast, emphasizes interpersonal harmony, the importance of others, and group cohesion (Bond, Leung, & Wan, 1982; De Vos, 1985; Hsu, 1948; Leung, 1997). That is, the normative imperative of Eastern culture is to "maintain...interdependence among individuals" (Markus & Kitayama, 1991a, p. 227). Internalizing the Eastern mandate fosters an interdependent (i.e., allocentric, connected, collectivistic) self-construal (Markus & Kitayama, 1991a, b; Triandis, 1989).

The cultural-self perspective casts doubt on the functioning of the individual self in Eastern culture and suggests that primacy varies by culture or, more specifically, cultural self-construal: The individual-self is primary among persons with (or in cultures that promote) an independent self-construal, whereas the collective self is primary among persons with (or in cultures that promote) an interdependent self-construal. We explored this culture-as-contextual-primacy hypothesis in three studies. In one study, we explored self-generated descriptions of the individual and collective self as a function of self-construal. In two studies, we compared enhancement of the individual self as a function of nationality and self-construal.

Self-Description and Self-Construal: Who Am I?

Trafimow, Triandis, and Goto (1991) report data that, in our opinion, provide evidence of the pancultural primacy of the individual self. These researchers primed either the individual or collective self of North American and Chinese university students. The students subsequently performed a self-description task in which they completed 20 statements beginning with "I am." Trafimow et al. coded descriptions of personal qualities as indicators of the individual self and descriptions of demographic categories and social groups as indicators of the collective self.

Chinese students and students whose collective self was primed listed more descriptions of their collective self than did American students and students whose individual self was primed. Of greater interest, neither culture nor priming moderated the relative frequency of individual- versus collective-self descriptions. Students listed more descriptions of their individual than collective self regardless of their culture of origin and priming condition.

Describing one's self predominantly in terms of individual qualities is certainly consistent with the individual-self-primacy hypothesis. Nevertheless, several caveats challenge a pancultural generalization of this interpretation. It is possible that the Chinese sample had only a minimal interdependent self-construal. Enrolled in a North American university, the Chinese students may have developed a predominantly independent self-construal. This acculturation account, however, is inconsistent with the tendency for Chinese students to list more collective-self descriptions compared to American students. Alternatively, the greater relative frequency of individual-self descriptions may be an artifact of the self-description task. Requiring students to describe the self with "I am" phrases may have biased self-descriptions toward the individual self (Brewer & Gardner, 1996). Furthermore, the coding technique may have disproportionately favored the tally of individual-self descriptions. Some of the attributes coded as descriptions of the individual self may have been considered by students as overlapping with the collective self.

We addressed these caveats with a conceptual replication and a refined procedure (Gaertner et al., 1999, Investigation 4). During an initial session, students completed the self-construal scale (Singelis, 1994) which assesses levels of independent and interdependent self-construal. A week later, students listed 20 statements that "generally describe you." This revised task does not mention "I" or "we" and, consequently, favors neither the individual nor collective self—"you" can refer to either self. Next, students were provided with explicit definitions of the individual and collective self, and they proceeded to indicate whether each of their 20 statements described one or the other self. We defined the individual-self for participants as "attributes and characteristics that are unique to you as an individual. That is, the individual self is composed of attributes or characteristics that differentiate you from all other people." We defined the collective-self for participants as "attributes and characteristics that you share with members of important groups to which you belong. That is, the collective self is composed of attributes or characteristics that make you similar to other people in your groups."

The results replicated those of Trafimow et al. (1991). Students with a higher level of an interdependent self-construal listed more descriptions of their collective self than did students with a lower level of an interdependent self-construal. More importantly, self-construal did not moderate the relative frequency of individual versus collective-self descriptions. Students listed more descriptions of their individual than collective self, regardless of their level of independent or interdependent self-construal. These results demonstrate the cultural consistency of individual-self-primacy.

Pancultural Enhancement of the Individual-Self: I am More Modest than Others?

When we introduced the individual-self-primacy hypothesis, we discussed research that points to a strong motivation to protect and enhance the positivity of the individual-self. The majority of such research, however, was conducted in Western culture and the cultural perspective has raised the argument that self-enhancement is a motive unique to Western culture (Heine, Lehman, Markus, & Kitayama, 1999). Although positively distinguishing self from others promotes the normative imperative of Western culture, such a motivation ostensibly is antagonistic to the Eastern imperative of maintaining connectedness. Consistent with this argument are cross-cultural comparisons indicating that European Americans and Canadians self-enhance more strongly than do Japanese, for whom a self-effacing (or critical) orientation appears characteristic (Heine & Renshaw, 2002; Heine, Kitayama, & Lehman, 2001; Kitayama, Markus, Matsumoto, Norasakkunkit, 1997). Assessing the literature, Heine et al. (1999) concluded that "the need for positive self-regard... is not a universal, but rather is rooted in significant aspects of North American culture" (p. 766).

Such an argument is certainly at odds with the individual-self-primacy hypothesis. The extant data, however, are not fully consistent with the cultural perspective. Implicit assessments of self-regard manifest individual-self enhancement in Eastern cultures, such as Japan (Kitayama & Karasawa, 1997; Kobayashi & Greenwald, 2003), Singapore (Pelham, Koole, Hetts, Hardin, & Seah, 2002),

Thailand (Hoorens, Nuttin, Erdelyi-Herman, & Pavakanun, 1990), and southern European countries (Nuttin, 1987). Furthermore, omnibus comparisons of self-enhancement between cultures potentially conceal an alternative effect of culture. As we subsequently elaborate, cross-cultural research needs to be sensitive to the dimensions on which self-enhancement is expressed and assessed.

Candid and unswerving self-aggrandizement is unsavory even in Western culture and yields mockery and disdain (Leary, Bednarski, Hammon, & Duncan, 1997; Paulhus, 1998; Schlenker & Leary, 1982). Rather than indiscriminately enhancing the individual self, Westerners (and, as we suspect, Easterners) enhance strategically (Sedikides & Strube, 1997). Self-enhancement, for example, is expressed most vociferously on important attributes (Alicke, 1985; Alicke & Govorun, this volume; Dunning, 1995). To the extent to which cultural mandates differentially imbue attribute dimensions with meaning and importance, we would expect to find cultural differences on the dimensions on which self-enhancement is expressed. Stated otherwise, the need to enhance the individual self may be a universal motive whose expression is culturally shaped.

We subjected the latter possibility to empirical scrutiny in two studies (Sedikides, Gaertner, & Toguchi, 2003). Across the studies, we implemented alternative operationalizations of culture. We compared the self-enhancement tendencies of Japanese and American students in Study 1 and of persons with an independent versus interdependent self-construal in Study 2. As determined by pilot testing, half of the attributes upon which participants could self-enhance were relevant to the individualistic mandate of Western culture (e.g., unique) and half were relevant to the collectivistic mandate of Eastern culture (e.g., compromising).

Participants imagined being part of a 16-person task force and interacting with the other 15 members (of the same gender, ethnicity, age, and education level of the participant) in an attempt to solve various business problems (e.g., budget, recruitment). Next, participants rated the extent to which each of the individualistic and collectivists attributes described themselves versus the typical group member (-5 = *much worse than the typical group member*, 0 = *as well as the typical group member*, 5 = *much better than the typical group member*). That is, participants compared self and other on individualistic and collectivistic dimensions, and the rating scale provided the possibility to self-enhance by positively distinguish self from other (i.e., positive numbers), self-efface by negatively distinguishing self from other (i.e., negative numbers), or not differentiate self and other (i.e., rating of 0).

The patterns of self-other ratings were remarkably similar across studies and revealed a pancultural motive to enhance the individual self on culturally relevant dimensions. Figure 10.1 presents the average self-other ratings on the individualistic (light bars) and collectivistic (dark bars) dimensions as a function of Nationality (Study 1) and self-construal (Study 2). Within-culture comparisons (i.e., comparing the magnitude of the light and dark bars within samples) revealed that Americans and persons with an independent construal self-enhanced (i.e., positively differentiated self from other) more strongly on the individualistic than collectivistic dimension, whereas Japanese and persons with an interdependent construal self-enhanced more strongly on the collectivistic than individualistic dimension. Likewise, between-culture comparisons (i.e., comparing the light and dark bars, respectively, across samples) revealed that Americans and persons with an independent construal self-enhanced more strongly than did Japanese and persons with an interdependent construal on the individualistic dimension, whereas Japanese and persons with an interdependent construal self-enhanced more strongly than did Americans and persons with an independent construal on the collectivistic dimension.

Furthermore, importance ratings obtained in Study 2 provide insight as to why self-enhancement varies across dimensions of social comparison as a function of culture. The importance ratings tracked the patterns of self-enhancement such that persons with an independent self-construal rated the attributes of the individualistic dimension to be more personally important and persons with an interdependent construal rated the attributes of the collectivistic dimension to be more personally important. Mediation analyses were consistent with the possibility that culture affected the perceived importance of an attribute, which, in turn, affected the extent to which persons self-enhanced. By shaping social conceptions of what is good, valued or ideal, culture affects the dimensions upon which the

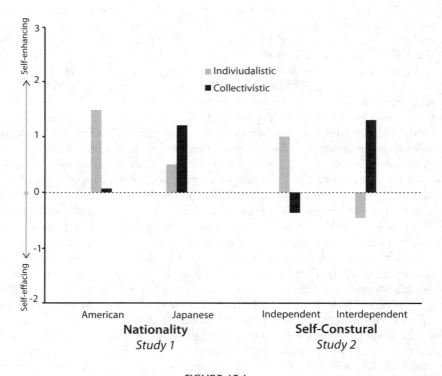

FIGURE 10.1

self-enhancement motive is expressed. Although cultures vary in terms of what attributes are considered important, members of those cultures share in common the universal need to enhance the individual self and they do so strategically on dimensions that are deemed important or culturally relevant.

Culture-as-Contextual-Primacy-Hypothesis in Review

The cultural perspective posits that culture molds the cognitive, motivational, and emotional structure of the self. Such a perspective is at odds with the individual-self-primacy hypothesis and implies that the essence of the self-concept varies as a function of cultural-context (or self-construal). However, the results of our experimental studies on self-definitional preference and individual-self enhancement tell a different story. Members of Eastern cultures and persons with an interdependent self-construal share in common with members of Western cultures and persons with an independent self-construal (1) a preference for describing themselves in regard to their individual self and, more important, (2) a tendency to strategically enhance the individual self. Our findings are congruent with an emerging literature on the panculturality of the individual self (Brown, 2003). Despite rumors to the contrary, the individual self is alive and well in Eastern culture.

NOVEL INGROUPS AND THE INDIVIDUAL SELF

In this section, we demonstrate the utility of the individual-self-primacy hypothesis as a framework for developing new or revisiting existing psychological theory. As an example, we reveal the influence of the individual self in a context in which existing theories attribute the regulation of social judgment to the collective self. The context is the minimal group paradigm (MGP; Tajfel, 1970) and the judgment involves intergroup perception.

The MGP provides a highly controlled context to examine the development and progression of intergroup relations. Methodological control is achieved by categorizing participants into novel groups (e.g., Groups W and X). Because those groups are novel, participants do not have ready-formed stereotypes specific to the groups, nor do the groups have a history of contact. Surprisingly, in this minimal context, participants favor their novel ingroup over the novel outgroup in terms of cognition, evaluation, and behavior (Brewer, 1979; Mullen, Brown, & Smith, 1992).

Prevailing theories suggest that the collective self regulates such ingroup favoritism. Social identity theory (Tajfel & Turner, 1979), for example, suggests that persons internalize group membership as a social identity (i.e., a collective self) and subsequently favor the ingroup over outgroups as a means of enhancing their social identity. Self-categorization theory (Turner et al., 1987) suggests that intergroup contexts accentuate perceived similarity among self and ingroup members on dimensions that distinguish the ingroup from outgroup and that shared similarity generates attraction to the ingroup. Common to these theories is the assumption that the collective self, derived from the salient ingroup, regulates intergroup relations.

In contrast, we suggest that the individual self regulates ingroup favoritism between minimal (or, more generally, novel) groups (for related perspectives, see Cadinu & Rothbart, 1996; Eidelman & Biernat, 2003; Otten, this volume). The scarcity of information about novel groups makes it unlikely that group members re*define* themselves in terms of the group. We find it more plausible that members define the novel group (at least initially) in terms of the individual self—a social object about which members posses a multitude of knowledge. What follows are descriptions of data consistent with the influence of the individual self on intergroup cognition, evaluation, and behavior in the MGP.

Intergroup Cognition

Schaller and Maass (1989) attribute a recall advantage for negative ingroup information to the additional processing required to reconcile the negative information with a positive ingroup expectation. We (Gramzow, Gaertner, & Sedikides, 2001) recently extended this explanation by demonstrating that the individual self provides the recall advantage. We conducted a two-session study to test whether the individual self serves as an information base when processing information about novel ingroups. In the initial session, participants judged whether each of 18 positive behaviors and 18 negative behaviors was self-congruent (i.e., "me") or self-discrepant (i.e., "not me"). One to 2 weeks later participants returned to the laboratory, and we categorized them into novel groups. We represented participants with the 36 behaviors which ostensibly were enacted by either ingroup or outgroup members. Participants read the 18 ingroup and 18 outgroup behaviors (counterbalanced for valence and presentation order) with the instructed goal of forming an impression of each group. Participants subsequently recalled as many behaviors as they could for each group, with half the participants beginning the recall task for the ingroup behaviors and the other half beginning with the outgroup behaviors.

Integral to our hypothesis was the finding from past research that information that is both negative and self-discrepant is more threatening to the self-concept than information that is simply negative or simply self-discrepant (Green & Sedikides, 2004; Sedikides & Green, 2000; Sedikides, Green, & Pinter, 2004). Accordingly, we hypothesized that, if the individual self serves as an information base about novel ingroups, then negative-self-discrepant information linked to the self via ingroup membership would receive additional processing to reconcile it with positive expectations about the individual self and, consequently, would be recalled more frequently than negative-self-discrepant information not linked to the self. Results were consistent with the hypothesis. The only intergroup difference in recall was for negative-self-discrepant behaviors: participants more frequently recalled negative-self-discrepant behaviors ostensibly performed by other ingroup than outgroup members. These findings indicate that the individual self guided the processing of information about the novel ingroup.

Intergroup Evaluation

We recently extended the self-as-information-base hypothesis to account, in part, for evaluative favoritism in the minimal group paradigm (Gramzow & Gaertner, 2005). Meta-analytic research indicates that individual-self esteem (i.e., global evaluation of one's self-worth as an individual) positively predicts the extent to which persons *directly* evaluate ingroups more favorably than outgroups (Aberson, Healy, & Romero, 2000). This tendency implies the possibility that the individual self serves as an evaluative basis of novel ingroups. Indeed, our own research indicates that evaluative favoritism of novel ingroups versus outgroups is predicted more strongly by level of individual-self esteem than collective-self esteem—a pattern that holds regardless of whether individual and collective esteem are measured 10 minutes (Gramzow & Gaertner, 2005, Study 1) or 7 days (Gramzow & Gaertner, 2005, Study 2) before persons are categorized into novel groups.

A third study in this line of research suggests that the global evaluation of the individual self automatically extends to novel ingroups via an unmotivated consistency process (Gramzow & Gaertner, 2005, Study 3). In an initial testing session, participants completed a measure of individual-self esteem and a measure of right-wing authoritarianism (RWA), which predicts ingroup favoritism via a social identity motive (Altemeyer, 1981). A week later, we categorized participants into novel groups and manipulated whether they completed a self-affirmation task. Fein and Spencer (1997) demonstrated that self-affirmation manipulations reduce the expression of prejudice that is motivated by a need to bolster the self. We obtained conceptually similar results with the measure of RWA. The self-affirmation task nullified the positive association between RWA and ingroup favoritism revealed by participants who did not self-affirm. On the other hand, individual-self esteem continued to positively predict ingroup favoritism, regardless of whether participants had the opportunity to self-affirm. Apparently, the global evaluation of the individual self extends automatically as an unmotivated basis for evaluating novel ingroups (Otten & Wentura, 1999)—a process anticipated by Groucho Marx who self-effacingly remarked, "I don't care to belong to a club that accepts people like me as members."

Intergroup Behavior

The tendency for members of minimal groups to allocate more resources (e.g., money) to ingroup than outgroup members is construed as evidence of a social-identity enhancement motive (Tajfel & Turner, 1979). Because participants cannot directly allocate money to themselves, self-interest is ostensibly absent in the MGP and the favoritism allegedly reflects a concern for the welfare of the ingroup. However, recent research suggests that individual-self interest is present in the MGP and contributes to the behavioral favoritism (Gaertner & Insko, 2000; Rabbie, Schot, & Visser, 1989; Yamagishi, Jin, & Kiyonari, 1999). In particular, participants allocate money to and *receive* money from other ingroup and outgroup members. Consequently, the allocation task fosters a structure of outcome dependence among ingroup members and participants can indirectly allocate money to themselves by reciprocating favorable allocations with ingroup members. Indeed, eliminating the potential for individual-self profit via reciprocation (e.g., informing participants that other ingroup members are not allocating resources) eradicates behavioral favoritism (particularly among males; Gaertner & Insko, 2000).

In summary, the individual self regulates much of the cognitive, evaluative, and behavioral responses in the minimal group paradigm. Rather than defining the self in terms of novel ingroups, it appears that the direction of inference is reversed. The individual self supplies an informational and evaluative framework that subjectively imbues novel ingroups with defining characteristics and social worth. Of course, we are not suggesting that all group-phenomena boil down to an individual-self analysis. The more general message is of the insight gained by (re)introducing the individual self into psychological theory (Aron & McLaughlin-Volpe, 2001; Higgins & May, 2001; Sedikides & Gaertner, 2001a).

ADDITIONAL CONSIDERATIONS

In this section, we anticipate and address issues that readers might ponder. We begin with two methodological issues and conclude with a more abstract issue.

Have We Tested Outcomes that Matter to the Collective Self?

As Crocker and Wolfe's (2001) contingency model of self-worth suggests, not all threats and enhancements to the self have equal impact; what matters is the extent to which self-worth is contingent upon the domain in which the threat or enhancement occurs. Consequently, a reader might question whether our comparisons of the individual and collective self were biased by feedback domains that lacked contingency in collective-self worth.

We believe that this was not the case. Indeed, we deliberately controlled for artifacts associated with feedback domain. In our laboratory and meta-analytic research we threatened (or enhanced) the selves on the same domain to avoid confounding target of feedback (i.e., individual vs. collective self) with domain of feedback. Furthermore, by premeasuring the importance of feedback domain to the individual and collective self, we empirically controlled for the possibility that the selves were *differentially* contingent on domain (Gaertner et al., 1999, Study 2). Even with this control, threat to the individual self elicited stronger responses than did threat to the collective self.

Have We Tested The "Real" Collective Self?

Readers might question whether our comparisons of the individual and collective self were biased in that we did not target a collective self that deeply mattered. In response to such an issue, we emphasize two points. First, our laboratory and meta-analytic research included a broad range of groups upon which a collective-self can be derived. Those groups included contextually defined groups (e.g., minimal groups), ascribed groups (e.g., gender), and achieved groups (e.g., university, sorority, political, and career affiliations). Second, given that the meaningfulness of a particular group likely varies across persons we purposefully included level of identification as a potential moderator. Neither our laboratory nor meta-analytic research yielded effects for group identification. Persons who weakly and strongly identified with the targeted groups evidenced stronger reactions to both threats and enhancements of the individual than collective self.

Confident that we provided a balanced test for the collective self, we acknowledge that a third form of self carries the potential to trump the individual self. The relational self (Brewer & Gardner, 1996; Sedikides & Brewer, 2001) is derived from dyadic interpersonal relationships with significant others, such as parents, siblings, offspring, romantic partners, and close friends. Given the developmental (Bowlby, 1969), and social (Baumeister & Leary, 1995) implications of interpersonal relationships, perhaps the relational self stands as primary. Although this is a yet-to-be-explored empirical issue, there is theoretical support for the continued possibility that individual-self-primacy reigns supreme. Self-expansion theory (e.g., Aron & Aron, 1986) suggests that interpersonal relationships influence cognitive, motivational, and emotional functioning to the extent they are integrated into the individual (or what Aron and colleagues refer to as the "personal") self. In particular, the experience of self-expansion is described such that "the other becomes part of the (personal) self, even confused with the personal self" (Aron & Mclaughlin-Volpe, 2001, p. 102). Aron and colleagues offer expansion of the individual self to explain acts of protection and concern for close others. Such a perspective construes the individual-self as a necessary ingredient for altruistic or other-serving actions and motives.

Theories that Emphasize the Collective Self: Much Ado about Nothing?

In light of our findings for an internal hierarchy that favors the individual self, readers might question the value or validity of theories that emphasize the collective self. Before rushing to the wholesale abandonment of such theories, readers should realize that neither our arguments nor data suggest that the collective self is unimportant, irrelevant, or unimpactful. We designed our research to explore the *relative* motivational and emotional standing of the individual versus collective self, not their absolute potencies. Indeed, our research would have been a pointless exercise and lackluster at best had we considered the collective self to be extraneous to social functioning. We readily acknowledge both the central role of collective self in human functioning and the often symbiotic relation between the individual and collective selves (Hugenberg & Bodenhausen, 2004).

Nonetheless, our findings offer an important message for collective-self theories. Self-functioning might differ considerably from what collective-self theories predict when motivational or emotional facets of the individual self are heightened. The meta-contrast principal of self-categorization theory, for example, provides a cognitive account for shifts between individual and collective self-definition in the form of contextually defined perceptions of relative similarity. Perceiving less similarity within than between social groupings likely promotes an individuated self-definition as self-categorization theory predicts. However, if an individual level threat was introduced into the latter situation (as we did in Study 1 of Gaertner et al., 1999), the cognitive basis of self-definitional shifts would likely play second fiddle to motivated needs of buffering the threat—such as by self-defining at the collective level. Optimal distinctiveness theory, as another example, offers a motivated account of self-definitional shifts in the form of the competing needs for assimilation and differentiation. As Pickett, Bonner, and Coleman (2002, Study 3) indicate, however, satisfying enhancement needs at the level of the individual self facilitates shifts to the collective self in the service of assimilation needs. In particular, persons who were positively differentiated from their ingroup were more willing to subsequently accept negative ingroup stereotypes than were persons who were negatively differentiated from their ingroup.

SUMMATION

We began our chapter pondering the motivational and emotional essence of the self-concept, and considered three possibilities: (1) the individual-self is primary, (2) the collective-self is primary, or (3) primacy is contextually established. We subsequently detailed our program of research that explores the primacy-issue. The initial stage of our research consisted of a series of laboratory studies and a more comprehensive meta-analysis that compared the relative reactions of the individual versus collective self to threat and enhancement. Those projects consistently yielded evidence suggesting that the individual-self is primary.

We broadened our empirical scope in the second stage of our research to examine the possibility that culture contextually moderates the fundamental nature of self. We enrolled in those studies persons who internalized independent versus interdependent cultural mandates and compared their relative self-definitional preference and proclivity to enhance the individual-self. Those studies revealed the cross-cultural vitality of the individual self in that independent and interdependent persons self-defined in terms of the individual self and strategically enhanced the individual self on culturally valued dimensions. In the third stage of our research, we examined the utility of the individual-self-primacy concept as a tool for understanding social functioning. Our minimal group research indicated that the individual self regulates cognitive, evaluative, and behavioral reactions to novel ingroups. In summation, the self-concept has a motivational and emotional hierarchy at the top of which sits comfortably the individual self.

REFERENCES

Aberson, C. L., Healy, M., & Romero (2000). Ingroup bias and self-esteem: A meta-analysis. *Personality and Social Psychology Review, 4*, 157–173.

Abrams, D. (1994). Social self-regulation. *Personality and Social Psychology Bulletin, 20*, 473–483.

Alicke, M. D. (1985). Global self-evaluation as determined by the desirability and controllability of trait adjectives. *Journal of Personality and Social Psychology, 49*, 1621–1630.

Altemeyer, B. (1981). *Right-wing authoritarianism.* Winnipeg: University of Manitoba Press.

Aron, A., & Aron, E. N. (1986). *Love as the expansion of self: Understanding attraction and satisfaction.* New York: Hemisphere.

Aron, A., & McLaughlin-Volpe, T. (2001). Including others in the self: Extensions to own and partner's group memberships. In C. Sedikides & M. B. Brewer (Eds.), *Individual self, relational self, collective self* (pp. 89–108). Philadelphia: Psychology Press.

Baumeister, R. F. (1998). The self. In D. T. Gilbert, S. T. Fiske, & G. Lindzey (Eds.), *Handbook of social psychology* (4th ed., Vol. 1, pp. 680–740). New York: McGraw-Hill.

Baumeister, R. F., & Leary, M.R. (1995). The need to belong: Desire for interpersonal attachments as a fundamental human motivation. *Psychological Bulletin, 117*, 497–529.

Bellah, R. N., Madsen, R., Sullivan, W. M., Swidler, A., & Tipton, S. M. (1985). *Habits of the heart: Individualism and commitment in American life.* Berkeley: University of California Press.

Bem, D. J., & Allen, A. (1974). On predicting some of the people some of the time: The search for cross-situational consistencies in behavior. *Psychological Review, 81*, 506–520.

Bond, M. H., Leung, K., & Wan, K. C. (1982). The social impact of self-effacing attributions: The Chinese case. *Journal of Social Psychology, 118*, 157–166.

Bowlby, J. (1969). *Attachment and loss: Vol. 1. Attachment.* London: Hogarth Press.

Branscombe, N. R., & Wann, D. L., (1994). Collective self-esteem consequences of outgroup derogation when a valued social identity is on trial. *European Journal of Social Psychology, 24*, 641–658.

Brewer, M. B. (1979). In-group bias in the minimal intergroup situation: A cognitive-motivational analysis. *Psychological Bulletin, 86*, 307–324.

Brewer, M. B. (1991). The social self: On being the same and different at the same time. *Personality and Social Psychology Bulletin, 17*, 475–482.

Brewer, M. B., & Gardner, W. (1996). Who is this "we"? Levels of collective identity and self representations. *Journal of Personality and Social Psychology, 71*, 83–93.

Brewer, M. B., & Roccas, S. (2001). Individual values, social identity, and optimal distinctiveness. In C. Sedikides & M. B. Brewer (Eds.), *Individual self, relational self, collective self* (pp. 219–237). Philadelphia: Psychology Press.

Brown, J. D. (2003). The self-enhancement motive in collectivistic cultures: The Rumors of my death have been greatly exaggerated. *Journal of Cross-Cultural Psychology, 34*, 603–605.

Bulmer, M. G. (1978). Group selection in structured populations. *American Naturalist, 112*, 389–399.

Cadinu, M. R., & Rothbart, M. (1996). Self-anchoring and differentiation processes in the minimal group setting. *Journal of Personality and Social Psychology, 70*, 661–677.

Cahoone, N. (1996). *History of the western mind.* Princeton, NJ: Princeton University Press.

Campbell, K. W., & Sedikides, C. (1999). Self-threat magnifies the self-serving bias: A meta-analytic integration. *Review of General Psychology, 3*, 23–43.

Caporael, L. R., & Baron, R. M. (1997). Groups as the mind's natural environment. In J. Simpson & D. Kenrick (Eds.), *Evolutionary social psychology* (pp. 317–343). Hillsdale, NJ: Erlbaum.

Caporael, L. R., & Brewer, M. B. (1991). Reviving evolutionary psychology: Biology meets society. *Journal of Social Issues, 47,* 187–195.

Crocker, J., & Wolfe, C. T. (2001). Contingencies of self-worth. *Psychological Review, 108,* 593–623.

Dawkins, R., & Krebs, J. R. (1978). Animal signals: Information or manipulation? In J. R. Krebs & N. B. Davies (Eds.), *Behavioral ecology* (pp. 282–309). Oxford: Blackwell.

De Vos, G. A. (1985). Dimensions of the self in Japanese culture. In A. J. Marsella, G. De Vos, & F. L. K. Hsu (Eds.), *Culture and self: Asian and Western perspectives* (pp. 141–182). New York: Tavistock.

Dunning, D. (1995). Trait importance and modifiability as factors influencing self-assessment and self-enhancement motives. *Personality and Social Psychology Bulletin, 21,* 197–306.

Eidelman, S., & Biernat, M. (2003). Derogating black sheep: Individual or group protection? *Journal of Experimental Social Psychology, 39,* 602–609.

Fein, S., & Spencer, S. J. (1997). Prejudice as self-image maintenance: Affirming the self through derogating others. *Journal of Personality and Social Psychology, 73,* 31–44.

Gaertner, L., & Insko, C. A. (2000). Intergroup discrimination in the minimal group paradigm: Categorization, reciprocation, or fear? *Journal of Personality and Social Psychology, 79,* 77–94.

Gaertner, L., Sedikides, C., & Graetz, K. (1999). In search of self-definition: Motivational primacy of the individual self, motivational primacy of the collective self, or contextual primacy? *Journal of Personality and Social Psychology, 76,* 5–18.

Gaertner, L., Sedikides, C., Vevea, J., & Iuzzini, J. (2002). The "I," the "We," and the "When:" A meta-analysis of motivational primacy in self-definition. *Journal of Personality and Social Psychology, 83,* 574–591.

Gramzow, R. H., & Gaertner, L. (2005). Self-esteem and favoritism toward novel in-groups: The self as an evaluative base. *Journal of Personality and Social Psychology, 88,* 801–815.

Gramzow, R. H., Gaertner, L., & Sedikides, C. (2001). Memory for ingroup and outgroup information in a minimal group context: The self as an informational base. *Journal of Personality and Social Psychology, 80,* 188–205.

Gibbons, F. X., Persson Benbow, C., & Gerrard, M. (1994). From top dog to bottom half: Social comparison strategies in response to poor performance. *Journal of Personality and Social Psychology, 67,* 638–652.

Green, J. A., & Sedikides, C. (2004). Retrieval selectivity in the processing of self-referent information: Testing the boundaries of self-protection. *Self and Identity, 3,* 69–80.

Greenwald, A. G. (1980). The totalitarian ego: Fabrication and revision of personal history. *American Psychologist, 35,* 603–618.

Hedges, L. V., & Vevea, J. L. (1998). Fixed- and random-effects models in meta-analysis. *Psychological Methods, 3,* 486–504.

Heine, S. J., Kitayama, S., & Lehman, D. R. (2001). Cultural differences in self-evaluation: Japanese readily accept negative self-relevant information. *Journal of Cross-Cultural Psychology, 32,* 434–443.

Heine, S. J., Lehman, D. R., Markus, H. R., & Kitayama, S. (1999). Is there a universal need for positive self-regard? *Psychological Review, 106,* 766–794.

Heine, S. J., & Renshaw, K. (2002). Interjudge agreement, self-enhancement, and liking: Cross-cultural divergences. *Personality and Social Psychology Bulletin, 28,* 578–587.

Higgins, E. T., & May, D. (2001). Individual self-regulatory functions: It's not 'We' regulation but it's still social." In C. Sedikides & M. B. Brewer (Eds.), *Individual self, relational self, collective self* (pp. 47–67). Philadelphia: Psychology Press.

Hogg, M., & Turner, J. C. (1987). Intergroup behavior, self-stereotyping and the salience of social categories. *British Journal of Social Psychology, 26,* 325–340.

Hoorens, V., Nuttin, J. M., Erdelyi-Herman, I., & Pavakanun, U. (1990). Mastery pleasure versus mere ownership: A quasi-experimental cross-cultural and cross-alphabetical test for the name letter effect. *European Journal of Social Psychology, 20,* 181–205.

Hugenberg, K., & Bodenhausen, G. V. (2004). Category membership moderates the inhibition of social identities. *Journal of Experimental Social Psychology, 40,* 233–238.

Hsu, F. L. K. (1948). *Under the ancestor's shadow: Chinese culture and personality.* New York: Columbia University Press.

Johnson, B. T., & Eagly, A. H. (2000). Quantitative synthesis in social psychological research. In H. T. Reis

& C. M. Judd (Eds.), *Handbook of research methods in social and personality psychology* (pp. 496–528) Cambridge: Cambridge University Press.

Kenny D. A., & DePaulo B. M. (1993). Do people know how others view them? An empirical and theoretical account. *Psychological Bulletin, 114,* 145–161.

Kitayama, S., & Karasawa, M. (1997). Implicit self-esteem in Japan: Name letters and birthday numbers. *Personality and Social Psychology Bulletin, 23,* 736–742.

Kitayama, S., Markus, H. R., Matsumoto, H., & Norasakkunkit, V. (1997). Individual and collective processes in the construction of the self: Self-enhancement in the United States and self-criticism in Japan. *Journal of Personality and Social Psychology, 72,* 1245–1267.

Kobayashi, C., & Greenwald, A. G. (2003). Implicit-Explicit differences in self-enhancement for Americans and Japanese. *Journal of Cross-Cultural Psychology, 34,* 522–541.

Kwan, V. S. Y., John, O. P., Kenny, D. A., Bond, M. H., & Robbins, R. W. (2004). Reconceptualizing individual differences in self-enhancement bias: An interpersonal approach. *Psychological Review, 111,* 94–110.

Leary, M. R., Bednarski, R., Hammon, D., & Duncan, T. (1997). Blowhards, snobs, and narcissists: Interpersonal reactions to excessive egotism. In R. M. Kowalski (Ed.), *Aversive interpersonal behaviors* (pp. 111–131). New York: Plenum Press.

Leung, M. (1997). Negotiation and reward allocation across cultures. In P. C. Earley & M. Erez (Eds.), *New perspectives on international industrial and organizational psychology* (pp. 640–675). San Francisco: Lexington.

Markus, H. (1977). Self-schemata and processing information about the self. *Journal of Personality and Social Psychology, 35,* 63–78.

Markus, H. R., & Kitayama, S. (1991a). Culture and the self: Implications for cognition, emotion, and motivation. *Psychological Review, 98,* 224–253.

Markus, H. R., & Kitayama, S. (1991b). Cultural variation in the self-concept. In G. R. Goethals & J. Strauss (Eds.), *Multidisciplinary perspectives on the self* (pp. 18–48). New York: Springer-Verlag.

Markus, H., & Kunda, Z. (1986). Stability and malleability of the self-concept. *Journal of Personality and Social Psychology, 51,* 858–866.

Markus, H., & Wurf, E. (1987). The dynamic self-concept: A social psychological perspective. *Annual Review of Psychology, 38,* 299–337.

Mullen, B., Brown, R., & Smith, C. (1992). Ingroup bias as a function of salience, relevance, and status: An integration. *European Journal of Social Psychology, 22,* 103–122.

Mullen, B., & Riordan, C. A. (1988). Self-serving attributions for performance in naturalistic settings: A meta-analytic review. *Journal of Applied Social Psychology, 18,* 3–22.

National Research Council (1992). *Combining information: Statistical issues and opportunities for research.* Washington, DC: National Academy Press.

Nuttin, J. M., Jr. (1987). Affective consequences of mere ownership: The name letter effect in twelve European languages. *European Journal of Social Psychology, 17,* 381–402.

Onorato, R. S., & Turner, J. C. (2004). Fluidity in the self-concept: The shift from personal to social identity. *European Journal of Social Psychology, 34,* 257–278.

Ostrom, T. M., & Sedikides, C. (1992). Out-group homogeneity effects in natural and minimal groups. *Psychological Bulletin, 112,* 536–552.

Otten, S., & Wentura, D. (1999). About the impact of automaticity in the minimal group paradigm: Evidence from affective priming tasks. *European Journal of Social Psychology, 29,* 1049–1079.

Paulhus, D. L. (1998). Interpersonal and intraphysic adaptiveness of trait self-enhancement: A mixed blessing? *Journal of Personality and Social Psychology, 74,* 1197–1208.

Pelham, B. W. (1991). On confidence and consequence: The certainty and importance of self-knowledge. *Journal of Personality and Social Psychology, 60,* 518–530.

Pelham, B. W., Koole, S. L., Hetts, J. J., Hardin, C. D., & Seah, E. (2002). *Gender Moderates the Relation Between Implicit and Explicit Self-Esteem.* Manuscript under review, State University of New York at Buffalo.

Pelham, B. W., & Wachsmuth, J. O. (1995). The waxing and waning of the social self: Assimilation and contrast in social comparison. *Journal of Personality and Social Psychology, 69,* 825–838.

Pickett, C., Bonner, B. L., & Coleman, J. M. (2002). Motivated self-stereotyping: Heightened assimilation and differentiation needs result in increased levels of positive and negative self-stereotyping. *Journal of Personality and Social Psychology, 82*, 543–562.

Rabbie, J. M., Schot, J. C. & Visser, L. (1989). Social identity theory: a conceptual and empirical critique from the perspective of a behavioral interaction model. *European Journal of Social Psychology, 19*, 171–202.

Roberts, B. W., & DelVecchio, W. F. (2000). The rank-order consistency of personality from childhood to old age: A quantitative review of longitudinal studies. *Psychological Bulletin, 126*, 3–25.

Schaller, M., & Maass, A. (1989). Illusory correlation and social categorization: Toward an integration of motivational and cognitive factors in stereotype formation. *Journal of Personality and Social Psychology, 56*, 709–721.

Schlenker, B. R., & Leary, M. R. (1982). Audiences' reactions to self-enhancing, self-denigrating, and accurate self-presentations. *Journal of Experimental Social Psychology, 18*, 89–104.

Schlenker, B. R., & Miller, R. S. (1977). Egocentrism in groups: Self-serving bias or logical information processing? *Journal of Personality and Social Psychology, 35*, 755–764.

Sedikides, C. (1993). Assessment, enhancement, and verification: Determinants of the self evaluation process. *Journal of Personality and Social Psychology, 65*, 317–338.

Sedikides, C. (1995). Central and peripheral self-conceptions are differentially influenced by mood: Tests of the differential sensitivity hypothesis. *Journal of Personality and Social Psychology, 69*, 759–777.

Sedikides, C. (2003). On the status of the self in social perception: Comment on Karniol (2003). *Psychological Review, 110*, 591–594.

Sedikides, C., & Brewer, M. B. (Eds.) (2001). *Individual self, relational self, collective self*. Philadelphia: Psychology Press.

Sedikides, C., Campbell, W. K., Reeder, G., & Elliot, A. J. (1998). The self-serving bias in relational context. *Journal of Personality and Social Psychology, 74*, 378–386.

Sedikides, C., & Gaertner, L. (2001a). A homecoming to the individual self: Emotional and motivational primacy. In C. Sedikides & M. F. Brewer (Eds.), *Individual self, relational self, collective self* (pp. 7–23). Philadelphia: Psychology Press.

Sedikides, C., & Gaertner, L. (2001b). The social self: The quest for identity and the motivational primacy of the individual self. In J. P. Forgas, K. D. Williams, & L. Wheeler (Eds.), *The social mind: Cognitive and motivational aspects of interpersonal behavior* (pp. 115–138). Cambridge: Cambridge University Press.

Sedikides, C., Gaertner, L., & Toguchi, Y. (2003). Pancultural self-enhancement. *Journal of Personality and Social Psychology, 84*, 60–79.

Sedikides, C., & Green, J. D. (2000). On the self-protective nature of inconsistency/negativity management: Using the person memory paradigm to examine self-referent memory. *Journal of Personality and Social Psychology, 79*, 906–922.

Sedikides, C., & Green, J. D. (2004). What I don't recall can't hurt me: Information negativity versus information inconsistency as determinants of memorial self-defense. *Social Cognition, 22*, 4–29.

Sedikides, C., Green, J. D., & Pinter, B. (2004). Self-protective memory. In D. R. Beike, J. M. Lampinen, & D. A. Behrend (Eds.), *The self and memory* (pp. 161–179). Philadelphia, PA: Psychology Press.

Sedikides, C., & Gregg, A. P. (2003). Portraits of the self. In M. A. Hogg & J. Cooper (Eds.), *Sage handbook of social psychology* (pp. 110–138). London: Sage.

Sedikides, C., & Skowronski, J. J. (1997). The symbolic self in evolutionary context. *Personality and Social Psychology Review, 1*, 89–102.

Sedikides, C., & Skowronski, J. J. (2000). On the evolutionary functions of the symbolic self: The emergence of self-evaluation motives. In A. Tesser, R. Felson, & J. Suls (Eds.), *Psychological perspectives on self and identity* (pp. 91–117). Washington, DC: APA Books.

Sedikides, C., & Skowronski, J. J. (2003). Evolution of the self: Issues and prospects. In M. R. Leary & J. P. Tangney (Eds.), *Handbook of self and identity* (594–609). New York: Guilford Press.

Sedikides, C., Skowronski, J. J., & Gaertner, L. (2004). Self-enhancement and self-protection motivations: From the laboratory to an evolutionary context. *Journal of Cultural and Evolutionary Psychology, 2*, 61–79.

Sedikides, C., & Strube, M. J. (1997). Self-evaluation: To thine own self be good, to thine own self be sure, to thine own self be true, and to thine own self be better. In M. P. Zanna (Ed.), *Advances in experimental social psychology, 29,* 209–269. New York: Academic Press.

Singelis, T. M. (1994). The measurement of independent and interdependent self-construals. *Personality and Social Psychology Bulletin, 20,* 580–591.

Spears, R., Doosje, B., & Ellemers, N. (1997). Self-stereotyping in the face of threats to group status and distinctiveness: The role of group identification. *Personality and Social Psychology Bulletin, 23,* 538–553.

Spindler, G. D., & Spindler, L. S. (1990). American mainstream culture. In G. D. Spindler & L. S. Spindler (Eds.), *The American cultural dialogue and its transmission* (pp. 22–41). New York: Falmer Press.

Swann, W. B., Pentfrow, P. J., & Guinn, J. S. (2003). Self-verification: The search for coherence. In M. R. Leary & J. P. Tangney (Eds.), *Handbook of self and identity* (pp. 367–383). New York: Guilford Press.

Tajfel, H. (1970). Experiments in intergroup discrimination. *Scientific American, 223,* 96–102.

Taylor, S. E., Lerner, J. S., Sherman, D. K., Sage, R. M., & McDowell, N. K. (2003a). Portrait of the self-enhancer: Well adjusted and well liked or maladjusted and friendless? *Journal of Personality and Social Psychology, 84,* 165–176.

Taylor, S. E., Lerner, J. S., Sherman, D. K., Sage, R. M., & McDowell, N. K. (2003b). Are self-enhancing cognitions associated with healthy or unhealthy biological profiles? *Journal of Personality and Social Psychology, 85,* 605–615.

Trafimow, D., Triandis, H. C., & Goto, S. G. (1991). Some tests of the distinction between the private self and the collective self. *Journal of Personality and Social Psychology, 60,* 649–655.

Triandis, H. C. (1989). The self and social behavior in differing cultural contexts. *Psychological Review, 96,* 506–520.

Turner, J. C., Hogg, M. A., Oakes, P. J., Reicher, S. D., & Wetherell, M. S. (1987). *Rediscovering the social group: A self-categorization theory.* Oxford: Basil Blackwell.

Turner, J. C., Oakes, P. J., Haslam, S. A., & McGarty, C. (1994). Self and collective: Cognition and social context. *Personality and Social Psychology Bulletin, 20,* 454–463.

Wallace, B. (1973). Misinformation, fitness, and selection. *American Naturalist, 107,* 1–7.

Walker, W. R., Skowronski, J. J., & Thompson, C. P. (2003). Life is pleasant—and memory helps to keep it that way! *Review of General Psychology, 7,* 203–210.

Wiley, R. H. (1983). The evolution of communication: Information and manipulation. In T. R. Halliday & P. J. B. Slater (Eds.), *Communication (Animal Behavior)* (Vol. 2, pp. 156–189). New York: Freeman.

Wilson, D. S., & Sober, E. (1994). Reintroducing group selection to the human behavioral sciences. *Behavioral and Brain Sciences, 17,* 585–654.

Wyer, R. S., & Frey, D. (1983). The effects of feedback about self and others on the recall and judgments of feedback-relevant information. *Journal of Experimental Social Psychology, 19,* 540–559.

Yamagishi, T., Jin, N., & Kiyonari, T. (1999). Bounded generalized reciprocity: Ingroup boasting and ingroup favoritism. *Advances in Group Processes, 16,* 161–197.

11

The Ingroup as Part of the Self
Reconsidering the Link Between Social Categorization, Ingroup Favoritism, and the Self-Concept

SABINE OTTEN
University of Groningen, The Netherlands

Theories on intergroup behavior are inevitably theories on the self. Linking intergroup behavior to group members' self-concept is an integral part of influential theories like *Social Identity Theory* (Tajfel & Turner, 1979; 1986), *Self-Categorization Theory* (Turner, Hogg, Oakes, Reicher, & Wetherell, 1987) and *Optimal Distinctiveness Theory* (Brewer, 1991, 1993). A core message of these theories is that the self can be conceptualized at different levels of abstraction, and that each of these levels is associated with certain patterns in social judgments and behavior. A common differentiation is that the self can be conceptualized at the personal level—*I versus others*—and at the group level—*us versus them*.

Undoubtedly, a great merit of traditional theories on intergroup behavior, like social identity theory and self-categorization theory, is to alert us that we cannot straightforwardly extrapolate from an unaffiliated individual's behavior to behavior a person displays when identifying with and acting on behalf of a certain group. Hence, the focus of these theories is on *differences* between the personal and the collective self and between determinants of interpersonal and intergroup behavior.

In the present chapter, several approaches are introduced that deal with the relation between the individual and the collective self. After a short survey of more traditional approaches on the self in intergroup contexts, which stress the differences between individual and collective identities, the focus will be on the *interplay* between the personal, uncategorized self and the self as a group member.

Specific attention will be given to theoretical and empirical work revealing that links between the individual self and the ingroup do contribute significantly to ingroup preferences. Hence, it will be argued that under certain conditions an *intra*group process—namely inferences from the individual self to the group as a whole—can explain an *inter*group phenomenon like ingroup favoritism. Evidence for the relevance of the individual self for understanding ingroup preference will be presented from both explicit and implicit measures. Finally, the theoretical implications of the findings and questions for further research will be discussed.

PERSPECTIVES FROM SOCIAL IDENTITY THEORY, SELF-CATEGORIZATION THEORY, AND OPTIMAL DISTINCTIVENESS THEORY

In the following, three influential theories on intergroup behavior will be introduced, all of which give a lot of attention to how the individual self functions and transforms when located in a group context rather than in an interpersonal context. Social identity theory (Tajfel & Turner, 1979) deals with the self in group contexts in order to understand intergroup differentiation, ingroup favoritism and outgroup derogation. Self-categorization theory (Turner et al., 1987) extended social identity theory, and asked under which conditions the self would be defined in terms of certain group memberships, and how the salience of the collective self affects perception, evaluation, and behavior. Optimal distinctiveness theory (Brewer, 1991, 1993), finally relates closely to self-categorization-theory, but has a specific focus on group preference and group size. Moreover, its main issue is not the situationally determined, malleable, and dynamic character of the social self, but the assumption that social identification is generally determined by two complementary drives, the need to belong, and the need to be distinct.

Social Identity Theory

Tajfel (1978) stressed the differences between the personal self and the social self. People behaving in terms of their personal identity will perceive themselves as *unique*, and will focus on differences between self and others. Social identity, however, is defined as "that part of an individual's self-concept which derives from his knowledge of his membership of a social group together with the valence and emotional significance attached to that membership" (p. 63).

Social identities[1] rest on characteristics that are *shared* with others; therefore, people behaving in terms of their identification as a group member are expected to show more homogeneity in their evaluations and behaviors than unaffiliated individuals, both within their groups and toward members of other groups. Within the group, perceptions of similarity will prevail, whereas clear differences will be perceived between the own group as opposed to other groups and their members.

Social identity theory (Tajfel & Turner, 1979, 1986) sees these processes as the immediate outcome of social categorization: Once a person identifies with a certain group, he or she will compare the ingroup to relevant (comparable) other groups. Ideally, these comparisons will render the ingroup as positively distinct; in this case, the comparison outcome helps establish or secure a positive social identity. Finally, as both personal and social identity form an individual's self-concept, treating and evaluating the ingroup in a biased way can be seen as a means to support or increase self-regard.

An empirical demonstration of ingroup biases as an immediate consequence of social categorization was most famously provided in experiments by Tajfel and his collaborators in the Minimal Group Paradigm (Tajfel, Billig, Bundy, & Flament, 1971), and has been replicated in numerous studies (for reviews see Brewer, 1979; Brown, 2000; Hewstone, Rubin & Willis, 2002; Mullen, Brown, & Smith, 1992). However, evidence for the underlying motive, a need for positive ingroup distinctiveness and a striving for positive self-esteem, is mixed, at best (see Abrams & Hogg, 1988).

Aberson, Healy, and Romero (2000) recently conducted a meta-analysis on studies testing the link between self-esteem and ingroup favoritism as implied by social identity theory. They report a pattern that runs counter to this hypothesis: At least on what they call "direct" measures of intergroup bias, that is on ingroup-outgroup ratings by individuals that were an active part of the ingroup, high rather than low self-esteem individuals showed most bias. On "indirect' measures, that is, when individuals rate the performance of a fellow ingroup member, no moderating effect of self-esteem was found.

Similarly, in a narrative review Rubin and Hewstone (1998) found only sparse evidence for self-esteem as a predictor of ingroup bias; similarly, evidence for a self-esteem enhancing effect of ingroup bias was weak. However, Turner (Turner, 1999; Turner & Reynolds, 2001) pointed out that deriving a firm link between self-esteem and intergroup differentiation is an oversimplification of social identity theory. For one thing, often the level of self-esteem measurement does not match the intergroup context. Rather than global self-esteem as a unique individual (as measured, for example, by Rosenberg's (1965) self-esteem scale, the esteem as a group member (as measured, for example, by the Collective Self Esteem Scale; Crocker & Luhtanen, 1990) needs to be considered. More importantly, Turner stresses that favoring the ingroup relative to the outgroup is but one of several strategies to manage a positive social identity. Nonetheless, we are left with a lack of clear evidence for a link between intergroup differentiation and self-esteem, and with legitimate doubts about a striving for positive ingroup distinctiveness as basic motivation underlying intergroup bias.

Self-Categorization Theory

With respect to the relation between personal and social self, social identity theory implies that they are linked insofar as they jointly form the self-concept. With respect to intergroup behavior, however, the personal self becomes relatively irrelevant. Not unique characteristics but characteristics that define the group as a whole become the defining features of the self as a group member. This idea is further elaborated upon in self-categorization theory (Turner et al., 1987). Self-categorization theory stresses that the self can be conceptualized at three different levels of inclusiveness: the interpersonal one (I vs. others), the intergroup one (us vs. them) and the superordinate one (ingroup and outgroup combined in an inclusive category).

A central point in the theory is that the self is a *dynamic* entity: depending on the context, people will conceptualize and perceive themselves on different levels of abstraction: (a) on the intragroup/interpersonal level as *me versus others*, (b) on the intergroup level as *us versus them*, and (c) on the superordinate level including both ingroup and outgroup in a common *we*. When a person self-categorizes as a group member, this implies two relevant consequences for the self-concept: self-stereotyping and depersonalization.

Self-stereotyping means that group members describe themselves and act in terms of prototypical characteristics of the respective social category. For example, on the annual celebration day for their Queen ("Koniginnedag"), many Dutch citizens will dress in orange irrespective of their regular color preferences. They do this while being fully aware that many fellow-citizens will do the same. Consequently, this process implies the accentuation of intragroup similarities, on the one hand, and of intergroup differences, on the other hand.

Inasmuch as self-stereotyping becomes stronger, the definition of the self in terms of personal, unique characteristics becomes weaker (Turner, 1999). A soccer fan in the arena watching his own team play will organize his world around the categorization "my team versus the other team." He will be well aware of the colors he and his fellow supporters are wearing, and he will know when to cheer and when to protest loudly. But at the same time he will care very little about his job, his family, or his specific food and music preferences. Turner (1984) labeled this phenomenon *depersonalization*: the "cognitive redefinition of the self—from unique attributes and individual differences to shared category memberships and associated stereotypes" (p. 528).

To sum up, both social identity theory and self-categorization theory lead us to the assumption that the personal self and the social self as defined by group memberships are fundamentally different. Rather than asking the question of which type of self is primary, these theories point to the situational variability and adaptiveness of the way the self is construed (see Sedikides & Brewer, 2001, for a rich collection of contributions about the relation between self-concepts on different levels of inclusiveness).

Optimal Distinctiveness Theory

Optimal distinctiveness theory (Brewer 1991, 1993) is closely related to self-categorization theory and incorporates the process of self-stereotyping as a core element. However, rather than analyzing the salience of certain social identities as determined by contextual conditions, optimal distinctiveness theory is more concerned with the motivational functions of social identities: collective selves can be more or less optimal in the way they serve need states of the individual. More specifically, the theory posits that people identify with social groups to fulfill two basic but opposite needs: the need to belong and the need to be different. Perceiving oneself as similar to other ingroup members fulfills the former need, whereas perceiving differences between ingroup and outgroup satisfies the latter. In contrast to self-categorization theory, which focuses on the cognitive determinants and the behavioral outcomes of self-stereotyping, optimal distinctiveness theory stresses more strongly motivational aspects.

A central question in self-categorization theory is to predict which social identity might become psychologically relevant in a certain situation. Here, the relation between intragroup similarities and intergroup differences, that is the meta-contrast, become the determining input for the self-categorization process (see Turner et al., 1987). Research on optimal distinctiveness theory goes a different way: For a given, typically quite relevant social categorization (such as being member of a certain university) either the sense of belonging to or the sense of being member of a distinct social group is jeopardized, and it is investigated how individual group members respond to this threat and try to restore optimal distinctiveness. For example, after hearing that one has a personality profile that is not typical for the average student at the home university, participants overestimated the number of group members in their group: The bigger the number of group members who belong and the higher the ingroup's heterogeneity, the higher the probability that the individual is still safely included (see Brewer & Pickett, 2002). Thus, we may argue that based on how the personal self is initially located within the ingroup (i.e., based on its perceived or communicated prototypicality), the definition of the ingroup will vary in such a way that the inclusion of the individual in ensured.

To sum up, like self-categorization theory, optimal distinctiveness theory assumes that *self-stereotyping* is a central process guiding group identification and behavior in terms of one's social identity. The individual self is compared against the standard of prototypical features associated with the ingroup. Whereas self-categorization focuses on the malleability of the self-definition, optimal distinctiveness theory adds the aspect of a malleable ingroup definition that is determined by the individual's need to belong and need to be distinct.

LINKING THE PERSONAL SELF AND THE COLLECTIVE SELF: THE SELF-ASPECT MODEL AND THE TRIPARTITE MODEL

The models previously described focus on how the conception of the self changes as a function of the situational context. An underlying assumption is that when an intergroup context becomes salient, then the personal self loses relevance. Social identity theory and self-categorization theory imply that there need not be a systematic link (e.g., a correlation) between one's perception as a unique person and one's perception as member of a certain group.

More recently, the *interplay* between social and personal identity has received more attention in social-psychological theorizing and research (as documented in Sedikides & Brewer, 2001). Self-categorization theory stressed that individual and collective self are somewhat independent, and that they can even have an antagonistic relation with respect to the salience of a certain self-definition (Turner et al., 1987, p. 49): When a group membership becomes very relevant in a certain situation—like for the soccer fan watching his favorite team play—then characteristics of the individual self may count very little. However, in everyday life, there are many situations in which identity-salience is less obviously determined, and in which both individual and collective aspects of the self-definition can be expected to be relevant. Accordingly, there is room for questions about whether the individual or the collective self is primary in social behavior (see Gaertner & Sedikides, this volume), and about conditions when the individual self cannot only coexist with the collective self, but may actually play a relevant role in social identification and people's functioning as group members. In the next section, two approaches will be outlined that are grounded in self-categorization theory, but that put more emphasis on the interplay between personal and social self and their *joint* contribution to intergroup evaluations and behavior.

The Self-Aspect Model

The self-aspect model (Simon, 1997) elaborates on the relation between the individual and the collective self. Central to this model are so-called *self-aspects*, which are defined as cognitive categories or concepts whose function it is to process and organize information about oneself (Simon & Kampmeier, 2001). Self-aspects do not only refer to group memberships (such as being a member of the Green Party), but can—among other things—also concern attitudes (opposing the death penalty), physical features (e.g., being tall), taste and style (e.g., always wearing black clothes), or traits (e.g., being anxious).

Irrespective of whether a self-aspect is referring to the individual self or to the collective self, it will be *relational*: it contains information about similarities and differences. For example, opposing the death penalty can only be a meaningful aspect of the self-concept inasmuch as it associates the self with others or distinguishes it from them. According to Simon (1997) both collective and individual self are based on self-aspects, with "the only difference being that the former is centered on a single self-aspect whereas the latter is based on a unique combination or configuration of social self-aspects" (p. 51). For example, when there are international championships in soccer, and the own national team plays, then—for those who consider soccer relevant—the collective self is fully determined by nationality. This self-aspect will determine when the respective person will cheer, when it will be disappointed, when it will be upset. However, a person invited for a job interview will rather self-categorize at the individual level, therefore being aware and trying to present a unique set of self-aspects that may be suitable to distinguish him or her positively from other applicants.

What defines whether a self-aspect becomes a defining part of the social or the collective self? To tackle this question, Simon and Hastedt (1999) asked their participants to list self-aspects that were positive versus negative and important versus unimportant to them. Later on, they rated how similar or different to themselves they perceive other people possessing this self-aspect (e.g., hard-working) and how similar or different to themselves they perceive people possessing the opposite self-aspect (lazy). Based on these data it was possible to calculate a ratio of the perceived intra- and intergroup similarities and differences as an index for self-categorization. The more the intragroup similarities exceeded the intergroup similarities, the more a certain self-aspect could be considered as reflecting a collective rather than a unique, individual self-aspect. The results revealed that only self-aspects defined both as positive and as highly relevant to the individual had a high probability to be associated with a collective identity.[2]

In line with self-categorization theory, Simon and Kampmeier (2001) argue that there are good reasons to assume that there is an antagonistic relationship between self-interpretation in terms of individual self-aspects, and in terms of collective self-aspects. Thus, when enhancing the relevance of the collective self (e.g., by introducing intergroup competition), then the relevance of the individual self should decrease, and vice versa (see also Turner et al., 1987).

However, individuality and group membership can also complement rather than contradict each other. A complementary relation becomes possible if group memberships do not challenge an individual's need for independence (not being reduced to a single self-aspect and thus not having to rely on approval on a single dimension) and its need for differentiation (being able to differentiate oneself from others). Illustrating this claim, Kampmeier and Simon (2001) could show that activating the one or the other need has different effects on self-categorization as a group-member depending on whether the salient ingroup is a majority or a minority.

For majority group members, it is the striving for differentiation rather than the independence motivation that reduces self-categorization on the collective level. However, for minority group members (being one of few), the differentiation motive can actually be fully reconciled with self-categorization as a group member. Thus, Simon and Kampmeier (2001) conclude that "self-interpretation as a distinct individual may be quite compatible with self-interpretation as an interchangeable group member as long as differentiation from outgroup members assures sufficient individuality" (p. 215). In this respect, the self-aspect model is similar to optimal distinctiveness theory (Brewer 1991, 1993; see above). However, Simon and Kampmeier add the distinction of aspects of individuality and their interaction with the minority versus majority status of the ingroup. Whereas self-categorization as a minority group member is especially suitable to be combined with the individual concern for being different, self-categorization as a member of a (typically more heterogeneous) majority group goes well together with the need for independence.

The Tripartite Model

The Tripartite Model on distinctiveness and the definition of the collective self is mainly concerned with the different functions of intergroup differentiation (Spears, Jetten, & Scheepers, 2002). The model assumes both an antagonistic relation between the individual and collective self and a joint contribution of both types of self to intergroup behavior. On the one hand, the more a group membership becomes psychologically salient in a specific situation (think of soccer fans watching their team play) the less will group members perceive themselves as unique individuals. On the other hand, in contexts where self-definition becomes the central issue, like when undergoing crucial changes in life (e.g., leaving school and joining university), "individual and collective self-categorizations may "infuse", complement and define each other" (p. 183).

The Tripartite Model distinguishes between different functions underlying the creation and perception of distinctiveness between ingroups and outgroups: *Reactive distinctiveness* implies intergroup differentiation resulting from a threat to the ingroup identity that originates in a high degree of perceived similarity between ingroup and outgroup. For example, a soccer fan learning that his home team scored the same as a relevant competitor might be eager to state that his or her team's soccer is technically superior. *Reflective distinctiveness* implies that intergroup differentiation takes place in response to a social reality that renders certain social identities salient (meta-contrast principle, Turner, 1984). To give a simple example, the different colors in which fans from competing soccer teams dress already enhance the probability that people will differentiate according to this categorization dimension. *Creative distinctiveness*, finally, serves an identity function; it aims at defining a (new) collective self. This form of distinctiveness is especially relevant in the scope of the present chapter.

In the case of creative distinctiveness, the individual self may become especially relevant: In line with self-categorization theory, Spears and collaborators assume that people are motivated to search for meaning in their group identities. When confronted with a new group that is not yet properly defined, such meaning and distinctiveness can be derived in two ways. One option is to define oneself as prototypical for the group as a whole. Members of a novel group may assume that they as a person represent central features of the group; they may hypothesize that there is a match between individual and collective self, and based on this premise they can define what is typical and distinct about their new group. If, however, people do not consider themselves prototypical for their group, then the second option, namely *intergroup comparison and intergroup differentiation*—rather than an assimilation of self and ingroup—will become relevant means to define the ingroup (see Spears et al., 2002, p. 151).

Generally speaking, perceived self-prototypicality enhances group members feeling to belong to a certain group, and it has also shown to affect commitment to the group and defensive reactions to threats directed against the group (Jetten, Spears, & Manstead, 1997). However, in the case of novel groups, prototypicality of the group member gets a specific meaning: the self is not compared with an already a well-established prototype of the ingroup, but, the other way round, features of the personal self may become the input for the definition of the group's prototype. This aspect is the central theme in the models on self-anchoring and differential social projection, which will be elaborated in the remainder of this chapter.

SELF-ANCHORING AND DIFFERENTIAL SOCIAL PROJECTION

"I would never join a club that would have me as a member"—this quote by Groucho Marx gives us a not very prototypical, yet illustrative example of the very process of self-anchoring: When people form an impression about a group they just joined or a group they were just assigned to, they may use their personal self as anchor from which they infer their ingroup judgment. Consequently, the representation of the new group will be a somewhat less extreme copy of the self-representation: my group is roughly as good (or as bad) as I myself.

This idea differs remarkably from the approaches that have been outlined before. Social identity theory and self-categorization theory focus on fundamental differences between the self as a unique individual and the self as a group member, and between personal and social identity. Optimal distinctiveness theory, though giving a central role to the relation between the individual self and the ingroup, defines the ingroup-prototype rather than the self as an anchor determining the quality of a social identity. The self-aspect model and the tripartite model, finally, specify conditions in which personal identity and social identity can add to rather than compete with each other. However, the models that we will be focusing on for the remainder of this chapter go further than that. Empirical and theoretical work on self-anchoring and differential egocentric social projection does not only render the individual self a compatible or a moderating variable in intergroup behavior. Rather, in these approaches the individual self is perceived as relevant and *necessary* constituent of people's representations of their ingroup. Instead of analyzing self-stereotyping—the adaptation of the self-definition to the ingroup's prototype—these models focus on *inferences from the individual self to the group* as a whole as a process underlying intergroup phenomena such as ingroup favoritism.

The idea that the self is not just a target of social perception but can also be a highly relevant anchor and guideline for our perceptions of others is well established in both theoretical and empirical work (see, for example, Balcetis & Dunning; Hodges; or Mussweiler & Epstude, this volume). However, in theories on intergroup behavior the idea of the self as a judgmental anchor for group judgments is relatively new, or has at least, until recently, not caught too much attention in the field of intergroup research. In this section, two closely related approaches are discussed: the self-anchoring model (Cadinu & Rothbart, 1996) and the differential projection model (Clement & Krueger, 2002).

Self-Anchoring

The starting point for the work by Cadinu and Rothbart (1996) on self-anchoring in intergroup relations was their dissatisfaction with theoretical attempts to explain that there is ingroup favoritism even toward completely new, arbitrary ingroups as established in typical minimal group experiments (Rabbie & Horwitz, 1969; Tajfel et al., 1971): "Overall in-group favoritism in the minimal group paradigm is a well-established phenomenon, but the exact reasons for this favoritism remain unclear" (Cadinu & Rothbart, 1996, p. 661).

Why should people try to derive positive self-regard from membership in a group that has not yet been defined? At least in the case of minimal groups, social identity theory's claim that a striving for positive ingroup distinctiveness is underlying ingroup favoritism seems debatable. As an alternative, Cadinu and Rothbart explain this effect in terms of two cognitive mechanisms, a self-anchoring process governed by a similarity heuristic and a differentiation process governed by an oppositeness heuristic: On the one hand, the ingroup representation is inferred from the representation of the individual self. The very process of social categorization implies that *ingroup and self share* one or more characteristics that define the respective social category. Based on the overlap between self and ingroup on the category-defining dimension, further similarities are assumed. On the other hand, social categorization is based on the information that *ingroup and outgroup differ* on at least the category-defining dimensions. The oppositeness heuristic implies that the ingroup-outgroup differences are generalized to additional dimensions.

Logically, an assimilation between self and ingroup and a subsequent differentiation between ingroup and outgroup could lead to both comparably favorable and unfavorable ingroup evaluations. However, it is well documented in social psychology that self-evaluations tend to be positive and above average (Alicke, Breitenbecher, Yural, & Vredenburg, 1995; Baumeister, 1998; Taylor & Brown, 1988). Therefore, when the self becomes the anchor for the judgment, and when a similarity heuristic is applied, then it should typically be a *positive* representation that is generalized to the ingroup. Moreover, as the outgroup evaluation is guided by the assumption that it is *different* from the ingroup, it applies that "because the in-group is assumed to be favorable, different comes to mean unfavorable" (Cadinu & Rothbart, 1996, p. 662).

Cadinu and Rothbart (1996) argue that social categorization per se implies the idea of differentiation (as already demonstrated by Tajfel & Wilkes, 1963). Initially, however, social categorization does not prescribe which category is the one that is positively distinct from the other. Yet, once people are personally associated with one of the two groups, the guiding assumption will be that the ingroup, like the self, possesses positive characteristics. In line with the latter assumption, Otten and collaborators showed that as an *immediate* consequence of being categorized as member of a minimal group, there is response time evidence revealing that the ingroup is more strongly associated with positive characteristics than the outgroup.

More specifically, Otten and Wentura (1999) showed that after subliminal priming with the ingroup-label, participants identified and categorized positive trait words more quickly as positive than after subliminal priming with the outgroup-label. Interestingly, the combination of outgroup primes with negative traits did not result in any response time advantage.

Further evidence for the assumed *positive ingroup default* stems from a study by Otten and Moskowitz (2000) who used the phenomenon of spontaneous trait inferences (Uleman & Moskowitz, 1994) to demonstrate that people do strongly and automatically associate a novel ingroup with positive characteristics. Adapting the basic paradigm, participants were first presented a full sentence and then a single word on the screen. The simple task was to indicate quickly as possible whether the single word was included in the previous sentence or not. Relatively prolonged response latencies for rejecting words implied by, but not included in, a previous sentence indicated that the respective trait was inferred from the behavioral description in the sentence. Otten and Moskowitz showed that participants made especially strong trait inferences after reading trait-imply-ing sentences describing *positive* behaviors by fellow *ingroup* members. Again, for sentences implying negative traits, there were no ingroup-outgroup differences in the response latencies.

In the experiments realized by Cadinu and Rothbart (1996, Experiments 1–3) participants were categorized as members of one of two minimal groups and then rated themselves, and either an ingroup or an outgroup[3] on a set of trait dimen-sions. In order to vary the accessibility of the self as anchor for ingroup evaluations, self-ratings either preceded or followed group ratings. As expected, self-ratings were most positive, but ingroup ratings also deviated positively from outgroup ratings. More importantly, members of novel, minimal groups construed their ingroup more similar to the self than to the outgroup, and they did so especially when self-ratings preceded ingroup evaluations. Outgroup ratings, however, were not affected by the accessibility of the self.

As previously mentioned, in Cadinu and Rothbart's (1996) studies, par-ticipants evaluated either the ingroup or the outgroup. Seeking evidence for the differentiation heuristic, Cadinu and Rothbart showed their participants test scores ostensibly obtained from members of the two groups. The experimental procedure thereby deviated from a typical minimal group situation, in which participants have no information about individual other group members.

Otten (1999) addressed this point by asking participants to evaluate all three entities, the self, the ingroup, and the outgroup, right after being catego-rized. Participants completed a presumably unrelated questionnaire about their individual self either at the beginning (prior to categorization) or at the end of the experiment. This questionnaire included the trait dimensions that were also evaluated for ingroup and outgroup. The results replicated Cadinu and Rothbart's findings; moreover, they also provide evidence that not only the salience of the individual self (manipulated by positioning the self ratings either before or after the group ratings), but also the salience of the intergroup sequence (manipulated by varying the sequence of ingroup and outgroup ratings) affected intergroup bias. Whereas ingroup ratings were *most positive* when the ingroup was evaluated right after the self, outgroup ratings were *most negative* when the individual self was not previously activated, and when outgroup ratings preceded ingroup ratings (see Figure 11.1).

A further study by Otten and Wentura (2001) analyzed self-anchoring by calculating the profile correlation between trait ratings on the self, on the one hand, and (minimal) ingroup and outgroup, on the other hand. In total, 20 traits—both positive and negative—were evaluated for each of the three targets. Results revealed that self-ratings significantly predicted ingroup bias in a minimal group paradigm. In other words, the more people assigned a certain positive trait to themselves as an individual (and the more they reject the notion to possess a negative trait) the more they were prone to judge their ingroup favorably on the respective dimension. Regression analyses showed that this effect holds for both ratings on positive and ratings on negative dimensions, but that it is stronger in the former than in the latter case.

A recent study provided some evidence that inferences from the individual self to the ingroup and their link to ingroup favoritism effects can also be shown in *realistic group contexts* Otten (in press). High school students evaluated their individual selves, their ingroup and an outgroup (teachers) on a list of 20 positive and negative traits (e.g., friendly, intelligent, impatient, egoistical). The task was to indicate, on a 5-point scale, how strongly the given trait applied to the target

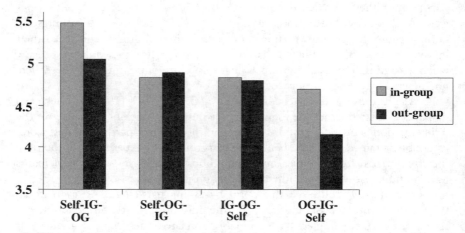

FIGURE 11.1   Ingroup and outgroup ratings as a function of the sequence of evaluation (7 = max. positive rating).

on each trait dimension. Self-anchoring as a dependent variable was calculated via the mean squared differences between self- and ingroup ratings (and self- and outgroup ratings, respectively). This study confirmed that the similarity of self-ratings and ingroup-ratings predicts how much individuals are biased in favor of their ingroup. Although the self-anchoring model predicts this effect, self-categorization theory cannot easily account for it, especially because the personality traits used as descriptors were not per se stereotypical for either of the two groups.[4]

Differential Social Projection

Krueger (1998) reviewed the role of social projection as process underlying the *false consensus effect*: When people infer an attitude within a broader population their estimates will be skewed in the direction of their own attitude. Inferring category characteristics from sample characteristics is an adaptive strategy in situations when no other information is available. Therefore, in the case of impression formation on novel, minimal ingroups, social projection research predicts that group members will project from what is typical for them individually to the new ingroup. Clement and Krueger (2002) showed that this process is *asymmetrical*: The ingroup vs. outgroup distinction defines the borders of the projection process. Only the ingroup, but not the outgroup becomes target of inferences from the self; as Clement and Krueger (2002, p. 219) phrased it in the title of their paper: "Social categorization moderates social projection" (see also de la Haye, 2001; Krueger & Clement, 1996; Mullen, Dovidio, Johnson & Cooper, 1992; Spears & Manstead, 1990).

The main difference between the self-anchoring model and the model of differential social projection lies in the assumptions about how judgments on (novel) outgroups are determined. Cadinu and Rothbart (1996) assume that the ingroup definition is inferred from the self-definition by application of a *similarity* heuristic, whereas the outgroup definition is derived from the ingroup definition by applying a *dissimilarity* heuristic. The differential projection model, on the other hand, postulates only one principle: Inferences from the self are an adaptive heuristic in case of judgmental uncertainty; as the social categorization determines that the ingroup is linked to the self whereas the outgroup is not, only the former will become target of egocentric social projection.

If we translate the differences between the two models into assumptions about correlations between the three entities, (individual) self, ingroup, and outgroup, Cadinu and Rothbart's (1996) model predicts a positive correlation between self-ratings and ingroup ratings, and a negative correlation between ingroup and outgroup ratings. Clement and Krueger's (2002) model predicts only the former correlation. The evidence for a positive correlation between individual self-ratings and ingroup ratings is now well established, whereas, especially for minimal laboratory groups, evidence for a reliable correlation between self- and outgroup ratings, or between ingroup and outgroup ratings is sparse (see Robbins & Krueger, 2005, for a recent meta-analysis).

Menzel and Otten (2003) extended work by Clement and Krueger (2002, Experiment 3) to examine differential projection in minimal groups with evaluative implications. Participants completed a 20-item personality questionnaire (including statements such as "I often ask other people for advice"; "I am an active person"). Then, they were categorized based on a short test that allegedly measured their "perceptual style" (figural vs. grounding-oriented; see Otten & Moskowitz, 2000). Group status was manipulated by claiming that this distinction correlated reliably with "visual intelligence" (defined as the ability to cope efficiently with the vast amount of optical information that has to be processed in everyday life). Half of the participants learned that the figural group would score higher on visual intelligence, the other half learned that the grounding group would score higher on visual intelligence. Following categorization, participants estimated for 10 statements from the initial personality questionnaire how many percent of the members of the in- and of the outgroup, respectively, would agree to the given statement. In the second part of the experiment, participants completed another, allegedly more valid test of their "perceptual style"; the scores on this test either confirmed or disconfirmed the initial categorization. Importantly, as the groups differed in status, a reversal of the category assignment implied either a loss or a gain in relative ingroup status. Following the second categorization, again, estimates of how many percent of the ingroup or outgroup members would agree with certain statements from the personality inventory were given.

Projection was measured by individual profile correlations between self- and group judgments (see also Otten & Wentura, 2001). The results replicated some of the main findings by Clement and Krueger (2002): Irrespective of whether projection was measured after the initial or after the second categorization, there was neither negative (contrasting) projection from self to outgroup, nor was there stronger projection to high than to low status ingroups. The latter finding implies that projection from self to ingroup is not primarily motivated by a striving for positive ingroup distinctiveness, but rather serves the goal to give meaning to the new group (see also Spears, 2001). As in Clement and Krueger's (2002) study, "projection did not completely revert after recategorization" (p. 227).[5]

Differential projection—with stronger correlations between self- and ingroup than between self- and outgroup-ratings—emerged strongly after the first category assignment. At the second stage (i.e., when categorization was either confirmed or disconfirmed), this pattern emerged only in the stable categorization condition (see Figure 11.2). In the disconfirmed condition, there was even a nonsignificant tendency to project more strongly to the outgroup (i.e., the previous ingroup) for those group members who changed from a high status to a low status group. Low levels of ingroup identification accompanied high levels of outgroup projection at time 2. Conversely, one could speculate that if ingroup identification would be especially high (which is hardly achievable within a minimal intergroup setting), then outgroup projection might decrease to zero or even become negative. In fact, Mullen et al. (1992) found a false uniqueness effect in inferences from the self to an outgroup when intergroup categorization was highly salient. In sum, the

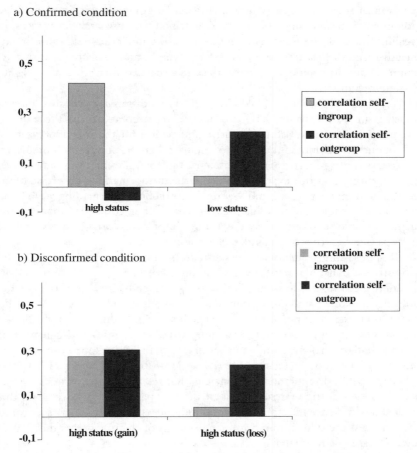

FIGURE 11.2   Differential social projection as a function of group status and (dis-) confirmation of categorization.

evidence suggests that—at least in a minimal intergroup context—people do not contrast outgroups away from the self. When the category distinction becomes blurred, the clear moderating effect of social categorization on social projection diminishes.

COGNITIVE PROCESSES UNDERLYING LINKS BETWEEN INDIVIDUAL AND COLLECTIVE SELF

In the studies summarized above, links between the individual and the social self were always analyzed on an explicit level. However, there is also a growing interest in what Devos and Banajii (2003, p. 153) call "research on the implicit social cognition of social identity." More specifically, the present section summarizes findings from studies using both memory data and response latencies as measures revealing firm links between representations of the individual self and ingroup/collective self. These studies complement the ones summarized above, as they tell us more about the cognitive processes that are associated with self-anchoring and self-stereotyping.

Gramzow, Gaertner, and Sedikides (2001) used *memory data* to argue that the self is an "informational base" for ingroup representations. In a recognition task, information that was both positive and typical for the individual self was most frequently attributed to the ingroup rather than the outgroup. Moreover, in a recall task it was negative and self-discrepant information that was remembered best, indicating that this expectancy-incongruent information is processed most deeply. Consistent with Otten and Wentura's (2001) findings regarding self-ingroup links in explicit intergroup evaluations, Gramzow et al. concluded that not only valence but also self-congruency determines impression-formation about novel ingroups (see Gaertner & Sedikides, this volume).

Response-time evidence on the self-ingroup link stems especially from work by Smith and collaborators (Smith, 2002; Smith & Henry, 1996; Smith, Coats, & Walling, 1999; see also Coats, Smith, Claypool, & Banner, 2000). Moreover, adopting the same paradigm Cadinu and de Amicis (1999) and Otten and Epstude (2004) report response time evidence mapping the findings from the self-anchoring/social projection studies as reported above. Smith and collaborators used a paradigm that Aron and collaborators originally developed to investigate closeness in interpersonal relationship (Aron, Aron, Tudor, & Nelson, 1991; Aron & Fraley, 1999). The method's rationale is that relationship closeness implies a mental overlap of the representations of the two partners. This overlap is then revealed by difference in response latency. Judgments about either partner can be made faster if the trait in question matches both of them, whereas they will be slower in case of a mismatch.

Smith and collaborators adapted this paradigm to an intergroup context. First, their participants did a paper-pencil task in which they rated for themselves as an individual, for their ingroup (e.g., a fraternity), and for the corresponding outgroup the applicability of a number of traits. Later, participants repeated either the self-evaluation (Smith & Henry, 1996) or the ingroup evaluation by responding "yes" or "no" for each trait shown on a computer (Smith et al., 1999). By relating the responses at the computer to those from the questionnaires, matches or mismatches were identified. Consistent with self-categorization theory, Smith and Henry (1996) found that *self*-evaluations were facilitated if they matched ingroup rating. Moreover, and in line with the self-anchoring model, Smith and collaborators (1999) found that *ingroup* evaluations were facilitated if they matched self-ratings.

Cadinu and de Amicis (1999) replicated these findings by manipulating in the same experiment whether either the self or the ingroup was the target in the computer task. These authors concluded that "common self-ingroup representations facilitate the access to both the self and the ingroup" (p. 226). Krueger, Acevedo, and Robbins (in press), reported the same pattern and pointed to the fact that within the group of traits for which self- and ingroup-ratings match, response latencies for self-ratings are shorter than response latencies for group ratings. They took this to mean that group ratings are matched with self-ratings rather than vice versa. Finally, Coats et al. (2000; see also Tropp & Wright, 2001) showed that the degree of response facilitation for matching as compared to mismatching self-ingroup combinations correlated significantly with measures of ingroup identification.

Recently, Otten and Epstude (2004) added a further analysis. Typically, in order to clearly identify matching and mismatching combinations of the evaluations of the three targets—self, ingroup and outgroup—traits are excluded if they receive an undecided judgment (e.g., a "4" on the 7-point scale) in the initial screening questionnaire. However, from the perspective of the self-anchoring model and the differential projection model, inferences from self to ingroup serve the function to reduce judgmental ambiguity. For minimal groups, Otten and Wentura (2001) argue that "the evaluative vacuum associated with a novel group can be filled by a "spillover" of general positive self-regard" (pp. 1051–1052), or, as suggested by the data from Clement and Krueger (2002), rather by a *spill-over of general self-knowledge*. Such an "evaluative vacuum" and the related ambiguity, however, cannot only be experienced with respect to *minimal* groups. We can also encounter judgmental ambiguity when we need to describe groups on dimensions that are not yet defined by a well-established group prototype.

Applying this reasoning to the paradigm as realized by Smith and collaborators (Smith et al., 1999), Otten and Epstude (2004) analyzed response latencies specifically for those ingroup traits that were rated "4" in the paper-pencil task, but which then had to be judged during the computer task with a forced-choice dichotomous response format. Again results revealed that responses matching the self-ratings were significantly faster than responses mismatching the self-ratings. Therefore, even though, typically, the response latencies per se only reflected close links between self and ingroup, but did not allow us to define whether the response facilitation for self-ingroup matches can be traced back to either self-categorization or self-anchoring, in the case of ill-defined (i.e., nonprototypical) ingroup traits we can in fact safely identify the latter process. Moreover, these findings show, consistent with the findings by Otten (in press) on the role of self-anchoring in explicit intergroup judgments, that projection from the individual self to the ingroup does not only play a role in minimal, but also in *realistic* group contexts.

Interestingly, in none of the studies by Smith and collaborators and in none of the adaptations of their design was there evidence for an effect of matches or mismatches with the *outgroup* judgments on response latencies when evaluating self or ingroup. This runs counter to the differentiation heuristic as suggested by Cadinu and Rothbart (1996) and is also—at the first glance—not fully in line with hypotheses that could be derived from optimal distinctiveness theory (Brewer, 1991) or from the meta-contrast principle as specified in self-categorization theory

(Turner et al., 1987). However, the two latter models can well be reconciled with this findings: For example, Brewer and Roccas (2001) argue that the gradients for the need to belong and the need to be distinct can vary as a function of social values (like individualism and collectivism); for individualists, group boundaries are set widely, and the distinctiveness striving on the group level is relatively weak; for collectivists, extending group boundaries and not differentiating sharply between in- and outgroup is costly, as they derive a main part of their identity from group memberships.

This reasoning parallels Simon and Kampmeier's (2001) predictions for majority versus minority members. Their self-aspect model suggests that majority members (like individualists) can identify with their group and at the same time see the individual self as independent, whereas for minority members (like collectivists) activating the collective self and viewing oneself as independent individual are more antagonistic self-views and will hardly operate in conjunction. The meta-contrast ratio is affected by both the degree of self-ingroup similarities and differences, and the degree of ingroup-outgroup similarities and differences. Thus, it is theoretically possible to assume that a very strong sense of belonging and of being similar to other group members can, even when combined with only little perceived intergroup differences, still render the intergroup context sufficiently salient. Typically, however, group identification in self-anchoring studies is not very high. We are thus faced with observing an intergroup phenomenon like evaluative ingroup bias that goes along with relatively low levels of perceived meta-contrast. Consequently, in these situations self-anchoring rather than self-stereotyping offers a parsimonious and convincing rationale for asymmetric evaluations of ingroups and outgroups.

SELF-ANCHORING VERSUS SELF-STEREOTYPING: COMPARISON, CONCLUSIONS AND FUTURE DIRECTIONS

From all the approaches summarized in this chapter, we can conclude that there are close links between the self as a unique individual and the self as a group member. At minimum, there is consensus that—as already pointed out by Tajfel (1978)—personal and social self both constitute a person's self-concept. Moreover, due to contextual conditions, a person may perceive and self-categorize him- or herself more on an interpersonal level (me vs. others) or on a group level (us vs. them).

According to self-categorization theory (Turner et al., 1987), there is a functional antagonism between levels of self-categorization such that the more salient the one level, the less salient the other. The self-anchoring model (Cadinu & Rothbart, 1996) and self-categorization theory both assume that when group membership becomes relevant there is similarity between how people describe themselves and how they describe their ingroup. However, the underlying processes for this similarity are conceptualized differently. Table 11.1 gives a survey of dif-

TABLE 11.1 Self-Anchoring versus Self-Stereotyping—A Dichotomous View on Correlates and Underlying Processes

Self-Anchoring	Self-Stereotyping
▪ Self as anchor; me → we	▪ Ingroup as anchor; we → me
▪ Joint salience of individual and collective self	▪ Depersonalization; situational dominance of the collective self
▪ Intragroup assimilation; the outgroup is psychologically *not* relevant	▪ Meta-contrast: intragroup assimilation *and* intergroup contrast; the outgroup is psychologically relevant
▪ Intragroup process	▪ Intra- *and* intergroup process
▪ Ingroup favoritism	▪ Ingroup favoritism and (possibly) out-group derogation
▪ "Self in Group"; belonging, mostly resting on the cognitive facet of identification	▪ "Group in Self"; group as relevant part of the self; all facets of identification relevant
▪ Especially minimal or novel groups; group-prototype absent or not clear	▪ Real groups with a defined prototype
▪ Self- and ingroup representations variable across group members; self-ratings and ingroup favoritism correlated	▪ Self- and ingroup representations homogeneous across group members; self-ratings and ingroup favoritism not necessarily correlated

ferent processes and correlates associated with self-anchoring, on the one hand, and with self-stereotyping, on the other hand.

Rather than starting a competitive argument whether the self-anchoring or the self-stereotyping process is most appropriate, Table 11.1 is meant to indicate that the two processes vary in their significance depending on social-contextual conditions. Self-anchoring will probably lose its relevance in situations where the salience of the intergroup context is strong, and the outgroup, rather than the individual self, is relevant in conjunction with the ingroup (for example, in situations with negative interdependence/competition between groups). Moreover when there is a well-established, strong prototype about the ingroup, self-stereotyping should be a more prominent process. However, when the ingroup is novel and still ill defined, inferences from the self should be the primary tool to form an ingroup representation.

Furthermore, whereas in studies about self-ingroup inferences, ingroup identification did not have a strong impact (Otten, 1999; Otten & Bar-Tal, 2000), self-categorization is strongly associated with ingroup identification (Turner, 1999). For self-anchoring to take place, people need only accept the category assignment; that is, they need to know which group they belong to. However, in terms of social identity theory and self-categorization theory, for social categorization to elicit self-stereotyping it also needs to have evaluative and emotional significance (Tajfel, 1978). Thus, the sometimes weak correlations between ingroup identification and intergroup behavior (see Hinkle & Brown, 1990; Mummendey, 1995) might also relate to the distinction between different components of identification (cognitive vs. affective and evaluative; see Jackson & Smith, 1999) and the self-anchoring versus self-stereotyping distinction as discussed in the present chapter[6]. Finally, a *similarity* between both self-anchoring and self-stereotyping is given by the assumed underlying motive to give meaning to a specific situation. Both approaches do not see self-enhancement as primary motive, nor a general striving for positive intergroup distinctiveness, but consider creating a meaningful link between ingroup and self most relevant.

Even though self-anchoring and self-stereotyping should both manifest in enhanced similarity between self-evaluations and ingroup evaluations, there are ways to disentangle these processes empirically. One example is the reference to ill-defined, nonstereotypical trait dimensions as done by Otten and Epstude (2004). Similarly, reference to minimal groups—as utilized in most studies reported above—allows us to identify rather straightforwardly whether there are inferences made from self to ingroup.

Moreover, the *variability in ingroup and self-ratings* might be indicative for the process that is operating. When self-anchoring is the process driving self-ingroup similarities, then there should be heterogeneity in both self- and ingroup judgments across group members (notwithstanding the preference for positive and typical descriptions as identified by Gramzow et al., 2001). Self-stereotyping, however, is (at least implicitly) based on the premise that there is a consensual ingroup prototype available; hence, such process should be reflected by a relatively low level of intragroup variance in evaluations of the ingroup.

From the self-anchoring perspective, we can expect a positive correlation not only between self- and ingroup judgments, but also between self-ratings and ingroup favoritism (as demonstrated by Otten & Wentura, 2001; Otten, in press). In terms of self-stereotyping, such correlations cannot straightforwardly be hypothesized. The latter reasoning also provides an interesting approach to tackle the inconsistent findings about the link between positive self-regard and ingroup favoritism effects (Abrams & Hogg, 1988; Rubin & Hewstone, 1998).

As indicated in Table 11.1, assuming that self-anchoring is the process that is driving positive and positively distinct ingroup representation is especially reasonable when dealing with groups that are not yet defined by a prototype, such as the artificial groups in the minimal group paradigm. However, is self-anchoring just a theoretical account for minimal groups? There are good reasons to doubt this: First, Otten and Epstude (2004) found that inferences from self to the ingroup facilitated ingroup judgments even in realistic group contexts (e.g., gender). Second, Otten (in press) provided evidence for self-anchoring in a realistic group context (teachers and high school students); ratings of the individual self correlated significantly with ingroup favoritism. Finally, Eisenbeiss and Otten (2002) investigated the role of self-anchoring in the group formation process for first-year psychology students. In their first week at the university, students evaluated both themselves and their new ingroup on a list of nonstereotypical traits. Supporting the self-anchoring approach, a high similarity between ratings of the individual self and ratings of the novel ingroup on nonstereotypical trait dimensions predicted higher levels of identification with the new ingroup.

Another possible restriction of the findings on self-anchoring and ingroup favoritism refers to the fact that the studies reported above all dealt with evaluative ratings. However, the minimal group experiments originally measured intergroup *allocations*. Thus, can the self-anchoring model really account for favoritism in the minimal group paradigm? It can, if we assume that anticipated reciprocity by fellow ingroup members drives ingroup favoring allocations in the minimal group paradigm (see Gaertner & Insko, 2000; Locksley, Ortiz, & Hepburn, 1980; Rabbie, Schot, & Visser, 1989). In terms of differential projection (Clement & Krueger, 2002), we can expect group members to assume that other ingroup members will choose the same allocation strategy as they chose themselves (see Krueger & Acevedo, this volume).

To conclude, this chapter sought to communicate that it is worthwhile considering the individual self when trying to understand how the self functions as a group member. Of course, we can imagine situations where the unique, individual self becomes nearly irrelevant—as in highly competitive intergroup contexts—and we can also imagine situations where a positive ingroup representation relies mostly on the individual self (as in minimal group contexts). We need not necessarily read evidence for self-anchoring and egocentric social projection from self to ingroup as evidence for a general primacy of the individual self above the social self (see Gaertner, Sedikides, & Graetz, 1999; Sedikides & Brewer, 2001; Sedikides & Gaertner, 2001). However, what we need to take into account when investigating intergroup behavior is the rich *interplay* between personal and social self, and between intra- and intergroup processes.

Researchers like Allport (1954), Sherif (1966), or Tajfel (1979) advised against simply extrapolating inter-individual processes to individuals' perception and behavior in group contexts. Rightly so, their focus was on the *fundamental differences* between the personal and the social self, and between interpersonal and intergroup behavior. Now that there is a well-established and excellent research tradition on social identities and intergroup behavior, however, it seems both safe and appropriate to acknowledge and disentangle the various ways in which individual and social self can blend.

NOTES

1. Recently, some authors argued that the term social identity should be replaced by the term "collective identity." As Simon (1997) noted, many self-definitions—as an individual as well and as a group member—are inevitably social, as they acquire their specific meaning in a social context (see also Ashmore, Deaux & McLaughlin-Volpe, 2004). However, as the term "social identity" is well established in the intergroup literature as referring to identities as derived from group memberships, I will use the two terms (social and collective identity, and social and collective self) interchangeably in this chapter.
2. Strictly speaking, Simon and Hastedt's (1999) data do not allow us to argue that positive and relevant features of the individual self were chosen as central feature describing a collective identity. It is also

possible that the positive and relevant features listed, in fact, got their valence and relevance from refer-ring to collective identities. The authors acknowledge this point, but argue that only a small number of obviously "groupy" self-aspects (like being female) were mentioned.

3. There was also a control condition in which participants were not categorized and, thus, evaluated unaffiliated groups. Results were broadly comparable to the findings for the outgroup ratings.

4. When self and ingroup are judged on a stereotypical trait dimension, then self-stereotyping, that is, inferences from the ingroup to the self, could similarly account for self-ingroup similarity and its link to ingroup favoritism. For traits that are not associated with the ingroup stereotype, however, only self-anchoring can plausibly account for self-ingroup overlap and its correlation with bias. Therefore, to allow for a reliable distinction between self-anchoring and self-stereotyping future research should systematically control for trait-stereotypicality.

5. Note that Clement and Krueger (2002) do not use the term "recategorization" in the sense it is used in the framework of the Common Ingroup Identity Model (Gaertner et al., 1993). The simply refer to a change/reversal in categorization, not to the joint categorization of in-group and out-group as part of a broader superordinate group.

6. A recent study by Schubert and Otten (2002) provided some evidence in line with this reasoning. The self-ingroup overlap as measured on graphical scales did correlate strongly with the cognitive component of identification, but was unrelated to evaluative identification.

REFERENCES

Aberson, C. L., Healy, M., & Romero, V. (2000). Ingroup bias and self-esteem: A meta-analysis. *Personality and Social Psychology Review, 4*, 157–173.

Abrams, D., & Hogg, M. A. (1988). Comments on the motivational status of self-esteem in social identity and intergroup discrimination. *British Journal of Social Psychology, 18*, 317–334.

Alicke, M. D., Breitenbecher, D. L., Yural, T. J. & Vredenburg, D. S. (1995). Personal contact, individuation, and the better-than-average-effect. *Journal of Personality and Social Psychology, 68*, 804–825.

Allport, G. W. (1954). *The nature of prejudice*. Reading, MA: Addison-Wesley.

Aron, A., Aron, E. N., Tudor, M., & Nelson, G. (1991). Close relationships as including other in the self. *Journal of Personality and Social Psychology, 60*, 241–253.

Aron, A., & Fraley, B. (1999). Relationship closeness as including other in the self: Cognitive underpinnings and measures. *Social Cognition, 17*, 140–160.

Ashmore, R. D., Deaux, K., & McLaughlin-Volpe, T. (2004). An organizing framework for collective identity: Articulation and significance of multidimensionality. *Psychological Bulletin, 130*, 80–114.

Baumeister, R. F. (1998). The self. In D. T. Gilbert, S. T. Fiske, & G. Lindzey (Eds.), *The handbook of social psychology* (Vol. 1, pp. 680–740). New York: McGraw-Hill.

Brewer, M. B. (1979). In-group bias in the minimal intergroup situation: A cognitive-motivational analysis. *Psychological Bulletin, 86*, 307–324.

Brewer, M. B. (1991). The social self: On being the same and different at the same time. *Personality and Social Psychology Bulletin, 17*, 475–482.

Brewer, M. B. (1993). The role of distinctiveness in social identity and group behaviour. In M. A. Hogg & D. Abrams (Eds.), *Group motivation: Social psychological perspectives* (pp. 1–16). London: Harvester Wheatsheaf.

Brewer, M. B., & Brown, R. J. (1998). Intergroup relations. In D. T. Gilbert, S. T. Fiske & G. Lindzey (Eds.), *The handbook of social psychology* (Vol. 2, pp. 554–594). New York: McGraw-Hill.

Brewer, M. B., & Pickett, C. L. (2002). The social self and group identification: Interpersonal and collective identities. In J. P. Forgas & K. D. Williams (Eds.), *The social self. Cognitive, interpersonal and intergroup perspectives* (pp. 255–271). New York: Psychology Press.

Brewer, M. B., & Roccas, S. (2001). Individual values, social identities, and optimal distinctiveness. In C. Sedikides & M. B. Brewer (Eds.), *Individual self, relational self, collective self* (pp. 219–237). Philadelphia: Psychology Press.

Brown, R. (2000). AGENDA 2000 – Social Identity Theory: Past achievements, current problems and future challenges. *European Journal of Social Psychology, 30*, 745–778.

Cadinu, M. R., & Rothbart, M. (1996). Self-anchoring and differentiation processes in the minimal group setting. *Journal of Personality and Social Psychology, 70*, 661–677.

Cadinu, M. R., & de Amicis, L. (1999). The relationship between the self and the ingroup: When having a common conceptions helps. *Swiss Journal of Psychology, 58*, 226–232.

Coats, S., Smith, E., Claypool, H. M., & Banner, M. J. (2000). Overlapping mental representations of self and in-group: Reaction time evidence and its relationship with explicit measures of group identification. *Journal of Experimental Social Psychology, 36*, 304–315.

Clement, R. W., & Krueger, J. (2002). Social categorization moderates social projection. *Journal of Experimental Social Psychology, 38*, 219–231.

Crocker, J., & Luhtanen, R. (1990). Collective self-esteem and ingroup bias. *Journal of Personality and Social Psychology, 58*, 60–67.

Devos, T., & Banajii, M. (2003). Implicit self and identity. In M. R. Leary & J. P. Tangney (Eds.), *Handbook of self and identity*. (pp. 153–175). New York: Guilford Press.

De la Haye, A.M. (2001). False consensus and the outgroup homogeneity effect: Interference in measurement or intrinsically determined processes? *European Journal of Social Psychology, 31*, 217-230.

Eisenbeiss, K., & Otten, S. (2002). From self-anchoring to self-stereotyping. Poster presented at the 13th General Meeting of the European Association of Experimental Social Psychology, San Sebastian, Spain, June 26–29, 2002.

Gaertner, L., & Insko, C. A. (2000). Intergroup discrimination in the minimal group paradigm: Categorization, reciprocation, or fear? *Journal of Personality and Social Psychology, 7*, 77–94.

Gaertner, L., Sedikides, C., & Graetz, K. (1999). In search of self-definition: Motivational primacy of the individual self, motivational primacy of the collective self, or contextual primacy? *Journal of Personality and Social Psychology, 76*, 5–18.

Gaertner, S. L., Dovidio, J. F., Anastasio, P. A., Bachman, B. A., & Rust, M. C. (1993). The common ingroup identity model: Recategorization and the reduction of intergroup bias. *European Review of Social Psychology, 4*, 1–26.

Gramzow, R. M., Gaertner, L., & Sedikides, C. (2001). Memory for in-group and out-group information in a minimal group context: The self as informational base. *Journal of Personality and Social Psychology, 80*, 188–205.

Hewstone, M., Rubin, M., & Willis, H. (2002). Intergroup Bias. *Annual Review of Psychology, 53*, 575–604.

Hinkle, S., & Brown, R. J. (1990). Intergroup comparisons and social identity: Some links and lacunae. In D. Abrams & M. Hogg (Eds.), *Social identity theory: Constructive and critical advances*. Hemel Hempstead: Wheatsheaf.

Jackson, J. W. & Smith, E. R. (1999). Conceptualizing social identity: A new framework and evidence for the impact of different dimensions. *Personality and Social Psychology Bulletin, 25*, 120-135.

Jetten, J., Spears, R., & Manstead, A.R.S. (1997). Distinctiveness threat and prototypicality: Combined effects on intergroup discrimination and self-esteem. *European Journal of Social Psychology, 27*, 635–657.

Kampmeier, C. & Simon, B. (2001). Individuality and Group Formation: The Role of Independence and Differentiation. *Journal of Personality and Social Psychology, 81*, 448-462.

Krueger, J. (1998). On the perception of social consensus. *Advances in Experimental Social Psychology, 30*, 163–240.

Krueger, J. (2000). The projective perception of the social world: A building block of social comparison processes. In J. Suls & L. Wheeler (Eds.), *Handbook of social comparison: Theory and research* (pp. 323–351). New York: Plenum.

Krueger, J. I., Acevedo, M., & Robbins, J. M. (in press). Self as sample. In K. Fiedler & P. Juslin (Eds.), *Information sampling and adaptive cognition*. New York: Cambridge University Press.

Krueger, J., & Clement, R. W. (1996). Inferring category characteristics form sample characteristics: Inductive reasoning and social projection. *Journal of Experimental Psychology: General, 128*, 52–68.

Krueger, J., & Stanke, D. (2001). The role of self-referent and other-referent knowledge in perceptions of group characteristics. *Personality and Social Psychology Bulletin, 27*, 878–888.

Locksley, A., Ortiz, V., & Hepburn, C. (1980). Social categorization and discriminatory behavior: Extinguishing the minimal intergroup discrimination effect. *Journal of Personality and Social Psychology, 39*, 773–783.

Menzel, D., & Otten, S. (2003). Die rolle der salienz fuer die projektion auf eigen- und fremdgruppe (The role of category salience for projection to in-groups and out-groups). Unpublished manuscript, University of Jena, Germany,

Mullen, B., Brown, R., & Smith, C. (1992). Ingroup bias as a function of salience, relevance and status: An integration. *European Journal of Social Psychology, 22*, 422–440.

Mullen, B., Dovidio, J. F., Johnson, C., & Copper, C. (1992). In-group and out-group differences in social projection. *Journal of Experimental Social Psychology, 28*, 103–122.

Mummendey, A. (1995). Positive distinctiveness and intergroup discrimination: An old couple living in divorce. *European Journal of Social Psychology, 25*, 657–670.

Otten, S. (1999). Unpublished data. University of Massachusetts.

Otten, S. (in press). Self-anchoring as predictor of in-group favoritism: Is it applicable to real group contexts? *Cahier Psychologie Sociale.*

Otten, S., & Bar-Tal, Y. (2002). Self-anchoring in the minimal group paradigm: The impact of need and ability to achieve cognitive structure. *Group Processes and Intergroup Relations, 5*, 267–284.

Otten, S., & Epstude, K. (2004). *Filling the gap in group evaluations: The self as reference point.* Unpublished manuscript, University of Groningen.

Otten, S., & Moskowitz, G. B. (2000). Evidence for implicit evaluative in-group bias: Affect-biased spontaneous trait inference in a Minimal Group Paradigm. *Journal of Experimental Social Psychology, 36*, 77–89.

Otten, S., & Wentura, D. (1999). About the impact of automaticity in the Minimal Group Paradigm: Evidence from affective priming tasks. *European Journal of Social Psychology, 29*, 1049–1071.

Otten, S., & Wentura, D. (2001). Self-anchoring and ingroup favoritism: An individual-profiles analysis. *Journal of Experimental Social Psychology, 37*, 525–532.

Rabbie, J. M., & Horwitz, M. (1969). The arousal of ingroup-outgroup bias by a chance win or loss. *Journal of Personality and Social Psychology, 69*, 223–228.

Rabbie, J. M., Schot, J. C., & Visser, L. (1989). Social identity theory: A conceptual and empirical critique from the perspective of a behavioural interaction model. *European Journal of Social Psychology, 19*, 171–202.

Robbins, J. M., & Krueger, J. I. (2005). Social projection to ingroups and outgroups: A review and meta-analysis. *Personality and Social Psychology Review. 9*, 32-47.

Rosenberg, M. (1965). *Society and the adolescent self-image.* Princeton, NJ: Princeton University Press.

Rubin, M., & Hewstone, M. (1998). Social identity theory's self-esteem hypothesis: A review and some suggestions for clarification. *Personality and Social Psychology Review, 2*, 40–62.

Schubert, T. W., & Otten, S. (2002). Overlap of self, ingroup, and outgroup: Pictorial measures of self-categorization. *Self and Identity, 1*, 353–376.

Sedikides, C., & Brewer, M. B. (Eds.) (2001). *Individual self, relational self, collective self.* Philadelphia: Psychology Press.

Sedikides, C., & Gaertner, L. (2001). A homecoming to the individual self: Emotional and motivational primacy. In C. Sedikides, C. & M. B. Brewer (Eds.), *Individual self, relational self, collective self* (pp. 7–3). Philadelphia: Psychology Press.

Sedikides, C., & Skowronski, J. J. (1993). The self in impression formation: Trait centrality and social perception. *Journal of Experimental Social Psychology, 29*, 347-357.

Sherif, M. (1966). *Group conflict and co-operation: Their social psychology.* London: Routledge, Kegan & Paul.

Simon, B. (1997). Self and group in modern society. Ten theses on the individual self and the collective self. In R. Spears, P. J. Oakes, N. Ellemers, & S. A. Haslam (Eds.), *The social psychology of stereotyping and group life* (pp. 318–335). Oxford: Blackwell.

Simon, B. & Hastedt, C. (1999). Self-aspects as social categories: The role of personal importance and valence. *European Journal of Social Psychology, 29*, 479–487.

Simon, B., & Kampmeier, C. (2001). Revisiting the individual self: Toward a social psychological theory of the individual and the collective self. In C. Sedikides, C. & M. B. Brewer (Eds.), *Individual self, relational self, collective self* (pp. 199–218). Philadelphia: Psychology Press.

Smith, E. R. (2002). Overlapping mental representations of self and group: Evidence and implications. In J. P. Forgas & K. Williams (Eds.). *The social self: Cognitive, interpersonal and intergroup perspectives* (pp. 21–35). Philadelphia: Psychology Press.

Smith, E. R., Coats, S., & Walling, D. (1999). Overlapping mental representations of self, in-group, and partner: Further response time evidence and a connectionist model. *Personality and Social Psychology Bulletin, 25*, 873–882.

Smith, E. R., & Henry, S. (1996). An in-group becomes part of the self: Response time evidence. *Personality and Social Psychology Bulletin, 20*, 635–642.

Spears, R. (2001). The interaction between the individual and the social self: Self-categorization in context. In C. Sedikides & M. B. Brewer (Eds.), *Individual self, relational self, collective self* (pp. 171–198). Philadelphia: Psychology Press.

Spears, R., Jetten, J., & Scheepers, D. (2002). Distinctiveness and the definition of collective self: A tripartite model. In A. Tesser, D. A. Stapel, & J. V. Wood (Eds.), *Self and motivation. Emerging psychological perspectives* (pp. 147–171). Washington, DC: American Psychology Association.

Spears, R., & Manstead, A. S. R. (1990). Consensus estimation in social context. In W. Stroebe & M. Hewstone (Eds.), *European Review of Social Psychology, Volume 1* (pp. 81–109). Chichester: Wiley.

Tajfel, H. (Ed.). (1978). *Differentiation between social groups: Studies in the social psychology of intergroup relations.* London: Academic Press.

Tajfel, H. (1979). Individuals and groups in social psychology. *British Journal of Social and Clinical Psychology, 18*, 183–190.

Tajfel, H., Billig, M. G., Bundy, R. P., & Flament, C. (1971). Social categorization and intergroup behaviour. *European Journal of Social Psychology, 1*, 149–178.

Tajfel, H., & Turner, J. C. (1979). An integrative theory of intergroup conflict. In W. G. Austin, & S. Worchel (Eds.), *The social psychology of intergroup relations* (pp. 33–47). Monterey, CA: Brooks/Cole Publishers.

Tajfel, H., & Turner, J. C. (1986). The social identity theory of intergroup behavior. In S. Worchel & W. G. Austin (Eds.), *Psychology of intergroup relations* (pp. 7–24). Chicago: Nelson-Hall Publishers.

Tajfel, H., & Wilkes, A. L. (1963). Classification and quantitative judgment. *British Journal of Psychology, 54*, 101–114

Taylor, S. E., & Brown, J. D. (1988). Illusion and well-being: A social psychological perspective on mental health. *Psychological Bulletin, 103*, 193–210.

Tropp, L. R. & Wright, S. C. (2001). Ingroup identification as the inclusion of ingroup in the self. *Personality and Social Psychology Bulletin, 27*, 585–600.

Turner, J. C. (1984). Social identification and psychological group formation. In H. Tajfel (Ed.), *The social dimension: European developments in social psychology* (Vol. 2, pp. 518–538). Cambridge: Cambridge University Press.

Turner J. C. (1999). Some current issues in research on social identity and self-categorization theories. In N. Ellemers, R. Spears, & B. Doosje (Eds.), *Social Identity: Context, commitment, content* (pp. 6–34). Oxford: Blackwell.

Turner, J. C., Hogg, M. A., Oakes, P. J., Reicher, S. D., & Wetherell, M. S. (1987). *Rediscovering the social group: A self-categorization theory.* Oxford: Basil Blackwell.

Turner J. C, & Reynolds K. J. (2001). The social identity perspective in intergroup relations: Theories, themes, and controversies. In R. Brown & S. Gaertner (Eds.) *Blackwell Handbook of Social Psychology: Intergroup Processes* (pp. 133–152). Malden, MA: Blackwell.

Uleman, J. S., & Moskowitz, G. B. (1994). Unintended effects of goals on unintended inferences. *Journal of Personality and Social Psychology, 66*, 490–501.

CONCLUSION

12

The Self in Social Perception
Looking Back, Looking Ahead

DAVID A. DUNNING
Cornell University
JOACHIM I. KRUEGER
Brown University
MARK D. ALICKE
Ohio University

S ocial and personality psychology has always been concerned with the question of how people come to understand themselves and their social world. Although research on self-perception and social perception has been at the core of the research enterprise, researchers have rarely taken a direct look at the intersection of the two. Classic and modern work has certainly uncovered many interrelations between self and social perception, but this work has, to a considerable extent, remained fragmentary. In the archives of social and personality psychology, one could find work on self and social judgment, but one would have to search through far-flung, uncatalogued, remotely connected sources.

Our goal in organizing a volume on the self in social judgment was not only to bring together diverse research approaches to this topic under one umbrella, but also to identify major themes and unresolved issues that lie at the intersection of the self and the social. So what did we learn? The foregoing chapters reveal four fundamental issues pertaining to the self in social judgment.

EMERGING ISSUES

Perceptions of Similarity

First and perhaps foremost, the self plays a central role as a source of information when people predict the actions and preferences of others. The notion of social projection harkens back to Freud's (1924/1956) depth-psychological construct, but it is now recast in a more general frame. Freud was interested in how projection serves unconscious needs, and he discussed its consequences to illustrate the operation of these needs. In contrast, contemporary work on projection shows that a great deal has been learned about how various ecological constraints can shape the effects projection has on perception and behavior.

One important constraint is the absence of direct knowledge about others. When this state of ignorance exists, people's best bet is to rely on what they know about themselves and how they think they would act. Projection then serves as a useful tool of mental simulation, while sparing the person the laborious and uncertain task of taking another's perspective. In the social world, a state of true ignorance with respect to the attributes or intentions of others may rarely be fully realized. Krueger and Acevedo (chapter two) suggest, however, that the standard one-shot prisoner's dilemma comes close to this kind of state. In its pure form, the dilemma aims to create a situation in which a player is left to his or her own devices. Any individuating information about the other player, as well as stereotypic knowledge derived from the player's membership in a certain social group, is deliberately stripped away. It is here that projection can do the greatest good by guiding a person toward cooperative behavior, inasmuch as he or she trusts that the other appraises the situation in much the same way.

When, however, there is information suggesting that others may be different—be it in terms of their idiosyncratic attributes or in terms of group-related stereotypic assumptions—projection should be tempered if best results are to be obtained. One such constraint is information about the situation in which others find themselves. Van Boven and Loewenstein (chapter three) report that people project too enthusiastically across situational boundaries. According to their dual-judgment model, people first predict how they themselves would feel or act in a different situation, and they then project these estimates onto others who actually are in that situation. Failing to fully appreciate the power of different situations to elicit different responses, people are left with *empathy gaps*. A person with an empty stomach thus overestimates how having a full stomach affects a person's decisions, and someone who has the benefit of hindsight knowledge fails to appreciate how the judgments of others who lack their knowledge may be different.

Both approaches outlined in these chapters share the assumption that social projection springs from an automatic, egocentric source, rather than being strategically engaged or withheld (see Ames, 2004, for such a perspective). Projection is seen as a perceptual default that can only be reduced with time and effort. A person would need to know when projection is ill-advised and then deliberately strive to keep it at bay (Epley, Morewedge, & Keysar, 2004).

Perceptions of Difference and Uniqueness

Whereas social projection involves the assumption of similarity between self and others, the second emergent issue involves the assumption of uniqueness, which typically involves the perception of personal superiority. The apparent conflict between the need to be like others and the need to stand out is widely recognized (Brewer, 1991; Brewer & Weber, 1994; Markus & Kunda, 1986). The self-enhancement perspective suggests that whichever orientation, similarity or uniqueness, permits a person to maintain a positive self-image, will predominate. The assumption that others share one's political beliefs, for example, renders those beliefs reasonable or justified. The same assumption, however, implies that one's cherished moral, social, or physical qualities are ordinary, and perceptions of similarity are curtailed when they threaten to diminish the luster of one's own valued attributes (Campbell, 1986).

Optimistic biases in general, and the better-than-average heuristic in particular, are the most thoroughly researched manifestations of the personal superiority assumption, and both cognitive and motivational factors have been shown to be relevant (e.g., Chambers & Windshitl, 2004; Dunning, 2005). Alicke and Govorun (chapter five) review much of this work, showing that experiments designed to control nonmotivational mechanisms reduce, but do not eradicate, the better-than-average effect. The better-than-average effect is larger inasmuch as people are at liberty to define the meaning of the trait dimension at issue in self-serving ways (Dunning, Meyerowitz, & Holzberg, 1989; Hayes & Dunning, 1997), and inasmuch as they see the relevant trait-related behaviors as being intentional (Kruger & Gilovich, 2004) or controllable (Alicke, 1985).

Gilovich, Epley, and Hanko (chapter four) also focus on the cognitive basis of personal superiority by distinguishing between two systems of reasoning. The first involves automatic and heuristic judgments, whereas the second requires a more careful deliberation of the available evidence. When the second system is invoked to correct and constrain automatic or "thoughtless" inferences, its efforts often fail to undo the rapid conclusions presented by the more primitive intuitive system.

Interestingly, the scholarship on personal superiority effects makes contact, in subtle but potentially important ways, with other issues discussed in this volume. For example, the two-systems account of self-enhancement proposed by Gilovich and colleagues is similar to previous discussions of anchoring-and-adjustment in social projection (Krueger, 2000). However, it should be noted that this shared theoretical outlook creates a contradiction. Whereas the projective stream of automatic thought leads to the idea that others are no different from the self, the self-enhancing stream leads to the idea that others are worse than the self. The reasonable and empirically sound assumption that most self-concepts comprise a majority of desirable traits implies that effortful curtailments of projection will lead to greater self-enhancement. Conversely, effortful curtailments of self-enhancement will lead to an increase of projection (Krueger, 2002). A person's choice of where to invest precious cognitive resources to correct automatic assumptions may indeed be a matter of motivational considerations.

This work of personal superiority also bears relevance to another self-enhancement bias long-observed in the psychological literature, namely, the self-serving bias in causal attribution (Miller & Ross, 1975). Attributions are self-serving when people take too much credit for their successes and too little responsibility for their failures. With respect to failures, the self-serving bias is an instance of the actor-observer effect. This makes contact with Malle's (chapter eight) meta-analysis showing that, relative to observers, actors are more inclined to distance themselves from negative behaviors by attributing them to situational factors. Consistent with the general self-enhancement bias, people tend to attribute their desirable behaviors to their good intentions and high abilities rather than to forces outside of their control.

The Self as Social Judgment Standard

The third main area of research is concerned with the role of the self as an evaluative standard. As Dunning and his colleagues have shown in a series of studies, personal strengths and weaknesses affect the way people view others (e.g., Dunning & Cohen, 1992; Dunning, Perie, & Story, 1991). In this volume, Balcetis and Dunning (chapter nine) account for a variety of common empirical findings within a general connectionist model. Here, self-related judgments and social judgments are viewed as an interconnected web of ideas that resolves itself, to the extent that it is possible, to a harmonious whole. With the internal consistency of the web being the primary driving force behind belief emergence and belief change, there is no need to assign casual priority to the self. Beliefs about the self and beliefs about others can influence each other. The consistency postulate thus reintroduces the question of when does the self influence social judgment and when is it the other way round?

Addressing the potential bi-directionality of the influence process, Mussweiler, Epstude, and Rüter (chapter six) argue that the self often constitutes the standard by which others are judged. However, when standards based on others are salient, self-evaluations may change. The same comparison between the self and another person can lead either to perceptions of similarity (assimilation) and or to conclusions of difference (contrast). If people begin with a hypothesis of similarity, they will see more similarity between themselves and another person. If they start with a hypothesis of difference, they will be biased toward seeing difference.

This analysis of the comparison process raises further questions. In particular, if people are biased toward seeing similarity or difference because of the initial hypothesis they bring to bear on a comparison, what determines the hypothesis that people begin with? Mussweiler et al. suggest that people start with a hypothesis of self-other similarity if there are salient signs of such (e.g., if the self and the other person belong to the same group), or when the presumption of similarity supports their self-esteem (e.g., when the other person is a revered character). But this first step of generating a hypothesis is still understudied. What other factors, especially those in the real world, bias people toward hypothesizing similarity versus dissimilarity between themselves and others? Future work could profitably focus on this issue, given the importance of that tentative hypothesis for the conclusions people ultimately reach when measuring themselves against others.

In Hodges's feature-matching model (chapter seven), the direction of social comparison matters. If the focus of a comparison is on the self, then features associated with the self will have more impact than features associated with another person; if the focus of a comparison is on the other person, the reverse will hold true. Unique features receive special weight in comparisons between self and others, whereas features that are shared with others are cancelled, at least when others are being described.

The cancellation of shared attributes may help explain a longstanding puzzle concerning people's self-views. As mentioned above, people tend to see themselves as unique—far too unique than they really can be (see Dunning, in press, for an extended discussion). This belief in uniqueness can be self-reinforcing, leading people to believe they are uniquely competent among their peers (Alicke & Govorun, chapter five). At times, however, the belief in one's own uniqueness can induce self-doubt and anxiety, as when people think of themselves as more inhibited, indecisive, and emotional than others (Miller & McFarland, 1987). If people go through their lives habitually canceling out the qualities others share with them, they may end up feeling more unique than they really are.

Malle (chapter eight) also offers new insights into the question of why people tend to exaggerate their uniqueness. He points out that people often have information about their own behavior that they do not have when trying to explain the behavior of others. They know their intentions and their reasons for choosing certain actions, whereas the intentions and reasons of others are removed from view. If explaining social behavior is a ubiquitous activity—and a generation of research suggests that it is—then it is again clear why people would come to view themselves as special. In short, people can point to all the reasons why they choose their actions, but such reasons are less accessible to explicate the actions of others.

Who's on First?

The fourth main theme is concerned with the status of the individual self relative to group-dependent, social, or "collective" selves. In essence, the question is which self is the one that people concern themselves the most with understanding and preserving. Is it a person's individual or personal self? Or is it their collective self—the one that is based primarily on the groups of which they are members. This theoretical yin and yang of individualism versus collectivism is not new. The influential sociological theory of symbolic interactionism, for example, has long maintained that the group matters to the self—that individual social perceivers, for example, are highly sensitive to how others see them and that they respond accordingly (Cooley, 1902; Mead, 1934). Numerous studies have shown, however, that people's ideas of how they are seen by the "generalized other" are more closely related to how they see themselves than how others actually see them (Felson, 1993; Fields & Schuman, 1977; Kenny & DePaulo, 1993; Krueger, Ham, & Linford, 1996; Shrauger & Schoeneman, 1979).

In their work, Gaertner and Sedikides (chapter ten) suggest that is the personal self that is on first. They reason that if collective self-construals were central to people's sense of identity, they would be as vigorously defended as individual self-construals. Instead, people feel worse when negative feedback is directed at them personally than when it is directed at their group, and they derogate this feedback more. This finding, although contrary to the current *zeitgeist* in cultural psychology (Markus & Kitayama, 2003), makes good sense in light of time-honored social-impact theory (Latané, 1981). According to this theory, a threat has a fixed psychophysical force, which dissipates geometrically with the number of people affected by it. Hence, the larger a person's group is, the less an individual needs to be concerned with the threat.

Inasmuch as a threat rouses a person's self-protective defenses, an opportunity to stand out engages his or her self-enhancement motive. If this motive is fundamentally egocentric, as opposed to ethnocentric, it should show itself under appropriate circumstances. Bucking the *zeitgeist* again, Gaertner and Sedikides show that not only Westerners reared on a diet of Protestant individualism think they stand above their peers; Asians, whose cultural-ideological views are rooted in the traditions of Confucius and Lao-Tzu, are not immune either. Members of collectivist cultures also self-enhance, and do so where it matters most to them, namely when their standing on such collectivist attributes as cooperativeness or family orientation is at stake.

Otten's review (chapter eleven) also suggests that the individual self-concept is on first. Its contents shape how people describe the social groups to which they belong. Because these contents are positive for most people, their perceptions of ingroups are positive too, but perhaps a little less so; hence self-enhancement. Descriptions of outgroups, which are less dependent on individual self-concepts, are even less positive; hence ingroup bias.

But is the self really on first at all? Is it really the self that produces all the phenomena that the various contributors to this volume have talked about? Expressing a contrary view, Karniol (2003) suggested that work in the tradition of experimental social psychology has been biased in its individualist cast of social perception (see also Foddy & Kashima, 2002). Karniol's alternative theory of *protocentrism* unabashedly puts social perception on first, ahead of self-perception. Much like self-categorization theory (Turner, Hogg, Oakes, Reicher, & Wetherell, 1987), protocentrism assumes that perception begins with generic or collectivist notions of what other people are like and what they are likely to do. Individual self-concepts are then derived from this generic template; specifically, people identify those attributes that they feel set them apart from the protocenter, and proceed to identify *with* them. Thus, when people tend to perceive others as similar to themselves, it is not because they start with the self and work outward—seeing people as similar because of some presumptions they have made about the self. Instead, people start with the procenter—some representation of what people are like in general—and then work inward to evaluate what they themselves must be like.

Karniol's (2003) suggestions are provocative and bound to generate a fair amount of research. Some of the present authors have already questioned the force of her argument (Krueger, 2003; Mussweiler, 2003; Sedikides, 2003). A common theme of this skepticism—and of the work presented in this volume—is that theories staked on the presumed primacy of the individual self are more parsimonious and easier to test than are theories built on more opaque notions of trans-personal collectives, such as the procenter. At present, it seems fair to say that the individual self remains a powerful heuristic for both people in the street and the researchers who study them, but it remains for future work to determine just how pervasive and powerful the impact of this individual self is.

WHERE TO NEXT?

How might the story of the social self unfold in the future? The chapters in this volume offer some stimulating leads, and we close with a small sampling of additional possibilities.

Self as Moral Standard

To date, one important function of the self has received relatively little attention, namely, the self as a moral standard. Arguably, people rely on their personal beliefs and values when evaluating religious ideals, when estimating groups norms or typical behavior, or when making utilitarian decisions.

Research on the better-than-average effect suggests that moral attitudes and behaviors have a special status because they yield the largest self-enhancement bias (Epley & Dunning, 2000; Messick, Bloom, Boldizar, & Samuelson, 1985). Indeed, self-enhancement is so much stronger in the moral than in the intellectual domain that this asymmetry has been dubbed the "Muhammand Ali effect" (Allison, Messick, & Goethals, 1989; Van Lange & Sedikides (1998). Like the great athlete, many ordinary people believe that they are better, though not necessarily smarter, than others.

Research that has directly compared different standards for moral judgment suggests that people have an egocentric outlook when judging the behaviors of others in the moral domain (Alicke, 1993). In these studies, participants were asked to indicate how they would respond to certain temptations, such as cheating on their income tax, driving while intoxicated, or employing an illegal immigrant. When evaluating the choices of others, people put great weight on whether those choices are the same as their own. This is so even when people recognize their own preferences in certain moral dilemmas to be inferior (as in the examples above) and concede that they would not want their own children to act as they themselves did.

One of the most interesting questions regarding the self in moral judgment concerns the extent to which people exhibit judgmental hypocrisy. Behavior is considered hypocritical if a person endorses one set of behavioral standards as moral while acting according to another (Batson, Thompson, & Chen, 2002). Moral hypocrisy is particularly striking when people holding social positions of moral guardianship commit the very sins they condemn in others.

In social psychology, attitude changes resulting from cognitive dissonance have sometimes been treated as a form of behavioral hypocrisy (Fried & Aronson, 1995; Stone et al., 1994). In a typical experiment, a participant who is subtly induced to behave in a way that is inconsistent with his or her attitude subsequently tends to assimilate the attitude to that behavior. By recognizing a new behavioral reality, this attitude change may not be hypocritical. Indeed, it could be argued that *failing* to alter one's attitude would be hypocritical. A person who disapproves of pornography, for example, is a hypocrite for not developing a more liberal view after hours of visiting pornographic Web sites on the Internet.

Moral hypocrisy is purely judgmental when people hold others to stricter standards than themselves. Examples are the alcoholic who disparages drug users, strict parents who disapprove of other parents' punitive behavior, or elderly people who forget their own past acts of conformity when berating younger people for yielding to peer pressure. Behavioral and judgmental hypocrisy are frequently related: People who commit behavioral hypocrisy by violating their personal standards often evaluate their own transgressions less severely than similar actions committed by others. A popular radio show host, for example, who routinely condemns extra-medicinal drug use, failed to take a more sympathetic view of drug addicts after his own dependency was disclosed.

Like social projection, judgmental hypocrisy has Freudian roots. The defense mechanism of reaction formation involves seeing characteristics in others that one denies in oneself. The classic example is the person beset with sexual guilt who views others as immoral. In a more general sense, this type of mechanism involves evaluating others with reference to one's insecurities. People who are unsure of their intelligence, attractiveness, or popularity, may be particularly harsh in judging others on these characteristics.

How Self and Social Cognition Differ

Many of the present chapters suggest that self and social perception are so linked that they cannot be separated. Yet, there are important ways in which processes of self-judgment differ from those of social judgment. After all, there are many instances in the literature in which the self and another person have performed the same behavior, but the conclusions reached about the self are quite different from those reached about the other person.

Malle highlights differences that might habitually arise between the conclusions reached about the self and those reached about other people. People have different information about themselves than about others, and that information can steer attributional processes to a different judgment when it is about the self rather than another person. People often know the reasons for their actions and the intentions behind them when they think about their own behavior; but such knowledge may not be available for others. They know the beliefs about the world that prompted their own actions, but may not know the beliefs that others possess that cause their actions. Without knowledge of such beliefs, people might more quickly attribute the behavior of others to desire than they do to themselves.

In the future, researchers might compare and contrast the processes underlying self and social perception and look for ways in which they diverge. Such an endeavor could start with the different types of information people have at their disposal when reaching self-judgments rather than social ones. That endeavor would also have to examine when the motives underlying self and social judgment are different. It is well-documented that people massage the conclusions they reach about themselves in order to maintain a positive self-image (Kunda, 1990), but they may not harbor that same motive about others. When would this difference in motivation produce the biggest difference in judgment based on the same information?

But a search for differences in self and social judgment might produce a paradoxical side benefit. If one looks at the existing literatures on self and social judgment, one finds that they tend to have different flavors. The literature on social judgment tends to dwell on the information that people have on hand as they try to evaluate others, as well as the types of information they seek (Moskowitz, 2005). The primary motive behind social judgments is often assumed to be the search for accuracy. In studies on self-perception, however, there is a greater variety motives. Besides having a need for an accurate understanding of self, often motivated to maintain or bolster self-esteem, or to find ways to ir self over time in a quest to realize a personal ego-ideal (Brown, 1998).

If one looks for differences between self and social perception, on (at least) a few. But then one should step back and ask if self and social are really all that different. Perhaps social judgment is also prompted by a motives, and one could draw inspiration from the self-judgment litera what types of motives might be at play. That is, work on self and social might serve to cross-pollinate each other to produce inspiration about fu and hypotheses to pursue.

The Boundary Between Self and Social

One last question has to do with the boundary between the self and the social—where does the self end and others begin? Gaertner and Sedikides tackle this question directly, asserting that the boundary of the self is set between each of our personal identities and the identity of any other individual. Otten, however, suggests that self-views can easily leak into perceptions of others within the same group. In the area of interpersonal perception, Aron and colleagues have found that people's self-concepts can, to a degree, merge with the concepts they form of significant others around them. At times, people treat these others exactly as their would themselves, as well as show some cognitive confusion about the traits that constitute the "self" and the attributes that make up the other person (Aron, Aron, & Smollan, 1992).

Perhaps selfhood is not a black or white affair, but rather a continuum. There are people out there who definitely fit into the category of "other people," but as one thinks about others who are more familiar, important, and closer to the self, thoughts about those others may take on a self-quality. As Malle noted, people know more about their internal lives—and the thoughts, desires, and intentions that inform their actions—than they know about the internal lives of others. And it shows. People are more likely to talk about their goals and thoughts when explaining their own behavior than when they try to explain the behavior of other people. When explaining others, people fall back on rather abstract and broad traits, such as whether the other person is, for example, aggressive or friendly.

With increasing familiarity and interdependence, however, others are seen and described in much the same way as people see and describe themselves (Idson & Mischel, 2001; Prentice, 1990). Their rich inner lives, filled with intentions, goals, and idiosyncratic interpretations become more appreciated. In short, people who are familiar and important are construed in many of the same ways as the self, as an active being who has nuanced and complicated traits, as well as complex thoughts and feelings. This suggests that the ways people have for thinking about the self is a continuum and that the ways they think about themselves can be extended, if not to all, then at least to some familiar others.

Parting Thought

The work described in this volume has taught us a lot about the intersection between self and social judgment, but there is still much to discover. Perhaps this is a good situation to be in. The psychology of the self has fascinated psychologists for over a century; the ways in which people sit in judgment of others has also been a central concern. Combining the two topics reveals many interesting phenomena and questions, and undoubtedly further study will reveal more. Young investigators can be heartened by the prospect that there is much more work to do on valuable and fascinating questions that can fill a career. The job is not done, and does not look like it will be any time soon.

REFERENCES

Alicke, M D. (1985). Global self-evaluation as determined by the desirability and controllability of trait adjectives. *Journal of Personality and Social Psychology, 49*, 1621–1630.

Alicke, M. D. (1993). Egocentric standards of conduct evaluation. *Basic and Applied Social Psychology, 14*, 171–192.

Allison, S. T., Messick, D. M., & Goethals, G. R. (1989). On being better but not smarter than others: The Muhammad Ali effect. *Social Cognition, 7*, 275–295.

Ames, D. R. (2004). Inside the mind reader's tool kit: Projection and stereotyping in mental state inference. *Journal of Personality and Social Psychology, 87*, 340–353.

Aron, A., Aron, E., & Smollan, D. (1992). Inclusion of the other in the self scale and the structure of interpersonal closeness. *Journal of Personality and Social Psychology, 63*, 596–612.

Fried, C. B., & Aronson, E. (1995). Hypocrisy, misattribution, and dissonance reduction. *Personality and Social Psychology Bulletin, 21*, 925–933.

Batson, D. D., Thompson, E. R., & Chen H. (2002). Moral hypocrisy: Addressing some alternatives. *Journal of Personality and Social Psychology, 83*, 330–339.

Brewer, M. B. (1991). The social self: On being the same and different at the same time. *Personality and Social Psychology Bulletin, 17*, 474–482.

Brewer, M. B., & Weber, J. G. (1994). Self-evaluation effects of interpersonal versus intergroup social comparison. *Journal of Personality and Social Psychology, 66*, 268–275.

Brown, J. D. (1998). *The self.* New York: McGraw-Hill.

Campbell , J. D. (1986). Similarity and uniqueness: The effects of attribute type, relevance, and individual differences in self-esteem and depression. *Journal of Personality and Social Psychology, 50*, 281–294.

Chambers, J. R., & Windschitl, P. D. (2004). Biases in social comparative judgments: The role of nonmotivated factors in above-average and comparative-optimism effects. *Psychological Bulletin, 130*, 813–838.

Cooley, C. H. (1902). *Human nature and the social order.* New York: Scribner's.

Dunning, D. (2005). *Self-insight: Roadblocks and detours on the path to knowing thyself.* New York: Psychology Press.

Dunning, D., & Cohen, G. L. (1992). Egocentric definitions of traits and abilities in social judgment. *Journal of Personality and Social Psychology, 63*, 341–355.

Dunning, D., Meyerowitz, J. A., & Holzberg, A. D. (1989). Ambiguity and self-evaluation: The role of idiosyncratic trait definitions in self-serving assessments of ability. *Journal of Personality and Social Psychology, 57*, 1082–1090.

Dunning, D., Perie, M., & Story, A.L. (1991). Self-serving prototypes of social categories. *Journal of Personality and Social Psychology, 61*, 957–968.

Epley, N., & Dunning, D. A. (2000). Feeling "holier than thou": Are self-serving assessments produced by errors in self- or social prediction? *Journal of Personality and Social Psychology, 79*, 861–875.

Epley, N., Morewedge, C. K., & Keysar, B. (2004). Perspective taking in children and adults: Equivalent egocentrism but differential correction. *Journal of Experimental Social Psychology, 40*, 760–768.

Felson, R. B. (1993). The (somewhat) social self: How others affect self-appraisals. In J. Suls (Ed.), *The self in social perspective* (Vol. 4, pp. 1–26). Hillsdale, NJ: Erlbaum.

Fields, J. M., & Schuman, H. (1976). Public beliefs about the public. *Public Opinion Quarterly, 40*, 427–448.

Foddy, M., & Kashima, Y. (2002). Self and identity: What is the conception of the person assumed in the current literature? In Y. Kashima, M. Foddy & M. J. Platow (Eds.), *Self and identity: Personal, social, symbolic* (pp. 3–25). Mahwah, NJ: Erlbaum.

Freud, S. (1924/1956). Further remarks on the defense neuropsychoses. In *Collected papers of Sigmund Freud* (Vol. 1; pp. 155–182). London: Hogarth Press.

Hayes, A.F., & Dunning, D. (1977). Construal processes and trait ambiguity: Implications for self-peer agreement in personality judgment. *Journal of Personality and Social Psychology, 72*, 664–677.

Idson, L. C., & Mischel, W. (2001). The personality of familiar and significant people: The lay perceiver as a social-cognitive theorist. *Journal of Personality and Social Psychology, 80*, 585–596.

Karniol, R. (2003). Egocentrism versus protocentrism: The status of self in social prediction. *Psychological Review, 110*, 564–580.

Kenny, D. A., & DePaulo, B. M. (1993). Do people know how others view them? An empirical and theoretical account. *Psychological Bulletin, 114*, 145–161.

Krueger, J. (2000). The projective perception of the social world: A building block of social comparison processes. In J. Suls & L. Wheeler (Eds.), *Handbook of social comparison: Theory and research* (pp. 323–351). New York: Plenum/Kluwer.

Krueger, J. I. (2002). On the reduction of self-other asymmetries: Benefits, pitfalls, and other correlates of social projection. *Psychologica Belgica, 42*, 23–41.

Krueger, J. I. (2003). Return of the ego—self-referent information as a filter for social prediction: Comment on Karniol (2003). *Psychological Review, 110*, 585–590.

Krueger, J., Ham, J. J., & Linford, K. M. (1996). Perceptions of behavioral consistency: Are people aware of the actor-observer effect? *Psychological Science, 7*, 259–264.

Kruger, J., & Gilovich, T. (2004). Actions and intentions in self-assessments: The road to self-enhancement is paved with good intentions. *Personality and Social Psychology Bulletin, 30,* 328–339.

Kunda, Z. (1990). The case for motivated reasoning. *Psychological Bulletin, 108,* 480–498.

Latané, B. (1981). The psychology of social impact. *American Psychologist, 36,* 343–356.

Markus, H. R., & Kitayama, S. (2003). Culture, Self, and the Reality of the Social. *Psychological Inquiry, 14,* 277–283.

Markus, H., & Kunda, Z. (1986). Stability and malleability in the self-concept in the perception of others. *Journal of Personality and Social Psychology, 51,* 858–866.

Mead, G. H. (1934). *Mind, self and society.* Chicago: University of Chicago Press.

Messick, D. M., Bloom, S., Boldizar, J. P., & Samuelson, C. D. (1985). Why we are fairer than others. *Journal of Experimental Social Psychology, 21,* 480–500.

Miller, D. T., & McFarland, C. (1987). Pluralistic ignorance: When similarity is interpreted as dissimilarity. *Journal of Personality and Social Psychology, 53,* 298–305.

Miller, D. T., & Ross, M. (1975). Self-serving biases in the attribution of causality: Fact or fiction? *Psychological Bulletin, 82,* 213–225.

Moskowitz, G. B. (2005). *Social cognition: Understanding self and others.* New York: Guilford Press.

Mussweiler, T. (2003). When egocentrism breeds distinctness—Comparison processes in social prediction: Comment on Karniol (2003). *Psychological Review, 110,* 581–584.

Prentice, D. A. (1992). Familiarity and differences in self- and other-representations. *Journal of Personality and Social Psychology, 59,* 369–383.

Sedikides, C. (2003). On the status of self in social prediction: Comment on Karniol (2003). *Psychological Review, 110,* 591–594.

Shrauger, J. S., & Schoeneman, T. J. (1979). Symbolic interactionist view of self-concept: Through the looking glass darkly. *Psychological Bulletin, 86,* 549–573.

Stone, J., Aronson, E., Crain, A. L., Winslow, M. P., & Fried, C. B. (1994). Inducing hypocrisy as a means for encouraging young adults to use condoms. *Personality and Social Psychology Bulletin, 20,* 116–128.

Turner, J. C., Hogg, M. A., Oakes, P. J., Reicher, S. D., & Wetherell, M. (1987). *Rediscovering the social group: A self-categorization theory.* Oxford: Blackwell.

Van Lange, P. A. M., & Sedikides, C. (1998). Being more honest but not necessarily more intelligent than others: Generality and explanations for the Muhammad Ali effect. *European Journal of Social Psychology, 28,* 675–680.

Author Index

Subject Index

A

above average effect. *See* better-than-average effect

actions defined, 156

actor-observer asymmetry, 155
  belief–desire asymmetry, 163–164, 168–169, 172
  belief marker asymmetry, 164, 169, 172
  meta-analysis of, 158–159
  reason asymmetry, 162–163, 167

adolescents, 61, 174

age
  estimating age of others, 44
  intentionality and, 159
  projection of attitudes and, 24
  self-other behavior explanations and, 174
  social projection decline over, 61

alignability, 133–134

altruistic intent, 73–75

ambiguity
  better-than-average effect and, 89
  self-other comparisons and, 120–121

anchoring effect, 70–71, 95, 103, 119, 134, 249

Asian culture. *See* Eastern versus Western culture

assimilation, 121–126, 272

athletic ability
  self-evaluation of, 111, 117, 119, 123, 188–191

attitude scales, 4

attribution theory, 157, 173

audience design, 168, 173

B

balance theory, 70

Bayesian framework, 7, 18–22

Beck Depression Inventory, 93

behavior explanations, 155–175
  causal history of reason explanations, 161
  classic model of, 157–159
  enabling factor explanations, 161
  future research, 174–175
  purpose of, 156
  reason explanations, 160, 171

better-than-average effect, 6, 8, 67–104, 271, 275
  and automatic judgments, 98–101
  boundaries of, 89
  under cognitive load, 99
  and comparison target, 90–92
  and controllability, 90
  and depression, 93
  and egocentrism, 95–96, 101
  and focalism, 96–97, 101
  and future research, 103
  and gender, 92
  measurement of, 88
  and motivational versus nonmotivational theories, 101–102
  and selective recruitment, 94, 104
  self concept and, 214
  and self-esteem, 92–93
  and self versus group comparisons, 97–98
  and trait ambiguity, 89

bias, 76–77

C

cancellation effects of feature comparison, 145–150
  consequences of, 145–146
  in self-other comparisons, 147–150